In Deadly Combat

In Deadly Combat

A German Soldier's Memoir of the Eastern Front

Gottlob Herbert Bidermann

Translated and Edited by

Derek S. Zumbro

With an Introduction by

Dennis Showalter

University Press of Kansas

© 2000 by the University Press of Kansas

All rights reserved

Published by the University Press of Kansas (Lawrence, Kansas 66049), which was organized by the Kansas Board of Regents and is operated and funded by Emporia State University, Fort Hays State University, Kansas State University, Pittsburg State University, the University of Kansas, and Wichita State University

Library of Congress Cataloging-in-Publication Data

Bidermann, G. H. (Gottlob Herbert)

[Krim-Kurland. English]

In deadly combat : a German soldier's memoir of the Eastern Front / Gottlob Herbert Bidermann ; translated and edited by Derek S. Zumbro ; introduction by Dennis Showalter.

p. cm.—(Modern war studies)

The editor's expanded translation of: Krim-Kurland : mit der 132. Infanterie-Division, 1941–1945 / G.H. Bidermann. [1964].

ISBN 0-7006-1016-2 (cloth: alk. paper)

1. Bidermann, G. H. (Gottlob Herbert) 2. World War, 1939–1945—Campaigns—Eastern Front. 3. World War, 1939–1945—Personal narratives, German. 4. World War, 1939–1945—Prisoners and prisons, Soviet. 5. Prisoners of war—Germany—Biography. 6. Prisoners of war—Soviet Union—Biography. I. Zumbro, Derek S. II. Title. III. Series.

D764.B4813   2000

940.54'217—dc21   99-055738

British Library Cataloguing in Publication Data is available.

Printed in the United States of America

10 9 8 7 6 5 4 3 2 1

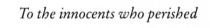

To the innocents who perished

CONTENTS

Photo sections follow pages 144 and 212.

PREFACE

The soldiers of the German Wehrmacht's 132d Infantry Division marched into Russia in 1941 with the profound belief that they were embarking upon a great crusade. They had been taught from youth that it was their responsibility to rid the world of Bolshevism, and in this naivety they had marched purposefully toward the east. Four years later, the remnants of this division, reduced by casualties to skeletal strength, sparsely clad in ragged uniforms, and surviving on carefully rationed horse meat, surrendered to the Soviet army.

As a close friend of the Bidermann family, I had long been aware that Gottlob Bidermann had served for a number of years on the Eastern Front, but the true extent of this service did not come to light until 1985. At that time I had been requested by the Federal German Navy to serve as translator and liaison officer to the commodore of a U.S. Navy Task Force during a port visit to Kiel, Germany. In the course of this assignment I was provided the opportunity to invite friends in Europe to participate in a special tour of the U.S. Navy warships that were present in the north German port. I extended an invitation to G. H. Bidermann to visit this display of NATO power, for which he graciously thanked me, adding, however, that for him the invitation had arrived "forty years too late." It was through this curious response that I was to learn the true extent of his experiences in Courland in 1945 and of the highly improbable rumor on which the beleaguered soldiers had placed their final hopes. In May 1945 word was widely circulated throughout the remnants of the Courland army that the United States and Great Britain had dispatched a fleet to the Baltic to evacuate Bidermann's division and thus spare it from destruction by the Soviet army. It was further rumored that the veteran Courland fighters would then join the U.S. Army on the Elbe River, where they were to engage the Red Army and push them out of central Europe.

Shortly thereafter I journeyed south to the Black Forest area to visit with Bidermann for the specific purpose of reconstructing and translating into English his experiences during the war. While in southern Germany I was provided a copy of a memoir, which he had privately published many years previously for the benefit of the veterans of his division.

Krim-Kurland mit der 132. Infanterie-Division 1941–1945 had been written over a period of several months in 1964, less than two decades after the ragged remnants of the division had marched into captivity as prisoners of war, and less than ten years after the last group of survivors was released from Soviet imprisonment. This memoir served as the foundation on which this book is based.

Many years after returning from the labyrinth of unnamed gulags and prison camps deep within the Soviet Union, the former Courland soldiers found themselves increasingly haunted by recurring scenes of violent death in combat. Like many of the soldiers against whom they had fought, they lived with the unspoken guilt of having survived the cataclysm in which so many millions had perished; and they increasingly found themselves awakened by the incurable, recurrent chimeras of the battlefield. The nights were broken by nearby screams of dying comrades as they perished under the submachine guns and flamethrowers of Soviet infantrymen breaking through a thinly held line. The sight and sounds of enemy soldiers trapped within the confines of a burning tank only several meters distant could not easily be erased from the consciousness, and the intervening years did not serve to diminish the repeated episodes of horror.

Through the writing of his memoirs, the former Wehrmacht officer attempted to soothe the psychological wounds and place the experience of war in a perspective that nonparticipants could share and to which all veterans of that particular phase of the apocalypse could relate. Relying on his own memory as well as sharing long-forgotten experiences with former members of his division, he brought together a manuscript that, with detached accuracy, effectively depicted the years on the Eastern Front as observed and experienced by the infantrymen.

As G. H. Bidermann explained in the introduction of his original manuscript, it is of little value to restate many of the brutal historical occurrences that characterized, and in some regard has come to represent, World War II. It is not the intent of this book through this omission even to suggest that such events did not occur. Nor does it serve the purpose of the book to place blame for the incidents of monumental importance and infamy that ensued. This is the story of the front as witnessed by the soldiers who fought there, and the events are limited within that same perspective. There is no examination of the causes of the war, nor can one detect underlying guilt, sorrow, or remorse for the undeniable political events and consequences that followed the German army throughout the odyssey. Many years ago Colonel Sepp Drexel wrote of Krim-Kurland: "The book is dedicated to the fallen—however, it is written for the living." And it remains for that purpose that this edition of the manuscript has been translated and published.

The task of conducting interviews, discussing events, and carefully examining aged documents and photographs with G. H. Bidermann extended intermittently over a period of several years. As translator and co-author of the account of those events that he experienced and witnessed during the war, I believe that several pertinent issues should be brought to the attention of the reader. I deemed it best to address most military ranks and units with the original German ranks and titles so as not to detract from the traditional Wehrmacht military structure. Professional historians may disagree or find error with a number of occurrences regarding place-names, strengths of opposing units, or specific dates of events. In that regard, it must be recognized that the primary sources of information for this book were gleaned from letters hastily written on the field of battle, yellowed photographs that resurrected long-forgotten names of individuals, and in some instances simply the fading memories held by Bidermann and a few surviving comrades who served with him in the east. Occasionally, official reports and unit war diaries were drawn upon for information regarding when and where a specific event might have occurred. Much of the information enclosed in the official documents and diaries stemmed from prisoner interrogations and documents captured on the battlefield. Thus, the official files themselves must not be regarded as infallible.

Many of the official documents were provided by the widow and son of General Fritz Lindemann. The existence and availability of the Lindemann family documents are owed exclusively to the fact that when the Gestapo searched the Lindemann residence in north Germany following the assassination attempt against Hitler, they overlooked the second Lindemann family residence near the Bodensee in south Germany. The general's personal files had been transferred to the second residence for storage and safekeeping some months before the assassination attempt.

It is not the purpose of this book to stand solely as a source of knowledge and information for events pertaining to the history of the Eastern Front. It must be considered, however, an accurate chronology of experiences and events as observed and acted upon by an individual who credulously marched to the bidding of an evil ideology. The survivors of this march spanned the immense distance from the role of invading conquerors to exhausted, isolated units locked in a fatal struggle against vast odds, and upon their experiences history has cast an ever-darkening shadow. While living within this shadow, these surviving witnesses of history's greatest contest of arms and industrial power may present us with myriad lessons of survival and defeat in a malevolent world. It is our responsibility to learn from those events and to heed the messages they continue to convey.

Derek S. Zumbro
Dornstettin, Germany

ACKNOWLEDGMENTS

I would like to express my heartfelt gratitude to Larry Malley, director of the University of Arkansas Press, who provided invaluable professional assistance that made the publication of this book possible. I am also greatly indebted to Michael Briggs, editor in chief of the University Press of Kansas, who exhibited unlimited patience and provided expert guidance from his initial reading of roughly translated excerpts to the completion of the manuscript. Most important, I wish to express my appreciation to Gottlob H. Bidermann for his willingness to engage in countless interviews, discussions, and written correspondence with me, during which he unfailingly provided explicit responses to my numerous questions. I also remain indebted to him for his contribution of personal photographs and archival materials for this portrayal of a soldier's story.

I also wish to thank these former members of the 132d Infantry Division, who selflessly provided important information regarding personal experiences, diary notes, photographic material, and official documents for G. H. Bidermann's original manuscript.

Lindemann, Fritz	Division commander. Information from his personal archives was generously provided by his surviving wife, Frau Lindemann, and his son.
Drexel, Josef	"Uncle Sepp," Commander, Infantry Regiment 436
Jahn (both brothers)	Battery commanders, Artillery Regiment 132
Bolte, Erich	Battalion commander, Artillery Regiment 132
Gassner, Hans	Battery commander, Artillery Regiment 132
Schuhmacher, Fritz	Squad leader, Fifth Company, Grenadier Regiment 437
Schmidt, Fritz	Regimental commander, Grenadier Regiment 437
Wetzstein, Hermann	Hauptfeldwebel, Twelfth Company, Grenadier Regiment 437
Volle, Erich	Battalion adjutant, II Battalion, Grenadier Regiment 437

Baur, Willi	Company commander, Sixth Company, Grenadier Regiment 437
Zoll, Erhardt	Company commander, Fourteenth Company, Grenadier Regiment 436 and 437
Hanselmann, Hans	Fourth Battery, Artillery Regiment 132
Weisensee, Dr. med Guenter	Medical officer, I Battalion, Grenadier Regiment 438
Busch, Albrecht	Regimental staff, Grenadier Regiment 437
Selle, Otto	Division staff, 132d Infantry Division
Lobermeyer, Franz	Regimental staff, Grenadier Regiment 438
Reiss, Otto	Division communications section
Bitsch, Richard	Division staff and battalion commander
Erhardt, Ulrich	Battalion commander, I Battalion, Grenadier Regiment 438
Sperger, Gottfried	II Battalion, Grenadier Regiment 437
Kohl, Horst	Battalion commander, Artillery Regiment 132
Geitz, Georg	Hauptfeldwebel, Ninth Company, Grenadier Regiment 437
Schramm, Fritz	Third Company, Grenadier Regiment 436
Wunderer, Eduard	Division chaplain, Protestant denomination
Thielmann, Fritz	Artillery Regiment 132
Herrle, Hans	Regimental staff, Grenadier Regiment 438
Krentz, Arthur Albert	Obergefreiter, Fourteenth Company, Grenadier Regiment 437
Ketterl, Franz	Company commander and battalion commander, Grenadier Regiment 438
Hohenadel, Jakob	Platoon commander, Fourteenth Company, Grenadier Regiment 438
Moehle, Friedrich	Hauptfeldwebel, First Pionier Company, Pionier Regiment 132
Stenitzer, Hans	Staff, II and III Battalions, Grenadier Regiment 437
Fleck, Guenther	Radioman, Eleventh Company, Grenadier Regiment 437
Lang, Friedel	Adjutant and company commander, III Battalion, Grenadier Regiment 437
Luecker, Ernst	Staff, I and II Battalions, Grenadier Regiment 437

and others

INTRODUCTION

Any memoir of frontline ground combat in World War II raises two fundamental questions: why did the author do what he did, and how did he endure it? Gottlob Bidermann tells a story increasingly unfamiliar at the turn of the century—a story requiring intellectual engagement as well as emotional response. Bidermann was a warrior for the working day. He was not a tanker or a pilot, but an infantryman. He served not in an elite division, like the *Grossdeutschland* or the *Panzer Lehr*, but in anonymous formations whose numerical designations resemble entries in a telephone book. Bidermann won no high decorations, none of the medals Adolf Hitler presented in person. His two Iron Crosses, his Crimea Shield, his Close Combat Badge were more or less standard awards for an infantry veteran of the Russian front who lived to wear them.

That did not make them easily earned. In 1942 Bidermann was in the front lines of the assault on the Russian fortress of Sevastopol—a close-gripped, six-month siege that cost the Wehrmacht one hundred thousand casualties but that remains obscured by the drive on Stalingrad. In 1943 Bidermann and his division moved north, to the Leningrad front—but in the final months of the epic battle for that city, when the correspondents and photographers had gone elsewhere for fresher stories. Bidermann finished the war in the Courland pocket, part of an entire army group trapped against the Baltic coast by the great Russian offensives of 1944. It was while the 132d Infantry Division was engaged in the vicious fighting in the swamps and forests of the Leningrad front that Bidermann was awarded more prestigious decorations—the German Cross in Gold, the Gold Wound Badge, and the Honor Roll Clasp. He would later earn the Tank Destruction Badge during the closing months of the war. The most remarkable aspect of the latter awards is that the bearer, as a junior infantry officer, survived the numerous wounds and months of countless engagements required to earn their bestowal. Again his experiences became a footnote, this time to the final destruction of the Third Reich.

Gottlob Bidermann is not "typical." No archetype exists for the German soldier of World War II, any more than for his counterparts in other armies. Yet Bidermann's war story is everyman's war story—a saga of the everlasting high privates and junior officers who, in the words of Bruce Catton, have no hope of stars on their shoulders and scant hope for any in their crowns.

Most English-language first-person accounts of World War II from the German side depict life among the high staff levels, the Luftwaffe's fighter units or Doenitz's U-boats, the panzer divisions and the Waffen SS. Johannes Steinhoff, Guy Sajer, Michael Wittmann—their stories appear and reappear on bookshelves and in footnotes. But most of the millions who served in the armed forces of the Third Reich had no celebration of their experiences and their sacrifices. They fought anonymously and died anonymously. Even the graves of those who fell in Russia were obliterated, some by a retreating Wehrmacht, others by a Soviet Union seeking retribution for its 20 million dead.

Those who survived found, in a Germany seeking to rebuild morally as well as physically, few outside their families who had time for or interest in their stories. At the end of the century, Germany has nothing like the proliferation of published personal recollections generated in the United States and Britain when veterans retired and opened footlockers and memories or when children went through their father's things after the funeral.

Those stories are by no means all triumphalist. Nevertheless, they describe a "good war," waged against enemies worth fighting and defeating. What can a German of the same generation say about his war? Bidermann's narrative is structured by the framework of the army in which he fought, by the nature of the Reich he served, and not least by a set of cultural and intellectual conventions vastly different from their British and American counterparts.

The German war memoir had its genesis in the experiences of 1914–1918. Like those of Britain, France, and the United States, it was the product of a limited, largely middle-class, group: the self-conscious and the self-reflecting. It also developed a set of conventions that strongly influenced the genre, because most war memoirists are neither authors nor intellectuals. Simply wishing to tell their story, they tend to do so in established frameworks. German memoirists of 1914–1918 tended to process the war in Hegelian terms, as part of a continuum characterized by cycles of destruction and renewal. The individual's war experience became a *Bildungsgeschichte*, a story of growth through a dialectic between personal engagement and organic, communal processes.

The Germans who recorded their experiences in Hitler's war came overwhelmingly from a generation that regarded those earlier memoirs as the norm for telling what Vietnam-era author Tim O'Brien calls a "true war story"—a construction depicting truths for which there are no words. They adopted as well a style of writing that Germans call *"heroisch-pathetisch"* not in the English usage of those words, but by employing a kind of elevated diction, combining romanticism and metaphysics.

Too often this phrase translates into English as self-pitying bombast, reinforcing a tendency for British and U.S. readers to interpret the conventions of the German war memoir as expressing militarism and proto-Fascism. French and British personal accounts of World War I focused on waste and betrayal, disjunction and fragmentation. The English-speaking world associates "real" memories of later conflicts with the disillusionment of Farley Mowat, the matter-of-fact diction of Audie Murphy, or the antic poststructuralism of Tim O'Brien. Yet to borrow another of O'Brien's concepts, all war stories are false—but all war stories are also true. *In Deadly Combat* merits reading on its author's terms.

Bidermann's terms are above all those of a front-line infantryman. *In Deadly Combat* was originally written not for general audiences, not even for German veterans, but for an in-group: the survivors of Bidermann's regiment and division. The author took no pains to explain organizations and terminologies with which his readers were likely to be intimately familiar. It is worth remembering as well that even as a junior officer, Bidermann was not necessarily au courant with every aspect of his parent formations any more than his American counterparts would be. Recent challenges to the authenticity of Guy Sajer's classic *Forgotten Soldier* depend significantly on details of nomenclature, equipment, command, and location that were highly unlikely to be noted and remembered by a man in the ranks. The same held true for platoon and company officers.

It is correspondingly appropriate to introduce here the German infantry of World War II. As in all armies, its basic building block was the division. But in contrast to the U.S. Army's practice of creating homogeneous, interchangeable formations, German infantry divisions were organized and equipped in waves, or *Wellen*—no fewer than thirty-five of them in the course of the war. Gottlob Bidermann's 132d Division belonged to the "eleventh wave," formed in September 1940, for service in the Russian invasion Hitler and the High Command were already planning. It saw action in the brief Balkan campaign of April–May 1941, but its war really began when it crossed the Russian frontier on 30 June. It is then that Bidermann takes up his narrative.

Initially the divisions in each wave had slightly different scales of armament, depending on what was available in the arsenals or what the Reich was able to scrounge from its latest conquests. Some divisions marched into Russia armed with captured French antitank guns and with French vehicles in their supply columns. The antitank company in which Bidermann initially served depended, for example, on light French tractors, Lorraine *chenilettes,* to draw its guns.

Organization was rather more standard than armament and equipment. The German infantry division consisted of three regiments, each with three battalions—for the 132d, the 436th, 437th, and 438th Infantry Regiments (IR). It had an artillery regiment of four battalions, sequentially numbered I through IV, in contrast to the American linking of four independent battalions under an artillery headquarters. Also in contrast to U.S. norms, the German division included an antitank battalion and a reconnaissance battalion with horses, bicycles, and a couple of light-armored cars. In accordance with standard German practice, all of these units in the 132d bore the division's number.

Engineer, medical, signal, and supply services were essentially the same in the German and the U.S. armies, with one essential variation. German infantry divisions were almost entirely horse-powered. At full war strength in 1939, a "first wave" division, with top priority for material, had over five thousand horses but fewer than six hundred trucks. The forced-draft, haphazard process of rearmament under the Nazis between 1933 and 1939 made it impossible even to consider developing Germany's auto industry sufficiently to motorize a mass army. The High Command, nothing if not logical, responded by designing a family of state-of-the-art horse-drawn wagons, with such refinements as ball-bearing wheels and rubber tires, for issue to units that would be marching in any case. The only major exceptions were the antitank companies and battalions, because they were expected to have to move quickly to counter enemy armor. Otherwise, throughout the war when the landser rode, it was an exception to a general rule—and too often the sign of an emergency.

Personnel casualties and losses of equipment led during the war to several modifications. The most important changes for the 132d Division were the 1944 reduction of each infantry regiment to only two battalions and the reconnaissance battalion's conversion to what was called a fusilier battalion—for all practical purposes a seventh infantry battalion directly under control of the division commander.

The reduction in numbers was, in theory at least, compensated by new equipment. The best way of evaluating that process is by examining in somewhat more detail the structure of the 437th Infantry Regiment, in which Bidermann served for most of the war. Students of the U.S. Army in World War II will find little here that is unfamiliar. The U.S. infantry regiment of 1941–1945 was, on paper at least, almost identical to its German counterpart. Indeed the tables of organization adopted by the United States in 1940 were conscious imitations of the German ones.

Each German infantry battalion had three rifle companies and what was called a machine-gun company, although like the U.S. battalion's heavy weapons company it included a platoon of mortars. The twelve companies of an American regiment were lettered sequentially from A to M, with J omitted. A German regiment's companies were numbered from one to twelve. The German regiment had a horse-drawn Thirteenth Company armed with short-range, close-support artillery pieces. The U.S. regiment had an organic cannon company with the same mission. Each regiment had as well an antitank company—number fourteen in the German regiment—with a dozen guns.

The antitank company was the only fully motorized unit in a German regiment. During most of Bidermann's service with it, the Fourteenth Company of the 437th was armed with twelve 37mm high-velocity guns. These were equivalents—the originals, indeed, of the pieces that the U.S. infantry would take into Tunisia in late 1942. Originally adopted in 1936, they were light enough to be moved by hand for short distances. That was about their only virtue as an antitank weapon by mid-1941. The little 37mm rounds bounced off Russian tank armor so often that the gun won the dubious nickname of "army door-knocker." Especially against the T-34s and the heavy KVs that came into service in the first six months of the Russo-German War, German antitank crews had to depend on holding their fire to point-blank range and aiming for a vulnerable spot like a turret ring or allowing the tank to pass and trying for a side or rear shot. Either was a high-risk option, demanding steel nerves and split-second timing from every man in the crew.

This tactical point is significant because the towed antitank gun was, for most of the war in the east, the backbone of German antiarmor defense. In sharp contrast to a U.S. infantry division usually able to count on an attached battalion of tanks and another of self-propelled tank destroyers, the German division had at best a couple of dozen improvised self-propelled guns at division level. The rest was up to the Pak gunners of the infantry regiments. Later in the war the 37mm gave way first to a 50mm, then to a 75- or 76mm gun, with correspondingly more effect on Russian tanks and assault guns. But the mind-set required by the gunners, and the infantry alongside whom they fought, remained the same. If the German landser of World War II was as formidable at close quarters as any soldier in history, it was in good part because he had no choice.

After his return from officer-training in 1943, Bidermann was not reassigned to the Paks. Instead, he commanded infantry units whose armament and dynamics had changed significantly since 1941. As was the case in the U.S. Army, a rifle company's building block was the *gruppe,* or squad. American infantry tactics depended on the individual rifleman and his semiautomatic M-1 Garand. The automatic rifle organic to each squad was a support weapon. A German squad, however, was built around its light machine gun; and the MG-42 plays a prominent part in the second half of Bidermann's narrative. In defense or attack, the rest of the squad, with their bolt-action Mausers, were expected to cover the gun crew and keep them supplied with ammunition. As long as the gun stayed in action, the position had a chance of holding out against anything but overwhelming numbers—or tanks.

With its high rate of fire and its quick-change barrel, the MG-42 compensated at least in part for the declining strength of front-line German units. Anybody able to scrounge one discarded his turn-of-the-century rifle for a submachine gun, either the German MP-40 or one of its Russian counterparts. The latter were popular for their ruggedness, their reliability, and not least for their difference, despite the risks of their distinctive sound drawing friendly fire. The AK-47 would acquire similar status for similar reasons among Americans in Vietnam.

Beginning in 1943, the hard-pressed German infantry also began receiving deliveries of the world's first assault rifle, the *Sturmgewehr.* With a smaller, lighter cartridge than its predecessors, it was capable of full automatic fire and proved resistant to the worst of weather conditions. Never standard issue, it was nevertheless available even in an ordinary formation like the 132d. Though Bidermann does not say so, it is logical to assume that he took a little advantage of his rank and made sure he had one of them most of the time.

The German infantry division had another unit foreign to its U.S. counterpart: a depot, or replacement battalion. That too was part of a comprehensive policy. Germany was divided into twenty-one military districts, and each division of the Wehrmacht was assigned to one of those districts as the source of its replacements. The districts were small enough to facilitate regional identity and large enough to prevent a particular town or district from losing most of its young men in the event of a catastrophe, as was the case with the British "pals' battalions" of 1916. The 132d Division began its life as a south Bavarian formation from District VII. Then it was transferred to District XII, including the Eifel, the Palatinate, the Saar, and after 1940, the reannexed province of Lorraine—where Bidermann reported after completing his officer-training.

In principle, recruits, recovered wounded, or men sent back for specialized courses would report to the depot of their regiment and from there be dispatched to the front, usually in organized detachments. Reporting to the divisional depot battalion, they would be sent forward as needed. As the war progressed, this system eroded. Men were assigned from any depot to any unit needing them, or thrown together in improvised battle groups to meet emergencies. The regional identities of regiments and divisions eroded, as Bidermann's text indicates. Nevertheless, the concept of maintaining unit identity as far as possible never completely disappeared.

To the end of the war, that cohesion contributed significantly to the German army's front-line effectiveness—especially improvised formations like the one Bidermann was periodically assigned to command. What he describes as an "assault reserve" or an "alarm company" was an ad hoc battle group that acted as an emergency strike force. Usually built around the regimental pioneer platoon, it might include cooks, clerks, walking wounded, stragglers—the sort of men few U.S. officers would choose for dangerous missions, even if they were the only ones available. But the 437th Infantry's Sad Sacks restored many a desperate tactical situation in the war's final months.

Never did soldiers fight better than Gottlob Bidermann, the men of the 132d Division, and the millions of others in Wehrmacht field gray. And never did soldiers fight in a worse cause. Were Bidermann and his comrades, as they so often insist, ordinary men doing their duty in extraordinary times? Were the obscene realities of Adolf Hitler's New Order something remote from the front lines? Here, certainly, are no stories of massacred prisoners or murdered civilians. Instead, Bidermann is at some pains to describe cordial relations with the peasants of the Crimea. He repeatedly insists that captured Russians were treated "correctly." Within the text's few connections to the Holocaust is Bidermann's description of the vicious see-saw fighting in a "Jewish cemetery" near Leningrad—an irony that was probably lost to Bidermann and his men as they struggled to survive in an unforgiving milieu.

Nor does Bidermann's text incorporate the ideological intensity described in general terms by Stephen Fritz and Omer Bartov as characteristic of the Wehrmacht as the war progressed. That is predictable in a memoir incorporating fifty years' reflection as well as four years' experience. It would be unusual for a self-defined "ordinary German," seeking to tell the truth that he remembers, to affirm at this distance the everyday importance of National Socialism in sustaining morale and military effectiveness. Similarly, the numerous vignettes of disillusion, pessimism, and cynicism need not be taken at full face value.

The closest Bidermann comes to affirming an ideology is his uncritical assumption that because the Germans were better soldiers than the Russians, they were also better human beings. Far from being a symbol and a rallying point, Adolf Hitler is as remote to the men of the 437th as the Germany he rules. And yet these two subtexts combine to tell a "true war story." By whatever blend of intention and memory, *In Deadly Combat* is a narrative of encapsulation. Bidermann's world is his unit, his comrades—"the outfit," *"der Haufen."* "The folk community" becomes a set of images preserved in worn photographs and fading memories. "Germany's mission in the east" is reduced to survival in the face of overwhelming odds.

Even "comradeship" becomes a construction. One of the more horrifying set pieces in this memoir is Bidermann's account of a military execution. The victim's original crime was stealing food and cigarettes from his unit's mail—certainly no small matter in any army at any time. But in Hitler's army, that offense carried penalties so severe that the thief committed premeditated murder rather than face being reported. What in the U.S. or British armies was a minor offense, in the Wehrmacht was part of a disciplinary system so brutal that in the course of World War II it executed fifteen thousand of its own men. It sentenced more than one hundred thousand to prison terms of over a year. It condemned thousands more to penal battalions where conditions were, in the words of one survivor, "like being on death row." *"That,"* as the distinguished historian Manfred Messerschmidt once said, "is what the Nazis called 'people's community'!"

Modern war's "depersonalization" and "objectification" of enemies are described as a precondition for "dehumanization," which in turn is a necessary first step to killing, whether on the battlefield, behind the lines, or in a concentration camp. But objectification requires interaction. To dehumanize someone it is necessary to see him. War also isolates, creating environments where everything "outside" some vital center is perceived through a soldier's equivalent of Sylvia Plath's bell jar. By the end of Bidermann's narrative, the Russians are less depersonalized than invisible. The Germans have been not demodernized but decivilized. The survivors of the 437th Infantry resemble nothing so much as a prehistoric band huddling around a fire, staring blindly into it as a talisman against nameless horrors hovering outside the small circle of light.

Dennis Showalter

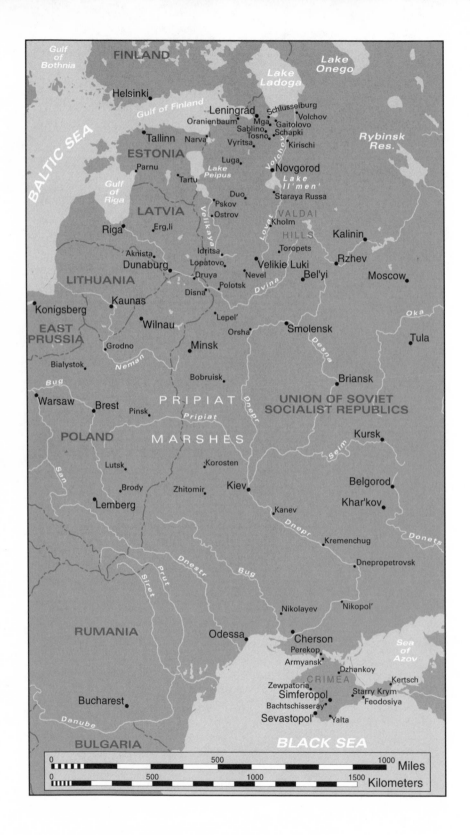

CHAPTER ONE

The March Toward the East

If there exists anything

mightier than destiny,

then it is the courage

to face destiny unflinchingly.

— Geibel

Thirty June 1941. A summer sultriness blanketed the endless plains of eastern Poland, and only the movement of the train swaying slightly beneath us brought us relief from the heat. The heavily laden transport rolled slowly through ragged pine forests and stretches of sandy, uncultivated land, and we passed tiny farms and villages and crossed meandering rivers on our way toward the east.

Except for children who occasionally waved to us from the dusty streets and roadsides, we were ignored by the local inhabitants. The men and women in drab clothing whom we observed from a distance became lost in the shimmering heat as the wheels of the Reichsbahn put them farther behind us. We passed the hours sitting or lying under a cloudless sky as we rested on the open flatbed cars between tightly secured weapons and vehicles.

In contrast to following the peacetime regulations that had previously dominated our lives, we were permitted to loosen the first button of our gray-green uniforms and roll back the sleeves for what little comfort we could enjoy in the sweltering heat. The initial news of the war with Russia was several days old, and we spoke little about the prospects of becoming involved in the fighting. Everyone was confident that this war against the Soviet Union, like the conflict with France and Poland, would pass quickly.

At dawn the walls and towers of Krakow, the holy city of Poland where the heart of Pilsudski lies within the cathedral, appeared. The transport slowly screeched to a halt beside a dusty rail-switching station, and within seconds we were ringed by a band of disheveled children who were ignored by the stone-faced military police sentries standing nearby. "Bidde um bror, Herr," they cried plaintively, with dirty hands grasping eagerly for the morsels we passed to them from our bread bags. We were permitted to detrain, and the children descended on us.

"Poor Poland," I thought to myself. I passed a slice of bread to an enterprising young girl in return for a tattered newspaper. It had been printed the previous day in German and Polish, and it was possible to read the first news about the operation in the east: advance on Lemberg. Gridnov, Brest-Litovsk, Wilnau, Kovno, and Dunaburg had quickly fallen into German hands. Ecstatic headlines announced that more than 2,582 Soviet aircraft and 1,297 Soviet tanks had been destroyed. Soviet-occupied Poland was being freed from the Bolshevik yoke.

The military police soon sprang to action with whistles and shouts, gesturing for us to reboard our transport, and we piled back onto the train. The rail cars groaned in protest and strained against the weight, and we began to move slowly forward as I read the contents of the newspaper aloud to our gun crew, all of whom lay listlessly and disinterested on the flat rail car. I glanced up from my reading and gazed back on the rail platform, now occupied only by the ragged band of children, and our journey to an unknown destiny continued.

On 1 July we came to a stop ten kilometers west of Pelkinie near Yaroslav, where we dismounted and proceeded eastward, the infantry forming a long column on foot, the unenviable fate of every infantryman. Our antitank gun moved ahead of us in the distance, pulled by a Chenilette tracked vehicle captured during the French campaign.

Our senses were immediately struck by the lingering smell of smoke and ashes, and soon we could observe the large craters and scorched vehicles that depicted the handiwork of the German Stuka dive-bombers. We eventually filed to a halt at a temporary roadside canteen where, under the watchful eyes of the ever-present military police, Swabian Red Cross nurses drew cold coffee from a horse-drawn field kitchen and ladled it into our outstretched canteen cups. In vain they asked questions about recent news from home.

We proceeded in a long gray column, leaving the Red Cross nurses behind, and marched farther toward the east. As dusk settled on us we located the vehicles and guns beneath the shelter of a small file of trees that sparsely lined the narrow road. Camouflage protection from aircraft was ordered, and we attempted to cover our position with thin branches.

At dawn we were overtaken by supply columns rolling along an arterial road running toward the distant sunrise. We spent another day following in the tracks of the supply unit, and late in the afternoon we encountered the enemy for the first time.

The dusty road was lined with endless columns of Russian prisoners in ragged khaki-brown uniforms heading in the opposite direction. Many of those without caps wore wisps of straw or rags tied to their close-cropped heads as protection against the burning sun, and some were barefooted and half-dressed, giving us an indication of how quickly our attacking forces had overrun their positions.

By their strange mixture of clothing they appeared to us to be barely soldiers, representing a mixture of White Russians, dark-skinned Caucasians, Kirgises, Usbeks, nomads with Mongolian features, an influx of people from the two continents covered by Soviet Russia. They filed past us silently and with downcast eyes; occasionally several of them could be seen supporting another who appeared to be suffering from wounds, sickness, or exhaustion. In school we had been taught that the Urals separated Europe from Asia; however, here we saw Asia in what we believed to be the heart of Europe. The long column of misery disappeared behind us, and as darkness descended we came to a halt. Beneath a star-covered sky we wrapped ourselves in camouflage-printed shelter-quarters, not to awaken until dawn.

The Fourteenth Panzerjaeger Company was assigned as the forward advance unit, and at precisely 0500 we marched. The crumbling ruins of burned-out houses stood as mute witnesses to the fighting that the city of Yaroslav experienced during the Poland campaign, which although only two years hence seemed a lifetime ago. With the crossing of the San River at Radymo we had Russian soil beneath our feet.

We passed a large German cemetery from World War I with a faded wooden sign above the entrance: "To the memory of those comrades who fell at Dubroviza." Our column was not permitted to stop long enough to examine the graves, and little did we realize how many cemeteries of our own would line the roadsides deep into Russia. We soon encountered fresh mounds of earth marked by rough birch crosses, topped with the unmistakable steel helmets of the German Wehrmacht. These first silent, bloody witnesses on the highway to the east were arranged in regulation rows and columns, and we attempted to divert our gaze but were always drawn back to the graves. We marched on without speaking, and the silent red-brown mounds of earth seemed to beckon to us as if to say, "Do not leave us here, . . . do not abandon us in this strange place."

Faint artillery fire could be heard from the direction of Lemberg. The condition of the roads became steadily worse, and dust settled thickly on the landsers, horses, and vehicles. Only the dim silhouette of the vehicle ahead of our platoon was visible as the sun stood like an orange globe in its zenith, barely penetrating the choking clouds of dust. Sweat and dirt combined to create bizarre shapes on the faces peering from beneath the heavy green helmets. Near Krakovize we again combined shelter-quarters to tent and spend the night.

Our odyssey into the void continued as we advanced toward an unknown destination. We encountered primitive villages lining the road, and Russian women and children peered at us intently from the shadows of doorways and gazed at us through the protection of rough-hewn windowpanes. The only men to be seen were ancient veterans of other wars.

When asked, the people of the villages would tell us of the Bolsheviki. The menace and terror of the Siberian penal camps could be seen in the eyes of these people as they spoke, and they told us that pictures of Christ and Stalin hung in the schools. When the village teachers asked, "Whom do you thank for your daily bread?" the children would be compelled to answer "Stalin." We were relieved that we were experiencing firsthand the effects of Communism and that what we were hearing could not simply be attributed to our own propaganda. Niedermeier remarked, "After having seen Russia, we now know how fortunate we are to be German."

On 5 July we moved through Lemberg. The city had been heavily hit twice during the initial course of the war, and the early morning haze revealed burned-out factories, ruined homes, and destroyed tanks with greasy, black smoke billowing from the still-hot carcasses. In one of the few partially intact sectors of the city a long line of people waited in front of a bread depot. They stared at us with listless eyes as we passed.

The Russian air base at Lemberg had been rendered unusable by the Stukas. Blackened aircraft and smashed equipment were scattered throughout the area, and during a pause on our march soldiers wandered among the wreckage, photographing one another alongside destroyed Soviet planes and curiously picking through the ruins, ever mindful of strict regulations against looting or the nonauthorized requisition of captured enemy equipment. The war with the Soviet Union being only a few days under way, we still observed anything associated with the Soviet army with curiosity.

Our march continued through the first half of July. For days great numbers of destroyed Russian tanks lined our path, and capsized prime movers with limbered field guns were scattered along the roadsides. In the fields one could see numerous abandoned Russian artillery positions that appeared to be intact, indicating how quickly our offensive had overtaken the Soviet defenders.

We were astonished at how well motorized the Soviet army was, as our own artillery was represented primarily by horse-drawn equipment reminiscent of World War I. The graves of German and Russian soldiers were now found to be close together, the German graves marked with rough-hewn wooden crosses to the right of the road, the Russians to the left. The Russian graves remained nameless, marked only with rifles and bayonets stuck into the fresh earth. The German graves were topped with the customary steel helmet, and from some of the crosses hung identification disks from linen string, waiting to be collected and filed.

On 8 July as we neared Brody on the wide, rutted road we passed supply units and cable-layers of the Seventy-first Division of the Sixth Army. The cable-layers advised us that the division had taken Lemberg with six hundred casualties and confidently reported that the war was to end within several weeks.

Our advance halted on the old Russian-Galician border. We expected to encounter strong enemy opposition when the Sixth and Seventeenth Armies reached the Stalin Line, a series of bunkers and heavily defended strong points. We were disappointed to learn that the 132d Infantry Division had received the assignment to remain in reserve, as most of us were eager to see action before the inevitable surrender of the Soviet Union.

Fourteen July passed without notice. Our existence remained marked by boredom; our environment consisted of one hundred-meter-wide transport roads, dust, mud, burning heat, thunderstorms, and an endless open space with only occasional clusters of sparse trees stretching to the horizon. Thatched-roofed huts of the collective farms could be seen in the distance, and we concentrated on them, like palms in the desert, to guide us to primitive wells. We had received word that the wells were often poisoned by the Red Army in retreat. Skeletal remains of horses left a lingering stench along our path, the smell that would remind us forever of the Soviet paradise into which we found ourselves marching ever deeper.

The advance slowed as we crossed through Jampol. Occasionally we were lucky enough to obtain a few onions and carrots from the villages that lined our path; more rarely a chicken or a couple of eggs served to augment the monotonous field rations. We reflected with longing on our time spent in Karnten and Zagreb before the onslaught against the Russians began, as there we had enjoyed cold beer and slibowitz.

The infantry continued to march from sunrise to sunset. Dusty, sweaty, and clammy without relief from the brutal climate, we penetrated deeper into Soviet Russia. Although it was against regulations, small panye carts, pulled by stout Russian ponies, were requisitioned to lighten the load of our field packs. As we left civilization as we knew it farther behind us, this habit became more commonplace. The sparse human habitation was primitive and probably lice-ridden, so nights were spent in tents, haystacks, or more often on the bare earth, sleeping rolled in the ever-useful shelter-quarter that each landser was issued. Members of horse-drawn units would be awakened at dawn by the nuzzling of hungry and thirsty horses.

We passed wood-framed schoolhouses, which were little more than rough halls decorated with the characteristic red stars and red-painted podiums for political gatherings of the Communist Party. Tattered, dusty pictures of Stalin and Lenin hung on the walls, and Stalin had introduced compulsory schooling where previously, during the era of the czar, the alphabet was hardly known. We were surprised that many of the schoolchildren could speak some broken German, and from captured propaganda material we learned that political education was a priority for the children.

On 17 July we received mail from home for the first time since our advance had begun, and ten days later the division entered the Ukraine and marched over Kasatin in a southeast direction toward Rushin. The Ukraine steamed in the summer heat. Over wide, sandy roads and on pavement of rough stones we came into a land of unending horizons.

Endless wide steppes and grain and sunflower fields bordered our way toward the east. Primitive wooden windmills dotted the horizon, and we used them as our drink and rest stations during the lonely march through a land that left us with unforgettable impressions of freedom contrasting with an overwhelming sense of emptiness.

We came to a halt in an unkempt acacia grove that offered sparse shade in an ocean of grass. The company had marched sixty kilometers in less than twenty-four hours on painfully torn and bruised feet. Dusty and channeled with streaks of sweat, faces browned by wind and sun peered from under heavy helmets to observe our domain. Hands slippery with sweat gripped the entrenching tools to tear holes in the earth. The command was given: "Dig in."

Stripped to the waist we hacked at the earth without speaking, and nearby the singing of bees reminded me of their own endless toil. Clemens and Gehr, the two tractor drivers, decided to locate the source of the bees in search of honey. Equipped with mess tins and armed with shelter-quarters and gas masks as protection from bee stings, they disappeared behind the gun position into a collective farm.

After an hour of labor I had constructed to the left of the Pak position a regulation earthwork, the high side facing our front, on which we would lay our rifles and grenades. The antitank gun stood well-concealed with branches and grass near the edge of the grove. A sandy road cut through the open field before us in an east-west direction, and in the shimmering heat of the afternoon sun the silhouettes of huts in a distant village were visible on the horizon.

To the left of the road Gefreiter Poell had placed his half-track to the rear of the position to be hidden behind the acacia grove, and he set to work camouflaging his Pak. Forward observers from the artillery and the mortar units moved ahead to their observation points with rolls of communication cable strapped to their backs. Only the occasional clatter of an entrenching tool, canteen cup, or mess tin broke the stillness of a seemingly peaceful world.

Folding my dusty tunic under my head for a pillow, I had just begun to doze in the afternoon sun when a rifle shot broke the afternoon silence. In one motion I rolled into the freshly dug foxhole, clapped on the heavy steel helmet, and brought my carbine to my shoulder. Staring forward, I could detect only emptiness and softly swaying grasses. During infantry defense drills it had been hammered into us to shoot at every disturbance, every moving leaf and blade of grass, in order to kill the enemy. Now with my heart pounding, thoughts raced through my mind: Would today be the day that I must kill another human being? Who shoots first, who hits first, him or me? Must I kill today in order to save my own life and the lives of my comrades? I pictured the rows of graves we had passed during our march with carefully placed crosses, identification markers hanging from them, and tried to shake them from my mind.

About six hundred meters to the left of our position the racing sound of rifle fire broke the stillness. Sounding at first like the familiar popping of carbine fire at the training range, soon wild shots snapped through the air and ricocheted above us. With burning eyes we continued staring forward, but we noticed nothing unusual before our position. Through the rifle fire the distinctive crack of an antitank gun sounded far in the distance.

Within a few minutes the incident was over. Dust and the acrid smell of burnt cordite drifted faintly in the air, and to our left an ugly black cloud billowed into the blue afternoon sky. We remained crouched in our positions; in hushed tones and with hearts pounding with excitement we tried to assess what had occurred. A short time later we learned through a courier that Poell's antitank gun had knocked out a Soviet armored reconnaissance vehicle and that an attack by a Russian rifle company had been repulsed.

Little did we realize that in the months and years that lay before us this short encounter would come to be considered as nothing more than a casual and insignificant brush with the enemy, and this first action of the regiment was little indication of the nightmarish years of fighting marked by deprivation, sorrow, and countless victims that lay before us. From this vast expanse many of us would never return, but at the time one didn't dwell on such thoughts.

I turned to my diary, the small pocket-sized book bound in black oilcloth, the corners already ragged and the pages stained with sweat and rain, to recount the incident.

The two drivers returned with mess tins dripping with honey, a satisfying addition to our evening rations. We ate the honey with the Komiss bread, welcoming the change from the usual ration of tinned liver and blood sausage, and we washed the bread and honey down with cold tea before preparing for another march at dawn.

Thirty July found us in bivouac at Michaelovka. During the course of the previous days some of the units had experienced attacks from Soviet bomber and fighter-bomber squadrons, which had proven to be ineffective in slowing our advance. The rifle companies and horse-drawn units marched throughout the night and covered about sixty-five kilometers to reach Kargarlyk on 31 July. The nightly password was issued, and rumors circulated of a pending attack to take place the following morning at 0700 along a wide front. We passed the summer night wrapped in shelter-quarters as we crouched in our grass-lined foxholes.

The rumors held true, as exactly at 0700, 1 August, we began our push forward toward the Soviet defenses near Mirovka. An immense open field lay before us, and our view extended over the steppe, which offered little protection save a gently rolling terrain with shallow depressions invisible to the untrained eye. This presented a great advantage for the Soviets, for as defenders they were able to dig into the safety of the earth with a clear field of fire before their defenses. We made final preparations to abandon our positions and to move across the open steppe.

With little effort we brought the Pak into position on the edge of a wheat field, which offered a wide field of fire facing eastward over the waving green sea, interrupted only by sparse potato gardens. The first rays of the morning sun danced across the wheat stalks of the Ukraine, and through the morning haze we could recognize the distant silhouettes of two villages on the horizon. We sat on the gun carriage drinking warm coffee in an attempt to dissipate the cold feeling within us. Everyone desired to appear nonchalant and spoke of things not associated with the war, attempting through conversation to conceal the anxiety clearly etched in sun-burned faces. Company officers gathered in tight circles several dozen meters away, speaking in low tones and glancing toward the enemy positions, occasionally raising field glasses to their eyes.

At 0650 our artillery had opened fire. The heavy projectiles screamed over us en route to predetermined targets within the enemy positions, and the infantry, burdened with weapons, ammunition, communications equipment, and explosives began to advance along a broad front. The movements seemed to follow as planned in exacting detail, giving an initial impression that nothing had taken place other than another training exercise at Pfarrkirchen or Dugo-Selo.

The captured French tractor clattered noisily up to our position. Limbering our gun, we climbed aboard and advanced, leaving a rising cloud of dust in our wake. We passed the armored reconnaissance vehicle knocked out by Poell on the previous day, and our eyes were drawn to the macabre and still unfamiliar scene of a half-burned corpse hanging with naked torso from one of the hatches.

The two antitank guns of the platoon lurched forward over the undulating ground, accompanying the advance along the sandy road toward Kargarlyk. The machine guns of the foremost infantry units were already engaged; the audible bursts of the MG-34s floated back to us over the wheat stalks. Behind us mortar tubes and artillery pieces pounded with dull thumping in contrast to the high-pitched bursts of small-arms fire.

Suddenly ricochets were whistling and bouncing among us, and we found ourselves scrambling for cover in the ruts and furrows of the road.

"Take cover!" screamed gun captain Hartmann. Through the ever-increasing roar from weapons of every caliber we could see his outstretched arms motioning and his lips moving. His commands remained drowned in the pounding thunder of weaponry. Finally the moment had come. It was now our time to face the enemy. Despite the gnawing fear within us, we met the inevitable with profound relief, which served to demonstrate how our priorities had shifted since our march had begun.

The gun crews automatically and mechanically set to work as they had done in drills countless times before. Gunners one and two loosened the limbers, locked the wheels. Gunners three and four spread the limbers wide apart while the aimer simultaneously adjusted for range by depressing the barrel to a horizontal position. The loader opened the bolt to the breech, and the handlers tossed cases of ammunition from the carriage. With one motion the first round was snapped into the open breech of the barrel to be smoothly loaded and locked, and the weapon was ready to fire. Hartmann knelt next to the gun with binoculars held to his eyes as he directed the aimer in textbook fashion: "Right end of the hedgerow . . . range four hundred . . . machine-gun nest. Fire!" Within seconds one round after another was leaving the barrel in response to his practiced commands.

We were able to observe an infantry platoon from the Fifth Company as it became pinned in a shallow depression under heavy fire from enemy machine guns. Under cover fire of the Pak—our rounds now struck directly within the enemy positions—the platoon worked its way forward. Clearly visible were the heavily laden infantrymen, advancing slowly through the wheat fields. Thin wisps of smoke revealed where the dry stalks had been ignited by tracer fire.

The collective farm at Klein-Kargarlyk, which was reportedly occupied by Soviet artillery observers, was taken under fire by the second Pak at a range of some six hundred meters. The straw-thatched huts of the collective began to burn brightly, with thick, black smoke rising into the clear sky.

We received the command to shift positions, and we advanced forward to the crossroads on the same bearing as the burning farm huts. Through the bursts of impacting mortar rounds and the pounding of machine-gun fire we were conscious of the cheers erupting from our parched throats as we observed the Russians abandoning their positions. As they attempted to flee from the farm along the dusty road toward the east, our machine gunners increased their fire, and again the rapid-firing MG-34 Spandaus sent streams of copper-jacketed rounds into the fleeing clusters of khaki-brown figures. To our right the first prisoners appeared with upraised hands and eyes wide with fright. They were quickly stripped of helmets and combat equipment, and they instinctively hurried toward our rear at a trot with hands clasped behind their heads.

While changing positions our tracked vehicle parted a tread. The Chenilette spun in an untimely half-circle and stopped, helplessly stuck in an open field within sight of the enemy. The drivers bailed out of the vehicle and desperately began to attempt repairs as we unhitched the gun and slipped into towing harnesses to pull it forward. The Pak designated as number one within our company left us behind as it advanced, bouncing along the rough road toward the sound of firing.

Sweat soaked through the gray-green uniforms and left trails on faces covered with dust and grime as the Ukrainian summer sun beat upon the dull green helmets. Exhausted, we hung gasping and panting in the towing harness as rifle shots cracked in a now familiar tone and plucked at the crusted, dry, road surface. Occasionally tiny mushrooms of dust erupted in erratic lines along the road near us as bullets fired from a heavy machine gun situated on the east edge of Klein-Kargarlyk impacted near us. With the protective armor shield facing forward, we again lunged against the harness to pull the gun farther, our faces strained with exertion and fear. An occasional ping rang sharply against the armor as a bullet struck it like a hammer, a deadly reminder that we were still under fire from isolated snipers.

Hartmann ran forward to reconnoiter a suitable gun position, his submachine gun swinging from his neck and a hand grenade clenched in his right fist. He directed us toward the right and into the edge of a wheat field. As we left the road we noticed a vague checkerboard pattern of fresh earth in the ruts where the Russians had blocked our advance route with their box-shaped mines. Hartmann's reconnaissance had prevented us from straying into them.

We paused to catch our breath in the sparse shadow of the steel gun shield. No tree, bush, or building was present to offer even faint relief from the burning midday sun. With heaving lungs I fell on my hands and knees for a moment. Others collapsed into the furrows on the edge of the road in a vain attempt to find shade; some merely stretched themselves on the Ukrainian earth.

I remained vaguely aware of the bullets from the Maxim machine gun again cracking nearby, and the pounding of my heartbeat gradually slowed while I lay in the dirt. The deadly projectiles continued to snap and whine over us.

The Russians attempted to zero in on our disabled vehicle now a hundred meters distant from where our efforts had brought the gun. Fountains of earth were thrown skyward, and a thick cloud of gray smoke engulfed the Chenilette as it was surrounded by impacting rounds. Despite the hail of small-arms fire snapping through the air about them, the drivers escaped unscathed and were able to repair the track. Leaping into the driver's seat, Clemmons slammed the transmission into gear, and with a racing engine the vehicle lurched forward and bounced over the open ground toward us.

The other gun, one hundred meters to our left, opened fire in an attempt to knock out the Maxim. It then moved forward, the tractor crawling down the left side of the road until it turned sharply into an immense wheat field that stretched to the horizon. The machine gun continued to keep the tractor under fire, the small-caliber ammunition having little effect on the steel-plated skin of the vehicle.

We greeted the arrival of our driver and the tractor with mixed emotions. We were desperate to shift positions, and the prime mover could now pull the heavy gun; however, we were fully aware that the vehicle would draw additional fire from the enemy positions. The thought of abandoning the gun in order to find shelter from the enemy fire flashed through my mind, but I just as quickly eliminated the unthinkable option and strained harder against the harness. Within a few seconds that seemed to last an eternity, the gun was hitched and under tow by the tractor, the motor screaming in protest as the gun bounced behind us over the uneven ground.

The Russians had pulled their artillery fire closer to their own lines, and the heavy projectiles of high explosives crept ever nearer to us, impacting among the most forward units. The incoming rounds shook the earth beneath us, and only with great effort could we hear the shouted commands above the explosions.

The Seventh Company, to the left of us, had become engaged in heavy fighting. As we advanced the Russians began to scramble from their positions to flee through the wheat fields toward Kargarlyk, some five hundred meters distant. Our forward machine-gun crews fired their MG-34s while standing in the waist-high wheat, each barrel resting across the shoulder of a crewman in order to maintain a clear field of fire. A number of the Russians were struck by the bursts of machine-gun fire and tumbled to the earth, disappearing among the wheat stalks.

As we moved forward we came under sporadic rifle fire from a group of Soviets who later surrendered, moving toward us with upraised arms, fear and exhaustion clearly etched in their faces.

The day's objective, a railway embankment in front of the village, had been reached. Twelve kilometers of territory were won in six hours of difficult fighting, and my thoughts dwelled on the insignificance of twelve kilometers: twelve kilometers—in an endless land, where unbroken fields stretched to the horizon before us from sunrise to sunset. I wondered how many more twelve-kilometer battles lay ahead of us during our march away from the setting sun.

We came upon one of our casualties lying motionless in the dirt on the road, his helmet still secured tightly to his head, sightless eyes staring into the sky. Russian prisoners were quickly employed to carry the wounded to a field dressing station. Escorted by our lightly wounded who marched along the edge of the road, the pitiful column wound toward the Second Battalion collection point to our rear.

Thus the regiment experienced its first clash with the enemy, and we had suffered our first losses as well. With no joy of victory in our ranks, the feeling of excitement quickly drained away to be replaced by an overwhelming sadness and longing to leave this place. As yet we had not experienced the true effects of prolonged warfare, which becomes an environment that sets aside all former bonds to family and culture and irretrievably replaces them with bonds to the comrade at your side. That was to come in the weeks, months, and years ahead. The journalists assigned to the propaganda company would write colorful reports on what had taken place and would also add that the dead and wounded had done their duty in service to the Fuhrer and the fatherland.

Our gun crew was assigned to perform a security detail, and as dusk fell we positioned the gun along the road near the battalion defense line. The isolated bursts of impacting mortar rounds echoed over the wheat fields and seemed to chase the sun as it sank slowly in the west, toward Germany. Our thoughts followed the sinking, fiery ball penetrating the evening haze to the horizon, and we thought of our homeland whose borders lay fifteen hundred kilometers behind us.

The front refused to sleep at night. Reconnaissance units from both opposing forces remained on the move, slipping through the darkness to locate the enemy positions. Again and again the Russian Maxim fire broke forth through the darkness, always answered by the ripping sound of our Spandau MG-34s, quickly joined by erratic rifle fire. The occasional detonation of hand grenades and the sharp reports of submachine guns drifted across the fields, and for long moments the defensive lines would be illuminated by glowing flares arcing skyward to hang, sizzling, above the line. In the early morning hours we were withdrawn from the sector and deployed two kilometers to the south in preparation for another attack.

Two August was marked by a break in the monotonous field rations, when we boiled freshly dug potatoes in an unnamed Ukrainian village. Oberschutze Fehr had already plucked a chicken, and together with the boiled hen and potatoes we ate peeled cucumbers.

Several hundred meters along the approach to the village on a small rise was Unteroffizier Aigner's burned-out half-track. During the previous day's fighting he had driven directly into a well-concealed minefield where the three men of the gun crew met their deaths. Two of the crewmembers were killed instantly. The antitank mine had severed both of Aigner's legs, and he had died that night at the medical collecting point. Their helmets could be seen clustered beneath a birch cross near the destroyed half-track; their graves added to the mounting casualties the war in the Soviet Union was costing the German army.

Not far from their rough grave site was a row of several dozen wooden box-mines dug up by the engineers. The soldiers had long since found an appropriate name for the deadly little boxes, referring to them as kindersaerge.

Word passed through the ranks of the infantrymen of how the division chaplain, Satzger, had risked his life to recover some of the men who fell wounded before the enemy during the previous day's fighting. We remained ever conscious of how the wounded were treated, as we lived every moment with the reality that we, too, could join them at any time without warning.

Many of the soldiers who had not previously been so inclined began to attend religious services, and with the growing consciousness of our own mortality we became more aware of the presence of the chaplain. As our casualties continued to mount, the chaplain, who wore no insignia of rank in the German army, came to play a more significant role in our lives. For far too many he would offer the last voice of reassurance and the last vestige of comfort before they, too, succumbed to mortal wounds.

Our lines of supply became more strained with each day's advance, and as our momentum slowed to a crawl we continued to experience ever-increasing sporadic shelling. Once my gas mask and entrenching tool were ripped away by a shell splinter, and my tunic was torn as well, but other than a bruise on my hip I escaped injury. The Russian rearguard elements continued to withdraw before us, attempting to burn many of the few mud and straw huts in our path and always leaving an ever-present cadre of snipers, who slowly extracted a deadly price from our ranks at the cost of their own lives.

On 3 August we spent most of the night lying in the middle of a turnip field. At length a reconnaissance platoon determined that a still-intact collective farm some five hundred meters distant was free of enemy troops, and in the early predawn hours we advanced to the tiny collection of huts. The company kitchen sent forward hot coffee and schmalzbrot. Our gun crew claimed one of the small thatched-roof huts, and we piled straw onto the mud floor and dozed for several hours, thankful that we were not still lying somewhere in the darkness among the turnips.

The following day we advanced farther toward the east until our forward reconnaissance units reported having reached the wide Dnieper River. The immense bulk of the Soviet army seemed to have evaporated, and victory appeared all but certain as we neared the banks of the Dnieper.

For weeks our routine had consisted of endless marching, interrupted only by sporadic resistance from small bands of Soviet stragglers overtaken by our advanced units. The occasional enemy dead now attracted little attention, and prisoners became a common sight, always rising from the terrain to approach us cautiously with upraised arms. Most often they would be simply disarmed and motioned toward the rear, often unescorted, to be collected by the reserve column.

The evening of 5 August found us in recently constructed defensive positions before Velikaya-Pritzki. The ominous thunder of heavy shelling continued without pause as our artillery pounded the enemy beyond the horizon. We waited nervously throughout the night for our offensive, which was to begin the next morning.

Our attack was launched at precisely 0550, with the Dnieper as the objective. Our artillery batteries fired smoke and high explosives onto a commanding height designated Hill 197, and from our position we could observe many of the enemy troops fleeing through the clouds of smoke enveloping the terrain features. Prisoners later stated that many of the Soviet troops had fled, panic-stricken, out of fear that we had used poison gas against their stronghold, and indeed sightings of enemy troops donning gas masks during the attack had been reported.

Within hours the ridge was captured by the infantry with minimal losses. At 0850 the enemy fought a deadly delaying action back to Hill 160, from where they continued to offer dogged resistance from carefully prepared positions.

Interrogations of exhausted prisoners indicated that the heavy concentrations of artillery fire were instrumental in draining the will of the defenders. In the late afternoon our own forces came under attack from squadrons of fighter-bombers who inflicted little damage.

On the morning of 7 August we labored to dig defensive positions into the earth near a village called Balyka, about one hundred meters from the Dnieper. From our position the wide Dnieper was visible, and we engaged in burrowing into the earth as quickly as possible in anticipation of fighter-bomber attacks as well as for protection from Soviet gunboats on the river.

Within hours heavy mortar rounds fired from boats maneuvering on the Dnieper began to impact on the slopes near us. A gun from the first platoon attempted to take one of the boats under fire without success, and our positions along the riverbank soon were blanketed with enemy mortar and artillery fire. Despite our extensive preparations, we were forced to withdraw from the positions to avoid suffering casualties inflicted by an enemy beyond our reach.

In this sector we found ourselves facing an enemy who held superiority in heavy weapons, and our own artillery units were now compelled to ration ammunition because of our strained supply lines. The depth of our penetration into the Soviet Union began to take its toll, and ammunition rationing served as a first indication of the shortages that we were to encounter with disastrous results in future battles.

The distant thunder of far-off heavy guns resounded faintly in our ears and was quickly followed by the roar of impacting projectiles echoing over the open terrain. The evening brought more attacks from the Ratas flying low over our positions, passing over us in what appeared to be no pattern of attack. We attempted to repel them with rifles and light machine guns, with little effect.

One evening I observed two rations-carriers from the artillery battery located behind us moving along the lower part of the ridge toward the front. The soldier in the lead carried the cylindrical thermos canister in a harness on his back, and they picked their way through the broken ground in the growing twilight, plodding slowly forward over undulating terrain torn by artillery shells and made soft and muddy from the intermittent thunderstorms.

Suddenly we were forced once again to dive for cover as a Rata began a surprise descent upon us from a low-hanging cloud bank, and the two oncoming figures scrambled for shelter behind the wall of one of the mud huts at the edge of the village. The plane loosed a burst of fire into the village as it passed overhead before disappearing into the gray thunderheads as quickly as it had appeared.

Moments later the two men could again be seen making their way past our position. They picked their way through the morass with difficulty, one following closely behind the other, curses clearly audible in the still air. The second man had slung his carbine and was holding both free hands against the sides of the canister in an attempt to salvage the remaining portion of their day's rations. The steel container had been cleanly punctured by a round from the aircraft's board gun, and the projectile had gone through the sides of the canister, leaving the hot contents pouring in twin streams onto the ground. Dodging the shell craters in the evening twilight, they wound their way through the muddy and torn earth toward the waiting men in the battery position. Still swearing and cursing the Ratas and Ivan, they stumbled slowly forward toward their destination. The soup for the artillery battery was to be carefully rationed that night; but however sparse the quantity, it would still be preferred over the monotonous "iron rations" of wurst and hard bread we were often compelled to consume while on the march.

On the evening of 9 August we were treated to schweinebraten, brought forward from the field kitchen by couriers, and the following morning we deployed forward again. The enemy had attempted to push armored units through a sector held by a neighboring division, and elements of the Sixty-eighth and our 132d Infantry Division were ordered to reinforce the sector.

The march was ordered for 0800. In preparation for the move we were provided with coffee and schmalzbrot. Despite the sickening odor of a dead horse that permeated the air from the edge of the road, we enjoyed the first meal since being treated to schweinebraten early in the evening of the previous day. During our short pause a band of Stukas flew over us, and we were able to observe them break from their formation and dive like hawks on an unseen prey. The screaming aircraft sirens threw panic and confusion throughout the enemy ranks as the Stukas dropped their bombs into the columns of Russian tanks and troop concentrations hidden from our view behind the terrain features. Clouds of black smoke mushroomed skyward through the still air, marking the locations of the vehicles that had fallen victim to the dive-bombers.

The Russians soon retaliated with air attacks of their own. Not having had time to prepare defensive positions, we dove for cover in the shallow depressions in the ground, only to be bypassed by the enemy aircraft. Behind us some bombs fell near a medical collection point without causing casualties.

On 12 August our pilots dropped artillery ammunition to the batteries in our rear area. The artillery units had fired ceaselessly while repelling the heavy Soviet counterattacks during the previous days, and the air observers reported that the Soviets were pulling their forces back toward the east over the Dnieper near Kanev. Our own units continued to press attacks, but enemy resistance had stiffened and we gained little ground.

My gun was situated near a railway embankment to secure the rail lines running toward Kanev and over the Dnieper. The front in our sector had remained quiet throughout the afternoon, and Hartmann and I set out on a short reconnaissance of our area.

Behind the rail line in an easterly direction along the edge of a small grove of trees we suddenly found ourselves staring into the muzzle of a Maxim machine gun not ten meters distant. Concealed beneath the shadows of low-lying branches, a blood-soaked figure in a khaki uniform was draped motionless over the gun carriage, as if resting.

Quietly releasing the safety catches of our submachine guns, we gingerly edged forward, surveying the scene before us. Lying closely together in a jagged row along the railway embankment we found a group of about thirty dead Russians. From their position it was obvious that during the previous day's fighting, a burst from a tank or aircraft machine gun had caught the platoon in a flanking fire, killing or wounding all of them instantly.

I slowly slipped forward to examine one of the casualties and observed that the lifeless hand of one of the corpses still grasped an open package containing a field bandage. The badly wounded Russian had vainly attempted to bandage himself, but, unable to staunch the flow of blood, had slowly died where he lay. His tunic was unbuttoned to the waist, his uniform black with the encrusted blood from a fatal wound. My gaze wandered from the first figure and fell upon a corpse wearing the uniform of a sergeant. The NCO was grasping one of the wheels of the Maxim carriage, his sightless eyes peering forward at the ammunition belt where it fed into the chamber of the weapon. Another held his rifle clenched in cold fists, his head resting against the ground as if asleep, the olive-colored helmet secured tightly under his chin.

Hartmann slipped past me and slowly approached two other figures lying closely together, side by side. One of the figures had draped an arm across the other in a last embrace, as if attempting to comfort a dying comrade. As Hartmann neared, a cloud of flies rose in protest, breaking the deathly silence, and I moved forward to join him in surveying the ghastly scene.

Moving silently among the carnage, Hartmann suddenly turned and slipped past me without speaking, heading in the direction from which we had come. Carefully avoiding the eyes of the dead, I quickly followed him.

In this abode of death, only the trees, still and quiet, appeared to be survivors and witnesses to the struggle that had occurred, hidden within this wooded glade. Despite having observed death many times over the past months, I unknowingly remained a novice as yet to the true brutality and horror of war. I could never at the time have imagined that in the months and years to come I would become benumbed to death on the battlefield and that such scenes would be commonplace to us all. In the months to come our reaction to the deaths we had witnessed would become callous and accepting. We would have searched the corpses for documents, collected weapons, and gathered equipment for our own use. At this early stage during our baptism of war, we remained burdened by the naive thoughts of pity for the dead and by our own aversion to physical contact with the bloody and torn bodies strewn upon the earth where they had fallen.

On 13 August we occupied a former Russian field position approximately ten kilometers northwest of the city of Kanev on the Dnieper. We had taken over the holes hacked into the clay by the enemy, who had occupied the heights only a few days previously. Experts at digging and camouflaging positions in the open fields, the Russians had constructed earthworks that consisted of circular holes about waist-deep, widened at the bottom to allow one to lie comfortably with enough room to stretch the legs. The clay held fast and was excellent for tunneling, so I confidently improved my position with my entrenching tool. Prior to our attack a rather small Russian must have occupied it.

I found the cool earth of my new dwelling comfortable, despite the sultriness of the hot Ukrainian summer day. Here I felt secure, with the sense that nothing could happen to me quickly or without warning. We crept cautiously forward into the open terrain to gather grass and straw, with which we camouflaged our antitank gun. In the evening twilight someone brought in a large bundle of straw, which was divided among the gun crews. With this we could plan on spending a comfortable night, providing that Ivan did not wake us.

The evening shadows disappeared as twilight turned to darkness, leaving rugged silhouettes of the uneven hills and deep ravines, the "balkas," to the east of us across the Dnieper. We would come to know them well in the future fighting.

The enemy had reestablished defensive positions approximately three hundred meters from our location in a small wood. To the left began a small valley lined with birch trees and heavy undergrowth that would have left an impression of peaceful solitude if not for the occasional

Maxim bursts that broke forth to harass our positions from this direction. We left one man on guard huddled behind the heavy armor shield of the Pak for protection from stray machine-gun and sniper rounds, and the sentry was relieved hourly while we spent the night within our straw-lined holes.

It is the nature of war to strike unexpectedly. A soldier may be temporarily lulled into a rare moment of false security—huddled in a crude shelter next to a warming fire during a cold night or sleeping soundly while curled up in a foxhole—only to be immediately thrust into an unforgiving and violent situation. Once again we were aroused from our rest by two rations-carriers who appeared from the darkness bringing the unwelcome news that we were again to shift positions and make preparations for another attack in the morning.

With the now-familiar coldness lying in the depths of our stomachs, we departed our comfortable foxholes shortly before midnight and were soon laboring under a star-filled sky to complete new positions farther to the right before daybreak. The occasional muffled clanging of entrenching tools was clearly audible to the enemy as we worked, and flares sizzled skyward through the night from the edge of a nearby wood. Time and again it was necessary to throw ourselves flat on the ground and lie motionless to protect ourselves from the Maxim fire probing our positions, the bullets popping through the air overhead and tracers leaving orange-red streaks arching and bouncing through the darkness.

During the early morning hours we received reinforcements in the form of two self-propelled guns, which rumbled up to our position on heavy tracks. Our initial concerns were that their throbbing Maybach engines would attract unwanted attention to our position. Despite our fears, their presence failed to attract more machine-gun fire, as the Russians were probably unwilling to reveal their locations to the armored vehicles.

Our attack took place at 1500 on 14 August. Following a ten-minute mortar barrage on the woods, the forward assault elements had closed in to within one hundred meters from the tree line when a Russian tank concealed on our left flank opened fire. It was spotted by one of the supporting self-propelled guns, and following a brief exchange of fire the Russian tank was left burning. Our heavy machine guns and mortars opened fire on the tree line in attempts to eliminate the ever-present enemy snipers, and we joined them in firing antipersonnel rounds into the treetops with our Pak.

With the destruction of the enemy tank, our attack pushed farther forward through the wooded area, and despite our concern the previous evening it was now comforting to have the support of the heavy assault guns. We were able to determine the location of the destroyed tank from the black cloud of smoke rising from the burning turret, and we heard rumors that one of the companies had suffered a number of casualties from the heavily armored vehicle before it had been located and destroyed.

We were facing the last obstacle defending Kanev. Although we had reached our assigned objective, we were again ordered forward after receiving reinforcements. Our assault resumed at 1800.

Our limbered gun was bouncing behind the tractor toward the city, following in the wake of the infantry assault company, when we suddenly came under flanking fire from an enemy field position. Having lain hidden to be bypassed by our advanced elements, the enemy now attacked the platoon with small-arms fire that impacted against the thin skin of the tractor and snapped through the air above us. At that moment the Chenilette motor stalled, and the vehicle lurched to a halt under a hail of fire.

With pounding hearts we grasped submachine guns and carbines and desperately scrambled for cover, the realization that we were caught on open ground gripping us with fear. Our machine gunner, Robert, with whom I had served since recruit training, seized his MG-34 and sprang to his feet to lunge forward under the weight of the machine gun. He sprinted toward the muzzle flashes revealing the enemy position, firing streams of bullets from the hip as he ran.

Completely surprised by this assault, a number of the Russians rose from their positions and stumbled toward us, arms raised in surrender. We were able to catch a further glimpse of Robert before he disappeared into the undulating terrain, firing bursts into knots of Soviets who continued to offer resistance. We rapidly unlimbered the Pak and prepared the gun for action; however, no longer knowing Robert's position, we were forced to hold our fire.

With submachine guns and rifles at the ready, we advanced to a small rise, and at the crest we found Robert lying over his MG with a single bullet wound through the heart. The bullet had exited through his back, and from this wound ran a crimson stream of blood. Hartmann knelt alongside the inert form and confirmed that he was dead, rolling him carefully onto his back.

Reaching for the linen string from which hung every soldier's identity tag, Hartmann broke the metal tag in two at the perforation before un-buttoning Robert's tunic to remove his identity book and watch. We gazed into questioning eyes staring skyward in the dusk, and the shock on his face seemed as to ask; "Why must I die now—why?"

Darkness descended on us as we carried the body back to our position. The experiences of the past weeks now seemed to consume my thoughts, and I pictured the graves left by the roadsides behind us. For the first time in my memory as an adult, I wept at the loss of an especially close friend. The following day the company commander wrote letters to the relatives of five men who had fallen during our most recent encounters with the Soviet army.

On 17 August shallow caves dug into a balka offered us protection from the fighter-bomber attacks. We had reached the heights of the west bank of the Dnieper, and now we found ourselves under erratic shellfire from Soviet artillery positions concealed on the east bank of the river. To the southeast of us was the city of Kanev, and a railway bridge led toward the east over the river. With the capture of this line we had seized the last avenue of overland retreat for the Russians who had been attempting to withdraw farther east during the previous night, and in the early morning hours isolated groups of enemy soldiers set out in boats to attempt an escape. Sporadic small-arms fire could be heard throughout the night as fleeing Russians came under fire from probing reconnaissance units.

Immense quantities of equipment and vehicles, including many American Ford trucks, had fallen into our hands. Hidden near the balka we found two abandoned but completely intact T-34 tanks that were battle-ready with fully loaded ammunition racks. We climbed into the tanks in a vain search for anything of use to us.

For several days I had been plagued with acute diarrhea, and I soon found myself incapacitated with a blinding headache accompanied by dizziness and severe stomach cramps. I soon developed a fever, and assisted by some of the lightly wounded I was ordered to the medical aid station in the rear.

En route we passed through the battlefield of the previous day, and the small depressions lined with bushes and birch trees appeared peaceful to our burning eyes, showing little evidence of the traumatic events that had occurred there. With the exception of isolated bomb craters and occasional scars from shell splinters, little trace of the war that had consumed this land was visible.

At the foot of an extended slope we passed three rough-hewn birch crosses garnished with bits of greenery and wildflowers. Under the surface of the freshly turned soil rested my good friend Robert, wrapped in a shelter-quarter, sharing a ragged birch cross with his fallen comrades, his battered, gray-green helmet perched on the cross to mark his place among the dead.

My thoughts quickly left the graves as the painful throbbing behind my eyes increased, and in a feverish delirium we stumbled through our advanced positions abandoned three days ago. The burned-out tank provided us with a good reference point.

Approximately one hundred meters farther we encountered a staggering figure with swinging arms and swaying body. The apparition was clearly attempting to follow a straight course, and two of us unslung our carbines and approached close enough to recognize a bloodied Russian army uniform beneath the layers of dust and dirt. His gymnasiorka was hanging beltless from his body. I approached him and seized his upper arm, looking into the parchmentlike face of an approximately twenty-eight-year-old soldier. The thin face stared back at me wide-eyed and unblinking. "The eyes of the insane," I thought to myself. From the encrusted blood on his neck and torso I was able to determine that he had received a severe head wound, as gray brain matter protruded from a closely cropped skull. A cloud of flies swarmed about the wound caked with black-red blood, and it was obvious that a bullet or shell fragment had ripped part of his skull away some days previously; he must have been lying unconscious in the undergrowth until shortly before our arrival. Two of us grasped him by the shoulders and led him with us toward the aid station, attempting to support him as he stumbled forward, unable to regain his balance.

Through a haze of pain I became conscious of a horse-drawn battery that halted alongside us in a cloud of dust, and a number of landsers assisted us in climbing aboard the caissons. They offered us water from field flasks, and the soldier in Russian khaki wedged tightly between us began to stammer. Through the croaking of his voice I could understand "Woti!" (water).

Exhausted, we reached the medical station, and from behind a feverish veil I observed how the wounded who had accompanied me were tended and the Russian soldier's head was bandaged. I was given a number of tablets, and the medical officer reported that a thermometer revealed a temperature of 39.8 degrees Celsius. I was then given warm tea in a field cup, and a medical orderly led me to a straw bed in a former schoolhouse.

I did not awaken before the afternoon of the following day, after having slept eighteen hours straight. Feeling fresh and wide-awake, I was provided a meal consisting of a healthy portion of bean soup and heavy black bread, which I consumed ravenously. Looking around, I was surprised to see that the area was almost deserted; the wounded occupants of the aid station were no longer present. They had either been evacuated or had been diagnosed as fit enough to be returned to their units, and only a small number of ill soldiers remained at the station, attended by the young medical orderly who had assisted me upon my arrival. He advised me that during the early morning hours the seriously wounded had been transported and that a medical officer had attempted to awaken me without success.

The following morning my fever was gone, and I was directed to return to my company. After a journey on a series of trucks and in pony carts I managed to locate my gun crew, who, during my absence, had again been sent back into action against enemy units that had temporarily broken through near Kanev.

CHAPTER TWO

Crossing the Dnieper

The sight of ragged individuals . . . approaching our positions with upraised arms became commonplace . . .

On 26 August we utilized all available time for reinforcing our positions. The overextended sector assigned to our division offered numerous landing areas for the enemy, and fortunately our heavy weapons were available to provide blocking and cover fire in the event of an attack.

During the night of 28 August we shifted to Kodorov on the Dnieper to reinforce a gun company that occupied a strategically important point on the line. This point commanded the heights of the bank on both sides of the river and was occupied by thinly scattered forces. The village was situated along an unpaved road where two balkas converged; and isolated, primitive dwellings lay scattered along the length of the small valley to the river. From the Pak position our view of the river was obstructed by trees, ragged hedges, and rustic clay cottages with thatched roofs and whitewashed walls. A large, prominent stone building served as a central reference point. Prior to our unexpected and unwelcome presence it had probably served as the village school. Below a steep embankment less than one hundred meters from our position the river flowed sluggishly to points unknown, and on the eastern edge of the village was a tomato farm. From the edge of the embankment the wide expanse of the river, which curved its way around small groups of islands, was clearly visible, and the eastern shore was thickly covered with a heavy growth of trees and bushes. A shallow island directly opposite us was covered with thick vegetation, effectively concealing all signs of Soviet presence.

Our supporting artillery battery, situated on a commanding terrain feature, was entrenched near a tomato kolkhoz which controlled a splendid view overlooking the enemy-held territory. The locations of enemy troop concentrations could be discerned through the vertical wisps of smoke rising from many cooking fires. Our artillery remained active and engaged in intermittent shelling in attempts to disrupt the enemy supply routes that lay hidden from our view. Otherwise, the front remained quiet.

Shortly after our arrival we sat in front of one of the huts, and I pulled my harmonica from its customary place in an interior pocket of my tunic. As I began playing folk songs, I was quickly surrounded by a motley collection of civilians, who appeared before us like shadows from the surrounding cottages. The melody, "Unshaven and Far From Home," brought the audience to life, and they clapped and sang their folk song "Stenka Rasin." In their bright scarves, the women and girls nodded to the tune; the old men and boys tapped their feet on the Russian clay to the music played from a German harmonica.

After an hour we received word from the commander of the panzer-jaeger platoon to spread straw in a former storage facility to use as quarters. Disappointed that we would not be quartered in the scattered rows of huts, we reluctantly obeyed. A large number of us felt as though we had entered a trap, for the building had only one entrance and was located in the center of the village, which offered no clear field of fire in any direction. At the very least we would have preferred to bivouac in an open area, to which we were accustomed.

Our gun remained limbered to the tractor twenty or thirty meters from us beneath a grove of trees, and a sentry was assigned to stand watch near the single door of the barracks. The clear sky brought a cool summer night, and approximately thirty of us settled into the improvised quarters, where we were soon immersed in a deep sleep.

Just before dawn we were startled awake by the sudden detonations of hand grenades near our shelter. A burst from a submachine gun hammered against the wooden rear wall of the storage shelter, and the guard sprang through the door into the darkness of the building.

"The Russians are here! The Russians are here!" he screamed.

I leaped into my boots, grabbed my equipment and ammunition belt, and scrambled along with Hartmann and several others toward the only exit. True to the discipline of the German Wehrmacht, our first thoughts were to get to the Pak, and we stumbled toward it through the darkness. I caught a glimpse of a glowing ember arching toward us from the edge of the stream and immediately recognized the burning fuse of a hand grenade. I instinctively dove behind the tractor and the grenade detonated harmlessly a second later.

The few men who managed to rally in the vicinity of Hartmann's gun at the onset of the surprise attack now opened fire with rifles and machine guns, kneeling behind the tractor or lying prone on the ground. As I pulled two grenades from my belt and tossed them in a wide arc over the tractor to the edge of the stream, Hartmann bounced a third grenade farther into the ravine.

As we suppressed the enemy fire, the chatter of Russian submachine guns slackened, and we received no more hand grenades from the streambed. In the interim more men of the platoon had sprinted from the building and attempted to reach our position. From the direction of the wooden bridge a new firefight raged approximately one hundred meters from us.

We suddenly caught a glimpse of the platoon leader dashing past us, screaming, "I've been wounded!" and he quickly disappeared into the darkness near the storage shed. Taking advantage of the pause in the firing, we unlimbered the Pak and began firing into the heavy undergrowth along the stream from where we could still discern the twinkling muzzle flashes of the Russian weapons. Bullets striking against the shield of our gun were clearly audible; but with several dozen antipersonnel rounds we managed to suppress their fire, and the Russians broke off any further attacks.

It had all taken place in less than ten minutes. Hartmann and I hastened into the storage shed where the leutnant was lying with a bullet wound through his thigh. Already being bandaged by a medical orderly, the wound was bleeding profusely although the orderly reported that no artery had been severed and no broken bone was noticeable. We left the two communicators and the leutnant's driver with him and returned to our platoon.

Hartmann assumed command of the platoon and ordered Burkhardt and me to establish contact with the company headquarters in the village. We cautiously stepped onto the bridge and immediately discerned the lifeless form of a Russian lying several meters from us, the silhouette of his body a stark contrast against the pale wood in the bright moonlight. The enemy had apparently broken off their attack and retreated, and within a few minutes we had made our way to the company headquarters located in a farmhouse.

The headquarters was filled with wounded tended by a medical feldwebel. Here we were told that at the time of the attack on our quarters the Russians had simultaneously launched an attack against another unit quartered in the east end of the village. We made our report, and to our relief we were immediately dismissed to return to the more familiar surroundings of our platoon.

After returning from the company headquarters we transferred the Pak to a more advantageous position about fifty meters from the warehouse. From this location we could cover an area extending from the top of the ravine to the bridge and would be able to take any further attacks under direct fire. We kept the ravine and the slopes to the right and left of us under close observation, but we detected no further enemy movement and received no further fire. There were reports circulating that the Russian attack had been repulsed and that the leutnant had received a heimatschuss.

We had just begun to feel secure in our new environment when suddenly, in the growing light of dawn, I observed to our left a small group of Russians pulling a heavy MG over a rise behind the schoolhouse. We scrambled to our assigned defensive positions and immediately opened fire on them with armor-piercing and high-explosive rounds, our antipersonnel ammunition having been expended. They dove for cover, leaving several dead and wounded on open ground. We fired into the location where they remained under concealment and into the abandoned schoolhouse to prevent them from establishing a machine-gun position. After several shots we observed several Russians retreating rapidly toward their rear, followed by the rapid hammering of our MG-34.

Suddenly the air directly before us exploded with small-arms fire. From a close range we came under fire from infiltrating Soviets, and the shouts of the Ivans were clearly audible from the cover of the ravine. Through thick bushes, trees, and small gardens of sunflowers, tomatoes, and bean plants the enemy again worked their way forward to our position, tossing hand grenades through the air that rolled to within ten paces from our gun before exploding.

We frantically pulled the last case of 37mm ammunition from our tractor as the gun-loaders shoveled and kicked a pile of expended shell casings away in an effort to clear the gun area. We had only thirty rounds of armor-piercing ammunition remaining, and as I stripped the last clip of rifle ammunition into the magazine of my carbine, a quick check with the others revealed that they had expended theirs as well. Hartmann had only a half magazine of ammunition for his submachine gun remaining.

The Russians attempted to push across the road to reach the storage building, and it was clear to all of us that we had to prevent them from reaching their objective at all costs to avoid being isolated from the remainder of the company, which would mean inevitable annihilation or surrender. At approximately 1000 the last antitank round was fired from the smoking barrel of our Pak. In attempts to deny us the use of our gun tractor, the Russians now assaulted the building directly, and soon it had been set ablaze by either tracer fire or molotov cocktails. Unable to know if there had been enough time for an evacuation of the barracks, we could only hope that the wounded officer had been taken to safety.

As we expended the last rounds of ammunition, I removed the bolt from the breech of the Pak and tossed it into the undergrowth before joining Hartmann in crawling through one of the ravines leading toward the west.

At times crawling on our stomachs through the underbrush and then scrambling from cover to cover, we were eventually able to reach an excavated cave cut deep into the clay of the ravine. There we discovered a number of the village inhabitants, peering fearfully toward the sound of the fighting with anxious faces. Obviously the village had been previously warned of the pending attack, and the villagers had crept into the hole to wait out the battle.

Ignoring the presence of the terrified civilians, we scrambled to the crest of the ravine. From this higher observation point we could see the Russians swarming around the storage shed some three hundred meters distant. From behind a tree I took careful aim and squeezed off several shots with my carbine at the figures, and Hartmann suddenly shouted that relief was en route. An infantry company and part of the now-dispersed unit that had been positioned next to us had assembled on the western side of the village. Hartmann and I wound our way through the underbrush down to the road, and we observed our company commander careening into the village in his sidecar.

Russian artillery rounds could be heard impacting far behind us. Our own heavy weapons took the embankments of the Dnieper under fire to block a Russian retreat, and our attacking companies pushed forward. Hardly thirty minutes had passed when, after searching the area, I was able to slide the bolt back into the breech of our gun, and within several hours the enemy had been thrown back into the river through counterattacks. The survivors who were attempting to reach the safety of the east bank with rafts and boats were taken under fire by our artillery.

We had repelled an attack by enemy forces four to five times stronger than our own, and we began the search for the wounded leutnant. Despite a sweep of the entire area we were unable to locate him, finding only a blood-stained officer's boot in front of the burned-out storage building.

During the search for the officer we came upon a Russian soldier chewing sunflower seeds in the garden of a nearby straw and mud cottage. Offering no resistance, he raised his hands high in surrender and approached us cautiously, glancing about fearfully and waving his open hands slightly as he neared our position. After a cursory search he was taken to regimental headquarters for interrogation.

The following morning the rifle company reported the discovery of an unidentified body where the stream met the Dnieper. We later learned from the company commander that the body was indeed that of the leutnant, who had been executed by a shot in the back of the neck, probably by a political commissar. There was no trace of two other missing members of one of the rifle platoons, and most likely they were taken over the Dnieper as prisoners. A Russian medical officer who was later captured after the encirclement at Kiev reported that the German prisoners captured in this area had been executed prior to the Soviet capitulation of that city.

We later heard reports that during the night of the attack the village schoolteacher and a Young Communist member, Olga, both of whom on the previous evening had joined us in singing "Stenka Rasin," had slipped through the balka under cover of darkness to swim across the wide river. On reaching the Soviet positions, they had provided detailed information to the Russian troops on the east bank, outlining our positions and strength before leading a Russian battalion unnoticed over the river and into the balka. Our quarters were situated near a bridge that provided a passage over this ravine into the village.

The war in the east had begun to exhibit its brutality. Nevertheless, none of us could foresee or comprehend that the bitterness and rage of the Russians following the invasion of their country would grow more intense with each passing year. Much of the civilian population was in opposition to this retribution, especially on the southern sector of the Eastern Front, where we were relatively well regarded. Many of the Russian prisoners captured early during the campaign had expressed a strong desire to fight alongside us against Stalin and the Soviet government.

As time passed the Communist leadership abandoned the call to sacrifice oneself for Communism and sought to make a strong appeal to the inherent patriotism of the people. To defend "Mother Russia" against the "invading Fascist intruders" became the patriotic duty for everyone, with absolutely no exceptions. Thus the conflict evolved into a war of the Russian people against the German aggressors instead of a struggle for survival of the party.

Unfortunately, the brutal measures of the Soviets could be compared with the conduct of the German occupiers in the rear areas, far behind the front. Through the excesses that took place against the Russian people the German soldier became, to the simple Russian, a fighter and supporter for a despised, murderous political institution. Because of this doctrine, established and mandated in far-away Berlin, countless atrocities were in turn committed on soldiers in the front lines, even though we front soldiers were unaware of the murder of thousands of innocent people through the Sonderkommandos of the system or of the excesses practiced for the "pacification" of captured areas by our Golden Pheasants of the National Socialist Party.

The commanders of the divisions on the front as well as many regiment and battalion-level commanders were at that time veterans and participants of World War I, who conducted and fought the war with the undeniable fairness instilled in the officer's corp of the kaiser's army. It must be added that during the entire campaign in the east, I never experienced a single incident when Russian soldiers who had surrendered were not correctly handled, or when captured enemy wounded were not medically treated exactly as our own. During the attack on Kanev prisoners were simply sent to the rear unguarded, as every available man was desperately needed at the front. However, I maintain the belief that from the masses of prisoners sent to the rear in this manner, many Communists and Russian patriots used the opportunity to slip into the undergrowth and eventually make contact with the ever-growing bands of partisans. The well-organized partisan units would become an increasing menace to our rear areas. As the war continued, the people came to trust and support the partisans to a great extent, and they were able to find shelter and protection everywhere.

Throughout the first half of September we continued to defend our positions on the banks of the Dnieper as the Soviets attempted to regain the west bank. On 14 September our first units pushed over the river. Following a reconnaissance on the Dnieper island north of Balyka, a successful landing was made and the Soviet defenses on the heights of the bank were assaulted. Despite strong enemy resistance, large numbers of prisoners were taken.

Two days later our company followed the foremost units as reserve and landed on the opposite bank. By exploiting the confusion of enemy forces, we successfully established a deep bridgehead that continued to be built up by more forces being pushed over the river into the breach. The German artillery batteries ceaselessly fired on enemy positions on the opposite bank from Kodorov, and simultaneously a line of fire was laid down to the east of the Dnieper tributary near Balyka. By nightfall the advance units had reached the area of Yaschniki.

On 17 September the reinforced Infantry Regiment 438 gained further ground against a weak but heavily resisting enemy near Balyka and Reschischtschev while attempting to make contact with advance elements of another corps along the Yerkovzy road. The attack objective was reached in the late afternoon following the elimination of pockets of resistance.

We continued to press onward, advancing to the vital main route from Kiev to the area of Yerkovzy, thus severing an important Soviet withdrawal route. During the night we received little rest as we dug into the hard earth to reinforce our line. We sweated and toiled in the damp air until dawn as the constant rumbling of motor vehicles and the clattering of armor drifted toward us from the enemy positions.

Throughout the day on 18 September we continued to strengthen our positions, although the enemy line had become quiet with little movement detected. As dusk approached we felt secure in the knowledge that the Soviet forces had withdrawn farther to the east, leaving only a rear guard to slow our advance.

The night suddenly exploded with impacting artillery rounds—and along the Rogosoff-Pereyaslaff road in the northwest area of Yerkovzy eleven enemy attacks were repulsed between the hours of 2210 and 0250. The sunrise bore witness to the effectiveness of our defense, as countless bodies clad in khaki-brown could be seen lying in heaps before our positions. Burning vehicles littered the landscape, sending plumes of oily black smoke skyward.

We received reports that a number of motorized enemy units had been completely destroyed, and the regimental staff proudly released to us a list of captured equipment: sixteen heavy and light MGs, eight heavy artillery pieces, nine trucks, two medical vehicles, two fuel vehicles, and six ammunition carriers. Four hundred prisoners were taken, the number increasing to 800 by 19 September. A number of detachments from Infantry Regiment 436, which had been assigned to clear remaining enemy forces from the east bank, had also reached their objectives with only light casualties.

During the next few days we brought in more than one thousand prisoners while combing the banks of the Dnieper. Convinced that the Soviet Union had lost the war, deserters were stealing boats and crossing the Dnieper in large numbers under cover of darkness in attempts to distance themselves from the Soviet army. The sight of ragged individuals either alone or in small groups approaching our positions with upraised arms became commonplace, and our confidence continued to mount that the war would be over before the first frost.

On 23 September our battalion was attacked by Russian infantry in surprising strength. We were able to repel the assault with light casualties, and the enemy was thrown back, leaving some light field guns and many infantry weapons littering the ground before us. We remained in our positions until word was received that the opposite bank of the Dnieper was clear of enemy forces and that our division was to be pulled out of this sector.

With the end of the fighting to the south and southeast of Kiev, the mounting casualties among our own forces were calculated. Each company had suffered an average casualty rate of 15 to 20 percent, and a rifle company of Infantry Regiment 437 had in the previous two months suffered an average of four dead, two missing, fourteen wounded, and two sick, a total of twenty-two men. The strength of our antitank company prior to operations had been between 100 and 120 men.

The equipment and weapons remained in relatively good condition, and the importance of properly maintaining all military property, as was constantly drilled into us during our basic training, had produced results. The official lines of supply and material between the troops and company headquarters became very informal as the troops learned to live from the land and from captured enemy resources.

With the beginning of the rain and mud season, the frontline units quickly learned that the native Russian pony carts were more reliable than the heavy horse-drawn wagons of our own army, which were designed for paved roads. The Russian panye wagons were used in ever-increasing numbers from captured equipment or, contrary to strict regulations, occasionally requisitioned from the civilians without authorization.

Our Fourteenth Panzerjaeger Company had lost two Chenilette prime movers to land mines, and others suffered damage to and wear on motors and tracks. Despite the efforts of our engineers, spare parts became unobtainable although we searched a distance of up to one hundred kilometers throughout the army and corps rear areas.

The troops had become masters at fending for themselves. From the end of August and the beginning of September the company attempted to make captured trucks usable. From the vast quantities of captured enemy material left behind by the retreating enemy, especially in the battlefield area of Kanev, our troops were able to assemble a large quantity of serviceable vehicles. The company commander brought in an entire fuel truck, which greatly augmented our inventory of "black," or unofficial, fuel supplies.

The Russians possessed large numbers of robust Ford heavy trucks as well as those of "Sis" manufacture. Those two types seemed to make up the entire inventory of trucks possessed by the enemy, and we always chose the American-manufactured Ford whenever possible, as many replacement parts seemed to be always available.

Due to this method of salvage and use, our army appeared to consist of vehicles of every type and description from half of Europe, sometimes making it impossible to obtain even the most simple replacement parts. We found ourselves growing envious of the uncomplicated Russian supply system. Although their inventory of weapons and equipment might not have been as varied or as specialized as our own, what they did have was reliable and could be logistically supported almost anywhere.

As in all armies, one of the main topics of discussion was the quality and availability of food. Our company field kitchen was able to work wonders as long as the lines of supply were capable of delivering essential items. During one of my visits to the field kitchen the company cook proudly showed me a cave where hundreds of sausages and smoked meats hung from long poles. I presented the cook with a number of captured Soviet medals and pistols as gifts for the kitchen personnel, and thereafter we were always guaranteed something more substantial than simply what the official system could provide for us.

On 25 and 26 September the main body of the division departed the former combat area on the west bank of the Dnieper. Once again long gray columns wound their way over undulating terrain on the march toward the south. The enemy forces, which had opposed us with tenacity in the previous weeks, had seemingly evaporated before our advance.

Throughout the month of October the division advanced through a Ukraine bedecked with the splendors of fall. The crops had been harvested; tall haystacks and threshing machines dotted the landscape, creating a picture reminiscent of America.

We marched in the direction of Krementschug, which conveyed to us the message that the city of Odessa on the Black Sea was still under siege. Rumors raced throughout the ranks that we and Rumanian units had been assigned to capture it.

On 17 October we learned that Odessa had fallen. The division wheeled toward the southeast and was assigned the objective of Nikolayev. While en route we passed through an area of ethnic German settlements that had been established under the direction of Catherine the Great of Russia some two hundred years ago; and here we clearly recognized places named after Karlsruhe, Worms, Speyer, Helenental, and other cities from our homeland. We encountered only women, children, and a few old men, as the Soviets had deported all men of military age.

In a simple but clean and strongly built stone house I located living quarters with a bedroom that could have been seen somewhere in the Pfalz two hundred years ago. A wide wooden bed covered with colorful pillows and topped with a large canopy stood inside. The farm women were speaking a dialect that is similar to what one hears in the Pfalz today. Helping ourselves to fresh milk and white bread, we made ourselves totally at ease in these surroundings.

Several days later we crossed the river Bug on a winding pontoon bridge that strained against the current and entered the harbor city of Nikolayev. Together with the company commander and some other men

I had the opportunity to see half-completed armored cruisers of about one thousand tons lying in the dry docks.

The march continued toward our new objective of Cherson. On 25 October we again crossed the mighty Dnieper, whose waters had drained us of sweat and blood some one hundred kilometers farther to the north. It was clear that the southern army elements had advanced ahead along the Sea of Asov and were now proceeding toward Rostov and that we were to link up with them as reinforcement. We soon found ourselves approaching the western outskirts of a forbidding, desolate area known as the Nogai Steppe.

After heavy fighting from 26 to 28 October the divisions of the Eleventh Army had broken through the narrow corridor of Perekop and had thus cleared the way for us to advance into the Crimean Peninsula. As part of Oberkommando des Heeres (OKH) reserve, the 132d Infantry Division became assigned to von Manstein's army. In breaking through the narrow corridor, it had been possible to employ only limited forces; however, it was now necessary to reinforce the army for a further push into and occupation of the peninsula.

As we advanced over the graves of the Tartars, the ancient protectors of the Crimea from northern invaders, we entered a new battlefield. Our division, together with the Fiftieth Infantry Division attached to the LIV Corps, was assigned to pursue the enemy relentlessly toward Bacht-schisseray-Sevastopol. It was also necessary simultaneously to sever the road to Sevastopol. The forward elements of the motorized units assembled in preparation for the attack.

On 31 October the enemy exhibited signs of full retreat. The advance elements thrust rapidly toward the south in long columns, leaving the horse-drawn units to advance more slowly toward the front. At Kara-Naymak the horses of both an entire infantry and artillery regiment were compelled to drink from a single well, other water sources having been poisoned by the retreating Soviets. The vast numbers of wagons and livestock clustered together left an impression of another time, of invading armies from another century sweeping across the steppe. Our growing sensation of becoming further isolated from the western world shadowed us into the Crimea.

We experienced a severe shortage of water, and the few deeply dug wells and cisterns not poisoned by the retreating enemy contained brackish water that varied from bad-tasting to undrinkable. The horses and soldiers had developed an unquenchable thirst as they labored in the tormenting heat, and the shortage of water for the horses became so critical that even the strongest and most healthy had to be rotated in the harness often.

The company mess attempted to make coffee from the brackish water, and sweetening it with saccharin resulted in a horrible-tasting broth that could be consumed only with the greatest amount of will power.

The range of march for the rifle companies and horse-drawn units now averaged fifty to sixty kilometers per day. The motorized reconnaissance and panzerjaeger units were able to make much better time and quickly reached the Alma Valley.

Running through the Crimean Peninsula in an easterly direction toward the Black Sea are three large valley ranges: the Alma, Katscha, and Belbek. The northern part of the peninsula is a vast salt steppe. Long basins for salt production were located here where the water from the Sivasch could be easily evaporated, leaving precious salt lining the basins, which was rare and difficult to obtain in many other regions of Russia. During our advance through the Ukraine we had noted how salt was used as a source of trade among the inhabitants, and it was more valued here than in our own homeland. Demonstrating to us the high value placed on this precious commodity, peasant women presented us with platters of salt and bread as an offering of welcome as we passed through villages.

The central Crimea is a flat, nearly treeless plain that nevertheless is fertile and well tended. Here, as throughout the entire Soviet empire, the farms had been placed under control of the collectives, the kolkhoz establishment. In the winter months snow and ice storms sweep over the region from the eastern Ukraine.

The Yaila Mountains lie in the south. They rise steeply from the level center to a height of two thousand meters and then fall sharply into the Black Sea on the southern coast. These mountains are thickly wooded, and the valleys running to the north bear heavy vegetation. Fruit plantations are seen here, along with the picturesque villages of the Tartars.

We soon advanced to a battlefield whose name was destined to haunt us for many months: Sevastopol. We closed upon its north and northeastern fortresses during the next few days.

During the first days of November we experienced little enemy contact; however, the advanced artillery batteries continued to lay a line of fire on our exposed west flank. On 2 November detachments from Infantry Regiments 436 and 437 departed the assembly area in the settlement of Chanischkoy and soon met strong resistance in the early morning hours. Despite enemy pressure from the left, we advanced in the direction of Adshi-Bulat and pushed through the enemy defenses to open the advance route.

With the gathering of darkness the strong enemy pressure on our left flank became more apparent, and the enemy concentrations were dispersed only by heavy artillery fire. It was rumored that due to personnel shortages, Russian volunteers from the prisoner of war camps were being used to augment artillery crews.

During the night, breakthrough attempts continued to be made by Soviet naval infantry units, and the attacks broke upon our strong defenses as the desperate Soviets attempted to push through our lines toward Sevastopol and to the coast.

In order to protect the open west flank and to silence an enemy shore battery on the Black Sea coast that hindered the advance of the division, units from Infantry Regiment 438 assaulted toward the west and southwest. A small advance unit later was able to reach a decoy position of this battery, where they found wooden artillery barrels pointing menacingly but impotently toward the sky.

The Russians were able to conceal the true position of the heavy battery, which was located farther south near Nicolayev. With the onset of darkness we were successful in taking the outerlying positions of the coastal guns after fierce fighting. An enemy ship operating on the Black Sea was observed, and our Pak took it under fire. During the night the enemy forces abandoned the coastal battery, and the surviving naval units were evacuated from the peninsula in boats, to be taken on board the large Soviet ships lying off the coast.

Leutnant Diehl from II Battalion, Infantry Regiment 438, along with twenty other comrades, met a soldier's death during this operation. It became obvious to us that the Russians held absolute control of the Black Sea, as Soviet warships could be seen silhouetted against the horizon as they cruised freely beyond the reach of our guns. During the previous day's fighting the Russian air force had been seen in enormous numbers; however, Moelder's fighter wing soon swept the sky clear of enemy planes.

On 3 November the advance section of my regiment, consisting of units from the motorized Fourteenth Infantry Panzerjaeger Company and the Ninth Bicycle Company, advanced upon a small Tartar village southwest of Evel-Scheich at midday, where we discovered an abandoned magazine containing Russian supplies, including numerous cases of Papyrossi cigarettes.

The advance continued along the Katscha Valley. In the rays of a setting sun the landscape appeared strikingly beautiful, with a narrow road running along a row of poplar trees and between fruit farms. From a distance of about fifteen hundred meters we could observe attractive, small Tartar houses with wooden porches and low roofs sprinkled among the valleys and along crests of the hills.

As we approached the edge of the settlement, the point element came under strong enemy fire, and I immediately opened fire with my Pak on a yet-unseen enemy in and among the houses. Under cover fire from our gun the officer in charge of the Ninth Company moved forward. Small-arms fire began to slam into the house wall behind us, leaving whirling clouds of dust as the bullets pockmarked the mud-colored buildings near our gun position. Our company commander continued to stand unshaken through the chaos, ignoring the rounds striking the wall behind him, while we lay flat or cowered behind the steel shield of the Pak.

Through the deafening explosions of the hammering machine guns I could hear the high-pitched screaming of a wounded soldier, and someone began shouting "stomach wound!" The nearest machine gun fired almost continually as the gunner emptied the barrel at swiftly moving targets. We continued to concentrate upon loading and firing at the distant figures scrambling between the houses, and the machine gun followed the enemy movements.

We attempted to give the impression that we were here in regimental force and not just a weak advance element with only a rifle company and two antitank guns. The ruse was successful, and we observed a number of Soviet soldiers, dressed in flowing, dark-blue navy overcoats, withdrawing along the valley floor toward the west to the sea.

The wounded landser was lying a few steps behind us on the edge of the road, his upturned helmet a few feet beyond where he lay. A medical assistant knelt alongside him and unbuttoned his dust-caked tunic to bandage the wound. Within seconds the soldier's screams for help had become unintelligible mumbles as he lay in the dirt. His feverish eyes appeared wide with astonishment against his chalk-white face, and he stared forward into blackness as the shadow of death quickly settled upon him. The medic removed the watch from the soldier's lifeless arm, and quickly began gathering personal effects from within the pockets of the ragged, blood-caked uniform. We turned away and busied ourselves with our own thoughts and responsibilities.

The thoughts of those gathered nearby remained deeply personal, and one could not escape feeling an intense pity for our brother in the gray tunic who had been struck; yet with these thoughts each man turned to concentrate upon himself, about how he could be the next to fall, the next to meet his destiny in Russia. We became at times possessed by these thoughts, as helpless against them as against the death that had quickly enveloped our brother soldier. Thus began the realization that we were being consumed by this foreign land.

One would hesitate and attempt to suppress these thoughts deep within oneself. During the fighting these suppressed emotions became entangled with every nerve and were strained to the breaking point through the repeated experience of indescribable terror. The cure for the turmoil within oneself was offered to us only in forms of action, in helping the wounded in every way possible, or in the wielding of weapons and equipment of war, the firing on the enemy. The infantrymen became consumed with a remorseless, ever-increasing rage; and the fevered minds could concentrate only on revenging fallen comrades, to kill the enemy, and to destroy. The highest degrees of rage would grow to suicidal levels, so near together lie fear and courage. During hours of calm we would sometimes discuss the impact on our lives of living with daily deprivation and danger, and the general consensus reached was that simple men of robust nature often dealt with the situation more effectively, with less personal stress, than do men who are usually considered to be intelligent or sensitive. There exist, however, no rules to guide this philosophy; and it remains inherent upon the momentary situation, which never duplicates itself as every situation in war is different, and the constitution of the fighter changes with time and experience as well.

It is often said that one becomes accustomed to it. One may become accustomed to the threat or constant presence of death; however, throughout the long years of the Russian campaign, helplessly witnessing the badly wounded soldiers in their agony always profoundly affected me far more than when a comrade met an immediate and painless death. He had met his death and was gone, but the cries of the wounded, of our own as well as those of the enemy lying alone between the lines, are often heard long after the guns are silent.

In the dim light of an early November sunrise I sat on the gun carriage of the Pak on guard duty when suddenly the crack of rifle shots and bursts of submachine gunfire exploded from very close range, the shots flying over and behind me. I sprang from the carriage and spun around to see a large number of Russians no more than fifty paces behind my position moving quickly among the fruit trees. I was immediately engulfed by an ice-cold sensation as I realized our small unit was cut off from our company. Throwing myself to the ground between the gun limbers, I nervously pulled the stock of my carbine to my cheek, took aim at one of the shadowy figures, and squeezed the trigger. The light rifle recoiled with the shot, and the paralyzing fear immediately melted from me. As I worked another round into the chamber of the bolt-action carbine, our machine-gun crew, alerted by the burst of gunfire, scrambled to their gun and frantically swung the cone-shaped muzzle to our rear. Within seconds they were raking the undergrowth among the trees with a sweeping enfilade. My Pak crew tumbled from beneath the shelter-quarters and raced to my position at the gun; however, it was impossible for us to bring the gun into action without endangering our own forces by the direct fire.

The Russians had succeeded in filtering between us and the Tartar houses where the troops of the Ninth and Fourteenth Companies were quartered, and we could see the company troops storming from the houses in the distance as they were alerted by the racing gunfire. A firefight quickly developed among the fruit groves as the Soviets brought a withering fire to bear on our position, and they in turn were taken under fire from our main body of troops. As our forces brought heavier fire on the enemy from both directions, the enemy assault unit was effectively destroyed and those Soviets not killed by the hail of gunfire were taken prisoner.

Prisoner interrogations revealed that the enemy force was part of the unit that had attempted to reach the coast through our lines during the previous day. The prisoners were clothed in navy-blue uniforms, which appeared to be recently issued and were still immaculately clean. The prisoners stated that they were members of an elite naval infantry unit, and we were impressed by the enormous amount of firepower that had been produced by such a small group of men. All were equipped with semiautomatic rifles or short-barreled submachine guns that were capable of firing seventy-two rounds from drum magazines.

I took one of the submachine guns and several drum magazines from one of the prisoners for my own use, as I no longer placed much faith in the slow-firing 98k carbine for close combat. I felt more confident equipped with the high-capacity automatic weapon, and it was to remain with me for many months.

Along a narrow road an ancient stone wall bordered by a vegetable garden ran between the scattered dwellings, and we knocked stones from the wall to create firing apertures facing our front. Behind our position we constructed a barricade from the loose stones as protection from enemy mortar and artillery fire directed on our line. In our sector we remained fortunate, as the high-explosive rounds continued to impact at a distance behind us.

As we labored to reinforce our fire position, we were again interrupted by an enemy counterattack. The Soviet naval infantry had crept through the thick undergrowth among the trees to within close range of us, and suddenly silent figures clothed in blue-black rose before us like fleeting shadows in the dawn.

The machine gun again exploded into action, accompanied by the barking of our mortars farther behind our line, followed seconds later by the impacting rounds tossing clouds of earth skyward some 150 paces from our position. The enemy advance ground to a halt, and they again evaporated into the undergrowth, leaving their dead and dying behind.

While sweeping the area we came upon an unwounded Russian who had become disoriented lying behind a ragged tree stump fifty meters from our gun position. With "Stoi! Ruki verkh!" and "Idi su da!" (halt, hands up, and come here) I ordered him to advance toward our position. He stumbled forward with his hands held high, a good-natured grin on his face. We removed two hand grenades and a full drum of ammunition from his belt, and a messenger escorted him to our company headquarters.

The ever-present, harassing mortar fire continued to haunt our daily lives with sporadic explosions erupting within our lines without warning. On one occasion, while searching the terrain features opposite us through field glasses, our company commander suddenly stumbled backward, his arms folded across his chest with both lacerated hands held high, blood spurting from open wounds and pouring over his sleeves. A razor-sharp mortar fragment had sliced through the glasses and cleanly severed some of the fingers from both hands. Other than the injuries to his hands he escaped unhurt, and his communicator accompanied him to the field hospital.

On 5 November the division was assigned to take the Belbek Valley near Duvankoy, Gadschikoy, and Beyuk-Otarkoy. The objective was reached that evening, and the assaults that followed during the next two days took the form of an arrow-shaped advance that captured a large expanse of outer defenses and field positions to the northeast of fortress Sevastopol. The heights near Makensia, the town itself, and the commanding terrain feature identified as Hill 363.5 were captured and held through heavy fighting.

On the late afternoon of 7 November the regiment ordered our guns to be emplaced on the defense line on the western perimeter of Makensia. Shortly thereafter one of the company Paks destroyed an enemy tank during a Soviet counterattack.

Our tractor bounced over the rough-cut road en route to our new destination, the western range of the Yaila Mountains. The high plateau lying before us was thick with forests and undergrowth; and as we observed them from a distance, the gently rising hills and shallow valleys from where we had just advanced gave the appearance of a smooth green and brown carpet. We were provided with a splendid view of the fields surrounding Bachtschisseray, and the rugged white limestone cliffs to the south were bathed in a soft pink glow against the setting sun. It depicted a serene environment; however, the sound of war resounded from our batteries on the heights, and in return enemy shells burst sharply on the plateau of Makensia.

About twenty paces from the trail we came upon a massive, concrete embrasure from which protruded the muzzle of a Soviet rapid-fire cannon, its steel glacis plate rising abruptly in the evening sky. Having only been recently abandoned, it was clearly one of the guns that had caused us such misery as it fired upon us days earlier from these commanding heights.

Heavy-artillery fire soon began bursting on the cliffs, and we sought protection from the white-hot shell fragments in the abandoned bunker. The design of the huge gun was similar to that of our own 88mm Flak, although on a larger scale, and on the heavy breech technical information as well as the caliber and year of manufacture, 1938, were deeply stamped in English. We surmised that it must have been manufactured for use as an English or American naval gun.

Moments after we had ducked into the bunker, Hartmann drew our attention to our munitions-carrier slowly climbing the steep rise behind us, and we prepared for its arrival. Without warning, at a distance of two hundred meters the triple-axle Ford suddenly exploded in raging flames, a plume of black smoke spiraling skyward.

The heavy load of ammunition began to detonate with sharp explosions, sending hot shrapnel and intact projectiles raining down on us. The vehicle, obviously having taken a direct hit from a hidden gun that struck the unprotected fuel tank, continued to shower the area with sparks and jagged metal for several hours. After the eruptions subsided we cautiously approached the vehicle, and eventually the flames died enough to enable us to pull the crumpled and singed corpse of the dead driver from the burning truck.

Again with the setting sun came rain. Under dripping shelter-quarters hanging from weary shoulders, the gun crews shoveled and hacked a grave into the stony ground for their dead gefreiter. The shallow grave was dug in silence, each member lost in those private thoughts that inevitably haunted us when we lost one of our own. The men tightly gripping the slippery entrenching tools, the shallow grave was dug, the identity tag was removed from the corpse, and his scorched remains were laid to rest wrapped tightly in a rubberized gas sheet. We shoveled earth on the grave and placed his worn and battered helmet on the mound covering him.

It was again difficult to imagine that his journey through life had come to an end, leaving only a steel helmet and a tiny mound of earth on a Crimean hillside. The rain intensified, washing the soil from the crumbling stones we had piled on his grave. In the darkness they gleamed chalk white, reflecting the light from flares bursting and floating in the distance over Makensia.

The cold rain fell throughout the night, running from helmet's rim into our collars as we muscled the gun through the thick clay into a defensive position. As dawn began to break against the horizon we shared hot ersatz coffee with a sentry manning a machine-gun position while he advised us of the strong Soviet counterattacks that had taken place in this sector throughout the previous days. Motivated by his story, we again tore into the earth, digging deeper and piling stones around our gun for protection from the shell splinters.

Suddenly and silently, from out of the darkness, poured waves of enemy soldiers. Elite troops of the Soviet Naval Infantry massed toward us, their ranks reinforced with work brigades drafted from the Sevastopol docks and factories. They assaulted our positions from the thick underbrush before Makensia, pouring toward us in dark waves, hoarse shouts of "Urrah!" erupting from the oncoming line. Springing to our weapons, we as the attackers had become defenders, and we prepared to defend our positions, step by step, as bitterly as the Russians had done on these same heights several days previously.

We opened fire with high explosives point-blank into the rows of attackers. The roar of battle smothered the cries of the Soviets; the frantic loading of our weapons concealed the terror that had enveloped our ranks. The heavy machine gun nearby burned belt after belt of gleaming ammunition through the feed tray, spent cartridges pouring from the hot receiver in an endless stream. Detonating mortar rounds erupted on the stony ground fifty meters before our defenses as our mortar teams behind us attempted to stem the advancing waves falling on us. Slowly the assault broke against our lines. The open ground before us was littered with the dark forms of the dead and dying. Only the cries of the wounded could be heard through the ringing in our ears caused by the firing of hundreds of weapons in close proximity. The early predawn air remained heavy and almost asphyxiating from bitter cordite fumes, and through the smoke and dust we could vaguely see the forms of wounded enemy soldiers thrashing in agony before our positions.

Within minutes we again faced another onslaught, and the sun climbed above the horizon to reveal the full horror of the battlefield. Pushed to hatred and thirst for blood through liberal rations of vodka, the Russians staggered and reeled ahead of the threatening pistols wielded by their commissars, their loud screams of "Urrah!" again lost in the deafening roar of exploding weapons. Over the din I heard the machine gunner cry, "I can't just keep on killing!" as he squeezed the trigger and held it tightly, sending a stream of bullets from the smoking MG barrel into the masses of attackers. Our Pak projectiles screamed and tore holes in the collapsing ranks. This attack ground to a halt hardly fifty paces from the muzzle of our gun.

We were positioned on a critical height strategically located near Makensia, and the Red Army was fully aware that if we were permitted to push through to Severnaya Bay their lifeline would be severed. Thus, in immeasurable numbers and multiple assault waves, spurred on by threats, coercion, and patriotic appeals from political commissars, the Russians threw themselves against us in charging ranks. Motivated by abundant amounts of vodka and facing the angry muzzle of a commissar's pistol for any sign of hesitation, they threw themselves against us again and again.

By afternoon we hardly remained conscious as we staggered through air thick with cordite fumes, ears ringing, bodies overcome and exhausted by the exertion and terror of battle. We stumbled weakly over our own legs as we attempted to clear the debris from our gun position. The machine gunners could no longer straighten the fingers of their right hands; the mortar crews could hardly lift their arms from exhaustion. Machine-gun barrels, rapidly changed during short pauses between attacks, lay on the ground in dull gray-white piles. Expended shell casings formed glittering heaps and were scattered everywhere underfoot.

A heavy silence had fallen on our line. The machine gunner and loader lay collapsed with exhaustion over their gun, staring blankly into the void from where the waves of attackers had come. The Pak crew had thrown themselves on the ground, still unable to comprehend the horror of the attack. Behind our lines the sharp clanging of entrenching tools could be faintly heard as the ringing through our fevered minds slowly subsided.

I recalled a story of how some defenders of a fortress during the Middle Ages stacked the dead in rows to be used as emergency defenses. Now a comparison came to mind. Dead and wounded Russians lay entangled and thickly scattered before our positions. The heavy underbrush that had protected their advance was shredded and torn by thousands of bullets and shell splinters.

With the setting sun we welcomed the protection of darkness. Throughout the night the screams of the wounded Russians lying in the no-man's-land before our lines continued to haunt us. We strengthened our position and labored under crates of ammunition. We observed no attempts by the Soviets to recover their wounded, either surreptitiously or under protection of a white flag. Sleep was impossible. Before our battalion sector, hundreds of enemy dead had hurriedly been counted at the risk of drawing sniper fire. Long afterward I could still hear the words of the machine gunner in my sleep, "I just can't keep killing!"

Miraculously, my Pak crew had suffered no casualties, although the battalion had suffered numerous losses. The Soviet waves had succeeded in penetrating a section of our line before being thrown back in hand-to-hand fighting. That evening, as we drew munitions and rations from headquarters, we found ourselves passing near the field medical station, and now with screams from our own wounded ringing in our ears we attempted to stumble onward.

Through the darkness we followed a pair of stretcher-bearers as they wound by shell craters filled with muddy water. We passed rows of our own dead, wrapped in shelter-quarters, waiting for their last journey toward the rear on the pony carts. On this night, however, they had to wait before embarking on their final journey with the German army, as the wounded had transport priority. We could see a young staff surgeon bent over an inert form, working endlessly, assisted by medical NCOs, sleeves rolled up in the dim light of field lanterns.

The shelter-quarters hung heavy with rain, stretched over the earthworks filled with wounded, and in the yellow light of a hissing lantern tetanus and morphine shots were administered. Lung wounds were tightly bandaged, arteries were clamped, limbs were wrapped, and shattered bones were set. Our wounded were laid in rows on piles of straw, evacuation tags hanging from their tunics. In filthy, torn uniforms, wrapped with blood-soaked bandages, they filled the air with a confusing mixture of screams, groans, whimpers, and stony silence as they awaited their journey to an unknown destination. In small groups they were transported to the rear on the pony carts.

A bad wound was psychologically shocking to a landser, regardless of how strong and courageous he may have been, and he would be quickly traumatized by what had smitten him. Overtaken by a feeling of helplessness, he found himself no longer the fighter but a man at the total mercy of his comrades.

Our only thoughts were to flee this nightmare, to escape from this place of filth, misery, and death, far away where no shells would fall. We hastened forward and returned to the familiar comfort of our gun, leaving the suffering behind us.

CHAPTER THREE

Makensia

Suddenly, through the

crosshairs of the gun optics, I found myself staring directly

into the round, black muzzle of the enemy gun . . .

Mid- to end-November 1941. The nights brought frost. Fortunately, in the Crimea no brutal Russian winter was expected, and we did not experience the suffering throughout months of subzero temperatures to the extent of our comrades on the northern front. In the northern and central areas of the Crimean Peninsula, the winters are much like those we experience in Germany, with frost and snow; however, on the southern coast, the "Russian Riviera," it remains relatively mild.

The days and nights had already revealed to us that the winter clothing issued in accordance with the Army Service Regulations for a German infantry division was entirely too light, especially for the soldiers in the foremost, exposed positions. In the front lines we were compelled to live in open earthworks or behind stone walls, with only a roof of light canvas assembled from shelter-quarters. In these primitive shelters we were exposed to the mercy of the elements and made more miserable with the onset of frost and rain. Rear support units, such as supply and staff, usually took advantage of the opportunity to seek out warm quarters and would house themselves in available Russian dwellings, despite the ability of the large-caliber naval guns from Soviet ships and fortresses to reach these targets far behind us.

Enemy fighters and Martin-bombers attacked the battery positions, medical treatment centers, supply columns, staff quarters, and other select targets on a daily basis. To add to this stress came the onset of the muddy season. When a thaw came, the trails and roads became bottomless mires; the heavy truck traffic would literally be brought to a standstill. Once again, the supply lines for the forward troops would find themselves reliant on the tireless Ukrainian ponies pulling primitive carts.

We in the forward elements had already become hardened by the deprivation and physical exhaustion constantly experienced throughout the previous months. Fighting, marching, and living under open skies while often suffering from thirst and hunger made the landsers tough and enduring, without a gram of extra fat on the ribs.

We learned the art of improvisation and self-sufficiency from the enemy. During the freezing nights, we insulated our bunkers and stone-wall shelters with blue navy overcoats stripped from the enemy dead in front of our positions. The Soviet army dead provided us with thick, brown flannel gloves as well. From somewhere far in the rear appeared instructions advising us that during the subfreezing nights the Wehrmacht socks could be used as gloves. Neatly written in precise, military terminology was the recommendation that the frontline troops should cut two holes in a sock for thumb and trigger finger. Someone was obviously not aware that our boots had been almost worn to scrap and that our socks were little more than rags, already with so many holes in them that we would have no difficulty in finding enough to poke all five fingers through.

Like the mud in the freezing weather that had descended on us, the front line congealed and solidified. The enemy relentlessly attempted to win back Makensia and the southern heights, as well as Duvankoy. Our own forces remained too weak to capture the threatening sea fortress by surprise attacks, and the situation was further complicated by our lack of tanks and heavy artillery. The Soviet fortress army was able to win enough time to reinforce and strengthen its position and to mobilize defenses. With the Soviet fleet holding absolute control of the Black Sea, the fortress was able to receive supplies and reinforcements from the Kuban salient and the Caucasus without difficulty.

Our own supply lines were extended for an untenable distance, stretching across the continent from the Crimea to the German homeland. Farther to the north, mechanical failures of the sensitive German locomotives became commonplace as they traversed the Ukraine in the bitter, subzero temperatures. Whenever a temporary thaw was experienced, the motorized supply columns became mired in the mud of the soft, unpaved roads of the southern Ukraine and northern Crimea. The hard clay roads that had proved to be easily traversable during the dry summer months had become virtually impassable for the mechanized units as they attempted to plow forward through the softened, rain-soaked earth. The supply question alone had become a critical problem for the entire Eleventh Army.

Because of the deteriorating supply situation, the heavy munitions were carefully conserved and could be used only sparingly. The rations became even more monotonous, consisting mainly of a tasteless barley broth mixed with a strange concoction of dried vegetables, derisively referred to by the infantrymen as drahtverhaue, augmented with the standard-army-issue cheese squeezed from tubes.

Shortly before being relieved by the Twenty-fourth (Saxon) Infantry Division on the front lines of Makensia, we found ourselves again harassed by the propaganda machinery of the Red Party. We had long since become familiar with the leaflets encouraging us to desert, as tons of them had been dropped on us since our crossing of the Dnieper an eternity ago. The nights were now often filled with the screeching of loudspeakers emitting endless political speeches and crude attempts to convince us to desert to the enemy:

German soldiers and workers, throw off the yoke of your oppressing imperialist and fascist clique! Come over to us, the farmer and worker's state. Clean, comfortable beds, beautiful women, good food and sweet wine awaits you! And your lives will be spared!

This would be followed by the Communist international, to which we usually replied with angry bursts from our machine guns. With monotonous regularity the routine would resume the following morning.

A short time after being relieved on the line, we learned that an area of the sector previously held by our unit was lost to the Russians. We were aware that this setback could just as well have occurred while we occupied the positions; nevertheless, our replacements were ridiculed by the landsers as the "tango division"—one step forward, two steps back. So heated became the relationship between the two infantry divisions over these words that one of our oberleutnants and an officer from Saxony were almost drawn into a duel, which had been illegal in the German army for a number of years. Only through the timely intervention of our commander was a serious incident prevented.

In December 1941, the company administrative and supply offices were located near Bachtschisseray, a village on the main road leading to Simferopol. It consisted of a genuine cobblestone street, over which rolled the main supply column to the Sevastopol front. Before our village was an open area through which motorized vehicles passed only at full speed and the pony carts clattered and bounced at a gallop.

The now-familiar phrase "in view of enemy forces" was known to every driver, and they were fully aware of the danger along this particular stretch of road, even without the signs that were posted to warn personnel of danger. Passing vehicles would predictably draw enemy shells fired from a great distance on the northern sector of the Sevastopol fortress. The heavy 305mm projectiles, fired from an armored embrasure on the battlement called Maxim Gorki I, blasted impressive craters along the road. Most of the landsers heard the name of the great Russian poet for the first time when they questioned the source of these screaming, howling shells that routinely impacted near our position. I never knew if the Soviets themselves had named this massive cannon after the poet, or if it was simply one of the battlefield nicknames that had become widespread by the landsers whose lives had been made miserable by its presence.

Bachtschisseray lay to the east of this road, artfully nestled in a picturesque valley. It was the old capital of the Crimean Tartars and was the location of the castle of the khan, complete with slender minarets and rich filigree work in arches. It was known for its 127 fountains, which, although dilapidated and worn, gave a distinct oriental impression of pre-Soviet grandeur. In the city bazaar we observed merchants who often bartered and traded items that would only be considered refuse by us.

When word was received that we were to be relieved on the line, we had quickly dispatched our drivers to locate suitable quarters for us in the designated rest area. With their usual efficiency, they immediately had arranged lodging in a small Tartar dwelling. It had a small veranda tastefully framed in carved woodwork, and water was drawn from an open cistern outside. The entire house consisted of two living rooms and was sparsely furnished. Along the walls were low benches for sitting and sleeping, and we were provided with a deep copper tub for bathing—a luxury long forgotten.

Two bent and wrinkled Tartar women engaged themselves in preparing hot water for us, and despite our protests they insisted on stripping the mud-encrusted, threadbare uniforms from our thin frames, followed by earnest attempts to scrub the layers of filth from our bodies as we soaked in unaccustomed lavishness. We finally submitted with relaxed grins to the cleansing, after which we removed stubbles of beard with hot water, soap, and razors.

We quickly developed a friendly relationship with the occupants of the house, and we traded bread and saccharin with them in return for tobacco and fresh vegetables. They made it clear to us that the Tartar people were never friends of the Soviets and that they deeply resented the "Russianization" of the Crimea, which had resulted in their becoming a minority of lesser status.

There were a number of women and children in the house who constantly came and went with abandon, as well as an old man who seldom spoke. All men of military age had apparently been swept up and conscripted into the Soviet army during its retreat. An old woman of undeterminable age would sit like a mummy with a pipe in her toothless mouth, always occupying the same place on her bench. The only time that I ever saw her round face break into a smile was on the occasion when a child was born just before Christmas. Then the old woman came to life and constantly waddled back and forth, caring for the new mother and infant.

Several days earlier we had seen a pregnant woman being carefully delivered to the house, and we experienced the birth of the little Ivan with his first cries in the room next to us. Afterward one of our medics provided them with clean bandages, and we donated the few sweets we possessed to the young mother.

Here the landsers and the Russian women celebrated the birth of new life, while a few kilometers distant the destructive mechanism of modern war could be heard in its full power as the sound of impacting shells echoed across the gently rolling terrain.

We were greeted throughout the day by the calls of the Moslem imam, and we heard his voice singing from the tower of the mosque five times daily as he called the Islamic followers to prayer, from sunrise to sunset.

When resupplying us during the Makensia operations, two transportation personnel with our supply column had managed to cross over the steep, partisan-infested Yaila Mountains and reach the coastal road near Yalta. With the senses of hungry jackals, they immediately located a captured Russian depot. Adjacent to the barrels of sauerkraut and applesauce was a large store of wine. It was already sealed and closely guarded by Rumanian troops and had been placed under the control of a strict German supply officer.

Our two soldiers pleaded for permission to take something with them from the depot, but their pleas and sorrowful tales of hunger, cold, and thirst in the forward lines were to no avail in softening the heart of the supply officer. The two decided to play on the sympathy of the Rumanians, so with a field lighter and cigarettes they located a cooperative guard who, during the night, helped them to load several kegs onto their vehicle.

The company supply feldwebel surprised us with three large wooden casks of Crimean wine, which arrived perched on the back of a supply vehicle. Told that we should draw a limited ration from the kegs, we drank the deep-red, priceless liquid from mess tins and field flasks as we sang "The Mills of the Black Forest Valley." Added to our repertoire were a few ribald lyrics, typical of soldiers since time began, and eventually we emptied our battered containers.

The driver devised a resupply system from a length of fuel line that ran directly from the casks through the open window to our quarters, where it could not be seen and controlled by our company spiess. Unhindered, we continued to drink our fill of sweet Crimean wine throughout the night, in the finest tradition of Peter the Great and Empress Catherine of Russia.

The following day an award document for bestowal of the war service cross was prepared in the company administrative office, and a justification for the award was written and acknowledged—for the obtaining of indispensable war material—wine. A vote was taken, and the company was unanimous in agreement that the award for our benefactors was in order.

Our wounded company commander had returned. Strict but just, he always led the company with exemplary fairness, never asking of his men what he could not or would not do himself. His lacerated hands had been treated in the field hospital at Bachtschisseray, where it had been necessary to amputate some of the mutilated fingers. With bandaged hands he made his rounds through the company quarters, greeting the landsers and inquiring about their needs. Despite his wounds, for which he could have been granted convalescent leave, he remained at the front in the company of the troops. Alois, his aide, assisted him in washing and shaving.

Weapons and equipment were thoroughly inspected. The drivers constantly checked their vehicles to ensure that the motors fired immediately, even in the subfreezing temperatures. We remained fully aware that our days of comfort and relative luxury in the rest area were numbered, and we could not escape the thoughts that soon our ordeal of waging war would resume.

A pre-Christmas religious service was provided by the division chaplains of both confessions in the khan's castle mosque in Bachtschisseray. The occasion would have remained in our memories as strikingly beautiful, if not for the recent horrors experienced on the Crimean battlefields that remained as yet unforgettable to us. According to the company schedule, and in strict observation of National Socialist political doctrine, attendance at religious events was voluntary, but almost the entire unit marched together to the mosque.

Foresight, strength, and faith remained the watchwords during these days of Advent. We longed for peace, and the initial excitement of war had been overcome by the strong desire to resume normal lives. We attempted to find comfort through the words of the priests and chaplains in gray, but our thoughts concentrated on home, the wounded, and the dead. In view of what we had recently witnessed together, and of what we had barely survived, the political philosophies and idealistic rhetoric that had brought us so enthusiastically into this foreign land had evolved into meaningless fragments.

The first assault on Sevastopol loomed before us. Together, with the Twenty-second (Lower Saxony) Infantry Division, we were assigned to attack the northern front of the enemy. This involved assaulting the complex system of fortifications, embattlements, and cliff positions on the northern sector of the Sevastopol stronghold and to push through to Severnaya Bay.

Fully aware that the northern sector held the heaviest defenses, we were advised that we must be prepared "to take the bull by the horns." With this drive the enemy was to be denied access to the harbor exit, cutting off any hope of further retreat for the remaining Soviet forces hoping to be evacuated by sea. The army command had drawn together all available resources for the attack. Only in the area of Kertsch did a

German division remain not committed to the assault. This division had been assigned the task of coastal security, replacing a weakly equipped Rumanian division of questionable reliability.

The pressing supply problems had rendered our complement of heavy artillery and munitions hardly sufficient to support a drawn-out, lasting battle. We were also desperately short of armored personnel, and the few we did have available were faced with the immense challenge of traversing difficult terrain while fighting their way through a fortified network of resolute defenders.

The Soviets lay deep within a series of fortresses of all types that controlled the battlefield. Our task became increasingly difficult as the weather worsened, bringing pouring rain that alternated with freezing nights to make life miserable for us in the trenches.

During the night of 16–17 December our companies trickled into the forward preparation areas. The strongly defended northern sector of the coastal fortress behind the heights towering over the Belbek Valley covered an immense area from our position toward the east. The rain quietly drizzled throughout the night, but with the sunrise the day broke clear and calm.

At 0500 the assault began against the fortress along the entire Sevastopol front. The division moved forward in a massive wave close behind an immense artillery- and smoke-battery barrage. The first assault objective, the heights west of a terrain feature designated as Hill 319.9, was taken. Due to deep emplacement of enemy defensive positions, further ground could only be taken slowly and through elimination of stubborn pockets of resistance. The enemy defended themselves with skill and bravery, fighting for every foot of ground. Despite the excellent observation positions from the batteries, very few enemy positions were actually visible to the assaulting landsers until they had approached within deadly range of the defenders. To the relief of the infantry, darkness fell early, forcing the foremost assault elements to halt for the night after reaching the first objective.

On 18 December the enemy continued to resist stubbornly from defensive positions situated on Lines 217 to 253 and extending farther south. Manstein's Eleventh Army continued to press the assault, pushing the divisions forward at first light toward the northern sector of the fortress. At approximately 0615 the enemy was forced from their defensive positions and pushed past the ravines and gorges south of Kamischly to the heights along Lines 226–228. By 1500 almost all objectives had been reached and further advance was again halted due to darkness.

In the predawn hours of 19 December the 132d Infantry Division moved forward in attempts to break through the enemy defenses and capture the heights northeast of Tschernaya and to secure the approaches to Severnaya Bay. Further attacks won ground very slowly against ever-stiffening enemy resistance. Constant counterattacks from desperate naval infantry units were effectively repulsed, and our advance was slowed by previously unreported mortar batteries and long-range naval guns, which covered the line of our advance with a heavy blocking fire. The objectives assigned for that day were finally taken in the early morning of 20 December. In the right sector of the division the town of Kamischly fell to Infantry Regiment 436, and after heavy fighting Hill 251 was captured by Infantry Regiment 438.

The divisions to our left remained hindered by thick undergrowth and almost impassible terrain. Our division, together with the Twenty-second Infantry Division, was able to penetrate deep into the fortress defenses. Our attack formations remained poised like an arrow pointing directly toward Severnaya Bay.

The enemy, aware of our attempts to win the harbor approaches, threw new strength into the defenses before us. Our point elements found themselves under a hail of bomber and fighter-bomber attacks, which took a heavy toll.

It was Christmas Eve 1941. Even during this holiest of times, a belief shared by soldiers fielded by both antagonists, the unforgiving god of war had taken no holiday. Upon the heights of Kamischly we settled into our holes and trenches dug into a former Russian field position. From the supply depot in the rear, the rations-carriers brought each man a special-issue ration consisting of a canteen of Crimean wine and a loaf of white bread. They also brought mail, the first we had received in many days.

In the light of a Hindenburg candle, huddled beneath the now faded and threadbare shelter-quarter, I opened a package from home with fingers stiff and sore from cold. The package was not very large; the authorized weight was limited to two kilograms. A feeling of homesickness swept over me as I eagerly tore open the crumpled wrapping, and the sweet smell of gingerbread filled our surroundings, contrasting sharply with the acrid smell of unwashed woolen uniforms, heavy leather equipment, grease, and oil. I had received a small candle mounted on a tiny star-shaped holder stamped from foil, a snip of evergreen twig from our Black Forest, a small bottle of Schwartzwalder Kirschwasser, and gingerbread, baked by my mother and packed with the greatest of care, using every bit of space possible for the long journey to the east.

The frost glittered on the moist wall of the shelter, and our breathing left clouds of vapor hanging momentarily in the still air before being consumed by the darkness. Pressed tightly together, Wolf and I crouched within the damp cave hacked into the Crimean earth, and we held our hands close to the inviting warmth of the Christmas candle.

We were no longer alarmed by the chatter of the Russian Maxim machine guns that stuttered in the distance, and we had come to ignore the shots cracking overhead. Our eyes stared into the candlelight from under the rims of cold steel helmets, battered and worn by the months of constant use. Wolf's downy cheeks revealed his youth; however, his eyes betrayed the years of a young man forced to grow old before his time. We had become old together and had developed a brotherhood between us, a closeness of spirit and trust that those who live in safety throughout their lives cannot know.

He pulled a harmonica from his tunic pocket and softly played the traditional songs from home, "O Tannenbaum, O Tannenbaum" and "Stille Nacht, Heilige Nacht."

Two landsers from the neighboring foxhole heard the harmonica and crept across the frozen ground to our position. With knees drawn beneath us, we were tightly pressed within the confines of our shelter, our bodies providing sparse but much-needed warmth for one another. The camaraderie that we experienced, the knowledge that each of us shared the longing to depart this place forever, softened the homesickness that we felt during these hours.

The contents of the Christmas packages were equally divided; the wine from the canteens sent warmth through our cramped limbs. Once again Wolf played the songs on the harmonica, and with voices hoarse with cold we sang softly to the music.

Outside, beyond the light of our candle, a flare sizzled skyward and cast ghastly shadows as it floated slowly over the frozen ground. Nearby, a Russian machine gun momentarily broke the stillness and was immediately answered by the bark of a sniper's rifle slightly forward of our position. Silence quickly descended on the lines again, although there remained no peace on earth.

After midnight the gun crews, led by the platoon commanders, assembled in the tank trenches that had been captured earlier the previous day by our infantry battalion. With picks and entrenching tools we set to work improving the trenches, no longer feeling the cold as we cut through the frost-hardened earth.

The sky was suddenly illuminated when a Russian, some two hundred meters distant, sent a flare sizzling toward the heavens. We threw ourselves flat on the ground and lay still until the flare, which floated lazily toward the earth for what seemed an eternity before striking the ground, sputtered furiously for a moment and extinguished itself.

We sweated and strained against the gun as we wrestled it into position, and the morning horizon was growing light as the last heavy cases of ammunition were finally in place. We rested against the walls of the tank trench, our still figures draped with shelter-quarters heavy with frost, and waited in silence before receiving word to post sentries.

In the growing light of Christmas Day we further explored the immediate area and found shelter in a former Soviet bunker near the tank trenches. The shelter was well-built, constructed of thick tree trunks lying in various positions and dug deep into the clay. The enemy, fully aware of the location of this structure, which they had abandoned only hours previously, soon targeted their former bunker. Once again we found ourselves under a barrage of artillery fire, and, just as during the countless barrages we previously had experienced, we resigned ourselves patiently to waiting out the hail of explosives falling about us.

In a corner of the bunker we located a small wood-burning stove. We engaged ourselves in roasting bread until the exploding projectiles from a 172mm gun crept closer to our position, shaking the earth and tossing fountains of dirt and debris skyward. With every explosion soil was shaken from the rafters, and hunks of earth rained on our shoulders and helmets. Instinctively we retreated to a far corner and pressed ourselves against the walls. Shell splinters and fragments of stone tore through the shelter-quarter hanging in the entrance and bounced throughout the bunker. The barrage suddenly died, and as silence enveloped our position we began to hope that the rain of shells was over; but suddenly we were overwhelmed by a tremendous explosion. Without warning, the blast from a massive shell exploded on the bunker and slammed us against the earth, leaving us dazed and almost unconscious.

We staggered weakly to our feet, choking on cordite fumes and groping futilely through the thick smoke, unable to hear the cries of our wounded through the ringing in our ears. The blinding dust and smoke eventually cleared enough to reveal a large hole in the ceiling, through which filtered the cold, gray light of the December day. Three of the thick timbers had been shattered like matchsticks by the enormous projectile, and tons of earth, which moments before had rested on the timbers, now lay piled before us.

We frantically began clawing at the mountain of dirt, using bare hands and helmets to shovel the heavy clay in attempts to free our missing comrades. With hands torn by stone fragments and wood splinters, we pulled two wounded men from the debris.

Boor was unconscious, with blood running over his face, and the other man had received injuries in both legs. He was unable to walk, and we suspected that he had suffered some broken bones. He appeared to be otherwise unhurt, and he remained talkative and alert, despite obvious pain.

Several minutes after Boor regained his senses we completed the bandaging of his wounds. Of a total of six men in the bunker, miraculously only two had received more than superficial injuries. Most of us had escaped serious injury or death due to our position at the rear of the bunker, and we had been saved by a heavy supporting wall when the shell struck directly on the center of the structure. When surveying the damage, we were all acutely aware of what fate would have dealt us if we had been directly beneath the impacting shell, where the shattered timbers and tons of earth had come to rest.

Our chimney and bunker stove were completely destroyed, and the cold began pouring through the exposed ceiling. We placed Boor on a self-propelled gun to be taken to the medical aid station. The shells continued impacting throughout the area, and a Russian Flak battery located on a railway line began taking our position under direct fire. Understandably, under these conditions the other wounded soldier refused to leave our position, choosing instead to wait until evening to be evacuated on the rations-carrier. I reluctantly agreed to let him remain with us until evacuation could be accomplished in relative safety.

Later that afternoon, the shelling increased to a steady, uninterrupted barrage, and our position fell under further direct fire from Russian small arms and howitzers. It became necessary to delay evacuation of the wounded soldier until the following morning. Several days later we received word that he had died from gangrene complications that developed in the field hospital. In view of the nature of his wounds I believe his death would have been avoided if he had received immediate medical attention from the field surgeon. Thereafter I was determined to act on my better judgement and to seek treatment as soon as possible for the wounded rather than to comply with their personal requests, which were usually made under the influence of great pain.

During the night of 26 December my gun crew crossed the tank trench and moved forward. At the bottom of the trench were lying a number of our comrades. They lay still and cold in death, wrapped in shelter-quarters for burial, and we filed past them with eyes averted. The casualties had been heavy, and we attempted to dwell on other things, on what destiny would hold for us within the next minutes or hours.

We lay before the rail embankment that led toward Mekensievy-Gory. Despite harrassing fire from enemy small arms, each Pak was flanked by two men digging in and camouflaging the guns with a cover of grass and branches. We had received no warm food throughout the previous two days, and Wolf and I volunteered to serve as rations-carriers. Shortly before dusk we worked our way toward the rear, following our tracks back over the tank trench and onto a rise, from where the enemy could be observed from a close distance. Machine-gun bursts cracked and sputtered behind us as we scrambled across the open ground, darting from cover to cover until we gained the safety of a small copse of trees. As we sprinted into the grove, a Flak gun positioned on the railway fired into the treetops above us, and we ducked instinctively as splinters and branches crashed to earth around us. With pounding hearts we finally reached our former bunker position and located the supply drivers, who issued us rations that had been reheated from the previous day.

While we were drawing our rations a number of Illyushun II fighters appeared on the horizon, and we watched them attack the foremost positions. They flew low and fast, dropping 50K fragmentation bombs directly on our company, banking and returning to the attack with board cannons and machine guns.

During a pause in the air attack we made our way forward in the growing dusk with the steaming ration canisters strapped to our backs. As we approached our position, the platoon commander, Oberfeldwebel Weiss, stared at us in astonishment for several seconds before leaping to his feet.

During our absence, my entire gun crew had become casualties. Two landsers had moved into our position immediately following our departure, and a brisance bomb had scored a direct hit on the foxhole. They had died instantly when the bomb struck, and the platoon commander had unknowingly reported Wolf and me as killed in action.

The men of the platoon wordlessly celebrated our return from the dead by hungrily devouring the hot food. We attempted to turn our thoughts from the loss of the two landsers. We had experienced too many casualties to concern ourselves at this moment with what could not be avoided, so we simply accepted the losses and continued to concentrate on our own survival. In the past six months we had crossed an enormous span of time and consciousness.

The strength of the infantry companies had been reduced from eighty to an average of about twenty men. Despite these losses, the companies had been continually thrust into the fighting ringing Sevastopol fortress, had succeeded in breaking through layers of the defenses, and in fierce fighting had captured numerous strongpoints.

Throughout the months of surviving in a brutal, unforgiving environment, each individual infantryman had exhibited remarkable endurance and adaptability while living in the open elements, under the harshest of conditions, with only field rations for sustenance.

My Pak platoon now consisted of only two guns, which were normally served with a crew of four men to each gun. With two additional men Wolf and I began training another gun crew.

On the evening of 27 December the infantry regiments prepared to launch a fresh attack. Part of the Fiftieth Infantry Division was assigned to strengthen the left-sector perimeter. At 0700, 28 December, our forces pushed forward. The attack had been precipitated by a massive barrage from our artillery.

The Nebelwerfer rocket launchers fired multiple projectiles that screamed over us, leaving long blue-white trails behind them before bursting on the enemy positions. Prisoners confirmed that the Nebelwerfers were much feared by the Soviet soldiers, who called them the "bellowing cows." We referred to the rapid-firing Russian katyusha rockets as "Stalin's organs."

We crouched in our forward positions and prepared to advance toward the enemy. The minutes passed slowly; the landsers nervously smoked final cigarettes in silence, thoughts racing through their minds of the impending assault, of wives and children, of mothers and fathers, of the bodies seen the previous night, lying still and cold, wrapped in shelter-quarters. Futilely, we attempted to concentrate only on the moment at hand.

The machine gunners again inspected the actions and feed trays of their weapons, ensuring that their gleaming belts of ammunition were free of mud and sand so as not to jam the sensitive locking mechanisms of the weapons. Hand grenades were stuck into leather field belts and into the tops of our knobelbeckers. A gefreiter silently crossed himself in prayer; others pretended not to notice.

As the final minute neared, the squad leaders sought to reassure the men, and with encouraging words they attempted to persuade us that with our battle-torn and weakened companies we could again accomplish the impossible. The artillery barrage crept ahead, and wordlessly the ranks moved forward.

After heavy fighting Mekensievy-Gory was taken. The numbers within the companies were fewer than ever. We positioned our Pak close to the Mekensievy-Gory train station, which offered us shelter next to a stone wall from the ever-present artillery rounds impacting at random throughout the area. The night was spent huddled beneath an immobilized Russian tank. During the night snowfall covered the torn earth like a white linen cloth, as if attempting to cover the wounds of war. Only a few ugly black splotches revealed the fresh impact locations of the shellfire, and the light from a full winter moon illuminated the gleaming landscape with a silver frosting. Before dawn Wolf and I requisitioned a white bed sheet from an abandoned house, with which we camouflaged the armored gun shield of the Pak.

In the gray morning light of 29 December we took shelter in a low stone house. It was solidly built, with thick walls of natural stone through which stared broken window panes. We later learned that it had previously been the home of the Mekensievy-Gory railway stationmaster. The air was cold, and we heated the stove built into the wall with splintered fragments of furniture. Somewhere Wolf found a small sack of potatoes, which we sliced for roasting on the iron stovetop. The aroma of the potatoes filled the primitive surroundings, and a wisp of smoke rose from our quarters into the still, milky morning sky.

The enemy continued laying heavy but erratic fire on the area surrounding the train station throughout the morning, and dark circles of soil left by exploding shells could be seen in stark contrast against the clean white snow. A mortar round detonated against one corner of the building but inflicted no casualties and caused only minimal damage to the structure.

We stretched our aching bodies on the floor, relishing the luxury of the heated room. Our appetites satisfied with the rare, hot meal of potatoes fried with onions, we rolled cigars from gold-brown leaves of Crimean tobacco, which we softened in the steam of a battered brass samovar. We also cut tobacco for our pipes and found ourselves deeply engaged in discussion concerning the best method for preparing tobacco to obtain the maximum aroma. One claimed that it is best after being soaked in fig juice. Another firmly asserted that corn schnapps is best, either of which we did not have. In order to end the ridiculous argument, Konrad recommended that we use horse urine, which was one of the few things in our army that we seemed to have in abundance.

The artillery fire increased as the sun climbed higher in the sky, reaching a crescendo as the god of war pounded on our positions, with impacting shells throwing geysers of earth skyward, seeking out the next victims. Our sentry took shelter alongside the low stone wall, and a nearby impact covered him with dirt and debris. His sun-bleached and ragged uniform was torn and dirty from the hail of earth, and he barely escaped death from the exploding shell. We found him lying prone on the ground, his arms shielding his face and his body and legs covered with bruises. We dragged him toward our shelter, ducking and throwing ourselves flat on the ground with each impacting artillery round.

I assumed sentry duty from within the house, peering through the pane of a shattered window. Gray-black trails from exploding artillery shells hung in the air, and I observed a number of new mushroom-shaped clouds rising within our area before the barrage fell silent. One hundred meters away two houses were burning brightly in the crisp morning air.

From my position I observed two landsers running through the streets between the huts of the village, dodging shell craters and holding their carbines at the ready. Two red flares sizzled skyward—the signal for us to prepare to repel an enemy attack.

The barrage of enemy fire had resumed, creeping forward and with most of the rounds appearing to land some one hundred meters behind our position. As our alerted platoon stormed out of the building to man our gun position, I heard the sharp crack of a tank gun mixed with the racing whine of rifle and machine-gun fire.

We leaped to our antitank gun located twenty paces from where the rail line intersected the road. Kneeling alongside the weapon, I cranked the barrel toward the direction from where I heard the tank and leaned over the gun shield to obtain an unobstructed view of our field of fire. A battalion messenger ran past, frantically yelling, "Panzer! Panzer!" Peering over the steel shield protecting the gun crew, I caught sight of the top edge of a dark turret as it moved slowly between the houses. Pressing my right eye against the rubber ring of the optics, I attempted to follow the heavy vehicle as it moved toward us, partially hidden along a side street. With a racing heart I rapidly rotated the barrel to rest where I had last viewed the enemy tank and adjusted the gun elevation for a range of 150 meters. With pulse pounding in my throat, I attempted to wait calmly for the tank to reappear on a rise in the street.

As predicted, the steel colossus moved menacingly into the sights with its heavily armored bow facing us. With a trembling hand I punched the firing button. The gun rocked back slightly, and it was possible to follow the path of the 37mm projectile through the gunsight. Horrified, I observed a trail of white smoke shoot skyward as the shell struck the turret. Ricochet!

"Panzer—forty meters!" I screamed without taking my eye from the optics. Our gun loader, Konrad, had already ripped open the case of special armor-piercing ammunition for use against heavy armor. With lightning speed Wolf slammed the heavy, red-tipped projectile into the gun and snapped the breech closed. Before I could again press the firing button, I felt the cold air and the pressure wave on my cheek as a heavy round screamed past us, barely missing our position. It impacted directly behind us into a burned-out truck, exploding and throwing hunks of metal throughout the surrounding area.

Once again, with the cross hairs of the sight firmly on the center mass of the tank, I pressed the firing button with the ball of my hand. With ears ringing from the detonation of our own weapon, we were unable to hear an impact of the round on the target. Wolf and Konrad had already reloaded our weapon when I observed a thin wisp of smoke climbing from the turret, followed seconds later by a blinding flash. A huge, black, mushroom cloud rolled upward into the frosty clear blue sky. A mighty explosion ripped the turret from its mountings as the racks of ammunition inside the tank began detonating, and the turret was left canted on the chassis, its long gun pointing awkwardly toward the sky.

A burst of machine-gun fire tore into the fresh snow directly before us. Through the ringing in our ears we heard a voice scream, "Tank on the right!" Four men gripped the gun carriage tightly, and straining and slipping on the icy ground we swung the gun to face another direction. I spied the second tank sluggishly turning among the village huts, and it slowly straightened its course before increasing speed. With plumes of smoke rising from exhausts, it accelerated toward us, smashing through a wooden garden fence at a range of about eighty meters.

The heavy tank rocked to a halt and the turret wound to face us. I rapidly attempted to find the target. Suddenly, through the crosshairs of the gun optics, I found myself staring directly into the round, black muzzle of the enemy gun as I frantically adjusted our weapon for windage and range. Exactly as I had zeroed in on the first tank, the enemy gunner now lined us up in his sights. Miraculously, I was but a fraction of a second faster, a fraction of a second that would determine whether we survived this day or if we would be buried in an unmarked grave on a long-forgotten battlefield. Our first round slammed through the heavy turret, and we observed the crew scrambling from the smoking tank.

"Tank at the front!" Again we swung the Pak around, and behind the burning wreck of the first tank we could see the ghostly silhouette of a third. The massive machine broke through the smoke like rolling death. It came onward, lumbering toward us accompanied by a number of Russian infantry who, with leveled rifles, mounted bayonets, and loud screams of "Urrah!" quickly gained the outermost line of houses in Mekensievy-Gory. With a shot that penetrated the thick, armored belly, this tank slid to a stop, the turret slowly turning toward us. We sent another armor-piercing round into the tank, and it immediately burst into flames. Wolf and Konrad reloaded with deadly speed as we fired antipersonnel rounds into the ranks of infantry. A lone machine gun joined us in defending our position, and the attack was repulsed.

I observed a fourth and fifth tank at a great distance, but the fleeting shadows of the turrets disappeared behind the crests of hills as we opened fire on them. The supporting infantry retreated, only to fall into the blocking fire of our mortar crews and artillery batteries.

At the Pak we threw our arms into the air and screamed unintelligibly at one another in uncontrollable elation. The entire action had spanned no more than a few seconds of indescribable terror, and we were consumed with relief for having escaped an almost certain death. After several long minutes of celebration, I began to reconstruct in my thoughts the excellent coordination exhibited among the men of my gun crew. Every movement, every action, and every word had been deliberate and had produced results. The endless drills and exercises with the gun, the curses, the complaints, the sweat, flesh, and blood spent during the past months had on this day saved our lives.

Our artillery batteries now opened fire, sending countless shells that rained on the ranks of the fleeing enemy. Poell and his crew dragged his Pak across the railway embankment to reinforce our sector. A single self-propelled gun rattled past our position toward the Soviet line, the crew hidden from sight beneath the heavy armor, and for the moment our defensive battle was over.

During the previous months the repulse of an attack would have been followed up with an immediate pursuit of the enemy by fresh, full-strength German units in counterattack. Fresh units could have penetrated deep into the Sevastopol line to capture the armored embrasure 626, later referred to in reports as "Stalin." This action could have then achieved a breakthrough to the bay, thus splitting the Soviet forces. Under the existing conditions, we had only battle-weakened companies available that did not possess sufficient reserves to carry through an additional push.

The companies of our infantry regiments had become too weakened through the months of constant casualties to fulfill assignments. The Ninth Company of our regiment now consisted of eighteen men; the acting company commander was a feldwebel. For weeks, the men had lain without relief before the enemy, beating back Russian attacks and then assaulting forward again. Added to the stress and deprivations of battle was a climate that took its toll on morale and fighting effectiveness: wet, cold days and freezing nights. In the trenches the Esbit stoves or a candle held beneath the cover of a ragged shelter-quarter provided the only warmth for aching joints and sore hands. We were painfully aware that our light-clothing issue would not suffice during a Russian winter.

In response to the calls on the public for assistance by our all-knowing leaders in brown, sitting far from the fighting in the east, clothing was being collected for the soldiers of the Eastern Front. The warm ski sweaters, fur vests, sport clothing, heavy blankets, wool socks, and mittens thus provided by the winter relief agency first reached us in February 1942.

By twilight, Wolf and I crept into no-man's-land to the second Russian tank that we had put out of action, the only one that had not burned of the three that had fallen to our gun. From an open hatch on the turret hung the body of the young tank commander. Together we pulled the corpse from the opening in the heavy steel armor, and I unbuckled his belt and took his gloves, pistol, and map case. We dismantled the gun optics, and in the process I noted that the crosshairs were sighted directly on the position of our Pak. We opened the breech of the gun and slid the heavy projectile from the chamber, letting it fall to the floor. We were painfully aware that this was the very projectile that would have killed our entire gun crew had we not been a fraction of a second faster. The tank had been knocked out by our single round, which had penetrated the turret just below the ammunition rack, instantly killing the Soviet gunner.

As the last traces of the sun disappeared on the horizon, the noises of the restless front increased, and under cover of darkness we crept back toward our quarters in the old stone house. As we were returning, we discovered a culvert under the railway embankment running toward the southwest large enough for a ten-year-old child to walk through standing upright. Inside the culvert, pressed closely together, we found a number of civilians, almost entirely women and children.

The women and girls were wearing thick woolen scarves wrapped around their heads and necks, and their bodies appeared to be large and stocky in their thickly quilted clothing. Through frightened, quivering lips they pleaded, "Vota nada" (we need water), and I replied, "Vota budid" (you will have water).

A middle-aged woman who appeared to be the boldest among them followed me with a pail, and I led her to the well behind our stone house. She thanked me with an unintelligible outpouring of words and much "spesiva" before trotting nervously back to the culvert. It was apparent that the tiny cluster of women and children had been crouching for several days in the confined area, where it was possible neither to stand upright nor lie prone. Packed closely together with drawn knees, they remained sitting like lost pearls in the dark confines of the culvert.

Unfortunately, it was the safest location for them to be during the heavy artillery barrages that constantly swept the area, and we could not offer them anything better in way of shelter. The following day a Russian aircraft bomb buried the tunnel entrance.

The next morning a lone Russian soldier, his rifle with fixed bayonet in hand and fur cap pulled low over his forehead, ran frantically past our quarters, his long overcoat flowing behind him. Through his hoarse cries of "Urrah!" we could not determine if he was drunk or had lost his senses. At a distance of twenty paces I called to him "Stoi! Ruki verkh!" A short distance away, he drew to an abrupt halt and looked about, finally fixing his eyes upon us. Instead of tossing his rifle aside and raising his arms, he squeezed the trigger of his rifle, firing at us from the hip as he charged forward with leveled bayonet. The bullet struck the stone wall of the house behind us, and with no other alternative I raised my carbine and shot him at point-blank range.

At midday our company commander, accompanied by two other staff officers, entered the stone house without prior notice. In acknowledgment of our accomplishment in repelling the tank incursion on the previous day, he awarded each member of the gun crew the Iron Cross, pinning the award on our tunics with bandage-wrapped hands.

Over the Christmas holidays our division was reinforced with a replacement battalion. I recognized one of the replacement personnel as Hans, from my home town in Württemberg. We had known one another since youth, and we were more than pleased to see that both of us had thus far survived the war. Hans had been shot through the neck during the early stages of the Russian campaign, and after recovering from his wound he had received orders to report to us as a replacement.

The men of the replacement unit had been en route to the front for weeks. The first phase of transport across the steppe was in cattle cars with no heat, after which the great distance from Perekop to the Crimea was covered by foot. According to Hans, all the men were glad to be back with the "masses" again, as it was only in the company of landsers that we now felt truly at ease.

One morning after a probe by a Soviet company against our defenses, we came on a Russian with an abdominal wound lying upon the railway embankment. Holding his hands over his wound as if in prayer, he was whimpering softly for water, and through his unintelligible pleas we heard him muttering "Christ" with a trembling voice. His pale face was drawn and turned toward the leaden sky, and his eyes flickered from one of us to another, seeking pity and relief from the hated enemy from whom he had been taught to expect no quarter. Hans departed for a moment before quickly returning with two Russian prisoners, who carried the badly wounded soldier back to the medical aid station on a makeshift stretcher that they had fashioned from army overcoats.

It was rumored within the company that a few days previously the division chaplain, Satzger, had inadvertently passed through the foremost positions during a visit to the front lines before suddenly finding himself surrounded by Soviet soldiers. Fortunately, a Russian soldier who could speak some broken German was among them, and Satzger talked the ten enemy infantrymen into surrendering and brought them back with him to company headquarters.

On this isolated battlefield we received little news regarding political or military developments in the world. News from home was scarce, and the theater of war around us overshadowed all else lying beyond our immediate realm. The overextended supply system was strained to its limits in providing us with desperately needed war material, and personal correspondence had to be considered of secondary importance.

When we learned that America had entered the war against Germany, we listened intently and somberly. Many of the landsers, regardless of rank or education, now believed that only the greatest of skill and luck could bring us total victory. However, despite the knowledge that the bulk of the world's industrialized strength was turned against us, never did we at that time realize the full extent of the defeat that was to befall us.

I recalled my father speaking of how all was lost for Germany with the entry of the United States into World War I. These comparisons were made, and within circles of close friends we discussed our dubious situation. Even the infantrymen, living in holes hacked from the frozen ground and fighting an enemy that seemed to grow stronger daily, came to realize that Germany could not hope to win a war against the entire world.

Nevertheless, our only hope and chance for survival was to place our trust in the leadership of the Crimean army and in the proven abilities of Generaloberst von Manstein. Eventually he, too, would follow the path of many of our most talented officers in refusing to bow to the impossible demands and the absurd political doctrines of the dictator in Berlin. Manstein's armies would be taken from him as the war wore on, leaving us in the field often to be led at the highest levels by party followers with little military talent. Some of these officers would attain a general's rank through what could only be recognized as misguided political appointments rather than through merit on the battlefield.

In the late afternoon of 31 December we learned through a courier that the front was to be pulled back, and the area now occupied by our forces was to be evacuated. During the night we pulled our gun over the embankment and onto the road that led northeast toward Kamischly. After several hours we arrived at the newly established forward lines, and by morning we were at the company assembly area near Bachtschisseray.

Initially we failed to understand why it was necessary to give up such a large area for which we had so heavily paid with the blood of our comrades. The two assault divisions had, over the days of Christmas, penetrated deeply through the Russian-held territory. From our forwardmost positions we had been able to hear the foghorns at night of the Russian ships on Severnaya Bay, the lifeline for the enemy. These deep penetrations had left our flanks dangerously exposed to an enemy who was continuing to be reinforced from the sea; thus the line had been adjusted to eliminate the possibility that we might be severed from our main battle group.

Before Feodosia, January 1942. The division war diary entry explained that due to "extraordinary events on the Crimea" it was deemed necessary to revise the planned assault against Sevastopol. Only later did we learn of the danger in which the Crimean army had found itself. On 25 December, the Russians had carried out successful landings near Kertsch, where only a single German infantry division had been positioned during the fighting at Sevastopol. Organized partisan units had received orders from the higher Soviet command to sever the supply route to the Crimea along the corridor near Perekop, and on 29 December and through early January the Russians landed at Eupatoria and in the harbor of Feodosia. Through tenaciously defending their position, the division occupying Kertsch was successful in halting the Russian penetration. Eupatoria was retaken by encircled reconnaissance units, and the partisan units were driven back.

The Forty-sixth Infantry Division at Kertsch fought a withdrawing action to the west to avoid being encircled, as only part of one Rumanian cavalry division, a supply unit, and a weakened pionier battalion were available as reinforcements. The situation for the army in the Crimea had become critical. During the first days of January 1942 the division marched through Simferopol, the main city of Crimea in the sector to the north of Karasubasar. Due to a thaw that turned all roads into a bottomless morass, headway was made only through the extraordinary efforts of the men and horses. In many instances teams of horses could be observed harnessed to motorized vehicles. The reliable animals were often able to make slow but deliberate headway through the mud, but the mechanized transports remained helplessly mired in place. With the further movement of units marching toward the east, the artillery and most of the supply units could move only on the hard surface of the Karasubasar–Stary road in order to make any progress whatsoever.

The assault on Sevastopol had cost the division such heavy losses that the division commander, Generalleutnant Sentzenich, deemed it necessary to dissolve one battalion in each regiment to bring the remaining battalions up to fighting strength. Sentzenich left the division on 5 January 1942 to be replaced by Oberst Lindemann, a brave and talented officer.

An offensive was scheduled for 15 January, and the 132d Infantry Division was assigned to push through and over Hill 132.3 to the Black Sea and on to the Bay of Feodosia. To the left was positioned the reinforced Infantry Regiment 213, and the sector to our right was assigned to the 170th Infantry Division.

Shortly before twilight we received reports of prepared Russian defenses southwest of Hill 132.13. Under cover of two machine-gun posts we pulled our Pak across the frozen, gray no-man's-land with the gun shield facing forward. We took up a position on a gentle slope, from where we could see the Bay of Feodosia. The Black Sea was visible to us for the first time, seen as a dark gray line on the horizon. We opened fire with our Pak upon a group of Russian vehicles and armor that was unwisely situated on the open steppe at fifteen hundred meters distance.

The Russians returned the fire from tanks and heavy mortars, and the impacting rounds burst on the crest of the slope behind us. During the exchange of fire a gunner manning another Pak in our company was killed by an exploding shell.

I carefully readjusted the range finder and sighted our Pak on a distant target. Once again we found ourselves facing the deciding minutes of life and death on the battlefield. If the enemy armor had our position fixed and were quicker and more skilled than we, then we would have found our graves on this hillside.

With a burning eye against the rubber eyepiece of the optics, I pressed the firing button and followed the path of our shell, holding my breath as the projectile was lost from sight against the tiny black target in the distance. The crew piled out of the armored vehicle, indicating that our shot had struck home and had disabled the tank.

A 105mm battery of our division artillery immediately opened fire, and within minutes the entire Russian-occupied field was enveloped in a thick cloud of dust and smoke. We continued to fire rapidly into the haze with antipersonnel rounds. The Soviet positions, which otherwise would have served as a bridgehead for a counterattack on our newly established lines, disappeared under a hail of artillery fire.

The protecting darkness swept over us, enveloping friend and foe and bringing an end to the exchange of artillery fire. During the night a reconnaissance platoon brought in several prisoners, providing information for pressing an attack the following day.

An icy wind whistled out of the northeast. We lay pressed tightly together in the trench dug alongside our gun, praying that we would not be tormented with rain or snow as we shivered in the darkness on the hillside. Covered by shelter-quarters and wrapped in bits of spare clothing, we passed the night on the frozen steppe before Feodosia.

Dawn provided scant relief as the sun sporadically pierced gray clouds, offering little warmth. At midday we provided security for the infantry units with our Pak as they advanced on Feodosia. Before us lay an open field of fire, and across the dry earth of the steppe the infantry moved relentlessly toward the sea, appearing as tiny, moving specks in the distance that eventually disappeared over the horizon.

During the initial hours of the attack the harbor had been bombed by Stukas, and we were able to detect burning houses, storage facilities, oil tanks, and expanses of factories in the approaches to Sarygol. Above the harbor of Feodosia a massive, black cloud of smoke hung in a clear winter sky.

From the positions to our rear the sound of rifle fire suddenly broke forth. One of the Pak support vehicles, which was parked some one hundred meters behind us in a depression, burst into sight with a wildly racing motor, pursued by erratic rifle and submachine-gun fire.

We swung the gun about to face our rear, with no visible sign of the enemy. Reaching our position, the driver, Fehr, fell breathlessly from the cab of the truck, exclaiming, "The Russians are behind us and have overrun the assembly positions!" He further reported that he was able to hear the alarm being sounded from regimental headquarters. He knew nothing of the fate of the other driver, other than that he also had been observed leaping into his vehicle within sight of the oncoming Russians, suggesting that perhaps the truck had been struck by a round that rendered it immobile. We later recovered the vehicle to find the driver slumped over the steering wheel, killed by a single shot to the head.

The attackers poured out of the depression. There were at least one hundred Russians streaming with a loud "Urrah!" toward our seven-man Pak crew and one machine-gun position. Rifle shots slammed into the side of the vehicle and ricocheted off the glacis plate of our gun. Hans took charge of the machine-gun position. Laying his machine gun across the ammunition trailer, he fired a long burst from a standing position. The first antipersonnel round from our cannon struck a tall Russian at the forefront, and his severed torso bounced across the ground. Through the roar of the weapons the cries of "Urrah!" grew lighter, the khaki-brown-clad bodies piled thick before us, partially hidden in the dry winter grass. Despite our desperate defense, they continued to creep slowly forward under the protection of rippling submachine-gun and rifle fire like a swarm of insects, resolutely crawling ever closer, refusing to turn back.

Through the magnifying optics of the Pak, the Soviets appeared large and terrifying, the muzzle bursts from their submachine guns filling the sight picture. I began to sight on the enemy soldiers independently. Those closest to us were lying motionless, but new shapes continued to appear from the depression.

Suddenly our machine gun jammed. Through a hail of rifle fire our munition-carriers wrenched more cases of ammunition from the caisson, and the loaders, soaked with sweat despite the cold, continued to ram one shell after another into the hot breech of our gun.

An unteroffizier lying next to me near the wheel of the carriage was firing short, sustained bursts from his submachine gun when he suddenly rolled backward, screaming with pain. We had no time to assist the wounded, only to fire, fire, and fire to save our lives. Having cleared the jammed feed tray, Hans opened fire again with the Spandau. The mound of spent shell casings behind the cannon continued to grow. Someone yelled, "Last case of antipersonnel!" The high-explosive ammunition was quickly depleted, and we continued firing at solitary figures with armor-piercing rounds. The ammunition bearers knelt with their carbines over the right side of the gun carriage and opened fire toward our flank as some Russians attempted to circle around us. Tossing hand grenades that exploded twenty meters before us, the Russians desperately pressed home the attack in an effort to prevent the protecting harbor of Feodosia from falling into our hands. Despite their individual courage, they vainly died in the attempt.

The roar of the weapons slowly subsided as the enemy survivors crawled back into the protecting depression. They were later taken prisoner by infantry units that were sent out for mopping-up operations, and the prisoners filed past our gun on their march toward the rear, bearing their wounded with them.

The wounded unteroffizier was still lying behind the protection of the Pak. We cut off his boot and bandaged the leg, which had been hit by a rifle bullet just below the knee. An exit wound was visible, which displayed a clump of bloody flesh protruding from the sole of his foot. We carried him to our only remaining intact vehicle, and Fehr drove him to the rear. We later learned that after cursory treatment, he was evacuated further to a central medical facility, where the field surgeons deemed it necessary to amputate his lower leg.

For the next twelve hours we continued combing our surrounding area and brought in additional prisoners, many of whom were wounded, and they were escorted to regimental headquarters.

Our rifle companies pushed onward, reaching the Black Sea coast. On the point was the First Battalion, Infantry Regiment 436; protecting their flank was Infantry Regiment 437. The town of Sarygol, a northern suburb of Feodosia, was firmly in our hands by late evening, and all approaches from north and south were secured. This action sealed the fate of the still unoccupied city of Feodosia. General von Manstein acknowledged in his official report that our 132d Infantry Division had led the decisive push to the sea.

On 18 January, the remaining Russian forces still holding Assambay broke through the German lines and harassed the combat units by destroying communications cables and creating a nuisance behind our lines. They suffered heavy casualties through concentrated artillery fire and after several days were scattered and effectively destroyed as a fighting unit. Throughout the fighting around Sarygol, enemy amphibious troops had suffered heavy losses, the dead lying thick in the streets and on the shore of the sea. During the night of 17–18 January three Russian tanks attempted to break out of the German encirclement but were knocked out by antitank mines planted by our pioniers along the southern edge of Sarygol. The division wheeled toward the northeast, and on 19 and 20 January we approached the defense lines to the east and northeast of Daln-Kamyschi, which was ordered to be held until the onset of the Kertsch offensive.

On 19 January Infantry Regiment 438 advanced west of the coastal road of Daln-Kamyschi and the surrounding heights. The movement was carried out according to plan against weak enemy resistance. In the morning hours the division headquarters was moved to Blish Baybuga. All movements experienced harassment from enemy aircraft, despite snow flurries and clouded skies.

Feodosia and the outlying areas had suffered heavy damage from Stuka attacks and artillery fire. A number of damaged transport ships lay in the harbor, and large quantities of war material had been abandoned in the areas evacuated by enemy forces.

On 20 January the enemy aircraft activity increased. During the evening, corps directives were received to prepare defensive positions along the Daln-Kamyschi line. On 21 January the division headquarters was moved toward Feodosia. The temperatures plummeted to minus thirty degrees centigrade. The Wehrmacht report of 19 January addressing the Battle of Feodosia stated: "German and Rumanian forces under the command of General der Infanterie von Manstein, in coordinated actions with Luftwaffe units under General der Flieger Ritter von Greim, have thrown back Soviet forces and have occupied the city of Feodosia. A total of 4,600 prisoners have been captured as well as 73 armored vehicles, 77 field guns, and large quantities of war material."

The successful termination of the battle for Feodosia eliminated any immediate danger for the army in the Crimea. In defensive positions on the narrow peninsula of Kertsch stood the XXX Army Corps with the 132d Infantry Division at the forefront, to our left the XXXXII Army Corps with the Forty-second Infantry Division, and the Eighteenth Rumanian Infantry Division in reserve. The attempts of the Russians to break out of the Feodosia sector toward Dshankoy-Perekop and to swing around the bulk of the Eleventh Army proved to be unsuccessful. As a result of constant breakout attempts by isolated Soviet forces, an order was received to concentrate on the mopping-up of all enemy resistance remaining in rear areas.

CHAPTER FOUR

In the Crimea

We quickly formulated an

attack plan. Heinz and Wolf hastily scrambled on all fours

toward the nearest cow . . .

We received the order to bivouac in Sarygol-Feodosia. The troops had been pushed to the extreme limit of endurance since the beginning of the Russian campaign, particularly during the intensive fighting in the areas of Sevastopol and Feodosia. The infantry companies as well as units of pioniers, panzerjaegers, reconnaissance battalions, the forward observers of the artillery, and the supply units had repeatedly demonstrated how good soldiers conform and react to a given situation, regardless of the strength of the opposition, when provided the proper training and leadership.

The respite from the front lines was savored by my Pak crew. We were situated near the company supply area in Sarygol, designated as regimental reserves. Immediately following the capture of the town, we located another solid stone house with two rooms situated near the railway, very similar to our previous quarters. The house was occupied by Mamuschka, an approximately fifty-year-old plump Ukrainian with a round, cheerful face, by Marussia, her thirty-year-old daughter, and Pan, the man of the house. Pan was born in the Crimea and was of slight build with a large, patriarchal moustache that hung from beneath the black lambswool cap that he was never seen without, even in warm weather. He was of an undeterminable age, a small, gnarled-looking man who could have been anywhere between forty and sixty years old. Before the path of war had rolled through their homeland, he had worked as a stationmaster for the Feodosia railway system.

We quickly grew accustomed to our three hosts, who occupied the front room of the house. Against the right wall of the building was an oven constructed of mortared brick with an iron facade, and the back of the room was filled by a large, wide wooden bed in which all three slept together. In the second room were two decorative iron beds, a dark-brown walnut armoire, and a night table that sported a well-tended house plant. I allowed myself the luxury of sleeping in one of the iron beds on a genuine mattress, and the others made themselves comfortable upon the floor. It was a warm and cozy house, and even the nightly sound of the large Russian naval batteries resonating from the horizon disturbed us little.

The only misunderstanding that we experienced occurred with Mamuschka when we callously pounded nails into the wall and along the front of the armoire for the hanging of our canteens, cartridge belts, and miscellaneous field equipment. Mamuschka paced rapidly back and forth shaking her head beneath her scarf, exclaiming repeatedly, "Nix karascho, nyeto kultura!" We immediately removed all the nails and she became calm again. The furniture at our disposal was somewhat old-fashioned and dated from the days of the czars. There was no evidence of new furniture to be seen. The house had been wired for electricity, but no power was available, so the old oil lamps typical of the Russian cottages were relied on to provide a dim but warm lighting within the dwelling.

The army rations remained sparse and monotonous; the bread ration had again been reduced. With the capture of the village we received a special addition to our rations, which now consisted mostly of canned meat. While rummaging through a Russian truck that had been partially destroyed by a shell from an assault gun, we found sacks of dried bread and long smoked sausages, which tasted similar to the Krakow sausages familiar to us in Germany.

In addition to looking for food, we searched an abandoned hut near the harbor where we found large pasteboard cartons filled with soap. With further investigation, we were surprised to discover large sacks of cornmeal and sugar hidden deep beneath the piles of soap. With these supplies at hand, Heinz, our baker from Karlsruhe, created an excellent meal of sugar-sweetened semolina, which we hungrily devoured with slices of Russian sausage. We stuffed ourselves full while sharing our bounty with Mamuschka, Marussia, and Pan, as they themselves had almost nothing to eat.

The word spread quickly throughout the company of how well our gun crew was living, and as a result we received a constant stream of visitors. Hans came to visit me as well, and we sat and talked of our homes in Württemberg, which lay three thousand kilometers behind us.

We filled a number of empty ammunition cases with the meal and sugar, and the trove remained hidden in full view among our stockpiles of ammunition crates. Because we always seemed to have additional rations, the company bestowed on us the honorary title "the riff-raff crew."

While searching the pier storage facilities we came upon two large liquid storage tanks. Hoping to find a bonanza of fuel for our vehicles, we inspected the containers closely. Inside we discovered three shivering Russian soldiers who had been standing up to their shoulders in oil for several days. Having been convinced that they would be shot immediately upon capture, they had chosen to die in the freezing temperatures or face the prospect of drowning in horrible conditions rather than surrender. We took them to the harbor commander's headquarters, where they were given other clothing, and there we left them to an unknown fate.

One afternoon, while searching through what we believed to be an abandoned factory, I stepped into a long passageway and slowly advanced forward. Suddenly, a hand grenade came bouncing out of the darkness, the time fuse sizzling and sputtering, and rolled to my feet. I lashed out instinctively and kicked it back into the darkened chamber, while simultaneously grabbing Heinz who, unaware of what was happening, had come up close behind me. I pulled him with me into a neighboring room as the grenade detonated, filling the air with dust and debris. With our ears ringing from the blast, we scrambled to our feet with submachine guns ready, and five Russians came stumbling toward us with upraised arms. The hand grenade had rolled back down the passageway and had exploded almost at their feet, and dazed but otherwise uninjured, they surrendered without further resistance.

The combing of captured and occupied areas was not without an uncertain degree of risk. I received personal satisfaction from knowing that although I was ultimately responsible for the safety of my gun crew, I could trust their judgment and physical ability to any limit. This faith in the abilities of one another had grown over the months on the front and matured to the extent that only death or wounds could separate us from this ultimate level of trust.

Following the winter battle of Feodosia from 15 to 18 January, the front on the narrow peninsula of Kertsch was reduced to static warfare. While the division held the sector from the "Icebreaker" on the Black Sea to the approximate middle of the Parpatsch line—Hill 50.6—the Russians occupied well-prepared positions opposite us. Their defensive line consisted of an extensive network of deep trenches, minefields, and tank traps.

All breakthrough attempts by the enemy from the end of February to early May were halted by the division with heavy losses to the Soviet forces, especially the assaults against the left wing on Hill 50.6. Despite enemy operations with tanks and a far superior number of rifle divisions, our defensive front continued to hold. Local penetrations through the line held by the Forty-sixth Infantry Division on our left and through the area covered by a Rumanian brigade were sealed.

Across the entire Eastern Front, the Russians attempted to win back ground lost to the German army the previous summer and in doing so to wrest the initiative from the German forces. They also used to great advantage the fact that the Soviets continued to exercise control of the Black Sea, and our troops and positions were more often experiencing naval gunfire from the Soviet fleet, which cruised the Black Sea at will.

The liberation of the Crimea remained a primary objective, as its possession would enable the Soviet forces to launch airpower against the weak flank of the southern front as well as to bring the Rumanian oil fields into bomber range. The loss of the Crimea to Soviet forces was to be decisive in determining Turkey's yet uncommitted role in the war. We later learned that the Russians had optimistically christened their attack the "Stalin offensive," and we did not spare any illusions that the Soviets would go to any effort to recapture the Crimea.

It was discovered through air reconnaissance that the enemy was steadily massing strength on the Kertsch Peninsula. The Straits of Kertsch had been frozen solid for several weeks and were capable of supporting traffic all the way to the Caucasus. This unexpected advantage to the Russians was to provide the Soviets with the possibility of transporting troops and material over the ice from the hinterland.

For both the German landsers and the Soviet infantry, a grinding, costly, trench war had begun, with troops laboring day and night constructing earthworks and obstacles. The shortage of wood and timber made the construction of bunkers difficult, and it was necessary to transport logs over great distances from the rear areas and from the Yaila Mountains.

The division's combat engineer units laid minefields and erected complex expanses of barbed-wire defenses. Through the tireless efforts and exertions of the troops, the enemy remained unsuccessful in attempts to break through our positions.

During the previous year, during our battle for Sevastopol, the Forty-sixth Infantry Division had captured the Kertsch Peninsula and harbor. Throughout this period of operations the Forty-sixth was under command of General Graf Sponek, who, when flanked by strong enemy forces at the end of December 1941, exercised independent command and ordered a withdrawal from the peninsula. This action was in direct violation of Hitler's nonwithdrawal policy. Subsequently, an investigation of the general's actions was ordered. Following Sponek's independent move, a directive from the commander of the southern front was released, which expressly forbade the awarding of any further decorations to this division. This measure of mass retaliation, which all of us considered wrong, was clearly the result of a direct order from Hitler emphasizing that the troops must unconditionally hold all positions, forbidding the withdrawal of forces from any captured territory.

The case of Graf Sponek demonstrated to us the conflict of principles into which a military leader could be thrust. In this instance, initiative had been taken by a trained general officer to save his forces from a perilous situation instead of obeying a sweeping order that did not take exceptional circumstances into consideration. Sponek knew that in the case of failure to fulfill his duty, he risked not only his profession but also his own life. By order of Oberkommando des Heeres, Sponek was subsequently relieved of his command. A courtmartial, presided over by Reichsmarschall Hermann Goring, ended after short deliberation with the sentencing of this brave and capable officer to death. Although this sentence was later commuted to life imprisonment, General Graf Sponek suffered the fate of many, and simply disappeared into the draconian National Socialist justice system. Although his fate remains unknown, it is most certain that he was executed during the purge following the 20 July 1944 attempt on Hitler's life.

Feldmarschall von Bock, Supreme Commander of Army Group South, was later to deliver to the Forty-sixth Infantry Division the following Order of the Day: "The Forty-sixth Division has consistently exhibited outstanding performance against the enemy since the beginning of January in the defensive fighting upon the corridor. As such, the division has earned, and is awarded, special recognition. Further recommendations for promotions and awards shall be reviewed for immediate approval."

As we continued to endure the horrors and depravity of an unforgiving war on the Eastern Front, our chances of escaping unscathed grew more remote. This belief was enforced by the widespread knowledge of the fate of German soldiers who fell into the hands of the Russians, of how they often died slowly and painfully in captivity. This awareness of Soviet brutality only instilled a will in the soldier to fight and resist to the last round and last breath. As humans we are often capable of great displays of courage, but for suicide we have no talent. The war in the east had degenerated to the point that we equated surrender to suicide.

At the end of February, the Pak crew entrenched the gun in the shelter of a terrain feature officially referred to as the Turtle. We sought shelter against the frost and icy wind in a crumbling shed previously occupied by sheep, and we made ourselves as comfortable as possible between the damp clay walls. The roof had fallen victim to numerous shell splinters, and we constructed our defense position with an almost circular field of fire. From the heights we could observe the Black Sea to our right. The town of Daln-Kamyschi with an imposing factory building dominated the foreground. Far to our right, on the cliffs that bordered the sea, was a clear view of the fortified position Icebreaker at a range of about fifteen hundred meters. In addition to Daln-Kamyschi, the Turtle, and the Icebreaker were various infantry positions such as the "Grasshopper," which lay near a former grain silo. To our left we had a view of the front that stretched beyond a frozen marsh up to a hill designated as 66.3. On a clear day at least a third of the Parpatsch position was visible to us as well.

We fortified our gun position approximately fifty meters' distance from our quarters and constructed a curved wall of earth for 360-degree protection from shell splinters and mortar rounds. It was possible to reach our gun position from our quarters in relative safety through a running trench that we hacked into the stony earth. We attempted to make our position as safe and as comfortable as possible under the conditions offered, and we longed for the simple wooden cottages that had been available to us at our previous location.

On 22 February I paid a visit to Hans. His gun position was located upon the hill of Korokel, on the shore of the Black Sea, for coastal defense.

Two days later he was killed. The panzerjaeger platoon of Feldwebel Falk was stationed three or four kilometers behind the forward lines as coastal defense near a prominent white house in the vicinity of Daln-Kamyschi. It was ordered that members of the platoons assigned to the quiet coastal sectors were to muster for a briefing, and on the morning of 24 February the visibility was limited by fog and mist, rendering far-range observations impossible for friend and enemy alike. Falk's platoon had assembled by the white house with approximately twenty men to receive instructions from the platoon commander, when a single incoming shell impacted almost at their feet.

From this platoon, five men, including Hans, were killed immediately or so seriously wounded that they died within hours. An additional twelve men received wounds that were not immediately fatal. Following this incident an order was released authorizing training to be conducted only in small, isolated groups.

Soon afterward another incident occurred when a number of forward observers were killed while massed together on a water tower near the factory of Daln-Kamyschi. In order to obtain a commanding view of the enemy frontal area, observers from an artillery unit, the infantry rifle companies, and several mortar platoons had situated themselves in an unprotected position. A direct hit from a single artillery shell on this observation point killed and wounded all the observers. Following this incident an order was issued forbidding the massing of observers in such a manner.

Operation Trappenjagd was prepared with the aim of driving the Soviet forces from the Crimea. In the antitank trenches of Feodosia, battalions underwent intense preparations for the planned assault on the enemy earthworks in the Parpatsch position. For the demolition of enemy wire obstacles, special explosives were prepared, and assault ladders were constructed for the storming of the enemy trenches.

Beginning at 0630 on 26 February the enemy laid strong artillery and mortar fire along our entire front. At 0830 the barrage abruptly subsided, and infantry units supported by heavy armor moved against us. Near Telegraph Hill a breakthrough was attempted by nine enemy tanks, one of which was destroyed by the Fourth Battery of our division's artillery regiment. Three other tanks were put out of action with lighter damage by the defensive fire from the Fifth Battery. The remaining tanks pulled back. Of nine attacking tanks, seven were destroyed or disabled and remained on the battlefield. By 1000 the attack had been beaten back along the entire sector, with the enemy withdrawing after suffering heavy losses.

The rainfall that had occurred throughout the night and continued during daylight hours had become a great advantage during the time we remained in a defensive posture. The ground became saturated and softened to the extent that movement over open ground could be accomplished only slowly and with great difficulty. Again at 1300 enemy forces attempted to assault Telegraph Hill. Through coordinated fire this assault was repelled.

On the morning of 27 February, the enemy pounded the division's defense lines along the Parpatsch with every available caliber of artillery. Pretargeted positions were taken under attack by bombers and fighter squadrons. The incessant barrages on the German lines were augmented by Russian gunboats and destroyers firing into the emplacements, on the factory, and into the division's artillery positions in and around Daln-Kamyschi.

With overwhelming numerical strength the Russians attempted to break through our positions. The thinly held German lines were facing seven rifle divisions and a number of armored brigades. In addition to those forces directly opposing us, the Russian army high command also held six or seven rifle divisions, one cavalry division, and two armored brigades in reserve to exploit the expected breakthrough.

The early morning sun presented a clear sky on 3 March 1942. Strong enemy movement on the Seytdshent road was detected, with trucks, marching companies, and horse-drawn vehicles filling the narrow roads. During the night enemy warships had concentrated heavy fire upon Korokel, and in the early morning hours the Russians fired on the town with approximately two hundred rounds from medium-caliber artillery. The barrage also swept along the coastal road and the strategically important railroad positions. After a short pause, between the hours of 1200 and 1400 heavy artillery fire fell on the positions of the Fifth and Sixth Batteries from the direction of "Moscow." In the Sixth Battery, a gun was heavily damaged and put out of action with the loss of several artillery crew members. During the night our batteries fired twenty-five rounds each on the road crossing near the tank trenches. During the morning hours enemy troop concentrations were taken under fire.

Strong enemy air attacks were launched on the neighboring left sector; friendly air activity remained weak. This artillery duel resulted in our batteries suffering two killed and seven wounded.

The divisional sector soon became polarized into a series of hotly contested strongpoints, with most heavy fighting taking place in the vicinity of Hills 50.6 and 66.3 as well as on the Turtle and Icebreaker, which fought off as many as a dozen enemy attacks per day. Numerous tanks were destroyed during the period between 27 February and 3 March and again when massive attacks were renewed along this sector from 13 to 20 March. Local penetrations into the Icebreaker, the Turtle, and on the perimeter of the left neighboring sector were quickly sealed through counterattacks.

We later learned that the Russians had broken through the Parpatsch in a sector that was defended by a Rumanian division, and the breakthrough could not be stemmed by the weakened German units on the Rumanian flanks. With this development it was necessary to commit a new panzer division into the line. This particular division had been organized and equipped in France and was largely outfitted with captured French tanks. The use of the new division had been planned for the spring offensive, but now it was compelled to churn through the deep mud to meet the Russians.

Splendidly outfitted in recently issued winter uniforms, the column roared and clattered past our positions to engage the enemy in the distance. We could not overcome the feeling that they looked on us with scorn as they swept by, perched high in the turrets of their steel chariots. We gazed enviously on the newly outfitted troops as we crouched in our earthworks and struggled through the mud in uniforms and equipment that were tattered, encrusted, and faded through months of exposure to brutal elements and constant use.

The neophyte panzer units charged bravely forward to launch their attack. With tracks grinding and engines roaring through the crisp air, they immediately smashed headlong against a Russian position, foundering in the deep mud in front of the enemy guns, fully exposed to antitank fire.

Included in their losses was a total of forty tanks, and after this disastrous probe they were immediately pulled out of the line and sent to a rear area for further training. They were forced to learn, just as we had learned throughout the previous months, that it takes much more than new uniforms and a vast amount of élan to survive on the battlefields of the Eastern Front.

In the usual, unforgiving tradition, the infantrymen thereafter referred to this particular unit as the "Eau de Cologne Division," meaning that they "came from the west and evaporated quickly." An official order was soon issued forbidding the use of the derogatory term, and it was no longer heard among the landsers in the foremost lines. It came as no surprise, however, occasionally to hear the term used for some time thereafter by soldiers who remained in the rear areas, usually far from the reach of the Russian guns.

On 23 March, the enemy assaulted the Icebreaker in battalion strength throughout the day. Infantry Regiment 437 had been supported with assault guns, but the enemy heavy-artillery and mortar fire blanketed the Icebreaker and the nearby factory, keeping the landsers pinned in their trenches and bunkers. During the night our batteries fired on the concentration of enemy troops in front of the Icebreaker.

The enemy was successful in capturing the Icebreaker after the German defenders expended all available ammunition. Through heavy blocking fire from our artillery batteries, the enemy was prevented from exploiting the breakthrough for a further advance. The Soviets had suffered massive casualties and were unable to reach the tank trenches east of the factory.

With supporting fire from artillery batteries and self-propelled guns, our infantry units were successful in retaking the Icebreaker by evening. The expenditure of sixteen hundred artillery rounds by our batteries had prevented a further enemy advance, despite Soviet ability to bring up reinforcements. Throughout the heavy ground fighting, air activity remained negligible, with only one enemy bomber and one Rata downed by our ground fire.

At 0440, 9 April, the enemy launched a surprise attack supported with heavy-artillery fire, which brought a hail of shells on our positions. At 0700 the enemy artillery fire lifted slightly in our sector, although the sector to our left continued to bear the brunt of the enemy attack. Tanks were brought into action, and by midday the attack had grown weaker. Enemy guns and numerous troop concentrations were taken under fire by our artillery batteries, and despite heavy pressure the enemy was able to launch another attack on our strongpoint, officially referred to as

"Siegfried." After several attempts, this attack was dispersed by artillery and infantry fire.

The Fifth Battery took a tank concentration under fire on the northernmost point of the marsh. Enemy air activity, consisting mostly of primitive Rata-like biplanes, was regularly encountered. These aircraft attacked any available targets with light bombs and machine-gun fire. At 1130 our Stukas launched attacks forward of Hill 66.3, and at 1500 they hit enemy armor concentrations. Our own airpower again resumed control of the airspace in our sector.

The enemy used the days from 9 to 11 April in last, desperate attempts to push through the Parpatsch positions and win back the Crimea as a closing phase of the Stalin offensive. They attempted to overrun the Parpatsch corridor with the overpowering force of half-a-dozen rifle divisions and the employment of almost two hundred tanks. The enemy was forced to break off the attacks under heavy losses, and again the Soviets exhausted all their available resources against our line.

Our division had played a major role in the successful defense of the Parpatsch position. Finally afforded the opportunity to catch our breath, we looked forward to a respite far from the constant shelling and threat of massed infantry attacks. Although there remained no possibility for the entire division to be pulled out of the line, single battalions from our infantry regiments were relieved and sent to temporary rest areas behind the front. Even for those fortunate enough to be given this break, the pause was not of long duration, and after a brief respite all were soon back at the front.

We received word that we were to be rotated from the front for rest. We plodded laboriously through the mud, following in the tracks of our gun mover toward the settlement of Blisch-Kamyschi. For the first time in many days the thunder of distant artillery grew faint behind us.

While in Blisch-Kamyschi, a member of our gun crew "requisitioned" a goose from the quarters of another unit without authorization or permission. The hapless fowl was prepared and quickly consumed by our ravenous crew. Shortly after our meal, the spiess of the offended unit appeared at our quarters, complete with the kolbenring badges of rank on his sleeve, designating his seniority within their company, and wearing the ribbon of the War Service Cross neatly in his buttonhole. He had also thought to bring a subordinate in tow to witness the event. The bones of the goose, stripped clean and lying on a nearby ammunition crate, did not go unnoticed by them during their investigation.

As gun commander, I was required to provide my name and unit. The grumbling spiess carefully noted the information in his report book, carried by all senior NCOs in their left breast pocket. We gave little thought to his threats of repercussion and disciplinary action, letting his words wash over us with little reaction. After many months on the front, there seemed to be hardly anything imaginable that could be worse than what we had so recently experienced, and we were fully aware that our destiny held only more punishment in the form of service on the Eastern Front.

The regimental headquarters was also situated in Blisch-Kamyschi. Several days later I received an order to report to the regimental command post. I attempted to present a respectable appearance, arriving punctually in a clean uniform, with field belt properly buckled and cap placed perfectly upon my head as called for in German army regulations. Alois, the company commander's aide, greeted me with a whistle before remarking, "You guys get enough to eat?" He interrupted his work to dash into the building and soon reappeared at the doorway, motioning me to follow.

The adjutant was seated at a table, intently studying a sheaf of papers piled between a number of field phones and map boards. I made a nervous attempt to click my heels together, an effort that failed miserably due to an ugly layer of fresh mud now coating the soles of my boots. I then announced loudly, "Gefreiter Bidermann reporting to the regiment as ordered!" The hauptmann let me stand silently for several long moments without averting his eyes from the desk. He then laid the papers on his desk and looked up at me.

"Gefreiter Bidermann, I have here," he selected a document from the corner of his desk and waved it in my direction, "a report regarding a theft. What was stolen?"

"A goose," I replied without hesitation.

"And who is responsible for this theft?"

"I am responsible," I answered.

"And from exactly where was it stolen?" he snapped.

Thoughts raced wildly through my mind. I had not been prepared to explain in detail what I had considered nothing more than a minor infraction. By my hesitation and my inability to answer immediately, he knew that I was attempting to protect the members of my crew who had committed the act. He then proceeded to lecture me on the virtues and importance of discipline and how noncompliance cannot, and would not, be tolerated. I was advised that a report of the incident had been forwarded recommending severe punishment. I felt a numbing sensation sweep over me. Never had I imagined that the theft of a goose would be taken to such extremes. I attempted to brush the thoughts and the possible severity of punishment from my mind and tried to concentrate on his words, which he continued to direct at me with the distinct sharpness of a Spandau machine gun. He finished abruptly, letting silence flood the room for several seconds. The hauptmann then pushed himself up from the desk and smiled.

"Take a seat, Gefreiter Bidermann," he said with a sudden, humane change in tone, motioning to an empty chair near his desk.

Alois immediately reappeared with three small cups fashioned from modified shell casings. He produced a schnapps bottle from beneath the desk and poured them full, and we drank to our old company. After a toast to various individuals of merit known to both of us, and after answering questions concerning the morale and welfare of the troops in the line, I was obliged to report in detail the last attempt of the enemy to break through our defenses following the capture of the Icebreaker, where Feldwebel Kowasz had fallen. Finally, after drinking a last round, I was dismissed without further threats.

Months later I learned that the senior NCO had actually requested punitive action in his report. Our hauptmann had endorsed and forwarded the report as required. Coincidentally, he had also forwarded with the report an eyewitness account of an incident, observed by several company members on the very same day, regarding a Fieseler Storch observation plane. The witnesses claimed to have observed the aircraft land in a pasture in the rear area of the division, and a number of officers had leaped from the aircraft and quickly loaded several sheep into the plane before taking off again. Luckily, the plane's identification number had been noted, and a subsequent, cursory investigation revealed that the Fieseler Storch was assigned to the corps staff. On receipt of this report, which had also included a recommendation of like punishment for those responsible for the theft of sheep, the authorities dropped the issue, and it was never mentioned again.

In April we received replacements on the line. The company was relieved from our positions in the factory, on the Icebreaker, and on the

Grasshopper, and we made preparations to turn over the gun position to a new crew from a sister regiment. After removing our personal equipment and light weapons from the pony cart, we left the Pak in the gun position and marched toward Sarygol.

With our departure we felt as though we had abandoned a part of ourselves to the enemy. For long months the gun had served us well as we had pulled it through the burning heat and dust of the Ukraine. In the fierce battles, during which we had relied desperately on its effectiveness against charging waves of enemy forces, the gun had never failed us. It had remained our faithful companion throughout the winter of mud, snow, and ice before Sevastopol and Feodosia. We had spent endless hours cleaning and polishing the low, double-armored, protective gun shield and the long, wide carriage. Not a speck of rust was to be seen in the barrel or on the carriage. It bore the scars of several deep scratches, the wounds of war, which had been carefully welded, and the right shield, which had been punched through by numerous shell splinters, had been patched by the maintenance company with a riveted plate. Several white circular rings painted on the barrel directly behind the muzzle brake indicated the destruction of the same number of enemy tanks.

I provided detailed instructions to the feldwebel in charge of the new crew in the care and maintenance of the gun. Breech and muzzle covers should remain in place, even in the most forward positions, to protect the delicate mechanism from dust and dampness. The days were growing warmer, but the nights remained cool; so as to prevent the buildup of condensation in the barrel, the breech cover was to be removed and the breech block left open during the night.

The morning sun warmed our bare heads as we savored the unusual luxury of marching, fully upright, in the open and under a clear sky, without the weight of steel helmets, entrenching tools, and gas masks. We finally reached Sarygol, the location of the former supply headquarters, where we could again enjoy the luxuries of sleeping and bathing, and we took time to visit the soldiers' club in Feodosia, which had been equipped with a movie theater. The survival at the front, living in filth and crawling through wet, muddy trenches or crouching in the dark, cold, clay bunkers seemed to be behind us forever, as we were provided the temporary illusion of peace in the spring sunshine of the Crimea. After several days, we were finally able to relax fully without the nerve-wracking anticipation of an enemy night attack hammering at our subconsciousness.

The two truck drivers, who had remained in the rear with the supply unit, had already prepared warm water and fresh clothing for our arrival. Mamuschka, Marussia, and Pan welcomed us with nods and grins. Pan even removed his lambswool cap in greeting, and we saw his stringy gray hair for the first time.

I reported the location of the crew to the company administrative unit. Hauptfeldwebel Kraemer was at the company headquarters, and our company clerk, Klampp, explained to me that other than the normal cleaning and weapons maintenance there was nothing notable for us in the schedule, which pleased us immensely.

The following morning we were abruptly awakened by the clamorous sound of excited voices nearby. Heinz had just arrived from drawing coffee rations, and he dashed in to inform me that our three Crimean hosts who had been providing us with quarters had obviously had something stolen from them during the night. I quickly pulled on my uniform and stepped through the timber-framed doorway into the morning sun. The outbuilding in front of the house was bordered by an ancient stone wall dating from the Ottoman Empire, and on the back side of the wall was a small wooden storage building with the door hanging loosely open.

Standing and weeping at the door were Mamuschka and Marussia, and Pan was pacing rapidly back and forth between the shed and the road, his dirty lambswool cap pulled low over his head. As I approached the scene, the two women beckoned to me excitedly and pointed into the shed. Peering inside, I observed only an empty stall; the dirt floor was littered with straw and manure from its recently departed occupant.

"Kurove zapzerap" (the cow is stolen), I heard them exclaiming. I was immediately overcome with sympathy for the pitiful figures before me, who obviously had only one animal, which had been carefully cared for and successfully nurtured through the winter. Between words and gesticulations I was made aware that it soon would have had calves and given milk. The trio had successfully kept the animal hidden from us, perhaps fearing that the strange invaders would requisition their single most valuable possession. Eight weeks previously, when we had first made our quarters here at their expense, I had known nothing of the existence of the cow, but I vaguely recalled seeing Pan slipping into the hut occasionally with a water pail or a bundle of straw under his arm. I attempted to calm them as much as possible under the circumstances of their terrible loss. "Kurove nassat" (the cow will return), I said, attempting to console them.

Incensed that someone would have entered into our chosen quarters and stolen from our benefactors, we began the search before midday. The Thirteenth Company had their support unit in the area, and inquiries brought no results from their company spiess. We passed through various rear-echelon units and a coast guard unit manning a heavy coastal gun, but we had no success. We vainly searched behind walls, in damaged warehouses, and in various dwellings scattered throughout the area. The cow remained lost.

Rumanian units were encamped in the western sector of Sarygol-Feodosia. We recognized the familiar wall of earthworks and tank traps that wound around the city in a half circle. As we walked along the perimeter, we discerned the soft lowing of a cow in the distance. Continuing along the wall, we suddenly came upon a number of cattle and sheep grazing on the thin, dry grass from last year and eagerly seeking the first green twigs of spring. Using the dwellings for concealment, we approached closer and soon left the last house to skirt the grazing animals in a wide arc until we could reach the earthworks. The earthen defenses provided us with additional concealment, which we fully used to approach within one hundred meters of the animals. Leaving the protection of the earthworks, we crawled around the edge of the wall and approached to within fifty meters of a small herd of approximately ten cattle and fifty sheep grazing contentedly under the guard of two listless Rumanian soldiers, crouching over a small fire with their backs to us.

We quickly formulated an attack plan. Heinz and Wolf hastily scrambled on all fours toward the nearest cow. It initially continued grazing, seeming oblivious of our presence, then began showing signs of nervousness as the two intruders approached.

Carefully, the two creeping figures isolated the cow and slowly herded it toward our prearranged location, being careful not to frighten the suspicious animal. The cow shied away from the oncoming landsers, always keeping a safe distance between herself and the two strangers. Along the edge of the earthwork stood several puddles, which served to entice the thirsty creature nearer; and as she approached our position and lowered her head to one of the puddles, four pairs of fists tightly gripped her horns. She struggled half-heartedly to free herself. A length of Russian communications cable was quickly looped about her neck, and with two men pulling from the front and two pushing from the rear we frantically dragged and pulled the reluctant creature rapidly along the earthwork to a depression. Here we chanced a quick glimpse over the wall—the Rumanians had noticed nothing. We led the cow closer to the safety of our bivouac area before expressing our satisfaction in our prize. We stroked the brown curly hair and remarked to one another the qualities of such a fine animal, although one of our members from a farming family observed that she was somewhat small and thin.

In the dusk of the evening, Wolf and Heinz led the cow back to our quarters. Mamuschka, Marussia, and Pan had given up their desperate search and were sitting dejectedly in the house as the two men led the cow unnoticed into the shed and secured the door. I stepped through the door to surprise them: "Kurove nassat!" (the cow is back!). They leaped to their feet as I beckoned to the unhappy trio to follow, and they halted in astonishment in the half darkness of the shed.

The animal raised its muzzle and sniffed its new owners cautiously. Pan then excitedly explained to me that their previous cow was a "malenki kurove" (a small cow) and that this one was "bolschoi" (large). With much "nitschevo" (it doesn't matter) and "charrascho" (it's all right), I attempted to explain to him that he could keep this one. Tears formed in the old man's dark eyes, and the women sniffed. Pan knelt before me and attempted to hug my knees, and only with effort was I able to successfully defend myself from this unexpected, undesired, and embarrassing display of gratitude.

That evening together with our hosts we celebrated "kurove nassat" with sweetened hot tea and with immense satisfaction for an accomplishment well done. During the previous months we had on occasion requisitioned from them chickens, geese, and eggs, and we were more than satisfied at having had an opportunity to repay their generosity.

The Crimean spring began early. In mid-April we again moved to our regular quarters in Feodosia-Sarygol, which were still available to us only because our driver successfully defended the place from other units during our absence, when we were in action on the Icebreaker, the factory, and on Hill 66.3.

The Fourteenth Company of Regiment 437 was now led by Leutnant Zoll, a professional officer who always had an eye and ear for all the small details and problems of the landsers. Every member of the company was permitted to come to him directly to address problems when necessary.

I once witnessed how David and Konrad, the two pony-cart drivers of the company, cursed our leaders in Berlin and particularly our Fuhrer in brown in their strong Swabian-Bavarian dialect when they were once again forced to evacuate their warm quarters in Sarygol for a troop movement. Of course the "Swabish greeting" heard from the two was not forgotten, and an officer of strong National Socialist beliefs would have considered the outburst grounds for a report of "defeatist attitude" or even "contributing to demoralization." Such offenses were punishable by assignment to a penal unit, or worse. Their reasoning was that where such slander is permitted it only breeds contempt and spreads defeatism throughout the ranks. Our company commander, a thoroughly professional officer who intimately understood life on the front from the perspective of the landsers, realized that as long as the men possessed the wherewithal to curse their situation, life remained normal in the trenches.

Regardless of their "criminal" behavior of being somewhat outspoken and of having volatile tempers, the two otherwise continued to prove themselves reliable and brave. Konrad had received the Iron Cross for his action while serving with my gun crew during the tank battle of Mekensievy-Gory. In February he had always managed with his pony cart to supply us with food and munitions, regardless of how harsh and extreme conditions had been in the Parpatsch line.

One night he arrived at our position earlier than usual. When asked about his early arrival, he indicated that he had taken a left turn after passing a marsh. He denied having taken a shortcut through a Russian minefield, which was clearly identified and cordoned off to traffic with white tape markers; however, this was the only possible route that he could have traveled such a distance in the limited period of time.

The only reason we could attribute to his successful traversing of the minefield was the probability that the earth was frozen over the surface of the mines or that the ice was not thawed between the pressure plates and detonators. Throughout the campaign on the Eastern Front, he seemed to have been watched by his own personal guardian angel and was to be one of the few in the company to survive the war.

Again the night brought freezing temperatures and total darkness. Although Konrad insisted on releasing his ponies to take him back to the headquarters after nightfall, I ordered him to remain with us until dawn. He obeyed without complaint and received a warm schnapps in reward for his compliance. After caring for the ponies and covering them with old woollen blankets, he secured the cart with a stick thrust through the spokes before returning to the warmth of the bunker stove. In spite of the nightly rifle and machine-gun fire, with occasional tracers bouncing and curving through the darkness, the ponies remained quiet. After having been faithful servants to the German Wehrmacht for so many months, they had become accustomed to the nightly sounds of the front. They stirred only slightly in the darkness and munched contentedly on the roofing-straw Konrad had brought to them. Even they felt the effects of our overextended supply lines, as the coarse straw was the only provision we could make available to them.

Konrad returned to the horses with the coming of first light, only to find their front hooves frozen fast in the deep mud. It was necessary to hack them free with a pick, and the sun was rising behind the Russian positions as he departed with "hub and hot" commands to the pair of horses. His departure was marked by the distant rattling of a Maxim MG on the line, and several of the machine-gun rounds impacted nearby. With the coming of daylight he made a tempting and not-too-distant target for the ever-watchful gentlemen opposite the line from us.

The next evening Konrad's cart again arrived at our position, bringing us much-needed supplies. Shortly after his arrival, he became visibly irritated at our complaints that the komiss bread smelled and tasted strongly of fuel oil. As a further wound to his pride, I accused him of having loaded the bread sack next to the diesel oil canister from which we drained fuel for our bunker lanterns and stove.

The following day he returned without the fuel canister, and we spent the night in darkness, using our last ration of oil to heat food and retain a semblance of warmth within the bunker. Despite the insults we had heaped on Konrad the previous day, the bread continued to taste as though it had been dipped in oil. Only weeks later did we learn that the bakery company personnel had discovered a number of grain silos in the Kertsch harbor, but prior to their withdrawal the Russians had poured fuel over the grain and ignited it. Fortunately, only the top layer had burned, leaving the remainder singed and foul-smelling. But, in the professional opinion of the German army, this was a windfall that was considered to be fully fit for consumption. In order to augment the critical supply situation, the grain was used for baking bread, which reeked of fuel oil and tasted like gasoline. Little did we realize that before our odyssey in the Soviet Union was over, we would long for a taste of a morsel only half so good.

After we moved into the Sarygol quarters there remained still one duty to our comrades yet to be fulfilled. We gathered clusters of the first spring flowers from the surrounding hillsides and searched out the division cemetery in Feodosia.

The fighting in the Parpatsch, the attack on Kertsch, and the capture of Feodosia had been costly to the division. Those who were killed in action or who had died of wounds in the field hospitals were buried in a parklike garden near a mansion that dated from the czar. The large, imposing house was built in an Ottoman style and was located on a height overlooking the bay, surrounded by pines and towering cypress trees. Our division's cemetery had been established here shortly following the capture of Feodosia on 18 January. Many of the graves remained marked with simple wooden crosses bearing only the inscription "unknown German soldier."

There had been several hundred of our comrades lying wounded in the field hospitals in Feodosia when the Russians landed early in January. During the landing that had forced Graf Sponek to conduct his fatal withdrawal, the wounded had been left behind in the care of the medical officers. After their capture by the Soviet forces, many of the wounded had been immediately shot by the Russians where they lay. Others, including a number of those who were unable to walk, had been stripped of their clothing and dragged to the edge of the sea, where they had been doused with water and left to die in the freezing temperatures.

These atrocities had been witnessed by some of the few survivors, and their testimony was underscored by accounts given by many men of the division who discovered the victims after the recapture of the city. The graves of these unidentified soldiers were located along the edge of the cemetery. In the center were buried those men from our division who had lost their lives in the preceding four months of action. A massive memorial stood at the head of the cemetery, and along the base, hewn into white sandstone, were the words, "For greater Germany they fell in the Battle for Feodosia—132d Infantry Division." Years later I received a photograph of the memorial from the personal effects of General Lindemann, and on the back the general had written, "Did they have to die?"

We searched for and located the graves of our company comrades and marked them with flowers placed carefully on the freshly disturbed soil. To this day they lie deep in Russian earth, the dead from the attack on Feodosia and Kertsch, from the Parpatsch, from the white house, from Hill 66.3, and from the Icebreaker.

The irony is, that for those who fell in battle, noted cemeteries and impressive memorials were built, but for those who died of wounds or sickness in the rear areas, even the boots could not remain on their feet. Through official orders, the boots had to be removed for use by someone else, as leather had become a scarce commodity. As the war continued, it became rare when the dead were afforded even a shelter-quarter in which they could be covered or wrapped. The corpse, mutilated and torn on the field of battle, would be placed into a shallow grave and simply covered with earth. The ashen, waxy countenance, with half-open mouth and dull eyes staring sightlessly at the sky, would seem to ask, "Why must I now die?—I have not yet lived—and before my journey you even pull the boots from my feet." My loyalty and my thoughts remain with you, beyond the grave to eternity; so rest in peace, my dear friends, my loyal comrades.

After suffering a major defeat in Feodosia, the Russian Forty-fourth Army retreated with the remains of its heavily mauled divisions to the strongly fortified Parpatsch position, and from 20 January remained entrenched in a well-planned defensive posture. The aim of the enemy was to halt a further German attack on the Parpatsch position, and behind this protective barrier, to rebuild and reequip the battered units as well as to position new divisions in preparation for a new offensive. The enemy was prepared to recapture the territory we were occupying at any price. The "sunny Crimea," the pearl of Soviet Russia, was considered strategically invaluable. The plan was to cut off the German Eleventh Army through a strike on Perekop, to surround and destroy it, and thus to bring about the collapse of the entire German southern front through the exposed right flank.

The recapture of the Crimea was a question of prestige for the Soviets as well. Through the planned offensive, the Red commanders hoped to end the danger of a permanent occupation of Crimea by the German Wehrmacht and to prevent a permanent presence in the Caucasus and Black Sea areas. In the words of a Soviet commissar: "Victory in the Crimea is the key to the overall defeat of the enemy." To carry through the plan of eliminating the German presence in the Crimea, a strong concentration of forces was built up on the Kertsch Peninsula and supported by the massing of hundreds of armored vehicles; they were confident of a certain victory.

From the end of January, new divisions were brought from the Caucasus near Kertsch and Kamysch-Burun, many marching over the ice to their assembly areas. On 25 January, the German strength stood at a total of four combined German and Rumanian divisions, with two Russian armies composed of nine divisions and two rifle brigades opposing them. By 26 February, the Soviet forces had been increased to twelve rifle divisions and one cavalry division, with an additional two rifle and two tank brigades as reserve.

Opposite the XXX Army Corps sector, which was held only by a single division, lay the Russian Forty-fourth Army with five divisions. The battered German units, which had months of difficult fighting for Sevastopol and Feodosia behind them, faced an overwhelming, superior enemy that was fielding fresh, totally reequipped Russian divisions.

In the weeks following 20 January, the front remained calm, with only minor harassing attacks that amounted to limited probes of the opponent's defenses, with few losses to either antagonist. During this period of time the Soviets systematically strengthened their forces. The great Russian offensive was predicted for 23 February 1942—a date traditionally celebrated as "Red Army Day." As a special gift to the Russian people, the Crimea was to be returned to them. The predicted date came and went. Due to the endless rain and low-lying clouds that blanketed the area, the attack had been postponed.

On 27 February the attack struck the entire front with an unimaginable fury. Seven rifle divisions, two rifle brigades, and two armored brigades assaulted in multiple waves of attacks. The XXX and XXXXII Army Corps positions came under merciless artillery barrages, with the pressure point of the ground attack falling directly on the latter. The goal of the attack was to capture the rail intersection at Vladislavevka, an important point in the perilous supply route for the German forces.

Further operations toward Feodosia and Dshankoy were planned to destroy German strength in those strategically important areas. The resulting attacks by three Soviet divisions consisting of sixty tanks, twenty-two batteries of all calibers, and strong air support were halted by a single German division—the 132d Infantry Division. All attacks were beaten back with heavy losses to the enemy. The Soviets eventually succeeded in breaking through the north wing of the XXXXII Corps but were quickly beaten back and the penetration sealed.

The enemy forces suffered heavy losses in men and material during the attacks, and to fulfil the requirements of remaining on the offensive, the units first had to be reequipped and brought up to strength in personnel. The enemy positions to the east and west of the tank trenches were first strengthened. The failure of these attacks to achieve a major breakthrough, and the subsequent decrease in enemy activity, served to indicate to the German commanders that the offensive strength of the enemy infantry was near exhaustion.

Despite immeasurable losses, the Soviet plan for recapturing the Crimea was not abandoned. The enemy force on the peninsula was reinforced through the middle of March with thirteen rifle divisions, one cavalry division, three additional rifle brigades, and four armored brigades.

The replenished enemy forces launched a renewed offensive against the positions of the XXX and XXXXII Corps. The Soviet forces now consisting of thirteen rifle divisions, three rifle and four armored brigades, reinforced by strong artillery and air force units, ran headlong against the German positions without success. The battered German line, although unable to be reequipped or strengthened, continued to hold.

The recent English-American influence in the war effort became more apparent. New vehicles of American manufacture could be observed in quantity. Medical supplies captured from the Soviet units bore descriptions and markings in the English language. Despite massive amounts of aid arriving from across the Atlantic, the situation remained unchanged. Prisoners and deserters repeatedly stated that the Russian soldiers had lost faith in a victory and that the aim of liberating the Crimea was personally ordered by Stalin to be successful at any cost. Thus the waves of Soviet soldiers continued to assault the German lines, spurred on through a combination of intense patriotism and fear of the political commissars.

On 9 April the enemy launched a renewed offensive against German positions on both sides of Koy-Assau, with most of the pressure on the XXX Corps. Eight rifle divisions and four armored brigades with strong artillery and air support assaulted the German positions until 12 April without success. Prisoners stated that the objective for 9 April was to have been Feodosia.

The 132d Infantry Division victoriously defended itself from combined assaults from four rifle divisions and two armored brigades consisting of approximately one hundred tanks of various types. Despite heavy artillery fire from approximately thirty-five batteries of all calibers, combined with heavy air attacks, the German infantrymen held their positions. A total of fifty-three tanks, among them the heaviest models, were destroyed, evidenced by the burning steel carcasses that exploded and smoked for days before our positions.

After again suffering disastrous losses—prisoners spoke of thousands of dead—the Russians eased their offensive on 13 April. According to the statements provided by deserters and captured documents, the Russian divisions had been bled white, forcing a reorganization and disassembling of the forces that had so recently opposed us in full strength.

Despite major defeats and innumerable casualties, the Russian command held fast to their original plan. Two more divisions were transferred to the Kertsch Peninsula; the artillery opposing the XXX Corps was strengthened by thirty-eight batteries, which were to become active on 1 May. For unknown reasons, this never occurred. Perhaps they expected a German counterattack, or perhaps the Soviets were awaiting still more reinforcements.

All attempts by the enemy, with vast superiority in troops and equipment, to recapture the Crimea and destroy Manstein's Eleventh Army met with defeat. The German soldier, especially the infantry, had prevailed against overwhelming odds while fighting under the most adverse of conditions.

The Trappenjagd offensive was launched during the night of 7–8 May near Feodosia. Artillery pieces, tanks, Flak units, munitions carriers, and foot-slogging infantry companies wound in endless columns throughout the night, concentrated along the few paved roads around the Bay of Feodosia as they marched toward the east. The enemy buildup and preparation areas behind the Parpatsch position had been taken by a penetration through the Soviet defenses and had to be exploited at any cost. Now was the chance to break out of the trench warfare in which the army had found itself mired.

The Russians fired their artillery in irregular blocking fire. The Soviet Black Sea Fleet also sent barrages into our marching area from their warships. It was possible to observe the muzzle flashes far toward the southeast as they cast a reflection on the dark water, and the horizon flashed erratically, like a far-away summer storm. The seconds could be counted between the sighting of the muzzle flash and the impact on our assembly areas. Despite the terrifying presence of the massive artillery employed against us, the shell bursts remained inconsistent and inflicted little damage.

Flying at high altitude over our heads and along the coastal advance route, a lone Russian aircraft rattled. Having grown accustomed to this routine nuisance, it had been dubbed "Iron Gustaf," "sewing machine of the watch," or "fog crow" by the landsers. This particular aircraft would spurt salvos of tracer fire toward the earth, and a few bombs would be dropped, which whistled annoyingly as they descended toward the earth, enough to demoralize the new replacements. The "old hares" had become very familiar with these primitive night fliers, aircraft pieced together from wood and canvas with a five-pointed red star displayed on the fuselage. One of the nightly experiences of the Eastern Front, they seemed to accompany us everywhere. The old gefreiters no longer bothered to react when they heard the droning of the motor accompanied by the whistle of the bombs, as they were fully aware that if a bomb could be heard, the impact point would be at least a hundred meters' distance.

The order for the attack on Kertsch was finally received. With this order, which meant a long-sought change in the static warfare, the morale of the troops in the line immediately improved. At 0300 on 8 May, a sudden, heavy Russian artillery barrage descended on us, and it ended just as quickly at 0310. At 0310 watches were synchronized, and at 0315 the entire front erupted with artillery fire. The fire plan ran according to schedule, down to the most minute detail. Observations still could not be determined because of darkness, and at 0338 came the first response from the Russian artillery, with a barrage on the factory area of Daln-Kamyschi. At 0350 a strong barrage of Russian mortar fire fell for a short time on the Icebreaker. The Russians were obviously now alert to our attack.

With the advance of the barrage, green and red tracer fire could already be seen east of the Turtle. At 0402 German fighters and Stukas were continuously in the sky, and they dove on the Soviet ground positions in long lines, peeling from formations high above the battlefield, their silhouettes barely visible against the dawn sky. At 0418 the first Russian Ratas appeared, which were immediately pounced on by the German fighter squadrons and destroyed. At 0430 the familiar sight of prisoners could be seen, being escorted to the rear in long columns. At 0444 the report from the First Battery arrived: "Direct hit upon gun, 2 men wounded, gun is out of action." Again at 0500: "The visibility allows for observed firing. Our infantry have overrun the tank trenches and with units from Infantry Regiment 436 have established a bridgehead by landing with assault craft." At 0535 the Russian fire from their Flak batteries had grown noticeably weaker. At 0545 all fire on the Baker bunker and enemy concentrations on Hill 50.6 was silenced. At 0625 the forward observers of the First Battery fired on enemy tanks visible in the foreground.

At 0630 the observers for the Second Battery were reported to have established a position on As-Tschaluke. At 0745 a reconnaissance unit was dispatched to reconnoiter positions for forward observation and fire positions. In the time from 0755 until 1100 the forward observers from the First Battery found nests of strong resistance in the Balka Pestcharnaya, and from the observation positions of the First Battery enemy columns marching toward the east as well as strong enemy movements south of Point 323 were taken under fire. At 1100 the Third Battery shifted positions in the area east of the tank trenches. At 1215, Point 323, the Moscow bunker, was reported captured by our infantry. Simultaneously, to the east of 323, the First Battery put an enemy tank out of action. At 1220 the unit headquarters was resituated. At 1345 the First and Second Batteries followed with a shift in position. Afterward, the forward observers directed blocking fire onto Hill 50.2, and darkness eliminated all further visibility.

CHAPTER FIVE

The Enemy

The Russian soldier proved to be an extremely tough adversary who . . . could endure the most adverse of conditions . . .

With the onset of our march into the Soviet Union, we found ourselves facing an unpredictable enemy whose methods, resistance, or loyalties could not be predicted or even estimated. We would at times face fanatical resistance from a handful of troops who would fight to the last round and, even when all resources were exhausted, would refuse to surrender. Other situations revealed an enemy who would surrender en masse with the least amount of resistance offered, seemingly without a clearly definable reason. Prisoner interrogations revealed that these variables had little to do with education, region of origin, or political leanings. A simple peasant would resist bitterly, whereas a trained military commander would surrender immediately upon contact. The next encounter would indicate that the opposite had occurred, seemingly without pattern or identifiable cause.

Trapped in a former copper mine near Kertsch, a number of officers and soldiers of the Red Army continued to resist throughout the entire occupation of the peninsula. When water supplies within their stronghold were exhausted, they resorted to licking the moisture from the damp walls in an effort to prevent death from dehydration. Despite the brutality exhibited by the antagonists on the Russian front, the opposing German forces developed a deep respect for these survivors who refused to surrender throughout weeks, months, and years of stubborn resistance.

In the early stages of the war we were facing a massive, unwieldy force that had been stripped of professional leadership, politically cleansed, and resurrected in the Communist ideology. The revolution of 1918 had led the political operatives in the Soviet Union to believe that only a steadfast political ideology, such as had prevailed during the revolution, would win wars. Thus in the prewar years between 1937 and 1938 Stalin had effectively stripped the Red Army of professional leadership in favor of politicoes, with whom he placed his destiny. These political appointees were successful in dismantling the army that had been created from the early years of the Soviet system. The large armored units were discarded and reorganized to employ obsolete cavalry tactics. Discipline was maintained according to lines of political reliability rather than military effectiveness. In 1941 these changes, brought about by Stalin's paranoia inherent in the Bolshevik system, were to cost the Soviet army millions of casualties.

It was the massive expanses of territory to be covered, the brutal climate of freezing winters and scorching summers accompanied by endless rain that turned roads into impassible quagmires in spring and fall, and finally the iron determination of the Russian people before the gates of Moscow and Leningrad that halted our advance. These factors provided the Soviet Union a respite in spite of the self-destructive policies inflicted on the Red Army by the Communist state. And then this philosophy took a turn.

The Soviet army reintroduced the ideology of an officer corps, replete with gold-laced shoulder epaulettes and jackboots. The traditional officer ranks and titles were resurrected to instill discipline, pride, and a sense of tradition in the beleaguered army. The doctrine that had vainly attempted to spur the peasants to sacrifice and struggle for the Communist state was abandoned, and the call to fight for Mother Russia and the homeland was fostered. Political officers, holding posts of importance in the Red Army, were soon to find themselves displaced by officers of military talent and merit. It was a series of massive changes born of desperation following months of sweeping successes by the German Wehrmacht.

As our early successes ground to a halt, we found ourselves burdened under increasing hardship in efforts to maintain mobility and to replace our losses. In contrast, the Soviet Union grew in strength. Its massive industrial capacity, much of it transported to the protection of the Urals, concentrated on weapons production on a gigantic scale. Food supplies and combat-support equipment began arriving from the United States in huge quantities. Against this overwhelming superiority in men and material, the landsers could not prevail.

The Soviets adopted the tactics of the Wehrmacht, and those advantages that were inherent in our military system were put to effective use by the Red Army. In contrast, the leaders in Berlin sacrificed immense numbers of soldiers to the same "hold at any cost" mentality that had almost brought the Soviet army to ruin in 1941. The tables had turned; Hitler obstinately refused to yield ground to enhance our strategic situation. Thus the Russians, with new-found strength, were able to pierce the thinly held lines and encircle vast numbers of German forces. The leadership of armies by political appointees, which had proven to be a hindrance to the effectiveness of the Soviet army, was demonstrated on an ever-increasing scale in the Wehrmacht. In the face of adversity and military setback, Hitler's reliance on politically loyal officers to oversee unwise, and at times absurd, policies began to mirror that of the Stalinist army in the prewar years.

The individual soldiers of the Red Army evolved into fighters distinctively different from the soldiers we had first encountered. The mentality of the Russian soldier changed from one of apathy and indifference to that of a patriot. The idea of belonging to an elite army that was alone saving the world from Fascism was instilled, and a sense of pride evolved that had long been absent from the ranks of the Soviet armed forces.

The Russian soldier proved to be an extremely tough adversary who, when properly motivated, could endure the most adverse of conditions. The standard-issue uniform in summer consisted of a loose-fitting, khaki-brown tunic and trousers of lightweight material. In winter, heavy woolen material of quilted design was used, which afforded excellent insulation against the cold climate. The heavy greatcoat was carried in all seasons, as it was used as a blanket and a uniform item, as the situation required.

The Russian soldier was issued boots several sizes too large, so as to enable him to wear them stuffed with straw or paper during the brutal winter months. This served as an efficient and a practical protection from the debilitating freezing temperatures, which caused so many casualties within our own army. In the latter months of the war, the Red Army forces were often equipped with large felt boots that offered excellent insulation qualities. Unfortunately, our boots were issued to fit very well, and on the Crimean front we considered ourselves fortunate that we experienced a much less severe winter than those divisions languishing on the northern fronts.

The weapons carried by our adversaries were of simple but practical design. During the early months of the war the infantry units encountered by our forces were armed with bolt-action rifles similar to our own carbines. As the war continued, we began developing new, automatic weapons that would deliver a much higher rate of fire to be used primarily in close combat. This tactic was employed by the Soviet army as well, and the short-barreled submachine gun fitted with the high-capacity drum magazine soon symbolized the Red Army soldier.

The Soviet soldier was a master at foraging and fending for himself. As the war progressed and the Russian supply lines lengthened relative to the Wehrmacht's defeats and withdrawals, the Red Army supported itself largely from the land it occupied. Armed with the submachine gun that held a high-capacity magazine, clothed in a uniform that suited the environment, and living from a sparse diet of whatever was immediately available, the Russian soldier proved to be a most able adversary.

The Wehrmacht marched into the expanses of the Soviet Union with maps and intelligence documents that proved to be deceptively inaccurate. On the German maps it was not uncommon to attempt to follow routes through terrain features that did not exist. A well-marked land route shown as an improved, major thoroughfare would actually be a primitive dirt track. It became common practice to use captured Red Army maps whenever possible; and these maps, known for their accuracy, were reproduced by the regimental staffs for our use, often with place-names in both German and Cyrillic lettering.

The Wehrmacht and the Red Army remained locked in deadly combat for almost four years, during which time the differences between the two forces, so apparent at the outset, became less obvious as the war continued. The German soldier, too, learned to master the art of improvisation and out of necessity lived largely from the land as the supply system slowly collapsed. Out of practicality and necessity even the uniforms became more similar, as did the weapons and tactics. Eventually the landsers found themselves better able to identify with the enemy, with whom they were engaged in brutal, unforgiving combat, than with the polished and sophisticated army they had known long ago in Germany.

We observed mass numbers of desertions from the Soviet army early in the war, and many of these deserters volunteered to serve our forces for a variety of reasons. Known to the landsers as hiwis, these workers were former enemy personnel who were previously members of the Red Army before being captured or deserting to us. Many of them volunteered to serve with us to escape the horrible conditions of the prisoner of war camps, far to the rear beyond the jurisdiction of the frontline forces, where they had faced unimaginable deprivations. There existed a distinction between those hiwis who came to us from the prisoner of war camps and those who had suffered starvation and forced labor under the regime of Stalin and had thus come to hate the Bolsheviks.

The freedom-loving mountain people of the Caucasus, the wandering nomads of the steppes, and the Crimean Tartars had defended themselves and their way of life for centuries against the Russians. Religion played no minor role as well, as the Islamic Crimean Tartars fiercely defended their religious freedom.

Included in the personal effects of General Lindemann were several letters written by Russian hiwis to relatives, accompanied by official translations provided by the field-post censor, as translated by Gefreiter Peter Teslyk:

Aliev Nambed, FPNr. 17 433
Do not believe anyone who tells you anything else. For twenty years we were prisoners of the godless Soviets, and we have hungered and worked day and night. Now we wish to help the German Army with all our strength and with our hearts. In this sense we perform our daily duties. God the almighty will give us strength to help defeat and destroy the godless enemy. Allah help us.

Sateirov Vetut, FPNr. 27 076 (Pi-Btl. 132, 3 Comp.)
From now on things will be better for us than ever would have been possible under the Soviets. For us Tartars comes a new, good era. In the future we will work no longer for others, but for ourselves.

Islamov Said Nallil, FPNr. 29 787 B
Father, on the 4th of April I arrived in the Crimea. Here we have found good conditions. We live together with the German soldiers, we eat and drink together. Every week we bathe. The soldiers are very friendly to us, and it is never boring here. When the officers arrive, they are not so arrogant, but are friendly to us. The officers are also friendly to the soldiers, and the soldiers respect the officers. The soldiers are never tormented, quite the opposite is true. The Bolsheviks always spoke of socialism, but when one makes a comparison, the socialism lies with the Germans, and the Bolsheviks have none.

True socialism is found in the German Army: Comradeship, equality, respect for one another, justice, and friendship. These qualities will guarantee a final victory.

A Tartar
I can tell you that on the 24th, partisans from the mountains attacked the villages of Taygan, Rayon and Karabusar. Afterwards, sixty Germans and fifty volunteer Tartars came and fought until the next morning to drive the partisans from the area. The partisans stole cattle, sheep, and horses.

Kurtamelov Vasim, FPNr. 16 691
I live for the German Army, and together we will destroy the Bolshevik enemy. I fight for the freedom of the Tartar people, and to free the Islamic religion from the yoke of Bolshevism. Every Friday we go the mosque and pray. If I survive this war I will become the village mola.

Sever Natur, FPNr. 12 963
Things are going well, do not worry about us. We have now become accustomed to things here, my German comrades are good people. Their generosity is difficult to imagine after having lived under the Soviets. The officers also live here with us. Write a prayer for me and send it.

Ablamit Metschit, FPNr. 00 462 (recon. bat. 132)
The mosque is again open, and everyone goes to pray. We live once again as we did in earlier times. Allah has again blessed us.

A letter written by a wife in response to correspondence received from a hiwi describes the suffering of the civilian population:

Hello, my husband!
Mafrem, I send my regards, and wish you the best of health. Your son Roslak, your daughter Narya, sister Aischa, and niece Lemara send their regards as well.
Mafrem, your brother has been released and now works in the village as barber. Mafrem, you have asked what support we have received. We have received nothing from the mayor. We receive bread once a week. There is no money, and when we request assistance, the mayor refuses. It was not necessary for you to report for service. Please do not ask how we are doing, as words are nothing, and we are not doing well. You probably have enough, and for that you have left your family. For that you can live alone, for when you return you will not find your wife and children.

In our own company we had Alex, a former Soviet soldier of Caucasian origin who had been taken prisoner by one of our units during the fighting. He had never seen the confines of a prisoner of war camp but had been employed caring for the horses and performing duties for the cooks. He remained a loyal and unshakable assistant for the support units to the very last days of the war. We also received many laborers from the prisoner of war camps who had volunteered for service.

The army did as much as possible to improve the conditions for a number of prisoners who, due to lack of transport, could not be moved from the combat sector. Our own rations were shortened to feed these prisoners, and the mortality rate remained at 2 percent as long as they remained under our immediate jurisdiction, which is remarkable when taken into account that most prisoners were exhausted or wounded when captured.

When the Russians successfully landed in Feodosia, the capture of one particular camp, holding five thousand prisoners, appeared to be imminent. Rather than face liberation by their Soviet comrades, the prisoners requested permission to march to the German lines at Simferopol, and this movement was conducted without the necessity of employing guards to prevent escapes. It is likely that they were fully aware of the treatment they would receive at the hands of the Soviets for having surrendered to the German army.

Numbers of former prisoners of war volunteered to fight in the rear areas against partisan units and proved to be effective in protecting sensitive communications and transportation routes. It was even reported that various bands of partisans and bandits would engage one another in open battle for control of certain political districts and geographical areas, thus establishing a distinction between those units that were organized and supplied directly by the Soviet government and those units that considered themselves independent from central control.

There existed partisan bands on the Crimean Peninsula as well. Operating from strongholds deep within the Yaila Mountains, they recruited from the local population and the scattered remnants of Soviet army units. Such partisan units had been preplanned and were well organized prior to the invasion, and deep within the mountains were large, well-established ammunition and supply caches. The partisan units consisted of a number of women, many of whom had lost their husbands, sons, and other family members in combat against our forces early in the war.

The southern coastal road came under frequent attacks, at times making it necessary to provide a heavily armed escort for supply convoys in order to ensure safe passage. For the most part the security units consisted of Rumanian troops or volunteer Tartar and Cossack companies, as German forces were used to the last man on the front. Even the local inhabitants found themselves in constant danger from the partisans. As had become commonplace throughout the Eastern Front, the partisans fought with brutality and lawlessness, presenting a constant threat in every rear area.

On 20 May 1942, we marched over the battlefield of the last twelve days toward the west. We passed the hotly contested Parpatsch position, the Moscow area, Hill 55.6, crossed over the tank trenches and traversed the Anglo-Indian telegraph line. In some areas the telegraph poles were splintered and broken; the cables draped in tangles from the stumps. The troops took advantage of the opportunity to gather copper cables to fill the countless needs of an army in the field. The telegraph line began in London, stretching through the North Sea, over the Crimea, across the Caucasus, and over Persia to Calcutta. Before falling victim to our war, it had linked two continents and for decades had served the world—especially English colonial politics—with peaceful purposes.

At the edge of a shallow valley we left the thin, wiry grass of the steppes and entered lush green fields surrounding a small village with clean cottages. Most of the cottages were made of light-colored stone with outer surrounding walls. The sweet smell of flowers met us here, and we soon discovered that this valley was the source for a trade in rose petals. Along the floor of the valley we found a sea of roses stretching to the horizon. The inhabitants came originally from Rumania and settled here during the time of Empress Catherine of Russia. During the summer season they gather millions of rose petals for processing, and from a thousand petals they receive one gram of rose oil. Under the control of Joseph Stalin, this industry, which had primarily served the upper classes from the time of the feudal barons, was exploited further to earn desperately needed revenue for the Soviet state.

During our earlier attack on Kertsch in this same area we had captured a small Russian tracked vehicle that had been abandoned fully intact by its previous owners. Before advancing farther toward Kertsch we had removed the alternator as a simple means of reserving the vehicle for our own use. After poring over maps and scouring the area, we located the vehicle standing intact on the side of a gentle slope, just as we had left it. With the installation of the alternator and a few adjustments it was ready for service, and we immediately put it to good use towing our Pak.

It was outfitted with the same type of Ford motor that was so commonplace among the captured vehicles, and despite a broken track link it
proved to be very reliable, providing us with months of uninterrupted
service. Outfitted with our new equipment, compliments of the Soviet
army, we marched onward toward our last objective in the Crimea: Sevastopol.

CHAPTER SIX

Sevastopol

A massive crescendo of fire erupted from the German lines. I adjusted the aim of the Pak on the predetermined target . . .

In early June 1942, the 132d Infantry Division was faced with its most demanding challenge of the war thus far. Since the recent winter battles, the enemy had been engaged in a concentrated effort to prepare and strengthen their defenses and had brought in fresh, newly equipped troops to reinforce the units that had suffered heavy casualties throughout their attempts to defend the Crimean Peninsula. The Soviets, strongly supported by supplies from the United States, also brought massive amounts of war materials into the assembly areas from the sea.

It was imperative that the Sevastopol fortress, which was made up of a complex system of defenses, be taken by the Eleventh Army. For the fortress to remain under Soviet control would serve to tie the German divisions to the Crimea at a time when they were badly needed elsewhere along the thinly held Eastern Front. The efforts to capture Sevastopol could not be abandoned, but had to be carried through to prevent its future use by the Soviets as a bridgehead from where offensives could be launched deep into the Ukraine. Once this penetration into the Ukraine could be accomplished, the Soviets would then be able to penetrate the German right flank, and possibly sever the lifeline of entire armies that were advancing farther to the east.

The Russians had long since held total control over the area with their Black Sea Fleet; thus this danger loomed over the German army in the

Crimea for as long as they held ground on the peninsula. Regular bombardments from large-caliber naval guns at a distance of twenty kilometers from the coast had become commonplace, and until July 1942, the naval strength of the Axis in this area consisted of only a small number of Italian patrol boats in the harbors along the Crimean coastline.

The position of fortress Sevastopol enabled it to control the entire area of the Cherson Peninsula. Armed with numerous modern coastal batteries of heavy caliber that could be trained to fire on the landward side, the fortress was protected by heavy terrain from that side as well. In the north, the Belbek Valley provided a natural earthwork for the foremost defenses. In the east, the heavy underbrush and thick woods served as a barrier to attacking infantry, broken intermittently by sharply cut valleys, gorges and ravines, often with steep, impenetrable sides that made large-scale troop movement impossible.

The forces destined to launch the final battle for Russia's strongest and largest fortress were facing commanding heights that offered a wide view for the defenders and presented the attackers with the immense task of penetrating deep valleys, steep ravines, and thick underbrush. Particularly imposing was the line delineating the north front, running along the Belbek Valley, with the fortress Bastion I, the armored battery Maxim Gorki, and the fortress Schischkova.

The LIV Army Corps under the able command of General der Kavallerie Hansen was assigned to lead the first assault on the fortresses, with support from the 132d, the Twenty-second, the Fiftieth, and the Twenty-fourth Infantry Divisions. Heavy batteries of calibers up to 800mm were brought up and emplaced in preparation for the attack scheduled for 7 June.

For seven days prior to the attack, a barrage blanketed the heavily defended enemy positions, and the battery Maxim Gorki drew special attention from the German gunners. The 132d Infantry Division, on the right wing of LIV Army Corps, was set into motion with the task of launching a frontal assault across the Belbek Valley, to take the Olberg under attack, and to push toward the southwest, placing themselves in position to storm the commanding heights of Bastion I and Maxim Gorki from the southeast. The neighboring unit on the left, the Twenty-second Infantry Division, would be in position to launch an attack only after the successful capture of the heights of the Olberg.

During the last days of May, the batteries of our artillery regiments were pulled into their new positions, which lay in the northern sectors. The following days the ravines and valleys resounded with the low thunder of countless artillery barrages, continually pounding the enemy positions in preparation for the attack to follow.

The batteries fired day and night on assigned sectors. The Fifth Battery attempted to establish an observation point on the Koberberg, from where the Soviet positions in the Belbek Valley could be observed. The ominous droning of aircraft from both antagonists filled the air during the hours of daylight as they sought their living targets, and dive-bombers could be seen periodically descending on the city in the distance. The enemy antiaircraft positions were successfully neutralized through the efforts of the dive-bombers and artillery fire, though with heavy cost to our Luftwaffe. Throughout the night Fieseler Storch reconnaissance aircraft circled over the Soviet lines, and the Russians attempted in vain to illuminate their locations with floodlights, which often swept the terrain at a level low enough to reveal any movement in our ground defenses. The activities of these aircraft also served to conceal the noise of our own motorized columns as they advanced toward the line.

We arrived at our position on 5 June, hastily digging into defenses at a distance of only one hundred meters from the foremost Russian outposts. Our captured Russian prime mover was used to bring the gun into position. As we were approaching our position we passed a heavy, 600mm mortar with an extremely short barrel, and our investigation revealed a weapon that was new to us. The gun crew advised us that when the mortar was fired, the barrel would compress in a telescoping action to provide a recoilless effect; and we were told that the weapon was deployed to the Sevastopol front for specific use against Maxim Gorki. During its firing, it was possible to see the giant projectiles in flight, and the landsers immediately dubbed them "flying coffins."

Our antitank gun was situated to the right of a steep cliff, concealed in a shallow depression opposite the emplacement Maxim Gorki. Throughout the previous night we had hacked a shallow trench into the rocky earth, the hard ground giving way only to the heavy picks that were carried in our tracked vehicle. The nights were of short duration, which enabled us only five or six hours of darkness during which we could work in relative safety before we would be visible to the enemy observers a short distance from our position.

The assault preparations against the coastal fortress neared completion. It was known that the fortress consisted of hundreds of concrete and steel-reinforced embrasures, belts of bunkers, armored batteries, deep trenches, barbed wire, and minefields. Situated deep within the cliffs were rocket launchers and mortar positions that could not be reached or neutralized by conventional artillery fire or air strikes.

The artillery, rockets, Flak, and assault guns pounded the enemy positions for five days prior to the attack. Thirteen hundred guns opened fire on predesignated targets and field positions. The squadrons of General von Richtofen's VIII Fliegerkorps bombed the Russian defenses mercilessly. The earth churned and was tortured in a murderous overture. Never before or never again during the war would the German forces mass such artillery, which more than equaled the one thousand guns used by Montgomery against Rommel's Afrikakorps at El Alamein.

The Nebelwerfers were assigned a special role in the assault plans. The heavy First Werferregiment, the Seventieth Werferregiment, and the First and Fourth Werfer Sections were attached to a special staff commanded by Oberst Niemann in the front before the fortress. Twenty-one batteries opened fire with 576 guns, including the First Werfer Battery with its 28cm and 32cm high-explosive and incendiary projectiles.

With each barrage, 324 rocket projectiles were fired per second from the barrels of this regiment on predetermined targets. The barrages served to demoralize the enemy troops as well as to physically destroy their defensive capabilities, and both attempts achieved the same end effect. A battery of six launchers was capable of firing twenty-six flaming projectiles with nerve-wracking screams, creating a terrible effect on the recipients. The shrapnel from these projectiles was not as effective as the splintering of artillery shells, but the explosive effect upon detonation, within a confined area or at close range, would rupture blood vessels with a benumbing shock wave. The enemy soldiers located within the immediate vicinity of the impact area were rapidly demoralized by the ear-splitting blasts, and basic, instinctive fear quickly gave way to terror and panic. The stoic Russian soldiers, usually insensitive even to the Stuka attacks, were often rendered stunned and helpless under these barrages.

Three exceptional artillery behemoths were sent into operation at Sevastopol: the "Gamma mortar," the mortar "Karl" (also called "Thor"), and the giant railway gun "Dora." All three were at the time considered wonder weapons of the conventional artillery forces and had been designed and manufactured for the specific purpose of penetrating reinforced concrete bunkers and fortresses.

The Gamma mortar was simply the Big Bertha cannon of World War I resurrected. The weapon fired 427mm projectiles that weighed 923 kilograms and had an effective range of fourteen kilometers. The immense barrel was 6.72 meters in length, and the weapon was served by a crew of 235 specially trained artillerists.

The Gamma weapon, in all its immensity, was a dwarf compared to the 615mm mortars Karl, or Thor. Designed for the specific purpose of destroying concrete embrasures, the 2,200 kilogram projectiles were fired from a weapon that had little in common with conventional mortars. The 5m barrel and the giant carriage provided the impression of a wheeled factory sporting an immense chimney, silhouetted at an angle against the sky.

Yet Karl was not the perfected model of artillery produced by our technology. The largest gun was located in Bachtschisseray in the Palace of Gardens, the old residence of the khan of the Tartars, and was officially christened Dora. The landsers referred to it as Heavy Gustav, and with its 800mm bore it remained the heaviest cannon of the war. Sixty railway cars were required for the transportation of the separate parts, which required assembly on location for the weapon to be rendered active. A high-explosive shell weighing forty-eight hundred kilograms, or almost five tons, was fired from a barrel 32.5 meters in length. It was also capable of firing a seven thousand-kilogram armor-piercing shell a distance of thirty-eight kilometers. The projectile and casing had a total length of 7.8 meters. If placed vertically, the ammunition would stand as tall as a two-story house. The maximum rate of fire was three rounds in an hour. Two Flak units were assigned as permanent security. The service crew, additional security, and maintenance personnel for this monster consisted of a major general, a colonel, and fifteen hundred men.

This obsolete military philosophy relied on conventional artillery pieces in a perverse, giant form that had so increased in dimensions that they became countereffective in terms of men and material required for support and use. Nevertheless, a single shot from Dora was reported to have penetrated thirty meters of earth to destroy a massive underground ammunition depot at Severnaya Bay near Sevastopol.

Deep in positions well situated and protected by natural terrain, the Soviets labored on their defenses while they waited for the attackers. The fortress was defended by seven Soviet rifle divisions, a dismounted cavalry division, two rifle brigades, three navy brigades, two naval infantry regiments, and various armored battalions with independent units, for a total of over 100,000 men. Ten artillery regiments and two mortar battalions, an antitank regiment as well as forty-five heavy-gun units of coastal artillery stood with a total of six hundred guns and two thousand mortars in the defensive line. These forces made up the enormous defense, all of which had to be overrun and captured or destroyed by the Eleventh Army with a force totaling only seven weakened German divisions and two ill-equipped Rumanian divisions.

We assembled at the headquarters of the II Battalion, 436th Regiment, on the evening of 6 June, where we were briefed that the attack would be launched the following morning at 0305. My gun crew was assigned to take a Soviet emplacement under fire that was situated half-left from our position and slightly higher in elevation. The target was clearly visible at a distance of three hundred meters from our position.

We spent the night crouching under our shelter-quarters in the narrow trenches dug behind our gun. In the early morning hours, while still cloaked in darkness, we shook ourselves free from the cover and warmth of our hastily improvised shelters, and in the crisp night air prepared to launch our barrage at precisely 0305.

At exactly the prescribed time, a massive crescendo of fire erupted from the German lines. As the sky in the east was showing the first hint of dawn, I adjusted the aim of the Pak on the predetermined target and opened fire—shot after shot—alternating armor-piercing and high-explosive rounds.

Within minutes I observed a red flare floating toward the earth through the smoke and darkness to our left, a signal to us from our own forces indicating that the assault elements were moving forward. I adjusted the fire accordingly, so as not to engage our own units storming toward the enemy positions. Despite the coming of daylight, the visibility continued to worsen, with steam, smoke, and clouds of dust covering the target positions.

An angry enemy had now been awakened, and we found ourselves taken under direct fire from the battery Maxim Gorki. Shell bursts of all calibers began to explode around us, including naval gunfire from the warships. Helpless to react, we could only cower in our shallow trenches, pray for survival, and wait out the storm. Countless impacts surrounded and seemed to engulf our gun, shrapnel filled the air, hissing and whistling overhead. We were showered with hunks of stone and earth as massive shells exploded nearby, tossing brown-black geysers skyward and leaving us numb with fear. The earth trembled, dust filled our eyes, it became difficult to breathe. We lay motionless, pressed against the earth in our trenches, as rocks and dirt rained on dull gray-green helmets. Our hands were clapped tightly over our ears, and we squeezed our eyes shut in vain attempts to block out the unexpected horror that had descended on us.

A member of my gun crew, who had bravely served through all our previous engagements, suddenly scrambled to a far corner of our trench, pulled his helmet from his head, and screamed over the roar of explosions, "I can't take it any more!"

Foaming at the mouth and his eyes wide with terror, he struggled to his feet in an attempt to spring from the trench. I threw myself on him and wrestled him to the ground as another shell exploded near the edge of the earthwork, sending white-hot splinters whistling through the air. Grinding his teeth, clawing and struggling wildly, he fought to escape. Rising quickly, I struck him hard across the face and threw myself on him once more. He lay motionless, staring wide-eyed at me, and I released him to seek shelter beneath the edge of the trench. He suddenly sprang forward as if possessed, and in one motion cleared the berm, sprinting bareheaded through the clouds of smoke and dust and disappearing toward the rear.

We again dove for cover as the hail of shells increased, and we never expected to see him alive again as we pressed ourselves against the earth in an attempt to escape the explosions and shell fragments. Later that evening, after the guns had fallen silent, he reappeared at our position as if nothing had occurred, and the incident was never mentioned.

The Fifth Company, Infantry Regiment 437, broke through the enemy trench system at the point of the cliff that lies on the northern side of the Belbek Valley. Reinforced by the enemy to serve as a secure strong point, the deep ravines of the valley provided the enemy protection from our artillery fire. Fritz, a friend I had known since our recruit training in Darmstadt, lay with his group in an assembly position before the cliff. He pulled a hand grenade from his belt, jerked the priming cord, and tossed it over his head into the enemy trench before him. At that instant a Russian infantryman opened fire with a burst from a submachine gun, and an explosive bullet tore into Fritz's arm, rendering him unconscious with shock. The accompanying landsers stormed forward through the smoke and dust. Regaining his senses, Fritz crawled along the earth to the rear to report the breach in the defenses. His grenade had killed the enemy gunner, which had enabled a small opening in the Soviet defenses to be exploited by landsers in gray-green, who continued to push forward rapidly, penetrating the enemy positions. The successes in our sector resulted in several hundred meters of ground won, while farther to our left our infantry company was able to overrun the forward defenses of the Belbek Valley.

On 7 June, a full frontal attack across the Belbek Valley was followed in the afternoon by the capture of the Olberg, which resulted in heavy losses to our troops. Despite the losses, with this winning of ground a linkup was made with the Twenty-second Infantry Division, and preparations were made for further advance.

From 8 to 15 June the regiment continued to press forward in operations that proved to be costly in men and material, each foot of ground being hotly contested in attempts to capture the commanding Neuhaus heights. During this period Infantry Regiment 213 was assigned to reinforce the division and was placed into action on the right wing. The Russians made numerous unsuccessful attempts to break through the lines on this wing in an effort to regain the Olberg.

A massive attack was scheduled for 17 June. New fire objectives were relayed to the artillery batteries, and shells bursting on isolated nests of enemy resistance could be observed from the front. At 0745 we received word that the GPU battlement had fallen to our infantry. At 0830 it was reported that the battlements Siberia and Volga had also been taken by German troops. Following an hour of fierce fighting, our infantry breached the line of defense that had been established among primitive dwellings near Bastion I, and at 0845 the Bastion was taken by the assault troops. At 1000 the enemy batteries, firing from positions near Bartenyevka, were silenced as well. At 1200 our foremost assault elements continued to hold Bastion against heavy enemy counterattacks. Between 1250 and 1315 each battery from our artillery regiment fired eighty rounds on Schischkova. Still, the positions remained resolutely defended by the Soviet infantrymen, who refused to yield a meter of ground. The landsers attempting to hold the Bastion became engaged in hand-to-hand fighting during the desperate Soviet counterattacks, and the battle swept back and forth as the positions were captured, overrun, and recaptured. The positions were littered with dead and dying. The walking wounded staggered and careened senselessly through the smoke that engulfed the defenses. The units of both antagonists became mixed inseparably as the soldiers shot, clubbed, and bayoneted one another. At 1445 the position Molotov was reported to have fallen to our forces.

Heavy Artillery Battalion 641 had been assigned to destroy the Maxim Gorki I stronghold with two 355mm mortars that were located four kilometers to the west of the Olberg. These massive projectiles, weighing one thousand kilograms each, were delivered to the breech of the gun with cranes. The mortars had previously seen action during the French campaign against the defenses of Luettich. The projectiles were designed not to explode on impact but were set with delayed fuses designed to detonate after the protecting concrete layers of the fortress had been penetrated. Shortly after the first rounds left the barrels of these monstrous guns, the report arrived from the observers that the fortress cupola had "flown from its mounting. . . . Maxim Gorki has been penetrated." The 305mm shells stored within the massive Russian battery began to explode, with huge fragments ricocheting wildly in the air. At last the battery fell silent beneath a cloud of dust and smoke.

The pionier and infantry units assaulted the hill. Within the concrete colossus, which measured three hundred meters long and forty meters wide, the occupants continued to resist stubbornly. When the fall of the emplacement appeared inevitable, some of the defenders made a desperate attempt to break out in isolated groups.

The pioniers worked their way into the defenses with demolition charges, flamethrowers, and smoke canisters. After the initial explosion, the Soviets continued to fire from embrasures and openings in the concrete, but a second blast tore open a section of the wall. A giant cave was exposed to the pioniers, revealing the detailed complexity of the fortress. Maxim Gorki was three stories in depth, a self-sustaining city with water and electrical power, a hospital, a canteen, and machinery rooms with munitions carriers, arsenals, and manufacturing equipment. Each room and every entrance was barred by double steel doors, and to gain entry every door had to be breached using demolition charges.

The pioniers pressed themselves tightly against the walls in anticipation of the explosions as they slowly worked their way deeper into the bowels of the concrete maze. As each door was blown open, the blast would be followed by hand grenades tossed into the smoke and gas-filled breach, followed by a momentary pause as they waited for the fumes to dissipate. Along the passageways lay the enemy dead, jumbled together in the darkness, the horrifying scene made even more surreal by the gas masks worn by the dead and dying.

Hand grenades continued to burst within deafening proximity; pistol shots cracked and whined through the confined spaces. After breaching a chamber, the intruders would be met by the slamming shut of a set of steel doors, and the process would begin anew. So it progressed, hour after hour, until the assault troops had penetrated deep within the fortress and were approaching the command center.

The Soviet admiralty ordered the defenders to fight to the last man—there would be no surrender. An enemy radioman reported to Vice-Admiral Oktiyabrski in a bunker located near the Sevastopol harbor: "The Germans are pounding on the doors, demanding that we surrender. We can no longer open the portals to fire, there are only forty-six of us remaining."

One half-hour later the Russians transmitted another message: "There are only twenty-two of us left, we are preparing to blow ourselves up and cease communications—farewell!"

And so it ended. The heart of the fortress self-destructed with the enemy at the door, and the battle for Maxim Gorki I was over. From a crew of more than one thousand defenders, only forty enemy personnel, too badly wounded to offer further resistance, fell prisoner to our forces.

Maxim Gorki fell at 1645. With the capture of this massive battery, the strongest enemy fortress along the north front of Sevastopol was in our hands. The backbone of the enemy defense system had been broken, and that evening our foremost line stood at the Schischkova position.

Visibility over the battlefield was often hindered during the daylight hours because of the bombing missions flown by our aircraft. The observation point of the First Artillery Battalion was situated on the height two hundred meters east of the tank trench. The Third Battery shifted positions and at approximately 0600 was again prepared for action northeast of the Neuhaus heights.

While on the Olberg I observed a Junkers 88 as it received a vital hit from an enemy Flak battery. One motor burst into flames, and the aircraft wound in a slow descent toward the north, a black plume of smoke tracing its path across the sky. While still over enemy-occupied territory an object appeared to fall from the rear of the plane and drop for a short distance. Suddenly a white spot appeared against the sky, growing larger until one could recognize a white parachute swaying gently toward the earth, growing larger with each passing second until it appeared that it would descend directly on us.

The wind carried the crewman toward us, but enemy Flak batteries and Soviet infantrymen began to open fire on the slowly falling target. Two of our machine-gun crews sprang to their weapons and fired belt after belt of ammunition on the Russian positions in an attempt to suppress their fire. Directed by the forward observers, we opened fire with a Pak, firing high-explosive rounds rapidly into the enemy positions, followed by mortars that added to the crescendo as the airman approached the earth. With our fire we successfully silenced the enemy guns for twenty or thirty seconds before the parachute swung over our position, and a crewman landed safely behind our lines with a bullet-riddled parachute. Several landsers raced to his location and assisted him to his feet. Breathing heavily, he expressed his gratitude between gasps and assured the rescuers that he was unhurt but was greatly relieved to have survived the harrowing experience and to have escaped capture, as the Russians were sitting in their positions only one hundred meters distant.

On another occasion one of the noncommissioned officers recently transferred to the company as a replacement claimed to have been a professional dancer before being called into service. He was very proud of his fitness and his physical appearance and always took extreme caution not to injure himself or to expose himself unnecessarily to danger. One afternoon a shell fragment sliced away a sizeable portion of his nose, and as I was bandaging his wound he stated his intentions to apply for a government disability pension, as he was certain that with this disfigurement his career as a dancer was finished.

We experienced rare occasions when individuals fresh to the front would surreptitiously creep along the earthworks, their hands held high in the air above the protection of the berm in hopes of receiving a heimatschuss to ensure a ticket home. In such an environment solid, dependable citizens would sometimes react in an unpredictable and strange fashion, earning themselves a reputation that during the course of a normal life would never have been considered.

The ranks of the rifle companies grew ever thinner. The days were sweltering with heat; the nights brought little relief. One lived only on cigarettes, cold coffee, tea, and the sparse battle rations that were issued daily to those in the foremost lines. It was impossible to wash regularly or to shave. The chalky earth absorbed any rainwater like a sponge, and where clear streams had run during the winter months there were now bone-dry beds caked with red-brown, cracked clay.

The demands placed on the landsers in the front lines escalated to inhumane levels. In many of the actions my Pak could not be positioned to engage the enemy due to the heavy terrain, impassible to all except the infantrymen slogging forward on foot. Almost all the Soviet trench systems and defensive emplacements had to be combated singularly, by the infantry and pionier units as they made their way slowly through terrain cut with ravines, thick with heavy underbrush, and wrought with danger from enemy mines. The enemy would be engaged, the position would fall with losses to both sides, and the landsers would advance to the next assigned objective.

I received the assignment to secure the road that ran behind the Neuhaus heights toward Mekensievy-Gory. During hours of darkness, when the advance would grind to a temporary halt, we assisted the infantry platoons in bringing forward ammunition and transporting the wounded to the rear.

During the night of 16–17 June, while at the headquarters of II Battalion, 437th Regiment, I saw Hauptmann Bernhard for the last time. The next day he was killed in action while assaulting a position west of the Neuhaus heights.

The dead from both sides lay thick in the ravines, and due to the danger from enemy snipers they could not be removed or recovered for burial. The oppressive heat soon bore with it the sickly sweet smell of decaying flesh, and after only a few days the corpses were swollen to the extent that the seams on the uniforms split. The faces and hands of the dead turned black, the hands stiffly extended in the air from the swollen bodies, giving a more ghastly appearance to the corpses than even this nightmare would ordinarily present.

A medical corpsman ventured between the lines to scatter chlorine over some of the corpses in a valiant attempt to lessen the stench and to help delay the onset of diseases. Despite the many months of constant exposure to death, I could never pass downwind of the ravines without being overwhelmed by nausea.

On 19 and 20 June our infantry regiments were withdrawn from the fighting, as the strength of the troops had declined to the point of being completely ineffective. One company listed only two feldwebels and a few troops thus surviving in the ranks, and many of the company commanders had been killed or wounded with no immediate replacements available. The forward artillery observers had also taken heavy casualties, and many artillery personnel had fallen victim to counterbarrages from the highly effective Russian artillery. Added to this steady erosion in manpower were casualties among communications personnel, pioniers, and reconnaissance personnel from Aufklarungsabteilung 132.

During the nights the droning of the Ratas overhead continued without interruption, and often we would be showered with propaganda leaflets printed with a crude attempt to entice the landsers to desert. One Soviet leaflet of June 1942 prompted:

Read and pass to your comrades. —

SOLDIERS OF THE 50TH, 24TH, 132ND, 170TH, 72ND, AND 28TH
INFANTRY DIVISIONS!
For seven months your high command has attempted to capture Sevastopol. This endeavor has cost you eighty thousand dead, and the goal has not been reached.

And it shall not be reached!

In four days alone, your June offensive on the heights 64, 4, 192, 0, 104.5, and in other areas of Sevastopol has cost you fifteen thousand men in killed, wounded, or missing, and you have still been unsuccessful in breaking through the Russian defenses.

You shall continue to be unsuccessful!

Russian Naval and Guard troops will continue to protect their homes, and will continue to line the approaches to the city with the graves of their enemies.

GERMAN SOLDIERS!
While your blood continues to flow in streams from the heights of Sevastopol, your cities at home are coming under daily attack by thousands of heavy British bombers. Cologne, Essen, Bremen, Emden, Rostock, Luebeck, and other German cities are being reduced to piles of smoking rubble.

Within days the English-American forces will land on the Continent and the Second Front in Europe will begin to roll. The units of Marshall Timoschenko continue to hammer with destructive strikes upon the Hitler Army in the Southern Army sector, and soon the day will come when the only escape route from the Crimean Peninsula will be blocked.

There will be no escape for you!

You still have a choice of two possibilities: senseless destruction and death for the criminal and inhuman policy of Hitler, or to give yourself up to the defenders of Sevastopol in order to save your lives.

SOLDIERS OF THE 11TH GERMAN ARMY!
Refuse to participate in any further attacks.
Desert from the foremost positions.
Surrender and you shall survive!

FROM THE HIGH COMMAND OF THE RED ARMY

On 18 June Infantry Regiment 436 moved into the northern area of fortress Schischkova, while Infantry Regiment 437 gained the southwest corner of Bartenyevka. Infantry Regiment 437, greatly reduced in strength, was then pulled off the line and assigned to the Forty-sixth Infantry Division as coastal security on the Kertsch Peninsula.

On 19 June Schischkova was fully occupied, and the Ninety-seventh Infantry Regiment won further ground to the southwest. On 20 June the strongpoint "Lenin" fell to that regiment, and on the next day the entire battery line was in the hands of the Ninety-seventh and the division pioniers. With that success the northern harbor had fallen to the 132d Infantry Division.

After fulfilling their assignment in the area north of Severnaya, the division was ordered to the left wing of the LIV Army Corps and was ordered to push south through difficult terrain to Gaytani. The division headquarters, formerly located in the Seamans' Home, was transferred to the Serpentine, and on 22 June to the Melzer Ravine north of Kamyschi. Infantry Regiment 436 was pulled out of the line following heavy losses and was transferred to the Kertsch Peninsula to serve as coastal defense. It was replaced by the Seventy-second Infantry Regiment. By 27 June the attacking forces were successful in penetrating the heavy bush area and capturing the heights of Gaytani in heavy infantry fighting. They then rotated to the left ninety degrees to occupy the Long Hill. With this move, the lines of the division were situated from east to west along the east bank of the Tschernaya. The neighboring division on the right was the Fiftieth Infantry Division, with the Fourth Rumanian Mountain Division on the left. On 27 June the division headquarters was transferred northwest to Tscherkes Kermen.

An assault was again ordered for 29 June, involving forces from the LIV and the XXX Army Corps. From the forward division headquarters on Bastion II the entire movement of the attack could be observed across the Tschernaya. Following heavy resistance, the German infantry units were able to capture the steeply sloped heights west of the Tschernaya. With clear visibililty, the observers were offered a spectacular view of storming infantry supported by assault guns and pioniers, and from this point they could observe the fleeing Russians as they were enveloped in an artillery blocking fire, with their motorized units suffering losses to Stuka attacks.

Thirty June brought more gains against ever-weakening enemy defenses, and at midday the point elements of the division pushed into the area south of Sevastopol. With this gain in territory the division headquarters was transferred to Inkerman-Sud.

On 1 July heavy artillery barrages and bombing raids were ordered on the beleaguered city at 1230. It was planned that the mass of the LIV Army Corps would take the eastern sector, and the 132d Infantry Division was ordered to push from the south into the city's defenses and capture the southern sector.

The goal of the attack from the south was to capture the southernmost third of Sevastopol on the first day, with the remainder of the city to be taken on the second. At 0900 the artillery and Luftwaffe bombardments were observed from the division headquarters, now located forward on Hill 73.0. The entire city appeared to have vanished beneath a thick blanket of smoke and dust.

In the event that only light resistance would be encountered, the division commander requested approval to push through the city center to the southern edge of the harbor, enabling the city to be taken in one day. This contingency plan was approved. The assault plan assigned the Forty-second Infantry Regiment to the right flank and the Seventy-second Infantry Regiment to the middle; and the left flank, sweeping through the western approaches to Sevastopol, was assigned to the Ninety-seventh Infantry Regiment.

At 1230 it was possible to observe the forward infantry elements penetrate the outer defenses of the city, and the artillery directed against the southern sector was lifted to prevent casualties to our own forces. At 1313 the war flag of the Reich was hoisted above the commanding Panorama heights as the infantry, now encountering little or no resistance, continued a rapid advance. At 1400 the division commander received a report from Oberst Maisel, commander of the Forty-second Infantry Regiment, that his forces had penetrated beyond the line of defenses, advanced through the city, and had reached Artillery Bay. With this report the city was officially in German hands.

The report was passed to the corps commander and was immediately endorsed and forwarded to be made available for a special broadcast by Deutsche Rundfunk. At exactly 2100, it was broadcast to the world that Sevastopol had fallen to German forces. Oberst Maisel was awarded the title "First German Commander of Sevastopol" by the division commander.

The German forces pushed onward through the heart of the city, which in large part had been reduced to rubble. In many areas the heat from burning buildings and bursting natural-gas lines became so intense that even driving through the devastated streets was difficult.

On the commanding features of the Panorama heights, overlooking the bay, stood the General Graf Totleben memorial to the defender of the city during the Crimean War of 1853–1856. Despite having been damaged by an artillery shell that had beheaded the statue, it was removed by the division and sent to Berlin to be displayed as a trophy in the Zeughaus.

The city's inhabitants slowly crawled from the cellars and underground shelters to greet their conquerors. Anxiously eyeing the German troops who moved in long columns at a snail's pace through the rubble, the surviving citizens immediately began plundering the food supply depots that had not been destroyed by artillery fire. Martial law was imposed as soon as possible to restore order to the tortured city. The supply depots and vital city facilities were put under guard, and labor crews were organized in efforts to resurrect life from the destruction that had descended on their world over the past weeks.

After weeks of difficult fighting and heavy losses, Russia's strongest land and coastal fortress was now firmly in German hands. Over the next several days, the landsers and Soviet prisoners set to work burying thousands of Russian dead still lying scattered throughout the areas where heavy fighting had taken place.

Some areas had experienced fanatical resistance. During the assault on Inkerman, an immense munitions depot built into a cliff was discovered. The huge facility had served as a Crimean wine processing and bottling factory before the war, and the Soviets had brought thousands of wounded soldiers and civilians seeking refuge into the massive complex for protection.

As the German troops approached, demolitions charges placed earlier in the base of the cliff were detonated. With a thunderous roar, the thirty-meter precipice collapsed along a length of three hundred meters, sealing the entrance and burying all occupants beneath many tons of earth. Among the casualties were members of a German reconnaissance unit that had approached the facility and had reached the entrance when the charges were detonated.

The merciless sun beat down on the city of Sevastopol, bringing sweltering heat with each sunrise. The city had suffered heavy damage from extended bombing and artillery barrages, but through the ruins one could see the beauty of what had once been there. Following destruction during the Crimean War in the 1860s, the czar had rebuilt the city in a late classical style. Many of the imposing facades had thus far survived this war and were still standing in exquisite beauty.

The harbor facilities were destroyed, and half-sunken ships lay in the water with bows and sterns angling upward from a surface choked with oil and debris. Fires raged throughout the area, and in the streets Russian prisoners of war shoveled passages through the rubble.

The battle for the Crimea was by no means complete. The Soviet coastal army had lost Sevastopol, but many of the forces escaped to new positions west of the city on the Cherson Peninsula. On orders from Stalin they were to fight in these positions to the last man if evacuation was not possible. A small number of high-ranking commanders and commissars were successfully evacuated by patrol craft, including the former commander of Sevastopol, General Petrov.

The heavy fighting on the Cherson Peninsula lasted until 4 July 1942. Russian units continued in their attempts to break through the German lines to reach the partisan bands in the Yaila Mountains. In thick masses, with arms linked to prevent shirkers from breaking ranks and holding back, waves of survivors launched attacks against our lines in the same manner that we had previously experienced at Makensia. Many of the suicidal attackers were women and girls from the Communist Youth organization. These poorly trained and unprepared forces suffered extremely high casualties, and the last remaining groups surrendered on 4 July after an unsuccessful attempt to escape the encirclement through ravines and gorges. On the Cherson Peninsula alone thirty thousand prisoners were taken during these mopping-up operations.

In the defeated city, the threat of disease remained great as myriad flies covered the dead and formed gray-black, swirling clouds over the wounded. The walls of the quarters were carpeted with the disease-spreading insects, and eating became laborious as it was necessary to clear the clusters of vermin from each bite of food. Despite efforts to avoid ingesting the insects, many flies were consumed with no apparent ill effects.

Even in peacetime, pestilence had descended on the city, brought to the Crimea by ship from Constantinople and into the harbors in the Caucasus. During our own siege, rats carrying bacillus virus had proliferated, but luckily the disease was kept in check. Without warning or explanation, the millions of flies soon succumbed to an epidemic that swept the area, and the flying vermin were mysteriously eradicated.

The English Cemetery served as a memorial to the first Crimean War. The Soviets had used the location as a command center, and the marble monuments erected to the fallen English soldiers were broken and strewn amid the remains of the dead thrown from their graves by the artillery barrages.

Numerous Russians lay wounded, scattered among the vineyards under a merciless, scorching sun. There was no water available to them where they lay, and they were quickly overcome with a sense of apathy as they lay waiting to die on the open ground. It became necessary for German medical personnel to attempt to save them, and Russian medical officers, nurses, and NCOs were brought from the prison compounds to assist in combing the hillsides in the search for wounded Red Army soldiers. The Russian doctors tore the rough wooden stakes from the ground and moved through the vineyards, using the poles as prods to persuade the ambulatory wounded to move to medical stations. For many who could not be persuaded with pokes and prods to rise to their feet, the doctors and medical personnel would spring among them, swinging the sticks wildly. With shouts and beatings the walking wounded would be forced to their feet and steered in the direction of the medical stations.

Leaning wearily against one another for support, covered with flies and wrapped in bloody bandages, the wounded would stumble in pairs or in small groups as they moved slowly toward their destination. Soon long, pitiful columns were making their way under a glowing sun toward the wells and the prisoner of war enclosures, and for many it would be a final journey.

Following the fall of the city, the division was assigned security duties on the Kertsch Peninsula, where we were to remain until ordered to the northern front on 27 August 1942.

On the seacoast, within clear view of the Caucasus Mountains, the division was able to recuperate in relative luxury after months of grueling combat. There was swimming and organized recreation, broken intermittently by occasional guard duty and training sessions. At Yalta, on the southern coast of the Crimea, often referred to as the Russian Riviera, a recreation area was established. Here, in the warmth of the summer sun and far from the shell bursts and the crack of the snipers' rifles, the landsers sat for hours playing skat. Two years later, Churchill, Roosevelt, and Stalin held a conference in this pleasant city that would determine the fate of millions.

The furlough restriction was rescinded, and a number of soldiers were permitted to take their earned departure from the front. I was elated to learn that I had been selected for this respite, and I soon boarded an overflowing furlough train toward Germany. Following my leave I reported back to the regimental headquarters in Kertsch. There I was advised that due to my participation in the action during which we destroyed the three Soviet tanks, I had been recommended and accepted for attendance at the Kriegschule (war school) as an officer candidate.

These carefree days in Yalta proved to be short-lived. The eastern migration of the German race, and the victories of the eastern gods, now stood at its zenith, or so reported the propagandists. The propaganda units declared that finally the dream, the idea of world domination, would now be coming to fruition.

But then the "victorious eastern warriors" took a furlough. Out of the sterile environment of the front they journeyed to the homeland, where they began to hear rumors of questionable actions committed by the Reich, and occasionally fantastic stories would circulate of the policies of political operatives far behind the lines in occupied territories. The soldiers returned to the front often dissatisfied, and sometimes disillusioned, as they came to realize that their experience in war had altered them forever. They had learned that in Germany they were no longer at ease, that the friends and comrades of their units had become the family, and that the war had become their life.

By summer 1942, the German armies had pushed the distance from the Don and Kuban to the Caucasus. They had reached the coasts of the Caspian Sea and the banks of the Volga. The name Stalingrad was already often heard, with no indication of what lay in the future for the Sixth Army on the Volga.

It had been initially planned that the Crimean army would cross the Straits of Kertsch, push through the Caucasus, and swing north to launch a planned offensive in coordination with the German southern wing. This plan was changed by Hitler, the man at the forefront of our command in Berlin, who was now occasionally referred to as the "Greatest War Lord of All Time." The capture of Sevastopol by the divisions of the Eleventh Army had stirred within Hitler the idea to use these divisions in the storming of Leningrad. Thus, the absurd plan to remove the core of the Crimean divisions from the southernmost point of the German advance and shift them to the northernmost part of Russia was put into motion. The urgent need for these forces to remain anchoring the southern flank of the Eastern Front was brushed aside. Perhaps the fate of the Sixth Army in Stalingrad could have been averted if the experienced Crimean divisions had remained on the southern wing.

Before the onslaught. The Fourteenth Panzerjaeger Company, Infantry Regiment 437, parades before onlookers in Munich on Heroes' Memorial Day, 16 March 1941.

Panzerjaeger crews on the march, June 1941. Due to a shortage of German heavy equipment, captured French Chenilette prime movers were used to tow the antitank guns. These prime movers proved to be ill-suited for the expanses of the Soviet Union, and of the ten Chenilettes initially assigned to Bidermann's unit, only two reached the Crimea.

Soviet prisoners of war file to the rear, late June 1941. Vast numbers of Soviet prisoners were captured by the enveloping of entire armies in pincer movements by highly mobile German forces. Later in the war, the Soviets used these same tactics to destroy the German Army Group Center in Russia.

Oberleutnant Vetter (adjutant, Infantry Regiment 438) rides on horseback past a massive Soviet armored vehicle abandoned by retreating Red Army forces near Lemberg, July 1941. Vetter was killed in action on 4 November 1941 before Sevastopol.

Destroyed Soviet armor along the advance route of the 132d Infantry Division near Lemberg, July 1941.

Suffering from thirst and exhaustion, a horse is coaxed to its feet, July 1941. The vast expanses and lack of support facilities in Russia and the Ukraine proved to be an enormous strain on men, animals, and equipment as the German army marched toward the east.

A battery from Artillery Regiment 132 passes German settlements north of Odessa in the Ukraine. The numerous German settlements were established by Catherine the Great of Russia in the eighteenth century.

An artesian well is put into use in northern Crimea. These wells produced brackish water, and lack of potable water soon became an acute problem for the advancing German army.

Soviet prisoners of war converse with Ukrainian women and children. The German forces were initially welcomed into the Ukraine, and large numbers of prisoners volunteered to serve with the invaders in the belief that they would be liberated from Communism.

Members of the Fourteenth Panzerjaeger Company under the command of Leutnant Zoll (*left*) establish an antitank position near the Dnieper, August 1941.

Russian prisoners of war captured during the fighting along the Dnieper, August 1941.

Captured and destroyed Soviet equipment near the Dnieper, mid-August 1941.

Gefreiter G. H. Bidermann with a 37mm Pak and
captured Ford truck, late September 1941. The
American-made Ford trucks were favored by the
landsers to augment their myriad support vehicles,
since replacement parts were readily available
from captured Soviet stocks.

An 80mm mortar crew in position before Makensia, November 1941.

Gefreiter Bidermann guarding an abandoned Soviet armored vehicle. This intact vehicle was placed into service to replace the weaker Chenilette for towing antitank guns.

Pak position of Obergefreiter Knappitsch in northern Crimea, early November 1941.

Infantry units move forward into their positions prior to the assault on the Sevastopol fortress, 17 December 1941.

Members of Infantry Regiment 437 prepare to assault the Sevastopol fortress, 17 December 1941.

Pak and crew in position at the factory before Daln-Kamyschi, April 1942. *Left to right:* Krentz, Spinnler, Albert, Bidermann.

The burned body of a Soviet crewman lies near his destroyed tank in the sector of Daln-Kamyschi, April 1942.

Infantry units moving into position near Daln-Kamyschi, April 1942. This position represented the southernmost point of the Eastern Front.

General von Bock (*left*) observes enemy positions with General Lindemann on 28 April 1942 during an inspection of the front prior to the assault on Kertsch.

Above and facing page: Landsers advancing toward objectives in Kertsch under artillery support, May 1942.

Destroyed Soviet armor before Bidermann's Pak position during the assault on Kertsch, May 1942.

Soviet prisoners captured during operations of 8–9 May 1942 in the area of Kertsch. The communications poles seen to the left of the column show the Anglo-Indian telegraph line that extended from India over Persia, through the Caucasus, across the Straits of Kertsch, and through Europe to England.

Landsers advancing through neutralized enemy positions on Kertsch.

Penetrating the defenses of Fort Todtlebena, Kertsch. The infantry units suffered heavy casualties in capturing these positions from a well-entrenched, determined enemy.

Major Sepp Drexel (*right*) and his adjutant prior to the assault on Kertsch by Infantry Regiment 436. Major Drexel was later awarded the Knight's Cross of the Iron Cross for action on the northern front and was one of the few senior officers of the division to survive both the war and imprisonment in Russia.

Cleaning the antitank weapon in the Kertsch sector, May 1942. Because of the cold nights and warm days, the weapon had to be protected from condensation that would quickly form on the sensitive optics and locking mechanism.

The morning following the capture of Sevastopol, Hauptmann Schmidt reports the status of his decimated battalion to regimental commander Oberst Kindsmiller near the village of Duvankoy, 18 June 1942.

Supply units advance across the Crimea toward Kertsch, May 1942. The vehicles and rail locomotives rapidly exhibited signs of excess wear due to dust, extreme temperatures, and distances traveled. The horse-drawn units, though reliable, were dependent on abundant sources of feed and water.

Obergefreiter Bidermann in Feodosia, February 1942.

The large military cemetery in Feodosia for soldiers of the 132d Infantry Division. Following the liberation of the Crimea by the Soviet army, all traces of this cemetery were eradicated.

CHAPTER SEVEN

Gaitolovo

The only color to appear

before our eyes in this frozen wasteland was the scarlet blood,

which covered the dead and dying who lay before our guns.

As the month of August drew to a close, a large part of the Eleventh Army departed the positions on the Kertsch Peninsula. Packed in rail transport for the long journey to the north, the various units of the division remained in transit for a period averaging eight to ten days before disembarking on the Leningrad front. It was mid-September before the division was reassembled and prepared for combat.

It was rumored that we were to assault Leningrad. In summer 1941 it might have been possible to take the city with the addition of the newly arrived divisions; however, at that time it had been decided that the population of Leningrad could be starved into submission, thus sparing the Wehrmacht many casualties. The Russians displayed resolute courage and steadfast determination in proving this to be a false concept, and they managed to supply the city in summer by ship and in winter by means of a railway laid on the thick ice over Lake Ladoga. Although many thousands died of starvation in the besieged city, the Russian people did endure and hold the front. From the German side, Leningrad became a costly war of attrition, a stalemate that continued to bleed us of our ever-shrinking resources.

The enemy quickly learned that new divisions had been brought in to oppose them on the Leningrad front. The Soviets immediately launched an offensive against our positions in an attempt to break our blockade from the landward side, and with this attack the Russians spoiled the planned offensive to capture the city. Instead of launching the final battle to capture Leningrad, the Crimean divisions were compelled to counter a deep Russian breakthrough, a move that evolved into open battle on the southern shore of Lake Ladoga.

The teardrop-shaped pocket extended along a front approximately eight kilometers wide and twelve kilometers deep into the German lines along a front defended by our Eighteenth Army. A counteroffensive was planned to strike the teardrop from the south, and our 132d Infantry Division was sent into action for this mission with the tasks of attacking toward the north and pushing through to Gaitolovo, securing the pocket to the west to prevent any breakout attempt, and building a new defensive line to the east as a defense against further attacks on our flank.

On the morning of 5 September the forward units succeeded in pushing through to Tosno. The enemy launched attacks with massed units along the eastern edge of the bottleneck, eastward to Mga, and succeeded in breaking through in several sections. The penetrations were repulsed by the newly arrived divisions from the Crimea, with the 132d Infantry Division remaining in reserve and assembling in the area of Mga-Sablino-Schapki.

As early as the following day the situation had changed, and the division once again was placed under the command of the Eleventh Army. On 8 September units from Infantry Regiment 436 and the Second Battalion of Artillery Regiment 132 were shifted to the front line. Every second day an average of seven to ten trains were loaded, and on the evening of 16 September the division was fully intact and was again prepared to engage the enemy.

Meanwhile, the enemy breakthrough had been halted in the area of Mga and was then sealed off by attacking the penetration from the north and south, isolating the Soviet force with a pincer movement that met at Gaitolovo.

Initially, the first attacks led by the 170th and the Twenty-fourth Infantry Divisions met with little success, and the 132d Division was sent into the attack toward Sogolubovka-Mga. On barely passable roads the regiments slogged toward their objectives throughout the period of 17–19 September. Every movement required extraordinary effort. The bunkers and defensive positions were situated in swamps with little or no shelter available, and the troops were constantly exposed to the saturated earth and clammy, cool air. Winter supplies were still lacking, and the troops suffered in the cold temperatures that descended on the shivering landsers with every nightfall.

The order to prepare to attack was received on 21 September. It was necessary to march throughout the night over rough-hewn corduroy roads to reach the preparation areas, and once again movement was severely restricted to narrow, muddy corridors through impenetrable forests. Only after dawn did the regiments finally reach their objective of Aprakssin. At 0800 a briefing was held by the chief staff officer for final assignments.

The distance from the bivouac area to the point of attack had been only two kilometers, but due to the poor roads and terrain conditions the transit required an excess of two hours. The attack was planned to be launched at 1200, and Regiments 436 and 437 were immediately aware that the timetable could not be met and that the attack would not be possible before 1400. The staff adjusted the schedule to the greatest extent possible, delaying the attack to 1300. Despite all efforts, the soldiers could not keep to the time schedule, and the attack was again delayed. The fact that the attack on Tschernaya was eventually launched at all remained a tribute to the individual efforts of the landsers, and the inevitable failure of the troops to push farther to the north to win more ground could only be attributed to the lack of time available for assault preparations.

Due to poor preparations the casualties suffered during this attack were disproportionately high. On 22 September the regiments suffered 510 killed in action, including seven officers, with an additional eight officers wounded and one missing. The battle strength of the four battalions was reduced to a total of sixteen hundred men, indicating that the first attack on Tschernaya had cost our forces 30 percent casualties.

On 23 September a further attack was ordered for 1000. The tanks and assault guns that were intended for support quickly become mired in the swampy terrain, unable to move over and beyond the Tschernaya River. Because of the impassable ground and the poor communications between the regiment and the battalions, the few morning hours of preparations again proved to be insufficient for the attack, and after an advance of merely one hundred meters the troops reported that they were unable to make further headway.

Three hours later, at 1300, a renewed attack was ordered. The push through the dense, swampy terrain to Gaitolovo was to be successful at all costs, but again the attack failed. Under cover of strong artillery support the attack was again attempted at 1530. The barrage was intense, as the entire corps and division batteries sustained an uninterrupted fire for a period of thirty minutes, completely blanketing an area the length of the assault line. Despite this expenditure of our last reserves of strength, our weakened forces had suffered too many losses and were too exhausted to make headway. Again the attack ground to a halt.

On 25 September, another attack was launched under the direct command of the battalion commander, which tore an opening in the Soviet lines and enabled a connection with the elements to the north near Gaitolovo. At 1230 the battalion entered Gaitolovo. The battalion commander, Hauptmann Schmidt, had accomplished this feat only through the use of his extraordinary leadership skills combined with his personal bravery in the face of overwhelming enemy strength. For this accomplishment, he was subsequently recommended to be awarded the Knight's Cross of the Iron Cross, and he did receive this highly esteemed decoration on 8 October.

The capture of Gaitolovo instilled within the ranks the attitude that once again they could accomplish almost any feat asked of them. It was widely believed that no intact enemy elements remained between the division and the forward elements of Regiment 437. The enemy did, however, succeed in opening a salient between the right wing of the regiment and Infantry Regiment 436 on 25 September that could not be closed, due to the weakening of Regiment 436. At this time the division should not have received further assignments, as all troops had reached the point of exhaustion from which no movement was possible. The Soviets obviously faced the same situation, and despite all attempts the attacks to win the two kilometers held by our regiment were unsuccessful.

On 26 September the division received another order to attack. The order was given to throw the enemy back over the Tschernaya and to hold the sector in order to establish a bridgehead from where our forces could close any openings torn through our lines. The weakened units were again unable to carry out the assignment against the heavily entrenched enemy.

A further attempt was made on 27 September, and Infantry Regiment 437 managed to reach the former Russian command bunker five hundred meters to the east of the Tschernaya Bridge, where they dug in and waited for the inevitable counterattack. With no support from either of our flanks, the embattled regiment could not prevent the Soviet forces from slipping past toward the west. The regiment continued to hold the position against heavy Soviet forces while Russian units flowed past the island of resistance to attack the German lines. On 30 September the Third Mountain Division launched an attack that relieved the beleaguered 437th Regiment, sealed the front on the flanks, and prevented an encirclement of the regiment.

The losses suffered during these days were exceedingly high, to the extreme that the regiment was only strong enough to remain on the defensive, lacking the strength to break even minimal Russian resistance. From 5 October the division was officially on the defensive, and on 11 October came the order for it to be replaced on the line by the Twenty-fourth Infantry Division. The shocked and weakened troops turned the positions over to their relief columns and made their way to the rest positions in the area of Vyritza.

During the fighting at Gaitolovo our division's Catholic priest had earned the name "the rucksack priest." He was constantly on the move with his worn field pack strapped to his back, from which he consistently provided the troops on the foremost lines with simple food items that had come to be regarded by the landsers as luxuries. He was always willing to assist the wounded, and on one occasion he personally located and rescued a badly wounded soldier who had fallen to a sniper's bullet in an exposed position on the line. His constant exposure to the front and physical risks for the benefit of the soldiers came to an untimely end when he received a severe shrapnel wound to his arm. Inflicted by a Russian mortar fired from the dense forest several hundred meters distant, the wound was severe enough to require amputation of the limb; thus the division lost a valuable soldier and friend. The division commander did attempt officially to recognize his numerous acts of bravery and dedication by recommending him for a high award; however, this recommendation was disapproved in light of the typical National Socialist philosophy, which was to refuse to grant such an esteemed decoration unless the priest agreed to surrender his cloth and collar.

During the weeks between 22 September and 7 October our battalion suffered a total of sixty-two killed, two hundred-eighty wounded, and thirty missing. Some twenty to thirty lightly wounded and sick remained with the battalion, leaving us with an effective strength of fifty combatants within the battalion.

During a short rest period between October and December in the area of Vyritza, extreme measures were employed to rebuild the regiment. Supply units, pionier platoons, transportation units, and other units deemed not immediately critical were combed through in the search for available personnel to serve in the infantry. The desperate battle that had recently been fought south of Lake Ladoga had been costly, and no replacements were available from other sources. There was little or no formal training for our self-supplied reinforcements prior to 28 October, when the order was issued to move to a newly assigned sector of the Eastern Front in the area of the Pogostya pocket. The winter months that followed brought little action, which offered the opportunity to train the recently assembled units and to recover strength until February. As early as February 1943, all units were again reported to be up to effective combat strength, despite the lack of extensive infantry training for replacement troops.

Shortly after our division was sent into action for a renewed attack, I was wounded again. A ricochet or shell splinter had struck my left foot and had penetrated completely through the heavy leather boot, leaving jagged entrance and exit holes. Fortunately the wound did not break any bones and appeared to be relatively superficial, indicating a swift recovery that would not require evacuation. While recovering in the regimental medical station I received notice that I was scheduled for immediate departure to the war school. Just as during World War I, the casualty rate for junior officers had proven to be extremely high, following the Prussian motto: "The life of a leutnant is first to live and first to die!" There existed within our regiment on the front no officers at the battalion or company level who had not been wounded, and many had fallen in action.

It was a strangely uncomfortable feeling to see the homeland again. My orders took me to Luneville, and from there to Chatons-sur-Marne, where the troop replacement command was located. Subsequent orders directed me to report to the war school in Milovitz, near Prague. As a reservist, which in the German army traditionally remained set apart from the regular, or "professional" soldiers, I remained dedicated but not overly enthusiastic regarding my impending promotion to the officer corps.

I was soon participating in the intensive classroom lectures and field problems, and due to my recent experience at the front I was called upon by the instructors to brief the officer candidates on various situations to be encountered on the Eastern Front. Suddenly and without warning the wound on my foot opened, and I was forced to spend a period of three weeks in a local military clinic where medical officers attempted to close the wound.

Unlike the American army, at this time the German army possessed no penicillin, and an even insignificant wound might develop infections that could prove to be fatal if they could not be held in check. Indeed, even at this late date in medical developments, a stomach wound was commonly fatal, and before going into action the landsers were often advised to eat very little, as a full stomach would increase complications and could prove to be fatal if penetrated by a bullet or shrapnel.

Throughout the period of time I remained immobilized in the clinic, I was frequently visited by Officer Candidate von Moltke, a descendant of our famous Prussian field marshal, who provided me with lesson plans and problems as they were presented in the class so that I could remain current with the curriculum as it was taught. One afternoon Major Richter, our class commander, toured the clinic and stopped at my bedside to speak with me. I was surprised to hear him ask about the well-being of Oberst Kindsmiller, with whom he had previously served. While reviewing the files of the officer candidates, the major had noticed that I had reported from Kindsmiller's command. Following World War I they had both served together in the Freikorps during the political upheaval of the 1920s.

During his visit he expressed concern that I would not be permitted to graduate with my class due to my prolonged absence. I then proceeded to show him the work I had been conducting throughout my convalescence, which pleased him immensely, and he departed after assuring me that he would attempt to intervene should my graduation and subsequent promotion be jeopardized because of my wound.

On 1 December I became a feldwebel and a leutnant on the same day. On 17 December the officer candidates of War School Class Eleven were driven to Berlin, where we assembled at the Sportspalast to hear a speech by Reichsmarschall Hermann Goring. Approximately two thousand newly commissioned officers from all branches of service were seated by the order of precedence of their combat decorations. As one of the students who had previously been awarded the Iron Cross, First Class, I was given the honor of sitting in the front row, only several meters' distance from the podium.

Suddenly, to the deafening tunes of stirring military music, the Reichs-marschall appeared and approached the podium. His corpulent frame was clothed in a resplendent ivory-colored uniform. At his neck hung the Grand Cross of the Iron Cross and the Pour le Merite, awarded for his accomplishments during World War I as a fighter pilot. As the only recipient of the recently resurrected Grand Cross, this ostentatious order appeared to overshadow the Kaiser's Pour le Merite. His breast was covered by glittering medals and badges, representing impressive feats of combat in another war long ago, as well as, in some instances, powerful political influence of a more recent past. Tightly gripped in his right fist was a massive, bejewelled marshal's baton.

He first spoke of political topics and eventually came to the subject of the Eastern Front, at last addressing the on-going disaster in Stalingrad. The remnants of von Paulus's Sixth Army had not yet surrendered to the overwhelming Soviet forces in the ruins of Stalingrad on the Volga; thus he still at this point spoke with conviction and authority. He addressed his promise to supply the beleaguered army with his Luftwaffe, a promise that we would later learn would not be kept. In his smooth, tenor voice he spoke of the sacrifices that we as young officers must face, of the perils that we must endure, of the resistance that we must meet, and, when the enemy has outflanked us on the right and on the left, we must harken back to the words from antiquity: "Wanderer, when you come to Sparta. . . ."

Thus we listened to the gallows speech. To emphasize his words, the Reichsmarschall began pounding the podium with his baton, using such force that I was certain that at any moment I might be struck with dislodged jewels.

Stalingrad! Wrapped within a political doctrine that abused the concepts of honor and of keeping the watch for the country, and firmly insisting that standing the ground—at any price—was essential, the Greatest War Lord of All Time—our Fuhrer in Berlin—committed an army to an agonizing death in the east.

As the war progressed, the extremely high casualties and the willingness of the German soldiers to offer themselves in sacrifice became an accepted norm. As the faulty leadership became exposed over an extended period of time, the willingness of the soldier to die for political beliefs began to fade, which in turn resulted in a general lessening of chances for the troops to survive the debacle of the Eastern Front. The code of honor, however, long inherent in the German soldier who stood to protect the fatherland with weapon in hand, remained within his consciousness. The soldiers continued to sacrifice their lives, not for the members of the party but for the fatherland.

The system continued to distance itself further from a humanitarian waging of the war. We remained unaware of the full extent of the orders for the liquidation and transport of Jews and other ethnic populations considered undesirable from the National Socialist viewpoint, but we became fully aware of those brave men who had faithfully served their country and who, because of a differing or conflicting political ideology, would simply disappear from our ranks.

The Sportspalast speech by the Reichsmarschall brought our formal officers' training to a close, and after outprocessing and receiving new orders, we were released for several weeks' Christmas furlough. On that very same evening I and two other war-school graduates decided to remain overnight in Berlin to celebrate our newly bestowed rank and title. Three nights later we boarded trains that would take us on our separate journeys. During several nights of reckless revelry we had unwisely succeeded in depleting our entire officers' clothing allowance, which amounted to approximately 1,500 Reichsmarks apiece. Exhausted from lack of sleep and appearing much the worse for wear, I proceeded to my home town of Stuttgart, where I arrived destitute and still wearing an enlisted rank's uniform with newly purchased officer rank insignia hastily sewn on the shoulders.

Several days later I received, as a Christmas gift from my parents and close relatives, several officer's uniforms, complete with newly purchased dress sword and dagger, as well as the many accessories still required by the Wehrmacht officers at that early stage of the war. Germany had reached the pinnacle of military success. Our forces held vast territory in the Soviet Union; victory appeared imminent. Despite massive odds, Rommel had consistently proven victorious against the British in Africa. We remained confident that the Sixth Army would prevail at Stalingrad and that in the east we would eventually emerge triumphant in our crusade against Bolshevism. As a commissioned officer with combat decorations, I remained the center of attention within my family circle. I spent a number of evenings with my Uncle Christian, who insisted on proudly introducing his young nephew, fresh from battle in the east, to all his friends. Several years later, in September 1944 when we lay under the shadow of impending, total defeat, Uncle Christian would die an agonizing death from burns received during an American air raid over Stuttgart.

During the early days of January 1943 I reported to Saarburg in Lorraine, where the Infantry Replacement Unit for my regiment was located. As I passed through the massive stone and iron gates of the former French garrison, the guard at the entrance sprang to attention and presented arms. Being a newly commissioned leutnant, I was somewhat taken aback by the unfamiliar greeting, and I sharply returned the salute before suddenly halting to scrutinize the sentry. Looking him closely in the eyes, I realized that it was my old friend Obulus Meissner from the Fourteenth Company. It remained a tradition in the German army for new leutnants to pay honor to the soldier who renders the first salute following commissioning, and we arranged to meet in a local bar to discuss recent and past experiences.

After reporting to the garrison administrative office, I located a number of friends from the Fourteenth. To my surprise, Josef Vogt, Sepp Klemens, Feldwebel Weiss, and Leutnant Huber were there. My old recruit corporal Jakob Hohenadel appeared as well. All of these comrades had been brought together as a result of wounds incurred on the front and had reported to the replacement command from various military hospitals in the area.

We received the inevitable work assignments and training objectives. On the second day the schedule demanded that we construct a circular defense point for an antitank position, to include the construction of tank traps and trenches. As officer-in-charge of this exercise, I requested an issue of necessary shovels and picks from the equipment room and learned that not a single tool was available. Even the most elementary items were nonexistent or in very short supply. To fulfill the assignment we searched for and located a large cache of new, unused tools hanging in neat rows on the wall in the basement of the garrison. Now properly prepared to conduct our training assignment, we confidently took tools in hand and, fully outfitted in combat dress, marched in ranks to the nearby training area.

On our return that evening I received the order to report immediately to the unit headquarters. There I reported as directed to a portly supply officer whom I found perched behind a massive desk strewn with documents. I was then subjected to a ludicrous tirade concerning the unauthorized use of tools reserved strictly for air defense. Stabbing the air with a thick finger to emphasize each word, he lectured me on the importance of the tools and sharply stated that, under no uncertain terms, the subject equipment was to remain in the cellar, ready and waiting for the inevitable air attack on our garrison.

The picks and shovels were returned unceremoniously and without further word to the basement to hang uselessly on the wall. It is possible that they remain hanging in the cold confines of this French garrison to this day, slowly rusting and turning dark with age, yet fulfilling the duty for which they were obtained by the Wehrmacht.

Having served so many months at the front among friends and comrades, it was not surprising that my days with the replacement unit were somewhat less than pleasant. This may have been due in part to my breaking with peacetime army tradition by socializing with my former enlisted comrades. Together with two other recently commissioned leutnants—Horst Lienhardt and Hans Durrmeier—I had invited a number of the old gang from the Fourteenth to the former residence of a French officer for an evening of drink and song.

During the evening the discussion inevitably turned to the others, the friends who remained on the northern front with our old regiment. We shared a feeling of alienation in our administrative surroundings. This was no longer our army, our environment. We belonged back at the front.

Immediately following my commission I had written to my former regimental commander, requesting that I be permitted to return to the 437th. Subsequently, the orders to report back to my old regiment were received in mid-January 1943. Together with Horst Lienhardt, I traveled in an overflowing furlough train returning to the front through Dresden, Konigsberg, Kovno, Pleskay, and farther toward Tosno.

As the final remnants of von Paulus's Sixth Army were meeting their destiny in Stalingrad, another theater of war arose to become priority and to draw full attention on the scale of political importance. Both Stalingrad and Leningrad exemplified by their names immense political, economic, and spiritual significance for the Communist state. Lenin, the father and spiritual leader of the Red Revolution in Russia, and Stalin, the iron ruler who, with whip and pistol ruled the Soviet Union as a Red czar, had given these cities their names. Thus the capture of these immense, heavily populated areas developed a significance far beyond simple strategic necessity, and they became rather a symbol of resistance that was to be defeated, regardless of cost, by our invading armies. Upon these two battlefields were to die hundreds of thousands.

Leningrad had remained encircled by the German forces since fall 1941. On 24 September of that year, Hitler had withdrawn the panzer corps and supporting units that had been reserved for the final assault on the city. With that move, the plans for a successful attack simply vanished; the troops could never again be assembled in such numbers and strength for a final assault against a weakened and unprepared enemy holding the city.

The vital mistake in delaying an attack on the city was exemplified by the nine-hundred-day battle for Leningrad that followed. The fighting south of Lake Ladoga and on the Volchov front, with which our division was involved from September 1942 to November 1943, resulted only in draining badly needed resources from which the Wehrmacht could never recover.

Only in the summer months was Leningrad entirely cut off by land. As the city is situated on the west bank of Lake Ladoga, numerous small vessels were able to deliver limited supplies to the beleaguered city. From west bank to east bank, which remained under Soviet control, the lake is only about thirty kilometers wide, the approximate distance across the English Channel at Calais. The lake remained the void into which all our efforts to blockade the city were lost.

The German Eighteenth Army held a fourteen-kilometer-wide corridor along the southern coast. The cities of Schlusselburg and Lipka remained the cornerstones on which our flanks were anchored. This narrow, dangerous corridor, called the bottleneck, ran through the heights of Sinyavino, and was otherwise flanked by trackless, impenetrable swamp. The entire southern section of this front was situated along the Neva, and the beleaguered Soviets made repeated attempts to break the ring sealing their city and were thus applying constant pressure on our east front. At the southern end of the bottleneck ran the Kirov Road, which connected Leningrad with the Urals.

Leningrad was dying. Soldiers and civilians, women, the elderly, and children were perishing from the starvation our encirclement had brought upon them. Those not engaged in building positions or working in the factories did not receive rations. Those who were eligible to receive a daily ration drew two slices of bread per day. Everything burnable was consumed by the need to heat dwellings and workplaces. Anything edible simply vanished. Even wallpaper was removed from dwellings and boiled to extract minuscule amounts of nourishment from the paper and paste. Schdanov, the military and political commander, drove the population without mercy in his untiring efforts to save his city and country. Women, the elderly, and young children were compelled to work in shifts for constructing the tank trenches. Those who could not work were by default condemned to die of starvation; all available food was required for those who could assist in defending the city. Production of weapons and war material continued at any cost. Tanks rolled off assembly lines almost within sight of the German troops, who remained in their positions at the very outskirts of the city.

The German strategic planners had apparently underestimated the winter's effect on Lake Ladoga. The large body of water froze solid for a distance of more than thirty kilometers. Unpredictably, a road was successfully constructed over a sheet of ice one-and-one-half meters thick, the road of survival for Leningrad. Throughout the long winter hours of darkness, heavy trucks rolled into the city bringing only the most essential war materials. The lowest priority was food. Gasoline became almost nonexistent. Schdanov next constructed a rail system over the ice during the cover of darkness. After the thaw, the Soviets established a pipeline along the sea bottom to deliver fuel and electricity. The electric power from the Volchov plant on the Svir supplied the armaments factories, which never stopped production.

In September 1942 our 132d Division played a major role in the breakthrough to Gaitolovo during the first battle south of Lake Ladoga. The offensive in which the Soviets attempted to break through toward Mga with the goal of relieving Leningrad by land became a catastrophic defeat for the Red Army.

The second great battle south of Lake Ladoga began on 12 January 1943, while our division was situated farther to the south on the Pogostya pocket and the Volchov. This phase of fighting rolled into our sector on 11 February. The White City on the Neva, the Cultural Pearl of Russia, the city that, until the Russian Revolution, had carried the name of Petersburg to honor the greatest czar, was to be freed from the German vise by a great pincer movement of the Red Army. For over two-and-one-half years the city of 3 million inhabitants, Russia's second largest, had endured the ring of German forces on the northern wing of the Eastern Front. Like

Stalingrad, the city that carried the name of one of the founding fathers of Bolshevism was of primary political importance and was to be freed.

In February 1943, the Soviets succeeded in breaking through the front and threatened to trap the German forces in the Oranienbaum pocket. Facing this disaster, the members of the 132d Infantry Division clung to their positions with stubborn resistance, and in doing so prevented a catastrophe whose dimensions would have equaled the Stalingrad debacle.

Many of my former comrades were missing when I reported to my old regiment; however, I soon felt at home again. I was immediately detailed to serve for two weeks on the Volchov front as platoon commander, which was a sector known for ever-increasing Soviet activity.

The climate and battlefield conditions that we were now facing in the area south of Leningrad differed greatly from those to which we in the units from the Crimea were accustomed. The terrain was swampy, choked with thick underbrush and birch trees, interspersed with shallow rises from which an intermittent defense network could be established. During periods of warm, thawing temperatures, water would seep into all positions, making it impossible to dig deeply into the ground for shelter. In place of trenches, a system of rough log barricades piled high with earth and branches dominated our defense line; the positions could be compared to the primitive palisades once constructed by the Roman legions.

A narrow rail track was laid through the swamp to enable the various positions at Pomeranya, Lipovik, and elsewhere to receive supplies. Other positions, such as these at Klosterdorf and Wasserkopf, were made accessible by constructing corduroy roads through the swamps from logs hewn from the dense forests. Over those narrow but effective roadways the troops were supplied by horse-drawn wagons, and the laboring of the animals to pull their burdens over the creaking timbers could be heard throughout the hours of darkness. The wagon beds were modified to be fitted with axles and wheel rims stripped from disabled military vehicles to create a miniature rail system.

Encouraged by the victories at Stalingrad and on the south wing of the Eastern Front, the Russians made vigorous attempts to put the offensives in the north into motion. During the severe winter months it was possible for their armored units to push over the frozen swamps, hindered only by thick stands of birch trees that prevented armored assaults on a large scale.

As a bitter cold descended on us, the Russians unleashed their offensive directly at Smerdynia. This second battle south of Lake Ladoga began in January. Infantry Regiment 437 was transferred to the XXXVII Army Corps on the Volchov front to support the defending divisions. After the sector was again stabilized the regiment was returned to the XXVII Army Corps, where it took up positions to the right of the division in the sector assigned to Group Weber. The division was responsible for defending a thinly held sector that extended along a forty-kilometer front.

At the end of January the enemy forces in the area of the Pogostya pocket became more active. Numerous reconnaissance patrols and attacks in company strength indicated that pressure was being applied in coordination with the operations conducted by the Soviets south of Lake Ladoga. No air reconnaissance was possible due to poor visibility until 9 February, after which large concentrations of enemy vehicles were reported traversing the roads in the Pogostya pocket. During darkness numerous campfires were observed in the area of Ssenino.

A change in the enemy soldiers themselves became clearly evident, as many of the positions were reinforced by large numbers of fresh troops wearing new snow-camouflage uniforms and equipped with drum-fed submachine guns of recent manufacture. The division confirmed that replacements had been assigned to the enemy sector opposite us and that a renewed attack was to be expected within the next one to two days.

The attack took place on 11 February. In the sector of Regiment 436 units of the exhausted Ninety-sixth Infantry Division were thrown into the line and came under attack by a force consisting of ten tanks with supporting infantry. The battle-weary, weakened regiment was unable to hold the front in the face of concentrated armor, and the enemy succeeded in breaking through. This attack was followed up the next day by enemy forces that had been reinforced with fresh troops during the night, and they penetrated to the southwest of Klosterdorf, eliminating all possibilities of a quick counterattack.

The exhausted troops manning the thinly held positions were able with superhuman efforts to halt the penetration at Klosterdorf; however, as late as 13 February a salient remained in the line along the wooden corduroy road that no longer could be closed. During the next two days the enemy had crossed the Klosterdorf road and had consolidated newly won positions. The Russians attacked the positions of the Sixth Battery of Artillery Regiment 132 with armor, and the troops were forced to destroy their guns before abandoning them in their positions.

The weapons did fall into enemy hands; and although the barrels had been destroyed, rendering them useless to the enemy, the loss of these assets to the division and regiment was irreplaceable and marked the first time during the war that the division had lost heavy guns, albeit temporarily, to the enemy forces.

On 16 and 17 February all attempts to close the gap in the line failed. Efforts to close it with battalions from the southern and western flanks were unsuccessful in penetrating the Soviet defenses, which were now reinforced with the arrival of enemy tanks that remained positioned along the road. The Russians were successful in repelling all attacks until 18 February, when units from the Ninety-sixth Infantry Division succeeded in freeing the roadway; supported with units from the 132d they were able to recapture the artillery positions with the now-useless guns still in their emplacements.

The glowing breath of battle descended with a vengeance on those who languished in the forests, swamps, and undergrowth between the Volchov and Lake Ladoga. The god of war would arise with daybreak as the light began filtering through the snow, and another day of death would begin. The slumbering swamps awoke from a frozen sleep to burst into life, and as on the previous day, the noise of battle would reign throughout the white wasteland. Like a cloud spewing forth fire and steel, the morning mists would rise and spread their seeds of destruction. For nearly two weeks the specter of death stalked the snow-covered swamps.

Each sunrise brought forth an intense barrage of artillery fire that impacted on the German positions. Mortars, heavy artillery, and antitank guns fired ceaselessly in greeting the day. As the bursting shells slackened in tempo, the landsers would crawl to their positions to meet the earth-brown waves of infantry filtering through the thickets, accompanied by tanks that crushed the slender evergreen branches of pines and alder beneath the wide tracks.

The overwhelming strength of the Soviets enabled them to break through several weakened sectors to penetrate the main battle line. The battle for the supply route burned fiercely. The enemy objective was to penetrate beyond the isolated defenders and strike deep into German-held territory; however, the determination of the German grenadiers, fighting to the last round, was to prevail.

The Russian attack bogged down in the thick underbrush of the swamp. The snow was pockmarked with black-brown craters. Torn branches and stumps hindered any movement. It was impossible to judge where the heavy-infantry support weapons could and would be brought into position. The tangled morass of ice, mud, and dense forests made it impossible to determine where to establish defense positions in preparation for the next attack.

During the night the Soviets again succeeded in breaking through a sector to push through the wilderness as far as the road, only to be finally stopped by a well-concealed Pak battery. The snow was heavily pockmarked with dirty-brown shell craters, the trees in the thick forests broken and stripped of greenery. Downed pines created obstacles across the swampy ground. Where was it possible to bring forward the heavy infantry weapons? From where could a counterattack be launched?

Again enemy armor penetrated our line, attempting to strike the firebase of our supporting artillery. Four of their massive steel vehicles were left burning; the remainder withdrew to the protection of the Soviet line. Following this failed attempt, they no longer limited themselves to traversing the narrow confines of the roadways, choosing to charge through the tangled wilderness rather than risk certain destruction on an obvious route.

Our antitank units responded accordingly. The crews disassembled the antitank guns, transporting them through the swamps on the backs of men and horses to reposition them at likely defense points. Often sinking up to their hips in the icy water and snowdrifts, the infantry plunged into the forests to meet and repel the enemy. Every step required an effort. Every meter of ground drained energy from the landsers. Simple rest became a luxury; sleep was possible only during intermittent lulls between threats of Soviet attack.

Every second day the enemy threw fresh forces into the ring. They appeared as an unending flood. The benumbed grenadiers would stagger to their feet, pull together into hedgehog defenses, and wait until the last second before retaliating with deadly effectiveness. The dirty-gray camouflage suits hung like sodden cardboard on the aching bodies, thawing during the day only to freeze solid again with nightfall. Between firefights the exhausted landsers lay in the snow, with drained, colorless faces and burning eyes pressed into the saturated ground. Dark swamp water soaked through the rotting uniforms and lay icy on the skin. With the moonlight the frost would return. From one day to the next the situation remained the same: no sleep, no bunker or shelter, no luxury of a simple fire to warm frostbitten limbs. Muscles grew stiff and unresponsive. Feet ached in the freezing temperatures; during the pauses between firefights our arms hung weakly at our sides.

Again would come the order that would tear us to our feet. Springing from our holes after hours of crouching together in the snow, we lunged forward through twilight in response to the order to counterattack. Surging ahead, we became possessed with the intent to kill the enemy where he lay, to kill as many of the soldiers wearing the rounded, white-washed helmets as possible, to destroy those forces that threatened hourly to strike and take our own lives. With a counterattack we momentarily gained a new life until our assault, like those of the enemy, would grind to a halt in the depths of the forest. The snow and mud weighed heavy with every step. In the pathless, frozen jungle there were no liberating, sweeping assaults to give one the opportunity to seize the enemy by the throat. We had been thrust into hell, from which there was no escape. To surrender meant immediate death. To survive was simply to delay the inevitable. Our tortured world became surreal and unclear; the encroaching undergrowth, the snowdrifts, and the splintered tree trunks hung silent with the secrets they had witnessed.

Wherever the Bolshevist rage was loosed on the defenders' lines, the attack would grind to a standstill against the nameless ranks of grenadiers. The line continued to hold. The Soviet attacks repeatedly broke upon the drained, frozen, and casualty-decimated ranks of soldiers from East Prussia, Westphalia, Bavaria, and the Rhineland.

As a Soviet attack supported by tanks penetrated a thinly defended wood and ground forward toward battalion headquarters, a Prussian feldwebel attempted to bring an antitank gun into the line but remained hindered by the thick limbs and stumps that prevented him from successfully positioning the weapon. Followed by bursts from a Soviet machine gun, he fought through waist-deep snow to a nearby artillery piece, the crew of which had all become casualties moments earlier. The feldwebel had never before laid hands on this type of weapon, and two grenadiers sprang forward to assist him. Rapidly adjusting for range and windage, he aimed and fired. It must work. And it did work. The first tank rocked to a halt and burst into flames, followed quickly by another, and for the moment the Russian attack faltered.

The Soviet lines now all but surrounded the weakened and exhausted battalion, which extended like an island of resistance deep into the enemy territory. The battalion had successfully repelled the attackers and had succeeded in keeping the supply route clear. Blackened hulks of destroyed enemy tanks along the perimeter bore mute testimony to the heavy fighting that had taken place within the narrow confines of the sector.

During one night an assault team was successful in destroying four Soviet bunkers and an enemy antitank position, but it became cut off and isolated in the ensuing firefight. After nine days and nights behind the enemy lines, with no rest under the unforgiving, freezing sky, two battle-exhausted corporals reached our lines at dawn, carrying a wounded comrade. They had wrapped him in a shelter-quarter, and thrusting a pole through the knotted ends, had carried him between them, moving among the enemy during the hours of darkness, burying themselves in the concealment of snowbanks during the days.

On reaching our lines they collapsed with exhaustion, and it was hours before they regained consciousness. Refusing an offer to be transported to the rear for rest, they then staggered to their feet and set out in the direction of their company. The following night their company assaulted and overran an enemy bunker complex with the two men at their front, destroying the last enemy bastion in the sector.

The weeks of battle in the swamps north of Smerdynia called upon the last reserves of strength and morale. A forest war, time-consuming and slow, brought endless fighting against a vastly superior enemy of unending strength. An attempt to endure against the worst possible conditions of unforgiving nature exacted a heavy toll on the grenadiers, the artillerymen, the engineers, and the Flak crews.

The main battlefront continued to run along a bulge in the line held by the regiment. The Seventh Company was positioned with the left wing extending from north to south within the narrow depression of the Lesna streambed. The fragile line then curved to the right with the front facing to the south, up to the forest's edge. The line then disappeared into the dense forest, running for several hundred meters in a straight line, then curving again to the right, facing the west and southwest. Within this extended salient, about thirty meters behind the line, was the company headquarters, consisting of little more than an entrenched hut covered with earth and snow. An adjustment in the defensive line had been conducted two nights previously, during which the right wing had been withdrawn, shortening the line to lessen the growing threat of being isolated and annihilated. Between the lines was a no-man's-land of dense thickets and evergreens.

On 15 February all was quiet along the line. With the silence a sense of discomfort had descended upon the isolated platoons holding a thin front. Seldom was it possible to hear only the deathly whisper of a winter wind passing through the treetops. Almost always did the front exhibit signs of life, be it from the occasional crack of a sniper's rifle or the methodical pounding of the Maxim positions as they probed our defenses.

The day before, the Soviets had probed the defenses of the salient along the length of the perimeter. Wherever they would appear—one could observe the ghastly silhouettes through the thick forest and deep snow at a distance of less than fifty meters at best—they were either destroyed or repulsed. Despite the apparent absence of the enemy, it was strongly felt that the Soviets were coming.

The salient was reinforced at the expense of the left and right wings. Two heavy machine guns were brought into position and were carefully concealed in the defenses. The sector where the line extended beyond the earthworks to turn sharply to the right was reinforced during the night by felling trees and stacking heavy timbers before the positions. At this location I directed that one heavy machine gun was to be situated at the turn on the line, where it would be afforded the maximum field of fire; and a squad led by an obergefreiter positioned a light machine gun in the sector center.

The grenadiers dug in, two shivering landsers occupying each snow hole, the holes situated ten to fifteen meters apart. The night remained brutally cold following a day of heavy labor in the snow; their feet stiff in their frozen boots, the grenadiers grew numb with cold and exhaustion. Huddled within the damp and freezing confines of the primitive earthworks, the occupants had little or no protection from the cold as it settled into the snow holes to torment them.

Suddenly the heavy MG broke the silence with an earsplitting roar, followed by a scream: "Alarm! Ivan!" The obergefreiter squeezed the trigger of the MG-42, firing quick, short bursts into the twilight, again joined by the heavy MG on the wood's edge. Carbines cracked between

MG bursts. The low drumming of the Soviet Maxim guns responded, joined by the high, shrill blasts of the always-present Russian submachine guns. Rounds whistled through the evergreens, sending branches laden with snow to the earth, and bullets carved long telling trails in the snow piled before the defenders' positions. The feldwebel at the heavy MG lay prone alongside the machine gun with his carbine at his shoulder, rapidly working the bolt and firing one clip after another.

The entire woods swarmed with Bolshevists. We first observed them thirty meters before our position, filtering through the undergrowth, sounds of snapping branches and ice breaking beneath dozens, perhaps hundreds, of heavy Russian boots. The machine guns roared and were joined by submachine guns and carbines, unheard above the pounding automatic weapons and grenade detonations.

The shouts of "Urrah! Urrah!" could be heard during split-second lulls in the roar of gunfire, and after several seconds of firing the shouts turned to screams, as the dead, wounded, and dying collapsed in the snow before our ranks. Bodies clad in earth-brown and white camouflage uniforms lay heaped in front of the machine-gun positions, and more Russians filled the gaps our steaming weapons left in the charging masses. The forest before us had become a concentrated killing ground. There was no need to search out targets as the Soviets threw themselves toward our line. Jumping, dodging, shooting, screaming, they pressed forward. Despite the overwhelming terror that swept over them, the grenadiers remained in their positions, refusing to panic. As if on a training exercise, the landsers controlled and sustained their fire, able to observe the field of fire directly before the line, unconscious of what might have occurred to their right or left. Some of the carbines had fallen silent; the situation became more perilous as the Soviet attack collapsed only six meters before the muzzles of the machine guns.

The forests echoed with the roar of battle for an hour. Seeing no end to the waves of attackers in sight, I desperately ordered our last reserve, a tiny squad of four men, to prepare for action. At that moment I received a plea from the platoon on our left for reinforcements. The line faced imminent collapse although the light machine gun continued to fire incessantly, the long ripping bursts accompanied by the continual detonation of hand grenades hurled forward by the desperate grenadiers.

The dead and wounded filled the forest. Our own losses remained relatively light—two dead and three wounded. Our casualties were light in proportion to the casualties we had inflicted on the enemy but were nevertheless irreplaceable. The firing on our right flank lessened, finally falling silent as the Soviet attack ground to a halt. The defenders, consisting of four or five weary grenadiers, remained on the alert, fingers on the triggers of weapons that slowly cooled in the frosty air.

Suddenly movement was observed in the direction of the Soviet line. An extremely tall Russian rose from the snow-blanketed forest at a distance of thirty meters, shouted unintelligible commands, and motioned with a raised arm to the left. A new wave of attackers swarmed in the direction indicated. The ranks of oncoming Soviets collapsed in the fire of the heavy machine gun, and the figures tumbled to the ground, the tall Russian among them.

The attack was finally broken. The Bolsheviks remained bogged in their tracks and began firing from snow holes, from behind shattered branches and ragged stumps, and from concealed positions within the evergreen forest. Slowly their fire became weaker, leaving the air filled only with the screams of their wounded who cried and thrashed in agony before our line. For more than two hours they had thrust themselves on the fragile position defended by the grenadiers from East Prussia, the Rhineland, Bavaria, the Pfalz, Baden, and Württemberg.

I became aware that the heavy machine gun had fallen silent and that the gunfire from carbines had slowly subsided. At the machine-gun position, the crew lay slumped alongside their gun. The corporal lay as if asleep behind the smoking weapon, the curved butt of the gun still pressed firmly against the shoulder of his battlesmock. His head was slumped forward; the heavy white-washed helmet rested against the smoking feed tray where the belts of brass and copper ammunition fed into the chamber. He had been the last man in his crew.

Slowly the cries of the wounded died to silence, and the stillness was broken only by the muffled sounds of Russians attempting to crawl back to their lines. Snow began to fall, and I was astonished with the realization that it was already past midday. The forest around us had taken on a new appearance during the assault. Entire trees had been downed by small-arms fire. The earth lay torn and pockmarked; branches and limbs hung from ragged stumps. The evergreens in the line of fire had been stripped of foliage and appeared as bare stakes upright in the snow. The only color to appear before our eyes in this frozen wasteland was the scarlet blood, which covered the dead and dying who lay before our guns.

The Soviets began firing mortars, the hollow thump from the tubes echoing through the forest. Their attack had been repulsed only moments before our own forces would have collapsed under the waves of attackers. During the last minutes they would have broken our line but for the fact that their strength was exhausted as well. A distance of approximately eighty meters of our line was held only by thick forests; the sound of carbine fire was no longer heard from its depths. We had repulsed the assault of a Soviet battalion, with few surviving to return to their own lines.

We later risked sniper fire and ventured out a short distance beyond our defenses to survey the carnage, and the grenadiers counted the dead. More than 160 corpses lay before the defenses, most of them in front of the heavy machine gun in the earthworks on the edge of the forest and scattered before the machine gun that had been manned by the senior corporal.

The body of the tall Russian who had led the last, fatal assault was also found lying in the snow. Thrust in his field belt we found a Cossack dagger, apparently carried by the soldier through a number of past battles. The dagger bore a thin layer of rust, and blade and sheath were sticky with a recent coat of blood. Filed into the handle were twelve notches of obvious significance.

"Panzer from right, Panzer from front, Panzer from left!" From all three directions the Soviet armor, mostly T-34s, attempted to smash through the division's defenses. Regardless of how many of the steel giants exploded and burned under the murderous fire from our concealed Pak positions, more always rolled forward to replace them. The front was severed through the thick forests between Klosterdorf and Smerdynia. The sound of battle grew to a crescendo.

A small combat group from Grenadier-Regiment Drexel continued to hold out between the tree stumps, crouching in snow holes and behind hastily constructed log barricades. They were supported by a Pak from the Fourteenth Panzerjaeger Company of Grenadier Regiment 436, commanded by Obergefreiter Kiermeier, one of the old veterans of the regiment.

Through the sound of battle, his experienced senses detected the high pitch of tank rounds coming from the right. From their position they observed only the impenetrable maze of tree stumps, piles of frozen logs, a massed tangle of branches and roots against which any attack would falter. The farmer's son from lower Bavaria continued to wait with the patience of a hunter, staring into the forest with the eyes of a lynx from behind the steel protection shield of the antitank gun. He was joined by the others in the gun crew, and they lay deathly still on the snow, attempting to penetrate the frozen jungle with their eyes.

The location of the oncoming Soviet troops was at last betrayed by the movement of a steel colossus grinding through the trees. Kiermeier motioned the others to hold their fire, allowing the enemy to approach closer as the oncoming waves unknowingly proceeded into the killing zone. Behind the first tank they discerned a second, then a third, a fourth, accompanied by ranks of Russian infantry moving ghostlike through the trees. Kiermeier remained unmoving at his position behind the gun shield, his eye now pressed to the rubber eyepiece of the gunsight. He centered the last tank in the crosshairs and with a strong fist firmly pressed the firing button.

The round exploded from the barrel of the Pak, striking the tank and spraying the interior of the turret with fire and red-hot steel. A thick column of smoke rose from the burning tank as the fuel and ammunition exploded with a roar. The steel carcass effectively blocked the withdrawal route of the foremost tanks as it showered the surrounding forest with splinters and glowing ashes. Kiermeier had already drawn a bead on his next target, and with two more shots the second tank burned brightly. The other tanks opened fire with cannons and machine guns, firing blindly into the thick undergrowth, unable to locate the source of the fire. The third and fourth began to burn and explode. Another round from the hidden Pak destroyed the transmission of the fifth, and the crew abandoned the tank and escaped the small-arms fire to flee to the rear with the retreating infantry. This gun crew later destroyed three more tanks—a total of eight for the day.

When the regimental commander received the report of the destruction of the tanks and the repulse of the enemy attack, he recommended the gun leader be awarded the Knight's Cross of the Iron Cross. Unfortunately, the battle group was authorized only one Knight's Cross to be awarded during this period, and the decoration was awarded to a general serving north of Smerdynia under General Lindemann.

Kiermeier was later awarded the Iron Cross for the destruction of the tanks, which resulted in the attack being repulsed, and Oberstleutnant Drexel offered a promotion to the gun leader. Kiermeier refused the opportunity, fully aware at this point in the war that the chances of survival remained greatest for those who remained with the soldiers whom they had fully trusted and served with throughout the campaign. The promotion would have provided him a more prestigious rank; however, it might have resulted in his removal from the gun crew to serve in another capacity.

On 20 February Infantry Regiments 405 and 408 attacked from the north in an attempt to cut off the enemy penetration on the corduroy road. The attack resulted in heavy fighting with severe losses, and in the evening the regiments succeeded in closing the gap in the line and mopping up the remaining Russian resistance. The roadway was free from point 38.9 to Klosterdorf, but our forces no longer possessed the strength to cut off and destroy any Soviet penetrations. Throughout the ten days of heavy fighting the enemy had suffered such severe losses that an attack northward toward Smerdynia was launched, and this successful offensive enabled us to stabilize the front, permitting the corps to withdraw the badly damaged divisions from the line. On 28 February Group Lindemann, badly battered and weakened by casualties, was temporarily replaced.

We were advised that the infantry regiments were to be changed in name to grenadier regiments. Perhaps the high command desired to demonstrate that through the use of hand grenades in close combat, the title "grenadier" would show recognition for special merit or ability in battle. It remained irrelevant to us if we were to be referred to as grenadiers or infantrymen, as our skill in using the grenades remained unchanged whether we were called grenadiers or not.

Following the desperate battle in which the Soviet thrust to Gaitolovo was repelled, we were relieved from our positions by the Twelfth Luftwaffe Field Division and transferred to a quiet sector of the front. The newly christened grenadiers marched in long columns from the log barricades on the line over the corduroy roads that cut through the swamps toward the rear. It had become necessary to constantly change the location of the rough-hewn roads and trails, as they came under frequent mortar and artillery fire when discovered by the enemy, who lay only a short distance away. The landsers marched in single file, bearing heavy equipment on their shoulders, occasionally assisted by the sturdy Siberian ponies that were always present among our ranks.

The division headquarters was transferred to Poprudka, and the new division sector was concentrated around the area of Moordamm. There we remained undisturbed, recovering from the ordeal of Gaitolovo, until 30 June, when we were again replaced by the 225th Infantry Division. This pause in activity took us to the area of Lyuban-Schapki-Uschaky, where we were able to concentrate on training the replacement personnel. Following the training period, the division was sent back into the line, again to a relatively quiet sector on the northwest front of the Pogostya pocket.

During the rest period of July 1943, the regimental commander, Oberst Kindsmiller, took quarters in a small house with a blue-painted front veranda. Among the tiny, scattered villages of rough-hewn wooden buildings a painted dwelling remained the exception, and the small but attractive forest house became the evening meeting place for the regimental staff.

Oberst Kindsmiller, fifty years old, had received a disabling wound during World War I as a young leutnant that had rendered his left arm stiff at the elbow. As a result of this wound, he normally carried this arm held in a rigid, formal pose behind his back, somewhat reminiscent of paintings of our Prussian ancestor, Frederick the Great.

The commander's birthday was celebrated during one of the midsummer evenings, and the junior officers of the regiment had prepared a surprise for him. We had previously coordinated with the soldiers' radio program Ursula, whose broadcasts were heard every evening in this sector, to wish the oberst a happy birthday and to dedicate a special broadcast to him. As we gathered for the impromptu birthday celebration, the broadcast suddenly announced that "the leutnants from one of our grenadier regiments convey their best wishes to their commander on his birthday, and on this occasion they have requested the following song be played in his honor." With these words came the haunting melody of the popular hit "Der Nacht-Gespenst."

The commander's initial reaction to our selection was to conceal his surprise at this broadcast, and he characteristically attempted to convey the impression that he was less than pleased. Of course he was impressed that we would so honor him with our efforts; however, it was apparent that our selection did not exactly fit his taste. He openly stated that the "Fehrbelliner Reitermarsch" would have been more to his liking. We remained nevertheless flattered by his reaction.

During the following days the enemy activity increased along our sector. Soviet aircraft again became a nuisance, overflying our positions at all hours, dropping loads of bombs and firing on vehicles and troop concentrations with board weapons. With the growing sound of aircraft engines, the landsers instinctively threw themselves into trenches or sought shelter among the trees. Every evening the thunder of artillery would increase noticeably, and the distant crack of detonating shells rolled over the treetops.

One July evening following a briefing at the regimental headquarters, I noticed Oberst Kindsmiller standing alone near the edge of the blue veranda. Gazing into the distance toward the north, from where the nightly artillery barrage was growing in intensity, he concentrated on a row of white flares slowly drifting through the darkening sky on the horizon. Although he used words barely perceptible from where I was standing, I heard him softly say to himself that "the Bohemian corporal" was certain to lose his war.

I did not consider this a denouncement, nor did I consider this to reflect a defeatist attitude from my commander. His words simply confirmed to me what all of us had begun strongly to suspect. The colonel was a fine professional officer and a great soldier. He was, as so many of us at the front had clearly come to recognize, an absolute realist. Four weeks later he was dead.

A rumor reached our position that several members representing a front theater group, on tour for the entertainment of the soldiers, were present at the division headquarters. Among the theater personnel were several women—news that immediately captured our full attention. The commander of Grenadier Regiment 436, Oberst Drexel, had offered to take full responsibility for the safety and protection of the theater members in exchange for a special presentation of their program for his regiment.

The division adjutant, Major I. G. Geyer, was less than enthusiastic about the prospects of permitting the ladies for whom he was responsible out of his sight. Major Geyer was sensitive to the fact that within the immediate vicinity of the division staff were our combat forces, which consisted of three grenadier regiments, an artillery regiment, various support battalions and administrative units, and to the myriad staffs required to administer the duties of an army. Like the good staff officer that he was, Geyer was aware of the problems that could develop with his acceptance of this proposal.

When it became known to the junior officers that the theater group had already exceeded their allotted time with the division and that Oberst Drexel's proposal had thus far been unsuccessful, a plan was formulated and presented to "Uncle" Sepp Drexel to liberate the two ladies from the clutches of the division staff. The assault group set out during the night, properly outfitted with lances and swords, wearing the customary beards and period costume to fit the occasion. At the forefront marched Uncle Sepp, closely followed by a raucous band of landsknechte who stormed forward like the wild army of Wotan and Florian Geyer, fully prepared to rescue the damsels at any cost. The band swept into the enemy lair, unrolled a parchment that proclaimed the official liberation of the maidens, and to the accompaniment of cheers and the swinging of broadswords, escorted the ladies through the forest darkness to the safety of our own camp. The liberation of the damsels brought us a night of socializing accompanied by some drinking and song, and thereafter the ladies were returned to the confines of the division.

The quiet sector of the front was soon to take on a different character. On the morning of 22 July our line came under heavy artillery fire in the area two-and-one-half kilometers southwest and three-and-one-half kilometers northwest of the Pogostya railway station. After an extended bombardment from "Stalin's organs" and mortar fire, the enemy struck with full force upon the section held by the Third Battalion, Grenadier Regiment 437.

According to prisoner interrogations obtained following the assault, the enemy had planned to coordinate this attack with a major assault on the north front to encircle our forces. This was to be accomplished by conducting a pincer movement from the east, which would then swing south to sever the extended salient in which our main battle line was located. This area was officially referred to by the German staff as the Sappenkopf.

Despite the heavy fire of our own artillery directed onto the assault line, the enemy was able to achieve a breakthrough two hundred fifty meters wide and three to four hundred meters deep to the west of the Pogostya railway station by 1215. This breakthrough, accomplished by overwhelming numerical forces, had been concentrated on the positions held by the Tenth Company, Grenadier Regiment 437. The attack remained unsuccessful against positions held by the two other companies in this sector. Through the use of our reserve, it was possible to push the

Soviet forces out of the left flank of the pocket and to restore this area of the main battle line by 1535, during which time the enemy was forced to abandon numerous dead and wounded on the battlefield.

Simultaneously, the Third Company, Grenadier Regiment 437, was successful in counterattacking along the right flank. Despite heavy enemy artillery that attempted to block the area to the south of the Soviet penetration, the remaining enemy forces were either forced to withdraw or were isolated and annihilated.

The enemy regrouped. During the lull in which he was preparing another assault, the landsers hastily evacuated their wounded. Cases of hand grenades were brought forward on pony carts for distribution. Machine gunners replenished gleaming belts of ammunition and cleared their weapons of sand and grit. Someone appeared with a container of cold coffee and a large canvas bag full of black bread, which was hungrily devoured while the forces were on the move. Medical personnel bandaged the lightly wounded, who then shouldered their weapons and returned to their platoons.

Incoming mortar rounds announced an end to the temporary pause on the killing ground. The Soviets then launched another stubborn attack against both flanks of the Sappenkopf area, again targeting the Pogostya station, and after one-and-one-half hours of fierce fighting succeeded in breaking through the Sappenkopf position at 1800.

Again, our weakening reserve units were pushed into a counterattack and were successful in severing the enemy lines for the second time within several hours. Despite concentrated artillery and barrages from "Stalin's organs," the Third Company, Grenadier Regiment 437, cleared the enemy from our lines to a distance two kilometers west of the Pogostya station by 2045. With this successful counterattack, a major thrust from the enemy was spoiled. The enemy plan was revealed and confirmed by interrogations of captured enemy personnel as well as through the numerous maps and supporting documents found on the battlefield.

The enemy had suffered relatively heavy losses, and the regimental situation report contained the list of enemy casualties—20 prisoners taken (2 officers), 69 confirmed enemy dead in the main battle line (15 officers), 100 confirmed enemy dead in front of the main battle line, 270 estimated enemy dead in front of the main battle line—and captured material—5 heavy machine guns, 12 light machine guns, 2 pistols, 6 rifles, 63 submachine guns, 2 antitank launchers, and 3 field telephones.

After repelling the last assault before darkness enveloped the combatants, the front fell silent. During the night the customary distant voices could be heard from the Soviet lines as we prepared for the ordeal that we were to sure to face with the dawn. As the sun rose over the treetops, the front remained suspiciously quiet; no enemy movement was reported. To our relief, we experienced no further enemy activity prior to being replaced on the line by the 121st Infantry Division.

Enemy propaganda leaflets were dropped from a Soviet fog-crow over Infantry Regiment 437 on 30 July 1943:

For us the war is now over!

COMRADES!

We—Feldwebel Ludwig Herbert, Obergefreiter Karl Beer, Gefreiter Gustav Goltze, Soldat Eugen Gieser, Soldat August Bartehl, Soldat Emil Kuhlen—from the 10th Company, I.R. 437 were taken prisoner during the 22 July 1943 Russian attack. We were correctly handled by the officers and soldiers of the Red Army. The wounded received immediate medical attention. The Russian soldiers even shared their cigarettes with us.

For us the war is now over. We need no longer fear the Russian artillery.

We know now that all that we were told by the battalion commander, Major Schmidt; the company commander of the 9th Company, Hauptmann Lindner; the company commander of the 10th Company, Leutnant Mika; Feldwebels Bienow and Einlehner about the atrocities and mistreatment we would experience should we fall into Russian hands were all lies. These ridiculous statements have been proven false by the excellent treatment we have received since becoming prisoners of the Soviet Union.

Please greet our relatives and friends.

(Signed) Feldwebel Ludwig Herbert
Obergefreiter Karl Beer
Gefreiter Gustav Goltze
Soldat Eugen Gieser
Soldat August Bartehl
Soldat Emil Kuhlen

A—100.24.7.43 30 000

In late July 1943, I was commanding the assault reserve of the regiment in the Maluksa position. One afternoon I was requested to report to the command post, where it was explained to me that a soldier condemned to death was to be executed by firing squad. Having received the appalling assignment to carry out the execution, I requested from the battalion adjutant the details regarding the case. If I was to be responsible for the death of one of our own, to ease my own conscience I desired to know why such a severe penalty had been imposed on the soldier.

It was explained to me that a member of the Fifth Company had observed a soldier steal a package from the postal transport en route to the platoon, from which he removed cigarettes and food for his own use. It was widely known throughout our ranks that a theft of this nature constituted a serious crime in the German army for which a severe punishment could be imposed.

Later, while standing alone on sentry duty with the perpetrator, the soldier who had witnessed the theft informed the culprit that he had seen the incident and that he should immediately return the stolen goods or that all details of the theft would be reported. The thief, obviously fearing the repercussions of his crime should it be made known, quickly sprang to the machine gun, pivoted the gun on its lafette, and shot the witness with a full burst from the automatic weapon at close range. He then tossed several hand grenades, which were always primed and within an arm's reach of the machine gun, and feigned an engagement of Russian reconnaissance troops before the position.

The wounded soldier did not die immediately but was taken to the medical station with severe chest and abdominal wounds, which shortly proved to be fatal. He temporarily regained consciousness, however, and was able to report the incident to the medical officer. The murderer was arrested, and a summary court-martial was convened. Subsequently, the perpetrator was sentenced to die by firing squad. There was no shortage of volunteers to serve for this purpose, and a platoon from the victim's company provided the necessary number of riflemen to carry out the sentence.

The following morning I began making the meticulous preparations for the execution. From the regimental headquarters I received the precise, official details of how it was to be conducted. Army regulations required that a two-meter stake be anchored vertically in the ground, supported from the rear. If possible, a retaining wall was to be located a short distance behind the stake for the purpose of stopping the bullets. Not far from the regimental headquarters I constructed a small, sandy berm, against which a low retaining wall was built.

The firing squad quietly assembled, accompanied by a feldwebel with a Luger pistol in his right hand. In the event the condemned did not die immediately, he would be required to fire the killing shot. As prescribed in the regulations, a medical officer was present. I quietly briefed the firing squad on how the procedure was to be conducted. As I spoke I scanned the faces of the soldiers who were to squeeze the triggers for any sign of nervousness or hesitation. The soldiers followed my orders and stood silently in ranks at their prescribed location, rifles at rest.

The execution was ordered to be carried through at exactly 1500. Several minutes prior to the time specified, the regimental legal officer arrived with a number of field police. Stumbling unsteadily among them was the condemned, who, with an ashen face, was still clad in our field-gray uniform, stripped of rank and all insignia.

Without hesitation several of the field police escorted the condemned forward, where he was quickly bound to the stake with his hands tied behind his back at the wrists. Wordlessly, a blindfold was placed over his eyes and tied securely behind his head. The escort then distanced themselves from the condemned, and the division chaplain stepped forward and spoke softly to him.

The silence lay heavy in the air. The condemned appeared to strain against the cords binding him to the stake; his head dropped upon his breast as the chaplain whispered words unheard by the firing squad. From several kilometers' distance on the front, the customary shell bursts and isolated rifle shots floated softly over the open ground to reach our ears. Despite the unquestionable guilt of the condemned, and the necessity of carrying through our assignment, emotions remained mixed when we were faced with the unthinkable task of shooting one of our own, of firing on the uniform worn so long by all present.

Thoughts raced through my mind. I was fully aware that in another place and another time this man would most likely have lived a full and productive life, and that his life had been stolen from him, like millions of others, by the folly and temerity of those beyond our power. My thoughts went to his family, his mother, father, siblings. I asked myself if they would ever learn the true fate of their loved one, of how he met his end in Russia. The laws of the front were harsh and unforgiving, and in this case the sentence could only be considered as just.

The execution squad remained in position opposite the bound soldier. I glanced about at those present, and I observed that all witnesses and participants had fixed their eyes upon the man to die. The firing squad exhibited grim, tired faces, void of emotion. The legal officer and the medical officer stood a short distance away, well beyond the line of fire, hands clasped behind their backs, faces expressionless. Only the feldwebel, with pistol in hand, looked at me expectantly.

I found myself looking at my watch. At exactly 1500, as if on the parade field, the commands came from my throat: "Zur Salve—hoch—legt an—gebt Feuer!"

With a roar the rifle bullets tore through the breast of the condemned; he rocked back against the stake, blood erupting from the wounds. He collapsed against the cords as all strength and consciousness left his body, and hung silently against the stake for several seconds. The medical officer strode forward to examine the still form. Despite the severity of the wounds, he detected a pulse and looked first at me, then shifted his glance to the feldwebel to motion him forward.

The feldwebel stepped forward, raised his arm, and fired point-blank into the head of the condemned, just behind the ear. Again the medical officer approached, examined the now-lifeless form, and called to the police escort. Two men loosened the form from the stake. Others then stepped forward, and the body was laid in a wooden box. Without another word, they disappeared in a cloud of dust as they drove away.

Having put that unforgettable experience into words, I must also state that this incident was the only such case that I experienced throughout the years on the Eastern Front. Never again was I even remotely aware of another incident of theft among the landsers.

In August 1943, our division relieved the 121st Infantry Division, which had suffered heavily during the fighting on the Neva along a ten-kilometer front. Since 2 August Grenadier Regiment 436 had come under command of the Fifth Mountain Division, which had experienced numerous assaults by an enemy heavily reinforced with armor and had suffered high casualties.

The days prior to the 132d Division's arrival on the line had remained relatively quiet; however, on 11 August the enemy launched a major attack. Attacking in regimental strength against the Poretschay bridgehead, the Soviets succeeded in breaking through the thinly held line but were later repulsed with heavy losses following our counterattack. A second assault launched in the evening was again beaten back with support from our heavy artillery. During the night the troops prepared for follow-on fighting. While attempting to resupply the exhausted units, the landsers came under constant bombing attacks as Soviet aircraft overflew the lines. Although the Ratas were lost to sight in the darkness, their droning would grow rapidly in intensity; then they would bank and sweep over the positions, dropping loads of bombs and tearing the earth with bursts from their machine guns.

On 12 August at exactly 0900, the enemy launched an attack along the entire front in full strength. It consisted of numerous waves of brown-clad infantrymen heavily supported by artillery fire, tanks, and overwhelming airpower.

These attacks in company, battalion, and regimental strength, which lasted an entire day, were beaten back either in brutal hand-to-hand fighting or with a combination of all available resources. Isolated penetrations were countered with assembled reserves. In the sector held by Grenadier Regiment 437, however, the enemy was successful in penetrating the forefront of the bridgehead and was able to enlarge the penetration to the south for a total of three hundred meters. The counterattack by the reserves remained mired and ineffective in the face of massive fire support from enemy artillery and advancing tanks.

During the night, nineteen enemy tanks were destroyed in close combat. Feldwebel Rein of the Seventh Company, Grenadier Regiment 436, distinguished himself by personally destroying two of the enemy tanks, then assumed leadership of the company after the commander was severely wounded. Leading the company against an overwhelming enemy, he beat back the Soviet attempts to sever the line and split the seam between the two regiment's sectors. His bravery and skill proved to be invaluable in preventing the regiments from being cut off and possibly annihilated.

On 13 August at 0430 the Russians again struck the line and, following an initial success in pushing back the German defenders, were unable to further penetrate the line held by the surviving landsers. At 0600 we counterattacked against overwhelmingly superior enemy forces supported by heavy artillery blocking fire but were able to make little progress in restoring the line to our old positions. As our own attack ground to a halt, the enemy again struck with renewed strength, penetrating the defenses with concentrated armor under heavy-artillery support. As the battle pivoted back and forth through the shattered forests and swamps, the Soviets were able to break through to the south and occupy the area northeast of Poretschay.

Again our regiment was thrown into the attack. In vicious fighting that lasted throughout the day, we finally succeeded in bringing the Soviet advance to a halt at 1700, and recaptured the Poretschay sector. After suffering numerous casualties, the Russians were stopped along the ridge marked as 54.1, approximately two hundred meters south of Barskoya Lake. This effort required the use of the last reserves of men and material and was successful only after heavy fighting throughout the afternoon.

The following day the II Battalion, First Grenadier Regiment, Reconnaissance Battalion 132, Pionier Battalion 132, and parts of the III Battalion, Grenadier Regiment 437, were pulled out of the line. Immediately reorganized into Group Schmidt, they were thrust back into action to recapture the sections of the main battle line along an area referred to in the reports as the Sandkaule. Despite heavy blocking fire from Soviet batteries, the attack won ground, and the units assigned to the left and right wings soon reached their objectives. The Russians counterattacked with massive air strikes, supported by artillery bombardments and concentrated armored units. Despite its initial successes, it was deemed necessary to withdraw Group Schmidt in the face of overwhelming opposition, leaving the Sandkaule heights to the enemy.

In the afternoon the enemy responded to the withdrawal of Group Schmidt with another assault. Despite the constant action experienced by the group throughout the day, they were successful in repelling the enemy strike and were able to push the Soviet forces back. During the fighting the group remained under almost constant attack from enemy fighter-bombers that dropped antipersonnel bombs and fired into the attacking landsers with board weapons. The evening saw the main battle line still in our hands, although the Soviet forces had paid heavily in their attempts to break through and encircle our beleaguered units.

The enemy used the night to reassemble his forces. Sounds of activity reverberated through the forests as the whine of Ford engines, accompanied by the rumble of T-34 tanks, was heard moving forward through the Soviet positions. The landsers resupplied their ammunition, bandaged the wounded, sent the severely wounded to the rear, and waited expectantly for what they instinctively sensed the following day would bring.

In the early morning hours silence fell on the vast expanse of forest. Exhausted soldiers lay behind makeshift barricades or crouched in hastily dug foxholes and attempted to sleep. In the gray light of dawn the snipers crawled forward and searched the ghastly landscape through rifle scopes for any hint of movement. With trained eyes pressed to the rubber ring shielding their optics, they slowly swept their field of fire from left to right, right to left, methodically following a mental grid, leaving no twig, no splintered tree, no parcel of torn earth unseen before them. On this morning the snipers' rifles remained silent, no enemy reconnaissance troops ventured forth, no sentries were placed. No Soviet snipers came forward to oppose ours in deadly duels. For the troops waiting behind the barricades, the silence that had descended upon the line remained a mixed, possibly ominous signal. The Russians were not digging in.

The sun had climbed above the treetops when, at 0900, the aircraft swept down on our positions. Bombs burst among the hidden ranks of defenders, followed by the sharp crack of mortar rounds exploding on preset targets. The landsers wormed their way deeper into the protection of the barricades, pressed themselves against the earth, and waited for the barrage to lift. After long minutes the explosions subsided, and the attack was launched. The gray-green figures sprang from the recesses of their foxholes, grasped machine guns and carbines, prepared the priming cords and stacked their supplies of hand grenades, and met the assault.

With massed waves of infantry the Soviets broke through the thinly held line in two sectors. Attempting a giant pincer movement, they thrust forward toward Schlossberg, Baracken, and the Jewish Cemetery. Despite the artillery barrages and fighter-bomber attacks, the landsers were successful in halting the advance.

The Second Company, Grenadier Regiment 437, distinguished itself in repelling this enemy assault, which had penetrated into the Nasiya sector to the west of Geisterwaldchen and was attempting to strike to the south. Nevertheless, we saw that it was now necessary to withdraw our forces from the Sandkaule heights. During the night of 14–15 August the landsers were withdrawn and hastily used to augment the field-replacement battalion. With this move it became apparent that the Poretschay bridgehead was to be evacuated to avoid encirclement of the forces still holding their positions on the line. During the night of 15–16 August the withdrawal was put into motion, and the positions were abandoned, save a one hundred-meter-wide section east of the Nasiya. The evacuation was completed by 0230.

With this withdrawal to terrain that offered better defenses, the threat of breakthrough was temporarily halted, despite our having surrendered ground. The main battle line remained unbroken throughout the sector held by the division, and the numerous attempts by the Soviets to penetrate the defenses ground to a halt.

In preparation for withdrawing the 132d Infantry Division from the line, the First Infantry Division relieved the badly mauled Grenadier Regiment 437 in the early morning hours of 16 August. The 132d Infantry Division began withdrawing from the positions that evening, having been officially relieved on the line by the 254th Infantry Division. Reduced by casualties and exhausted to the point of incoherence, the grenadiers had successfully defended the line through almost seven days and nights of uninterrupted combat against overwhelming odds. With this final withdrawal, the participation of the 132d Infantry Division in the Poretschay bridgehead drew to a close.

During the course of this battle, the enemy had thrust these divisions and armored units into the battle: 364th Rifle Division, with parts of three regiments; 374th Rifle Division, with two regiments; 165th Rifle Division, with two regiments; 378th Rifle Division, with two regiments; 311th Rifle Division, with one regiment; 256th Rifle Division, with one regiment; 503d Armored Battalion, with fourteen tanks; 35th Armored Regiment, with fifteen tanks; 50th Armored Regiment, with fifteen tanks; 77th Independent Engineer Battalion.

Twelve to fourteen enemy battalions were reported as decimated. Twenty-four tanks were destroyed, ten of which were knocked out in close combat with light weapons. The Russians had suffered extremely high casualties during the intensive Soviet attempts to break the defense line. With the withdrawal of our division, the battle south of Lake Ladoga came to an end.

At 0800, 18 August, General Lindemann turned over command of the 132d Infantry Division to his replacement, Generalmajor Wagner. Simultaneously, the sector held by that division was officially turned over to the 254th Infantry Division. General Lindemann wrote a letter of departure to his division:

132nd Inf. Division   Division Headquarters
Commanding General   18 August, 1943

Soldiers of the 132nd Infantry Division!

Called to other duties and responsibilities, I have today relinquished command of the division, which I have had the honor to lead since 5 January

1942. I reflect back upon this period of time with immense pride and satisfaction. In every battle, in each engagement, we remained victorious. In attack we defeated the enemy forces, often to their total destruction. In defense we remained the lords of the battlefield, never having once lost an artillery piece to the enemy. Welded together into six battalions following the battle for Sevastopol, the division struck the enemy again in January 1942, and fighting through ice and snow, through mud and rain, defeated the enemy during the winter battle of Feodosia and pushed them to the sea. After many victories during the defensive battles from February to April, 1942, in the area of Daln-Kamyschi, the division broke through the line on the Parpatsch position on 8 May and thrust rapidly ahead from Kamysch-Burun to the harbor of Kertsch, where we witnessed the last enemy transports fleeing before us.

On 7 June, 1942 the division was transferred to the north front of Sevastopol to assault the Oelberg. The Neuhaus heights were taken while fighting fiercely under the most adverse of conditions. With the assault on the "Bastion," the armored battery "Maxim Gorki," considered the most modern and strongly defended battery that existed at that time, and the capture of Fort Schischkova, the entire northern fortress system fell to our forces. After our push through to the "battery-tongue" on the north edge of the harbor, the division struck toward the west over the Tschernaya and on 1 July captured the city with an unparalleled and daring sweep from the south. With this success the special report was issued announcing the fall of the mighty fortress.

The division was then transferred to northern Russia, where the brave regiments immediately engaged seven Soviet divisions in brutal combat throughout September 1942 in the swamps and forests of the Gaitolovo pocket. During this phase of bloody fighting all breakthrough attempts by the Soviets were successfully repelled.

In the defensive battle of Smerdynia in February 1943, an overwhelming force of five Russian divisions, two armored brigades, and two rifle brigades collapsed against the iron defenses of the division. The enemy losses exceeded seventy-five tanks due to the steadfast defense exhibited by the brave men of the division while facing an overwhelming enemy.

During the last days of my command, the division successfully repelled all attempts by the enemy to break the main defense line during the 3rd battle south of Lake Ladoga.

Despite the heavy artillery and mortar bombardments, despite the endless attacks by enemy aircraft which occurred day and night, the brave men of all the division's units successfully repelled every enemy attack, inflicting grave losses upon an overwhelming enemy force. Whenever called upon, the junior officers and non-commissioned officers successfully met every challenge, repelling and often totally destroying the enemy forces opposing them.

The iron curtain of protection provided by our artillery units never failed us in the heat of battle, and through their skill and professional abilities they were able to repel the most aggressive foe, to include armored units. The enemy forces were often demoralized or destroyed by our artillery prior to coming within range of our infantry weapons, thus sparing our infantry numerous casualties that otherwise would have been inflicted without this support.

Our anti-tank units, through skillful use of various weapons, were successful in the destruction of twenty-four enemy tanks, of which seven fell to the infantry in close combat. This feat deserves my special recognition! Also in these instances the victory in defense lay with us.

Soldiers! On the march through the waterless steppes of southern Russia, during the fighting in the ice-covered or burning heights of Sevastopol, or upon the plains of the Kertsch Peninsula, in the mud and swamps of Gaitolovo, through the hip-deep snow of Smerdynia and in the pock-marked terrain south of Lake Ladoga and the Nasiya, you have accomplished the seemingly impossible.

My unending gratitude and my special recognition goes out to my exemplary commanders, whose names shall be eternally recognized in the history of the division, as well as to the officers and non-commissioned officers, the independent fighters who held steadfast against all odds, and whose countless deeds often remained unwitnessed and unspoken, but were of decisive importance to our survival and to our subsequent victories.

I thank all branches of service for your endurance and your selfless comradeship. I now take leave of a division that has been welded together through the heat of battle experienced in the expanses of Russia, and my thoughts remain with our 4,520 dead, who sleep their eternal rest on the banks of the Dnieper, on the battlefields of the Crimea, and in the contested forests to the south of Lake Ladoga.

I know that the closing words I once issued with my very first daily order as new division commander, "trust for the trustworthy," have been echoed many times. I depart from my old division with the unbreakable bonds of comradeship and unity of spirit. I wish the division, and each and every member, the very best soldiers' luck, and I close with the recognition:

The 132nd Infantry Division—Hurrah!
　　All for Germany!
　　(Signed) Lindemann
　　Generalleutnant and Division Commander

CHAPTER EIGHT

Dyatly

Screams of the enemy

wounded broke forth, and I rolled into the trench, falling

directly on a wounded Russian. . . .

August 1943. Nasiya-Grund, Sandkaule, Jewish Cemetery, Geisterwald, Poretschay, Voronovo—those are the names of insignificant battlefields that remained burned into the memories of those who survived. Sweeping back and forth, the deadly contests raged for days, weeks, and months throughout the forests and swamps near Leningrad. This was a killing ground where many thousands of men and machines were pitted against one another, the soldiers killed without remorse or mercy over hotly contested, jagged terrain. Small road crossings were defended to the last bullet; a small rise in the swampy terrain would suddenly gain importance and become a citadel where the combatants fought bitterly to the end. In this tangled jungle uncounted brave souls died and were lost forever in unmarked graves.

At one time there was a dense, green forest with thick undergrowth and majestic pines. The air was filled with the singing of birds from the lush undergrowth and from high in the tops of the stands of birch and alder trees. Then came the armies. The earth was torn and overturned by an endless hail of bombs and artillery shells. The fresh green of the forest no longer dared show itself, lest it be destroyed again. Nature turned its face in anguish from the scene of grenade and bomb craters; of thick tree trunks splintered from machine-gun bursts; of expanses of woods set alight by tracer bullets, leaving only blackened posts through which men dashed headlong into battle, straining beneath loads of war material—carbines and submachine guns, linen sacks filled with the deadly weight of hand grenades, steel gray-green canisters of belted machine-gun ammunition, antitank weapons, and mines. In desperation they dodged the shell bursts and sought the very shelter they had stripped from the earth. Ragged limbs of dying trees pointed agonizingly toward the heavens, void of all growth and life in this man-made hell. Through skies clouded with the smoke and dust of battle, the sun appeared only as an orange glow as it tried to penetrate air choked with debris.

There was once a stream, crystal clear, winding its way through this land to join the river Volchov, eventually meeting Lake Ladoga. In previous years the intelligentsia and wealthy visitors from Petersburg would come to enjoy the lush forest canopies, to escape the heat and oppression of August in the city. Now the Nasiya's land was crushed and torn, the once clear-running stream choked and muddy, tormented and poisoned by the dead lying thick in the forests—the ugly debris of war. The green meadows fed by clear water were now muddy swamps, churned and spoiled by the evil that had befallen this place. The crisp air was heavy and putrid with the stench of dead soldiers and horses, grotesquely swollen in the summer heat.

There was once a village, marked by picturesque wooden cottages and houses with slate roofs sporting a layer of soft moss. The windows were framed with carefully fitted shutters and windowpanes, finely carved with stylized Russian ornamentation cut long ago. The houses typically had sported a covered entrance lined with benches. Here would sit Gregor and Ivan with Dunya and Tamara in the evenings, smoking Papyrossi and gazing at the evening sky, the same sky described so well by Nikolai Gogol in *Dead Souls*.

Then came the soldiers. First the dwelling was destroyed, with only an ugly black mound remaining, the chimney rising awkwardly and painfully from the ashes. An explosive projectile fired from a distant Russian gun soon brought the chimney and oven crashing to earth, adding the rubble of burnt brick and mortar to the blackened ruins.

The ruins were then occupied by a half-dozen landsers. They hastily removed the entrenching tools from their belts and hacked at the earth, burrowing deep beneath the blackened timbers and ashes. They then stacked the bricks from the destroyed chimney and carried bits of shattered tree trunks to reinforce their position. With the skill and expertise learned from many previous battles, they constructed their fortress facing the east and created gun positions from the ruins. When their afternoon of labor met their satisfaction, they carefully positioned their machine gun and readied hand grenades by removing the safety cap from the base of the wooden handles, then stacked them in a neat pyramid nearby. They opened cases of ammunition, inspected and loaded flare pistols. They then waited for the darkness, when they would face the next attack.

During the night the darkness was suddenly shattered by explosions. Muzzle flashes illuminated the positions of ghostlike figures moving rapidly through the wooded glade. The landsers grasped hand grenades and crouched behind their machine gun with hearts pounding and terror gripping their limbs. Suddenly Russian submachine-gun bullets snapped and whistled over their helmets. In one motion the machine-gun crew pulled the primer cords from their grenades, lobbed them into the darkness, and waited expectantly. The blasts of the grenades swept over the tiny cluster of figures, accompanied by the screaming of a wounded Russian. Grasping the machine gun, the crew leader fired a ripping burst into the darkness. The others joined in with carbines and submachine guns. The screams grew faint, and the terrifying sound of bodies crashing through the undergrowth was heard as the enemy patrol retreated.

In the ghostly light of magnesium flares the silhouettes of the attackers faded into darkness; the probe was momentarily repulsed. The grenadiers crouched in their holes and prepared for the next onslaught, and over the broken terrain drifted the unmistakable, throbbing sound of engines. Tanks were coming. The German artillery batteries began firing salvos over the ruins into the enemy positions; the explosions of heavy-caliber shells drowned the whine of engines and the grinding of the heavy steel tracks. The Russian armor slowed, then hesitated and waited.

With dawn came a barrage crashing from the barrels of more than one thousand enemy guns. The Russians commanded the skies, and Soviet aircraft dropped antipersonnel bombs and strafed the German positions with machine guns and cannon. The landsers pressed themselves tightly against the earth. Huge chunks of brick and stone flew through the air; the dirt walls of the positions collapsed on the heavy field-gray helmets of the grenadiers. The earth shook and trembled in agony. A soldier pulled his helmet over his face in a vain attempt to end the nightmare—to hear nothing, see nothing, feel nothing.

At this moment gun-loader Gregor Bogatkin of the Soviet Baltic Front slammed another 152mm projectile into the already hot breech of his howitzer. The attack was launched by the 364th Guards Division and Thirty-fifth Armored Regiment. The projectile screamed through the air, slammed into the earth and exploded, burying four cowering soldiers in field-gray beneath earth and debris. Only a crater remained where the four had crouched in their position. From the earth protruded a single hand, half-opened, gold wedding ring gleaming lightly.

As the barrage of artillery fire and salvos of rockets crept forward, the two remaining survivors of the six-man crew who had burrowed deep into the ruins caught their breath and began to move. They found themselves lying on their MG, half buried in sand and stones. Their tiny earthwork had collapsed beneath the pounding barrage. Through the forest they clearly detected the ominous, familiar sound of rumbling engines. The Russians were coming, with tanks, T-34s, accompanied by infantry.

The dim silhouettes broke forth into the clearing from the forest's edge. The two attempted to fire their MG, the same weapon that had so faithfully protected them in battles past. Instead of the rapid, ripping burst so characteristic of the German automatic weapons, only one isolated shot left the barrel—then silence—a jammed feed tray. The sensitive feeding mechanism was choked with sand from the shell bursts. The gun leader spun the gun about, and both men frantically attempted to work the bolt free. Bracing their weight against the weapon, they desperately attempted to clear the chamber and force the charging handle to the rear with their heavy infantry boots. The mechanism remained frozen in place.

The clatter of the tracks grew louder as the enemy neared; the "Urrah!" of the attacking infantry approached ever closer. One of the landsers sprang to his feet and dashed toward the other position to locate another weapon, but there he found only an empty crater, at the edge of which a lone hand was projecting from the earth. At this moment Gunner Sergeant Ivan Tschernikov, in the lead tank of the Thirty-fifth Soviet Mechanized Brigade, squeezed the trigger of his 76mm cannon. The shell ripped through both of the German's legs below the knees. With a scream the grenadier slammed to the earth and cried for help. No one heard the screams, and he crawled toward the rear, dragging the stumps of his legs behind him.

The tank reached the now defenseless position. Two stick grenades exploded harmlessly beneath the heavy tracks. The tank rolled over the MG nest, paused, and with rumbling engines it turned on its tracks, crushing the hole, burying from sight all traces of the desperately defended position.

The T-34 rocked forward and pushed on through the German line until it, too, met its destiny. An 88mm projectile from a hidden Tiger lying in wait beneath heavy branches and foliage ripped through the turret of the Russian tank, tearing it from the chassis, and the massive vehicle began to burn. The forest reverberated with the angry sound of small-arms fire, which slowly subsided. Another attack had been stopped.

The First Battalion was no longer reporting. Shells rained on the headquarters and buried the battalion commander, Hauptmann Gusel and the adjutant, Leutnant Vogel, together with their staff. The communications equipment was smashed; the radiomen were dead. Scores of wounded staggered or crawled toward the rear or were carried in shelter-quarters by landsers stumbling through a hail of artillery and katyusha fire toward the regimental aid station.

Hurriedly I briefed the small remaining group of landsers and prepared to launch a counterattack with the regimental reserve, which now consisted solely of a combined infantry-pioneer platoon. Moving rapidly through the deafening din of battle, we dashed from shell crater to shell crater, battling with submachine guns and hand grenades until we reached the Sandkaule. There we took a number of benumbed Russians prisoner, many of whom were wounded and unable to retreat.

The night brought no rest. Flares sizzled across the sky and illuminated the tortured land in a silver light, showing the way for the Russian bombers to bring their loads of death. The Jewish Cemetery was defended by a small group of landsers led by Hauptmann Scheckenbach, and Russian assault troops infiltrated behind them. During the night our couriers and ammunition supply-carriers received sporadic fire from the darkness.

I selected two groups of the old hares to take with me, names I had come to know well, men whom I knew would never falter: Kammermaier, Herfellner, Obermeier, Juckel, Macklsdorfer, Mackinger, Feuerstein, Wagner, Ganser, Martin, Holzmann, Kurz, Doser, Hack, Hipp, and others. We quickly prepared ourselves for action, stuffing our boots and belts with hand grenades and spare submachine-gun magazines. Three light machine guns were slung from the hip. Several canteens were passed through the tiny group at the last moment in a vain attempt to quench a nervous thirst.

We plunged into the darkness and across a crater-strewn field, leaping from cover to cover, shooting into the trenches and holes, screaming and flinging hand grenades to our front, to the left and right. Furtive shadows in khaki-brown darted before us, figures in olive-colored round helmets with the small packs on their backs characteristic of the Soviet soldier. They scattered into the darkness like rabbits in the night, and we took seven prisoners.

The supply column followed our trail and located us at the Jewish Cemetery. There we eagerly broke into the containers of food and ammunition, wordlessly devouring the meager rations of cold wurst and bread.

The battle raged for seven days and nights. The regiments of the antagonists, bloodied and weary, refused to withdraw or stop to rest. To withdraw meant defeat. To halt for rest meant death. For the survivors of this hell, these swamps and forests, these jagged stumps and tortured earth would remain as burning memories of the battle from which many would escape only through death.

At long last, on 16 August the bulk of the division was withdrawn from the battle line south of Lake Ladoga due to heavy losses. Regiment 437 remained on the line, and on 17 August Oberst Graf Schwerin von Krosigk assumed command of the First East Prussian Infantry Division while it still occupied the forward positions.

During the night Oberst Kindsmiller of my regiment proceeded forward to the Eleventh Company's headquarters. The unit was still clinging tenaciously to its positions in the Jewish Cemetery. For seven long days of fierce fighting, and under direct fire from armored vehicles, barrages of artillery shells, and tons of bombs dropped from endless waves of aircraft, Hauptmann Scheckenbach, nicknamed "Stubborn Ferdinand," had refused to yield to the overwhelming attackers on the Jewish Cemetery heights. Following a Soviet breakthrough in a left sector, his position became a strongpoint and was responsible for breaking waves of attacks, thus preventing a collapse of the entire left wing. Although Soviet infantry managed to infiltrate behind the position and entrench themselves firmly among the artillery and bomb craters, the Eleventh Company continued to hold.

During the night Hauptmann Scheckenbach summoned his runners. Gefreiter Fleck, the nineteen-year old courier of the Second platoon, crawled and raced through the torn landscape from his platoon position toward the company headquarters. Although the landscape had shifted and changed appearance constantly under incessant barrages, he instinctively found his way through the darkness. Throwing himself prone on the earth and lying motionless when sizzling flares would light up the sky, Fleck eventually arrived at the headquarters, gasping for breath and soaked with sweat. Slung over his shoulders and around his neck he carried four Russian submachine guns he had gathered from enemy dead strewn across the moonscape terrain as he had made his way across the contested ground. These weapons were particularly valued as trade items with rear-echelon logistics-and-supply personnel, and an experienced landser was never one to pass up such an opportunity.

"Our only supply line has been cut by a Russian penetration," explained Stubborn Ferdinand. The five couriers were given their assignment: get through the Soviet lines and return with enough food for two days.

During this time Oberst Kindsmiller had completed his briefing, and the five couriers were assigned to escort him back with them to regimental headquarters. The couriers carried two ration canisters per man, wearing one slung across the chest, the other strapped in a harness across the back. In addition to the German MP-40 or a captured Soviet PPSH submachine gun, they carried grenades stuck in their belts and in the tops of their boots. Thus burdened for their assignment, they plunged into the darkness, the oberst between them in the center of the file, carrying his stiffened left arm in the characteristic pose behind his back.

Orientation became more difficult as the party slowly picked its way through the tortured landscape in the darkness. After traversing several hundred meters, the leading courier had just approached the edge of a large shell crater when a heavy machine gun exploded into action at point-blank range. Simultaneously, a flare sizzled skyward and burst, illuminating the area. Gefreiter Fleck had instinctively thrown himself prone at the instant the machine-gun bullets cracked overhead. He stripped himself of the ration canisters and rolled into the shell crater to find the other four already in position, weapons trained over the edge, caps removed from the hand grenades. They immediately assumed that they had walked into an ambush and were prepared to give their lives only at great cost.

In the brief silence that followed, they recognized hushed German voices whispering in the darkness from the direction of the machine-gun position. One of the couriers shouted, "Don't shoot; it's your own people!"

The machine gun remained silent. Within the crater the men took a cursory count. Someone was missing. They called into the darkness for the oberst and received no answer. Seconds later the courier from the Second Platoon located Kindsmiller's still form lying ten paces from the crater. The courier pulled the body upward by the shoulders and grasped the motionless officer around the chest. His hands came away sticky and warm. Immediately joining the courier, the others unbuttoned Oberst Kindsmiller's tunic and found a wound directly over the heart.

The nineteen-year-old gefreiter lifted his commander onto his shoulder and stumbled toward the MG position. The men of the MG crew from the neighboring regiment could hardly imagine the catastrophe and were speechless with horror when it was revealed to them that their burst had killed their commander.

The situation along the line in this sector was so precarious that all sentries had been forced to remain alert, fingers on their triggers in preparation for another attack. Just hours prior to this fatal mishap an infiltrating Russian patrol had been repulsed at this very spot, and all noise and movement outside the line had to be considered enemy activity.

This tragic incident had cost the regiment its most talented and respected leader. Oberst Kindsmiller had been with the men since the formation of the regiment in lower Bavaria, throughout the Balkan campaign, and during the entire course of operations in Russia. His death was a heavy blow to the regiment as well as to the division. Two days later he was laid to rest among his soldiers in the cemetery at Sogolubovka. It was said that the funeral was carried out with full military honors under the direction of the division and the army corps.

This cemetery served as the grave site for the division through the two battles at Lake Ladoga, and the division medical center had been established nearby. At the cemetery a large birch cross was erected in the shadow of a well-preserved Greek Orthodox church. A few months later the German army evacuated the area, and there remained no crosses to be seen on the graves of soldiers. To deny Soviet intelligence information regarding the formations involved in the vicinity, as well as to keep the names and numbers of the fallen from the enemy, military cemeteries were often stripped of any indications of burials and markers when an area was evacuated. Following the war, the Soviet government then made additional efforts to eradicate any remaining signs or monuments that the invaders might have erected to honor their dead. Those who fell on the vast expanses in the east now lie in lost graves.

As the army continued in its attempts to satisfy the unrelenting appetite of the battlefields for military leaders, the feldwebels and obergefreiters began to play a more critical role in leading and commanding the combat forces. But the eternal "old gefreiters," many of whom became noncommissioned officers, constituted the backbone of the army.

A common joke circulated that reflected the tone and disposition of the landsers on the Russian front. It was supposed that when the victorious armies would eventually return from the east, a great parade would be held in Berlin. Marching columns would be observed by thousands of onlookers lining the Unter den Linden, and the magnificent ranks in all their finery would pass beneath the Brandenburg Gate. At the forefront would ride the generals and their staffs, resplendent in polished staff vehicles, with regimental banners flying. Following closely would come the unit commanders, accompanied by their staff officers, awards gleaming on their breasts, dress swords at their sides. Behind them roll the communications vans, the supply and logistics units, smartly riding in freshly painted kuebelwagons. Then come the field artillery batteries, heavy guns pulled by rumbling half-tracks and teams of groomed horses, all fittings polished and in perfect order. The entire procession would be led by Reichsmarschall Goring, outfitted in a resplendent white uniform piped with crimson and gold. Hanging at his throat is the Grand Cross of the Iron Cross with oak leaves. His entire entourage would ride in half-tracked vehicles for effect.

The parade passes by, the music eventually comes to an end, and the crowd, duly impressed, starts to disperse. Suddenly, trailing the magnificent parade at a distance, a ragged landser—one of the eternal gefreiters—wanders into view. His cracked and worn boots reflect the distance walked from the steppes of Russia. Wearing a tattered and faded uniform augmented by bits and pieces of Russian military equipment, he sports a week's stubble of beard and is burdened with gas mask, entrenching tool, mess tin, shelter-quarter, rifle, and hand grenades. Battered and dented field badges pinned to his tunic indicate numerous engagements and multiple wounds suffered. As he approaches the Brandenburg Gate, he is stopped and asked to what extent he has contributed to the victory. He shakes his head, a look of bewilderment on his face, before responding, "Nix ponemayu!" The single survivor from the decimated infantry regiments during the long years on the Eastern Front, he has forgotten the German language.

Whenever the old gefreiters were wounded, or more seldom, disabled due to sickness, they would go to great lengths to avoid being sent to a replacement company or to be reassigned as a replacement to another unit being newly formed. Through experience they had learned that they were more likely to survive with their old unit, where everyone knew one another and knew those on whom they must depend with their lives. Individual units were composed of officers and NCOs who had suffered deprivations and had experienced fear together for years on the front, and to be separated from these familiar surroundings and faces could be traumatic. With each loss of a battle-experienced member, the gap could often be filled only with personnel from supply, staff, or Luftwaffe units with little or no infantry combat experience. And as the numbers of the old veteran gefreiters declined, the casualties among the new men would rise accordingly.

On one occasion we received a group of replacements shortly after being relieved on the line. A feldwebel escorted them to their new company, and as was customary I spoke with the new members, asking each individual his name, formal occupation, background, and so on. Among them were four soldiers from Alsace, and one of the short, stout gefreiters looked vaguely familiar to me. It suddenly occurred to me that he had been the "kitchen bull" at the replacement center, where I had received basic training as a recruit.

I asked him if he had ever served with the Panzerjaegerersatzkompanie in Darmstadt, and he replied with a hearty "jawohl, Herr Leutnant!" I then requested that he report to me later at the company headquarters. He appeared as ordered, completely outfitted with correct battle dress, including gas mask and helmet. I initially put him at ease with light conversation, and then I revealed to him that I had been a recruit under his direction in the past. He immediately sprang to attention with a look of distress on his face as I related numerous incidents of harassment and verbal abuse that my friends and I had endured under his tutelage.

I specifically mentioned one interesting incident during which he had discovered two tiny, encrusted drops of coffee in the massive aluminum coffee canister I was engaged in cleaning, after which I was berated, insulted, and duly informed of the importance of cleanliness for the welfare of the army. I was then compelled to spend the remainder of the afternoon cleaning the kitchen equipment until each item met his satisfaction. To his immense relief, I then slapped him on the shoulder and remarked about the incredible trials one must endure to become a soldier. He proved to be a brave and very reliable member of the company.

On 22 July the Russians attacked the Sappenkopf with overwhelming strength, and we were thrown into battle as regimental reserves to close a local breakthrough. During the course of the heavy fighting a twenty-year-old Alsatian received a severe wound, from which he subsequently died while being transported toward the regimental aid station. That evening his platoon feldwebel gathered together the soldier's effects. It was customary to separate those items to be sent to the relatives from those things that would not be appropriate for the family. During the course of these unpleasant duties, the feldwebel approached me and requested to speak in confidence. He then revealed to me a letter written by the fallen soldier's mother:

Our dear son, you have now been sent to distant Russia as a German soldier. There will come a time for us in France when the sun shall shine again. We have heard that the Russians treat the Alsatians very well. The neighbor has told me that she wrote to her husband imploring him to surrender to the Russians. Throw away your rifle and go to the Russians. Surely they will treat you well.

Other things followed, the common things that are written by distraught mothers to sons at war far from home. Leaving the letter in my care, the feldwebel wordlessly departed. It was my duty to pass the letter to higher command. I failed to do so, although it was quite obvious that the writer neither trusted in, nor desired, a "final victory" for Germany. It was quite clear as well that the soldier's mother was willing to risk even her own life in an attempt to save her son from the fate that was befalling so many on the Eastern Front. I made a conscious decision not to bring additional hardship on the soldier's family. The fact that a grieving mother in Alsace did not support Germany's military endeavors, or our political system, would certainly have had no bearing on determining our victory or defeat in this world at war. In losing her son, she had already suffered more than a mother should have to bear.

On 28 August 1943, I celebrated my twenty-third birthday on the operating table in the field medical center. I had recently been struck in the upper left arm by shrapnel from a shell fired by a Russian artillery battery south of Lake Ladoga. Despite cursory medical treatment, the wound had become infected, and it was suspected that fragments of my uniform had been carried into the wound by the jagged steel. After examining the wound, the regimental surgeon, Dr. Heger, ordered an operation, for which he used an anesthesia that supposedly put the patient into a trance, during which all questions asked would be truthfully answered.

As I regained consciousness I became aware that a large number of friends from the regiment—Fritz Schmidt, Bouquet, Deuschel, Rech, and others—were gathered about to witness the effectiveness of the truth serum. Under the encouragement of Dr. Heger, they were very convincing when telling me of incredible things heard while I was under the influence of the medication. Not surprisingly, most of the questions asked were concerning certain experiences with females. In order to hinder the usual aftereffects of the anesthesia such as nausea and vomiting, a bottle of kirschwasser was provided, with the understanding that it must be shared by all those present. The evening of drinking and song was broken only by the new jokes and rumors that now abounded—at my expense—concerning my supposed social life as revealed during the operation.

Despite suffering subsequent pain and a fever from the wound, I remained among the troops until receiving orders for a furlough several days later. I soon departed for the homeland, accompanied by Dr. Heger and Hauptmann Dedel. At the end of our furlough, we met as planned in Lyuban, where we climbed aboard the train that carried us back to our regiment deep in Soviet Russia.

THE VOLCHOV-KIRISCHI BRIDGEHEAD

Those units of the 132d Infantry Division that were relieved to the west and south of Poretschay were then sent into the Dratschevo area to assume operations in the sector previously held by the Eighty-first Infantry Division at the Volchov and Kirischi bridgehead. With the exception of occasional clashes between reconnaissance patrols from both sides, as well as isolated skirmishes along the perimeter of the bridgehead, the area assumed by the division on 20 August remained quiet. On 27 August Oberst Altmann, commander of Grenadier Regiment 438, was killed while inspecting the forward lines of the Kirischi bridgehead.

Without warning, an order was issued on 11 September to plan for the pending evacuation of the bridgehead by the Eighty-first, the 132d, and units of the Ninety-sixth Divisions. The positions in the area of Kussinka and south of Myagray were to be abandoned as well.

On 14 September preparations for the evacuation began. All excess material not immediately required for the fighting units was either transported or destroyed, including reserve ordnance and fuel. The transportation of the material was carried out over a period of five days, and upon completion of the final phases, all assets deemed of value to the enemy such as bridges, roads, railways, dwellings, and wells were prepared for destruction by the pionier units. The sky filled with heavy black smoke as all supplies and equipment not removed were systematically destroyed by the landsers as they prepared to withdraw.

The evacuation and withdrawal plan for the combat units required five days to complete. For the purpose of hindering any follow-up action by the enemy, certain features were designated as strongpoints that were to be abandoned only during the last phase of the operation. Included in the strongpoints were areas within the Kirischi bridgehead and important railroad positions.

The evacuation order was set into motion during the night of 1–2 October with the withdrawal of the Second Company, Grenadier Regiment 437, which had been designated the bridgehead reserve. Only one railway was available for the movement of an entire division, which now consisted primarily of horse-drawn artillery and dismounted infantry. However, the evacuation was flawlessly executed without interruption from enemy forces and with no losses in men and material.

During the interim, the main line was held for another twenty-four hours until the landsers quietly abandoned their thinly held positions at midnight. Soon after the last platoons had initiated their march out of the pocket, the enemy began cautiously probing the empty German positions with reconnaissance patrols and light-infantry units.

No large-scale enemy movement was detected, however, until the afternoon of 5 October, when enemy-tracked vehicles piled high with infantry were observed moving into the area of Irssa-Dubrovo, and they were quickly taken under artillery fire. After the last battle-weary landsers crossed the Volchov during the night of 2–3 October, preset demolitions charges were detonated, completely destroying the railroad bridge and rendering it unusable to the enemy.

By midnight on 5 October the division was occupying new positions at Kussinka and had completed defensive preparations. With the withdrawal of the last rear guard from Grenadier Regiment 437 and Fusilier Battalion 132 on the morning of 6 October, Operation Hubertusjagd came to an end.

We received more propaganda leaflets from the Red Army that month:

For the soldiers of the 7th company, Infantry Regiment 437, 132 Infantry Division!

GERMAN SOLDIERS!

Hitler has led you into a catastrophe. In attempts to conceal this fact, your high command speaks of a "Flexible Defense" and a "shortening of the front line."

The Hitler clique has in the course of two years on the Eastern Front waged a war that has murdered millions of young Germans and made widows and orphans of millions more, only to gain a so-called "shortening of the front line."

You yourselves can judge the gains of the "flexible defense," as the Red Army has already thrown the Germans behind the banks of the Dnieper, occupied the city of Saporoschye, cut off the Crimea, and is now successfully fighting in the suburbs of Kiev and Gomel. The German Army is bleeding to death on the Eastern Front.

The fascist dictators have earlier said that you must sacrifice yourselves for the victorious end of the "Blitzkrieg." Now they say you must fight to the last man for the "flexible defense" to succeed. You can easily recognize the lies of the fascists. But what price must you continue to pay? Here are a few facts from the tragic history of your company:

2–7 November 1941

During the fighting before Bachtschisseray (in the Crimea) the company lost not less than 62 soldiers out of a strength of 180 men. The company again was reinforced, and after a short pause was thrown into the battle for Sevastopol. After this phase of fighting only 16 men remained.

In September 1942 the company was re-organized and its losses replaced on the Volchov Front, and it was then engaged in the fighting at Gaitolovo on the Mga. After this battle only 15 of 100 men remained.

11 October 1943

The 7th Company had already been withdrawn when it once again was hastily ordered to support the 12th Luftwaffe Field Division. Your commanders threw you into a counter-attack that needlessly cost you heavy losses in defeat. The 7th Company was beaten back and left a third of its soldiers lying upon the battlefield.

SOLDIERS!

You are spilling your blood for Hitler, a sacrifice that benefits neither yourselves or the German people. Nothing can save you from this carnage.

Break from this army of Hitlerite oppressors, otherwise you will face destruction.

The 26 soldiers of the 1st Company of your regiment who, together with their company commander Oberleutnant Rudolf Kremer, gave themselves up to the Russians on 12 March 1943, can show you the path of survival. For them the horrors of war are over. After the war they will return to their homeland healthy and sound.

Whether you return to your families or as fascist invaders are destroyed upon Russian soil depends entirely upon the decision you make.

Decide, before it's too late.

Often the Russian propaganda units used crude photo montages assembled from the pictures and names taken from identity documents that had been confiscated from German prisoners or collected from the dead. In our sector, as well as on all other fronts, Soviet aircraft dropped tons of such leaflets over our lines. The soldiers enthusiastically collected them and put the leaflets to good use at the latrines, as paper for this purpose was always in short supply.

The communications unit of the division retained a special reconnaissance and interception platoon. This unit would dispatch specially trained teams behind the enemy lines to tap into the land-line networks; thus, the telephone communications of the enemy could often be intercepted and overheard. In this manner we could hear the messages of the Russian officers, and through the often coarse language we learned that women were playing an ever-increasing role on the enemy staff as communications technicians or logistics officers.

We intercepted Russian propaganda as well. In one instance we intercepted the orders of the day issued to a rifle company opposite our position. This order detailed the plan and time line for capturing the strategically important railroad crossing at Kirischi and the largest wooden match factory of the Soviet Union. Later interceptions announced in great detail the assault on Kirischi against a strongly fortified enemy, and its subsequent capture by the brave Soviet soldiers. In reality Kirischi had been systematically evacuated by our forces prior to the execution date of this order.

On another occasion we overheard a regimental commander berate a junior officer for failing to capture booty during an operation. "How can I capture anything," the exasperated officer responded, "when the Fritzes take every scheissdreck with them!" The word "scheissdreck" was spoken in German.

One night our main battle position was penetrated by approximately fifty Soviet soldiers. Using great skill and stealth, they successfully climbed through the fortification in an area thinly guarded by sentries without a shot being fired. After discovering the infiltrators within our lines, the soldiers manning the two machine guns on the right and left flanks of the area of penetration took the enemy under fire. Several of the Soviets fell dead or wounded, the remainder scrambled through the darkness to escape through our lines. During the encounter not a shot was returned, and at dawn we discovered by examining the bodies of the Russians struck by the machine-gun fire that no firearms were among them. Still clenched in their cold fists were opened razors with which they had planned to silently cut the throats of our sentries.

WEST OF NEVEL

On 4 December we were on the offensive again. With the assault reserve of the regiment, I arrived at the small stream where it cut through a triangular wooded area. To our left Schmidt's battalion was engaged in heavy fighting, and opposite us tanks were moving into position toward our location. I ordered that absolute noise discipline be observed along our sector and that only clearly recognizable infantry targets be fired on when and if necessary. I immediately requested reinforcement in the form of a Pak with crew, not knowing when we could expect the arrival of this direly needed weapon.

Ahead of us and to our left was located Feuerstein's squad, which held a commanding view of the battle area and of the stream ahead. Suddenly a machine gun fired from Feuerstein's position. A Russian company had been observed moving along the length of the stream, providing infantry support for two T-34 tanks. When taken under fire the Soviets had fled behind the protection of the tanks, one of which immediately rocked to a halt and pivoted its massive turret toward the hidden MG nest. A direct hit from the heavy gun struck the machine-gun position, instantly killing Feuerstein, who had faithfully served under my command for many months.

Additional tanks immediately opened fire from the tree line opposite us. Standing with Juckel and Sepp in a shallow trench, we were observing them through binoculars when a tank round struck a nearby tree to our left and sent it crashing to the ground. Juckel slowly turned his head to face me, and I saw that only a small stump was remaining of the ever-present pipe between his lips. A shell splinter had cleared the rim of his helmet and had cut cleanly through the head of the pipe, and he muttered softly, "That one got me," and sank slowly to the ground.

His left upper arm was red with blood soaking through the white camouflage battle smock, and I unbuttoned his blouse and tunic to see that a large shell fragment had nearly amputated his left arm just below the shoulder. Taking a mess-tin strap, I bound his arm tightly just below the armpit until the flow of blood ceased. Throughout the incident Juckel had not made a sound, but he now smiled faintly and remarked that it appeared that he had finally received his long-awaited heimats-chuss. I helped him to his feet, and he disappeared toward the rear, steadily marching upright without assistance.

Some weeks later I received a letter from a hospital in Vienna, which opened with the words, "My dear leutnant." Juckel wrote that with the exception of a left arm he remained in one piece. He also added that he lacked tobacco for his pipe, as the hospital did not consider tobacco to be a priority item for their beleaguered supply system. I underlined this passage of his letter with a red marker from my map case and passed the letter on to the regimental supply officer, Haertel, with a request that some tobacco be sent to him. To my immense satisfaction and surprise, I received another letter approximately four weeks later thanking me for fulfilling his implied request.

The next day we welcomed the arrival of a 75mm Pak and crew. We were immensely relieved to receive the antitank gun, as we were otherwise without effective protection from the Soviet armor that lay opposite us. Once again I found myself in my long-forgotten element of the panzerjaeger, and I spoke with the crew while refamiliarizing myself with the weapon. We carefully positioned the gun and lay in wait, but no tank presented itself as a target.

The following day we crossed over a bridge constructed of inflatable boats spanning a tributary that separated us from the III Battalion. The enemy took notice that reinforcements were arriving and attempted to advance with their tanks, two of which fell prey to our 75mm Pak; the remainder hurriedly withdrew to concealment.

During the night two of the tanks, with infantry piled on the chassis, broke through the lines in the area held by Schmidt. Some of our companies were thrown out of their positions, and I counterattacked with the reinforced Pionier Platoon 437 as assault reserve. We advanced to a small depression 150 meters from the earthwork system where the Russians had penetrated. Selecting two squads to take into the counterattack, I left the remainder, numbering approximately sixty men, lying two hundred meters behind us in a depression. The plan was to take as few men as I deemed necessary for the initial assault in order to minimize casualties; the remaining men were to follow up the assault after our initial thrust.

On a preplanned light signal, the forward observers ordered our artillery support to open fire, and within seconds our artillery rounds were impacting hardly thirty to fifty meters before us. As the explosions crept forward and enveloped the enemy trench systems, we advanced and soon began receiving sporadic fire from the Russians. A submachine gun opened fire on us at close range from a concealed trench, striking one of the machine gunners in the shoulder.

With no time to lose we stormed the positions, firing from point-blank range and tossing grenades into the earthworks. I threw myself on the edge of a trench, from where I could distinctly hear the hushed voices of the Russians less than a meter's distance below me as they crouched in the darkness. Fearfully remaining in their position, they did not trust themselves to peer over the edge of the berm; otherwise, they could have simply pulled me into the position with them. With a pounding heart, I pulled the priming cords from two hand grenades and waited until the last second before rolling them over the berm and into the trench below me.

The grenades exploded with a cloud of dust and smoke, and holding my pistol over the edge of the trench I fired a number of shots into the unseen targets. Screams of the enemy wounded broke forth, and I rolled into the trench, falling directly on a wounded Russian. I shouted for the men to follow, and Schorsch stormed into the trench system and secured our left flank, his machine gunner firing bursts from the hip with his MG-42.

Sepp, Humpert, and the others followed me into the defense network. From our position we observed a group of Russians to our right spring from the ground and dash through our fire along the perimeter of the earthwork system to a tank squatting ominously in the darkness farther to the rear, its silhouette visible against flashes of our bursting artillery shells. Within a few minutes the Russians had been pushed from the trenches, and a number of them sought shelter in a depression. As we regrouped and prepared for a counterattack, Sepp Sturm collected a handful of grenades and, running toward the perimeter, he pulled the lanyards and tossed the grenades one after another into the depression. The Russians left a number of dead and wounded behind them, and we took twelve prisoners.

Following this attack by our small group, the Russians lost the initiative for assaulting the position, and throughout the following days they displayed no further inclination to attack. I immediately recommended Sepp Sturm to be awarded the Iron Cross, and this award was presented to him the following morning by the regimental commander.

On 14 November the 132d Infantry Division was relieved in their sector of the Kussinka front by units of the Ninety-sixth Infantry Division and the Twelfth Luftwaffe Field Division. We were then transported by rail to Army Group Loch to reinforce the front west of Nevel near Pustoschka.

At this location the division was not sent into action as a unit immediately, but it served as assault reserve for the defense and reinforcement of the threatened divisions. With the exception of the units remaining in the area of Issakovo, all of its battalions were used for defense and attack by the Eighty-first and 329th Infantry Divisions.

It was planned that the 132d Infantry Division would attack toward the west from positions south of Nevedro Lake in support of the offensive launched by the Sixteenth Army at the end of November. This offensive was planned with the objective of enclosing in a pocket the Soviet units that had broken through south of Pustoschka. This attack, which would have freed the vital supply route to Sheglovo–Lopatovo using Grenadier Regiment 436 and units of Police Regiments Sixteen and

Nine, was launched on 29 November. In the face of overwhelming enemy strength, the units advanced toward their objectives of Vassilyeva, Pustky, and Height 192.7; however, due to heavy losses suffered during the previous months, for which there had been no replacements, the assault ground to a halt.

A second attack was planned for 10 December following the completion of another supply route reaching the areas of Idritsa, Nischtscha train station, Lushiy, and Lopatovo. The division planned to use Grenadier Regiment 436 and Grenadier Regiment 174 for the renewed attack. However, the plans were never carried through, as the division was redesignated Battle Group Wagner and, combined with the Third Estonian SS Volunteer Brigade and the Latvian Police Regiment, Riga, was assigned to reinforce the sector between Drissa and Yasno Lake. It was expected that an enemy offensive from the area of Nevel would fall on this sector and that the enemy would strike in the direction of Polozk. This expected attack threatened the entire right wing of Army Group North.

The new division sector, which extended for a distance of fifty kilometers, remained quiet, with the exception of minor reconnaissance actions, until mid-January. Throughout these weeks the units remained at work reinforcing and building defenses, roads, and bridges. The rear echelons were evacuated of all civilians, following an increase in the partisan activity throughout the dense forests that were so prominent in north Russia.

On 12 January 1944 the enemy launched their expected attack. Throughout the early days of the new year, enemy activity had been observed in the areas of Neschtscherdo Lake, Yasno Lake, and Nevedro Lake. The Soviets attacked in a northwest direction with the goal of freeing Idritsa in the northern area of the division sector.

The enemy quickly won ground against weakly held positions defended by foreign units and police detachments and penetrated toward Pustoya, Mogilino Lake, and Sviblo Lake. The Latvian Police Regiment Riga, operating farther south between Yasno Lake and Gussino Lake, was able to establish a blocking line along Puchariza-Issbischtscha-Sagatya-Schulyatino-Dyatly. By the evening of 12 January the Soviet advance was halted, and the police regiment reinforced their positions through equipment and command-and-control assistance provided by the 132d Infantry Division.

On 14 January the division received orders from the Sixteenth Army to engage the enemy forces that had broken through along the line on the southern edge of Dubrovo to Aleandrovo. This attack was launched at 2000 and succeeded in containing the enemy forces. On 15 January at 0630 the enemy struck back with a strength of eight to nine battalions against our weakly held sector, which was now defended by three understrength companies. The enemy forces, heavily supported by air-craft, artillery, and multiple rocket launchers, struck the line at Pucha-riza, Issbischtscha, Sagatya, Schulyatino and Podberesya. Regional breakthroughs at Puchariza, Sagatya and Schulyatino were contained in a counterattack, and heavy fighting north of Tschaiky and Lushiy took place in the area following close combat and direct fire support from field artillery.

Throughout 16 January repeated attacks against Dyatly and the posi-tions to the northeast were successfully repelled, and the 120 grenadiers manning the defenses at Dyatly were ordered to counterattack at 1800. The counterattack threw the enemy forces back and sealed the salient to the west of Sagatya. On 19 January 1944 the division turned over the sec-tor to the newly arrived 290th Infantry Division.

January–February 1944, near Dyatly. The thermometer read twenty degrees below zero. The Soviets had again broken through the thinly held German lines. Weakened security battalions, many consisting of foreign units, were compelled to surrender their positions under pressure from the strong enemy forces.

I moved forward with my men along a well-worn roadway in the winter night. The landsers moved instinctively with rifles at the ready. The dirty-white battle smocks gleamed faintly in the darkness as the col-umn wound its way forward. We were assisted by the use of three pony sleds, which were heavily loaded with weapons and equipment. It was a night of total darkness, and although our eyes were long accustomed to the night, each man could only faintly discern the soldier several paces ahead of him. I attempted to follow the planned route carefully, occa-sionally finding it necessary to scan the crumpled map in the dim glow of a field light hidden beneath a shelter-quarter.

After several hours of marching we arrived at the headquarters of a foreign security battalion, and during the next hour confusion reigned as we attempted to gain information about the area. After several frustrating attempts to communicate with the occupants of the position, a German officer was located, but he was able to provide little definitive information on the situation or the lay of the front, so I was again left to my instincts.

We set out, following a narrow trail that led us toward the southeast. Hours earlier I had been instructed by the regimental commander to establish a new defensive line on a small terrain feature in this area. Our destination was a small rise in elevation referred to on the map as the village of Dyatly. As we approached the area of the village, we suddenly received fire from submachine guns and machine guns on our left. We returned fire, and the guns immediately fell silent.

With field glasses I searched through the breaking dawn for the huts and buildings that would reveal the location of the village to us. As the horizon grew lighter, it occurred to me that in the darkness we had bypassed the village, the remains of which were now barely visible immediately behind us. Having fallen victim to the war, the village now consisted only of several blackened chimneys standing among the barely recognizable ruins of burned cottages. A low fence and a well came into my view through the binoculars, indicating the location of a former dwelling, the remains of which were covered with a thin blanket of snow.

Quickly issuing commands, I ordered Feldwebel Staffen to the right flank with his platoon. Feldwebel Bernhardt was to remain at our present location. We established the machine-gun positions among the ruins of the village as isolated rifle shots began breaking forth in the growing light.

With the coming of dawn I was better able to assess our surroundings. The village was situated on a commanding height that descended evenly on all sides in a gentle slope. Approximately one kilometer distant on another terrain feature was Staffen's platoon. Unknown to me at the time, while carrying out my directions the platoon commander had fallen victim to a Soviet sniper hidden in the forest, who had fired a single shot that struck him in the head.

Later in the morning we were cautiously approached by an officer whose red-piped collar tabs, indicating artillery service, were visible beneath his field jacket. The hauptmann introduced himself as the forward observer of a battery located barely two kilometers to our rear and stated that the guns were fully ready to provide us with support. With this comforting information we continued to prepare for the inevitable Russian attack.

For the remainder of the day the forest lay silent. The forward observers joined us as we engaged in building a banya deep in the earth to serve as a headquarters. As the temperature continued to fall with the ensuing darkness, I permitted the men to rotate the sentry duties on their positions to give them the opportunity to warm themselves, as the lighting of any fire would draw immediate fire and was thus strictly forbidden. I had long since learned that rotating sentries as often as feasible would result in the sentries remaining more alert and less prone to fall victim to the effects of cold and fatigue.

The Soviets had planned to attack the foreign security units that had occupied this area before our arrival. With taut nerves we lay in our snow holes and waited as darkness descended on us again. Just before midnight the unmistakable sounds of commands and shouts were heard from the Russian positions. Then came the ominous sound of heavy boots treading through the snowdrifts. We steeled ourselves to wait until the ghostly figures broke into the open before us, and the MG-42 immediately on my left opened fire with a long, ripping burst.

Flares arched skyward, and the air was filled with the explosions and screams of open battle. Tracer bullets bounced and ricocheted through the darkness. With deafening bursts, the support promised by our artillery battery began falling with unerring accuracy on the ranks of attackers. The enemy was beaten back amid bursting shells, but not before my friend and squad leader Herfelder fell mortally wounded.

The following day the enemy repeated their attacks, which were again repulsed. The dawn of the third day found us still clinging to the battered positions. Again and again the ranks of shouting enemy forces attempted to overrun our positions, now with the support of mortars and artillery batteries, which lay barrages on us in preparation for the assaults.

I was required to hold a line one kilometer in length—with only forty men. Along our neighboring front to the right was a five-hundred-meter breach in the lines, which reportedly was manned during the hours of darkness by a reconnaissance unit.

During the night of 16–17 January the Russians were active again. Under the cover of darkness they circled the village to our left with a strong assault force, silently penetrating an area where we had no support and striking the small team located in that sector. From our positions we could observe muzzle flashes and the explosions of grenades. After about an hour Sepp Sturm appeared, creeping on all fours through the darkness toward our position. He had suffered a grazing wound to his shoulder, and his camouflage battle jacket, mess tin, canteen, and even his entrenching tool were riddled with bullet holes from the Soviet sub-machine guns. During the evening twilight the Russian unit had overrun our left wing, and Sepp had taken cover in a depression while bullets cracked around him and riddled his jacket and equipment. He had waited until he was certain that he was no longer being observed and then made his way back to our position.

We reinforced the shrinking perimeter around the banya. In the darkness I was standing in the chest-high trench when I observed to my half-left a light signal behind the hulk of a burned-out tank. The light would blink intermittently behind us for several seconds, remain inactive for approximately a minute, and then the signal would be repeated.

As I was preparing to send a team to investigate the light I observed the silhouettes of twenty or thirty figures moving rapidly toward the signal barely twenty paces away. I instantly opened fire with my submachine gun at the figures now vaguely visible against the white snow, and the alarm raced throughout our position.

All our machine guns were positioned on their lafettes facing the front and could not immediately be brought to bear on the infiltrators. We took them under fire with small arms and hand grenades. I was vaguely aware of the glowing fuse of a Russian grenade as it flew past me from the darkness, and I was then enveloped in a soft, sinking sensation and knew nothing else.

As I slowly regained consciousness, I felt light-headed and unable to orient myself to my surroundings. My legs radiated with pain, and I felt paralyzed, unable to move any part of my body. Slowly I realized that my battle smock was pulled over my head, and as I began to regain movement I could feel pain that encompassed my every limb. I was suddenly shivering with cold, and the ringing in my brain ceased as I reached up and pulled my heavy jacket from my face. After several seconds I had regained enough sight to discern through the darkness the comforting forms of Sepp and Juckel bending over me, their familiar eyes peering from under the distinctive silhouettes of the whitewashed Wehrmacht helmets. During the heat of the assault they had managed to drag me out of the direct line of fire and away from the Russians charging through the snow.

The Russians ravaged the banya with molotov cocktails. The strongpoint on our left had been overrun, and in our sector there were only ten of us remaining. As dawn appeared on the horizon, we received reinforcements in the form of one feldwebel accompanied by twenty-five men, who had been dispatched from a Silesian division. With our reinforcements in tow, we reoccupied the right flank of the village, from where the Russians held a small ravine barely one hundred meters distant, which offered them concealment and protection from our artillery.

With the coming of dusk we attacked. We assaulted and overran the enemy position without artillery support, and together with Sepp and Jukel I closed on a depression into which a Russian had fled with a shoulder-fired antitank weapon. I was able to detect his crouching form in the growing twilight just as he squeezed the trigger, and the hot projectile roared past, burning my battle smock and tunic between my arm and hip. I struck him squarely in the chest with my assault rifle and he tumbled backward as Juckel sprang forward and thrust the muzzle of his submachine gun in his face. The terrified Russian stared at us, eyes wide with fear, and lay motionless. Pulling him to his feet, Juckel instructed a radioman to take him to the rear.

The Russians quickly counterattacked, storming out of the darkness and throwing hand grenades. The feldwebel of the reinforcement unit, who had performed with great courage and reliability while serving with us, was struck by a bullet in the abdomen, the force of the round spinning him backward before he collapsed. Again we beat back the attack, and against overwhelming odds we recaptured and held the village of Dyatly.

With the coming of daylight we risked sniper fire to examine our tiny battlefield. We discovered a warm shelter of straw within the knocked-out tank at our rear and determined that either a partisan or an infiltrator had used the tank as an orienteering point to vector attacking forces through our thinly held lines. It would have been a simple matter to penetrate through the gaps in the line and to mass attackers at our rear, by whom we would have been easily annihilated. Only the signal light had revealed the position and the plan, and its discovery had prevented our certain destruction.

During another incident a lone individual wearing a German officer's rank insignia on a uniform with red artillery piping on his shoulder boards and collar tabs appeared suddenly in our midst. His unexpected presence, here on the front line without the customary battle dress and armed only with a pistol, aroused my immediate suspicion. When I challenged him to halt and to provide his name and unit, he suddenly wheeled and wildly fired two shots in my direction. I returned fire with my submachine gun; however, he had plunged into the darkness and disappeared.

It became obvious that infiltrators were penetrating our lines dressed in captured uniforms, and it was rumored that in some sectors Russian assault units were being led by personnel dressed in our uniforms who spoke excellent German. It was known that our sentries were occasionally confronted by plaintive cries for help, delivered in flawless German, which emanated from the Soviet lines. This was clearly an attempt to exploit the landser's natural sense of compassion for his comrades in order to lure our soldiers to their deaths.

With a reinforced infantry-pionier platoon and an alarm company, I assumed command of the sector northwest of Dyatly in February. During the first few days we suffered numerous casualties in dead and wounded. The Russians dug themselves in along a trench system that ran the length of a wooded height and occupied positions within 150 meters from our location. We remained under constant danger of sniper fire and received machine-gun fire whenever we exposed ourselves to the enemy position. In an attempt to end the harassment, we called mortar fire on the positions opposite us; however, the Russians clung tenaciously to their trenches and continued to deliver deadly sniper fire.

At length I positioned a heavy machine gun on the line and carefully adjusted the lafette to train on the exact point where I had last observed the light-blue muzzle flash of a sniper's rifle in the early morning hours. In addition to the machine gun, we trained the Pak directly on a suspected enemy position. As the evening twilight fell, we again found ourselves under fire, and on command the machine gunner opened fire, accompanied by the Pak. Belt after belt of 7.92mm ammunition raced through the feed mechanism of the MG–42, and the Pak fired high-explosive shells directly into the Soviet line. We instantly repeated this process whenever fired upon, and within a week it was said that we occupied the quietest sector of the entire regiment. Indeed, our own reconnaissance units reported that in the sector opposite us the enemy now employed a limited number of snipers and machine-gun crews and used these only during hours of darkness. They would immediately withdraw into their rearward area at dawn. For the next several weeks we suffered no further casualties along our sector of the line.

As I made my nightly inspection of the line one evening in mid-

February, a machine gunner reported that a large dog had been sighted about thirty meters from our position. I asked if the animal had been wearing a harness and pack strapped to its back, and the solider replied that it was possible; however, due to the poor light he could not be certain. I then ordered that all such animals be shot on sight. In previous engagements the Russians had sent dogs into our positions with armed mines strapped to their bodies. These animals had been trained to seek food under tanks and vehicles with engines running and would thus strike the detonators against the vehicle chassis. Using these tactics, the Soviets could also dispatch the animals through the barbed wire of our positions, opening holes in our defenses or destroying tanks and other irreplaceable equipment. The explosives would kill any personnel within a radius of several meters, and the shrapnel could inflict serious wounds at an even greater distance.

The following morning I inspected the area in front of our position and located large doglike tracks. That evening one of the animals was shot between our lines in an area from which it could not be recovered. The evening of the next day, as I was making my way through our positions back to the company headquarters, a large animal bolted hardly ten meters distant, sprinting rapidly through the dusk toward the enemy line.

I opened fire from the hip with my submachine gun, and the animal tumbled and lay motionless in the snow. Immediately a burst from a nearby Maxim forced me and the nearby sentries to dive for cover, but later we were able to recover the dead animal from between the lines. It proved to be a fully grown wolf, which had obviously been feasting on the numerous corpses in the area between the Russian and German positions.

The animal was of heavy build, with a pointed muzzle and powerful jaws. The ears were short and round, the thick winter fur was a gray-beige color along the flanks and faded to light brown on the underside and was almost dark brown along the back. Sepp skinned the wolf, nailing the pelt to the side of our shelter with wire staples to dry after treating it with salt and birch ashes. After several days it was pronounced cured despite a slightly pungent ordor, and Gefreiter Doser bundled it together and carried it back to Germany on furlough. Within a week it was being professionally prepared by Weissgerber in Stuttgart, and it remained one of the few souvenirs I retained from the entire experience on the Eastern Front.

From 11 to 12 March the division, as well as additional regiments provided by the 120th Infantry Division, remained engaged in heavy combat near Schwary. From 13 to 19 March units of the division were placed under the Thirty-second and Eighty-third Infantry Divisions. The fighting at Rog remained fierce and brutal, with every meter of ground being desperately defended by the beleaguered landsers. From 29 March to 4 April the division remained in defensive fighting along Neschtscherdo Lake and near Lobovo. The Red Army was unsuccessful in repeated attempts to penetrate the German defenses, despite overwhelming superiority in tanks, artillery, and aircraft.

The snow and ice slowly receded. On Easter 1944, a Russian company attacked over the frozen Neschtscherdo Lake but was repulsed, leaving the ice strewn with dead. Prisoners who were taken reported that the Soviets believed the west bank to be poorly defended, and some of them attempted to convince us that the lake was no longer passable due to the recent thawing temperatures. We were fully aware that the lake remained frozen with ice one-and-one-half-meters thick and that it would probably remain passable at least until the end of April or early May.

On Easter morning after I departed the headquarters following a situation briefing, the members of the company presented me with an Easter basket carefully constructed with available articles from our position. Lying on a layer of soft moss were a dozen round, olive-colored Russian hand grenades, which had been recovered from the bodies of the attackers and carefully arranged within the basket. Thus we celebrated Easter 1944.

A heavy machine-gun crew with Infantry Regiment 437 in action during the fighting in the forest north of Smerdynia, February 1943.

A heavy Russian tank destroyed before the positions of Infantry Regiment 437 during the battle for Smerdynia. Note the enemy dead in the immediate vicinity of the armored vehicle. The Soviet practice of infantry riding on the chassis of tanks into battle could prove to be devastating if the armored vehicle was struck by a heavy-caliber Pak projectile.

Landsers advancing toward the line on a corduroy trail laid through the marshes of the Volchov front, early 1943.

A log road leading to the forward positions of the Volchov front, early 1943. Motor vehicle tire rims were adapted for use on carts and wagons as an improvised rail system.

Leutnant Bidermann (*left*) inspecting defensive positions in the forests of the Volchov front, February 1943.

Receiving a resupply of ammunition south of Leningrad on the Volchov front, February 1943. This photograph was taken just hours before a Soviet breakthrough attempt. The bunkers constructed from heavy logs in the marshy terrain proved to be effective protection from light mortar and small-arms fire.

Soviet armor destroyed during the winter battles near Klosterdorf, March 1943. The thick forests and impenetrable swamps made large-scale assaults by armored units difficult, forcing them to traverse known trails and roadways.

Bidermann (*kneeling, with visored cap*) and Hauptmann Dedel providing instruction for Luftwaffe replacements in the use of infantry weapons. Despite having received only cursory training a short distance from the foremost lines, Luftwaffe replacements quickly adapted to the brutal conditions of combat in the frozen forests.

Leutnant Bidermann (*mounted, on left*) leads a company of landsers from Infantry Regiment 437 through Schapki, south of Mga, July 1943.

Constructing corduroy roads through the marshes near the Maluksa position, July 1943. The terrain limited large movements of supplies to these roads, which were constructed only through the intensive labor of the pionier units.

Russian prisoners captured during a breakthrough attempt in the Maluksa sector, July 1943. During this Soviet assault, four Russian officers and numerous enlisted were killed before the German positions.

A staff meeting near Schapki, June 1943. *From left to right:* Oberst Altmann (commander I.R. 438), killed in action, August 1943; General Lindemann (division commander), mortally wounded by Gestapo officials in Berlin, September 1944; Oberst Kindsmiller (commander I.R. 437), killed in action, August 1943; Major Schmidt (commander, III Battalion, I.R. 437), and an adjutant.

Unteroffizier Stennich at the entrance to the communications bunker in Mga, south of Lake Ladoga near Leningrad, August 1943. Stennich was killed in action on 18 January 1944 near Dyatly.

The final salute. The burial of Oberst Kindsmiller, who was killed by friendly fire on 17 August 1943. The burial took place at the military cemetery at Sogolubovka. The battalion commander, Major Schmidt, is third from left.

The Volchov railway bridge south of Leningrad. This strategically important bridge linked the main railway route from Moscow to Leningrad. Trees and branches were placed on the bridge to conceal troop movement from Soviet ground reconnaissance units.

On furlough with relatives in Stuttgart, September 1943. Uncle Christian (*sitting, center*) died from severe burns received one year later during an American bombing raid.

Bidermann (*center, with binoculars*) with soldiers assigned as assault reserve, Infantry Regiment 437, west of the Nevel sector. Note the variety of uniforms and camouflaged equipment, including white-washed helmets.

A 50mm Pak crew in the forward positions near Dyatly, mid-January 1944. The landsers had just received warm coffee after several days of bitter combat.

Feldwebel Bernhardt (*left*) briefs Leutnant Bidermann on the strength of Russian positions after returning from a reconnaissance patrol, March 1944. The soldier in the camouflage battle jacket on the right is equipped with MP-40 "schmeisser" magazine pouches.

Receiving mail and packages in the Klosterdorf sector, April 1944. Deliveries of mail had already become erratic and unpredictable at this phase of the war.

Bidermann (*third from right*) with members of Infantry Regiment 437 who have just been awarded the Iron Cross, Second Class. The Second Class medal was worn on the field uniform only on the day of receipt; thereafter, only the ribbon was worn.

Absendestelle:	...te Meldung	Ort	Tag	Zeit
Batl.Gef. Stand	Abgegangen			
	Angekommen			

An   Lt. Steinhardt.

Ihr habt Euch prächtig verhalten. Anerkennung des
Rgts. soll ich übermitteln.
Den ganzen Tag griff der Gegner den Batl.-Ab-
schnitt an. Stellung wurde gehalten. 1 Panzer
bei Kirche u. einer unweit des Batl.-Gef.-Std.
abgeschossen.
Es gibt Frontkämpferpäckchen.
Munition beim Batl.Gef.Std. abholen.
Ich brauche dann die Stärken u.Verluste, Munition-
verschuß ungefähr.
Die Art. die kurz schoß, war 1.schw.Mörserabt. Ist
festgestellt u. wird nicht mehr vorkommen.
Bitte uns weiter durch Melder über die Lage
unterrichten.
Die Pioniere müssen laut Rgts.Befehl ihren Ab-
schnitt wieder besetzen. Machen Sie sich stark
durch Bildung einer Reserve.
Herzl.Gruß an Radeja.   Horrido !
                        Ihr Bidermann Oblt.u.Btl
                                Adjt.

F.d.R.d.A.

A Russian village burns west of Nevel, winter 1943–1944. The civilian population suffered terribly as the war enveloped them, often leaving villagers without food or shelter in the brutal environment of winter.

Facing page: Message from Oberleutnant Bidermann at battalion head-quarters to Leutnant Steinhardt in command of Luftwaffe replacements in the front positions. The message commends the unit on their recent performance in combat and credits them for the destruction of Soviet armor. They are advised to receive rations and ammunition resupply, and a status report of casualties and ammunition expenditure is requested. Also noted is that artillery rounds that fell short originated from the First Heavy Mortar Battalion, and the message states that this will not recur. It is further requested that the situation report be sent by courier, and the unit is to be advised that in accordance with orders from the regiment the pioniers will reoccupy their sector. They are requested to reinforce their sector with the building of a reserve force. Of particular interest is Bidermann's closing, in which, as opposed to ending the message with the customary "Heil Hitler!" he has used the traditional "Horrido!" taken from a German army Alpine Corps song. Leutnant Steinhardt was killed in action in November 1944.

The painting of the Holy Madonna, which hung in a sanctuary near the church in Pikeliai. The painting received a burst from a Soviet submachine gun during an incursion into the German defenses. Although the painting was restored after the war, traces of some of the bullet holes that encircled the countenance of the Virgin are still visible.

General Fritz Lindemann, commander of the 132d Infantry Division from January 1942 to August 1943. General Lindemann was involved in the assassination attempt on Hitler that occurred 20 July 1944, and the Nazi government offered a reward of 500,000 Reichsmarks for his capture. Shot by a Gestapo official during his capture in Berlin, the general died of his wounds on 22 September 1944.

Leutnant Gottlob H. Bidermann, Infantry Regiment 437. The portrait was taken in early 1944 while he was serving on the northern front in Russia.

CHAPTER NINE

The Oncoming End

The few survivors within our

old circle of friends had become inseparable, and only wounds

or death could break the bonds of comradeship....

On 23 June 1944, the Russians struck Army Group Center along a front four hundred kilometers wide. The entire central front from Vitebsk to Kiev stood in flames. With full-strength, well-supplied divisions heavily supported by armor, aircraft, and massive amounts of aid from the United States, the Red Army launched an attack against the exhausted German lines at Rschev, Smolensk, and farther south.

The Russians were now inflicting damage on the German army in the same manner that we had inflicted it on them in 1941 and 1942, during the periods of our great victories. Due to the obstinacy of Hitler, our generals could not proceed with the action needed to prevent the encirclement of entire armies. Offensives on an enormous scale cut through our foremost lines, raced deep into the hinterland, and cut off vast numbers of men and material, forcing mass surrender or annihilation of the ensnared units.

In the Bobruisk pocket, far south of our position at Yuchnovo, the trapped divisions were defeated and annihilated. The survivors of these huge encirclements that took place during the first days of July found themselves on their bitter way to the gulags and prisoner of war camps.

The reasons for the collapse of the central front were clear. We simply had too few soldiers, tanks, and resources to hold the enormous areas to be contained in the east, and our supreme commander in Berlin refused to accept this reality. There now existed no divisions possessing the strength of our units that had won earlier victories. From the regiments that originally were composed of three battalions, there were now only two greatly weakened battalions remaining. The pionier units and the artillery regiments were likewise weakened, having suffered severe losses in combat or having been stripped of personnel to serve as infantry.

In Germany, within the Reich itself, again and again new divisions were raised in attempts to hold the many fronts against an ever-stronger enemy, but the old divisions, those that had been on the front since the beginning, never received full replacements for the vast losses that had occurred over the years. One of the most serious problems that faced the landsers at the unit level was the fact that most of the experienced officers and noncommissioned officers had been killed or had suffered serious, debilitating wounds at the front and were no longer with us.

Moreover, the Wehrmacht never fully developed or learned the tactics and methods of retreat. The German soldier was taught to view retreat solely as a defeat, with no advantages forthcoming. Even in the early years, in the Reichswehr, the study of retreat, to include using this often necessary tactic to our advantage, was discouraged. After 1936 even the lesson plans for the teaching of a fighting withdrawal were stricken from the curriculum. "Attack" and "halt" were the only two methods of warfare hammered into us. In this regard, the Wehrmacht had entered into the war unprepared.

The collapse of Army Group Center in June and July resulted in chaos. This was clearly exhibited by the countless units observed on the roads and bridges, fleeing to the rear seemingly leaderless and without direction, while other weakened units attempted to make their way through the mob toward the front to engage the onrushing enemy. Some battered units were overcome with panic, and they streamed toward the west on foot and in vehicles of every description. The confusion, the panic-stricken landsers, the jamming of all movements along the passable roads would earlier have been considered as an inconceivable scenario, but the collapse of discipline and order had become reality.

The Russians were able to increase the turmoil and confusion through constant attacks with their air force, which bombed and strafed all roadways and rail lines, leaving shattered, demoralized fragments of once-proud regiments strewn in their path. The strategic reserves were unable to make their way through the chaos to the front and remained jammed in the tangle of vehicles and men. The movement of entire units had become impossible. And the highest commander, to whom credit for the catastrophe should be awarded, was not present to witness what his decisions had wrought. As always, the soldiers in the field bore the brunt of these mistakes and paid with their lives.

Army Group North was impacted by the collapse of the central front, as was the XXX Army Corps to the south. At the end of June the enemy right wing broke out of the heights before Polozk. The 132d Infantry Division was holding a wide sector of the front before Yuchnovo-Moskatschevo and the Velikaya sector. During the night 28–29 June, a police security regiment moved forward to relieve the battered landsers holding the positions of the First Battalion, Grenadier Regiment 437. With sixty men remaining in the Second Company, we crawled from our defenses in the swampy ground that we had held for weeks against overwhelming numbers of the enemy opposite us. We marched past the destroyed tank from the winter battle, its sides now streaked with rust and the hatches frozen open like gaping wounds, and we slowly wound our way along the splintered and scarred corduroy road through the swamp. Mess tins, entrenching tools, and assorted equipment rang softly on the steel helmets hanging from our belts, and the Ivans sent departing shots after us.

Five kilometers behind the front the battalion mustered at the edge of a small wood that offered a semblance of concealment from the ever-present aircraft. Our company spiess, Novotny, supplied us with warm food and other small items that we had been unable to receive during the weeks we had been on the line. We spent several hours sitting along the edge of the road or lying beneath the ragged pine trees, relishing the first warming rays of the early morning sunshine. It was a luxury once again to be able to stand erect without danger, once again to enjoy freedom of movement without the fear of meeting a sniper's bullet.

The obligatory schnapps bottle made its rounds. The younger and less experienced landsers, recent arrivals to the weakened company, rejected offhand the burning, home-brewed drink that left us with an unaccustomed tingling in the throat. We owed this rare amenity to the talents of Feldwebel Rohrer, who had skillfully fashioned a distillery from a battered Russian field kitchen that we had captured during the Crimean campaign. The stove had been modified for our use with a complicated tangle of copper tubing and bits of rubber fuel lines and had been fed a diet of potatoes and rhubarb gleaned from abandoned villages or captured from partisan caches.

As we passed the bottle, we felt an instinctive bond that only the survivors could know. Together we had known wind and heat, life and death. We had experienced hails of bombs and shells. We had tended our wounded, buried our dead, and moved forward to the next encounter, knowing that eventually, we would meet the end of our journey. Most of us owed our lives to the skill and self-sacrifice of others in our company, many of whom were no longer with us. We, the survivors, lay on the Russian soil, the smell and touch of which had become so familiar, and dozed in the summer sun.

As we lay quietly in small groups, consuming the schnapps and immersed in discussion of those things not associated with war, our idyll was interrupted by the rhythmic sound of approaching horses. Sitting upright, I observed a recent arrival to the division, Oberstleutnant Katzmann, approaching with several members of the regimental staff. He reined his horse to a halt several meters from my position. Rising stiffly to my feet, I drew myself to attention and rendered a salute, greeting him as respectfully as possible under the given circumstances.

"Good afternoon, Herr Oberstleutnant!" I called, holding my salute. He glared at me momentarily from his position on horseback before sharply returning the salute.

"Leutnant Bidermann, you are drunk!" he stated loudly and emphatically.

"Yes, Herr Oberstleutnant!" I replied. "I am drunk."

As I remained standing, perhaps unsteadily at attention, the staff officer began to upbraid me for my condition. After several long seconds of a stern tirade, I noticed Feldwebel Pinov rise to his feet and approach our location. With a long, glowing cigar hanging from one corner of his mouth, he marched forward. "What is going on here?" he abruptly demanded, his normally clear and precise demeanor obviously affected by the abundant quantity of schnapps consumed by the roadside. "No one talks to our leutnant like this!" He suddenly brushed past me and approached the mounted oberstleutnant, exclaiming, "We don't let anyone treat our leutnant like a recruit!"

I desperately moved forward in an attempt to grasp him by the shoulder to stop his verbal assault, and Katzmann sat upright in the saddle with indignation, alternately shifting his glare from me to the oncoming feldwebel. Before I could stop him and before Katzmann could utter a sharply worded reply, Pinov had grasped the reins of the mount's halter at the bit. Quickly leaning over as if to speak softly to the horse, he pulled the large animal toward him as he held tightly to the halter. Suddenly the lit cigar touched the sensitive muzzle of Katzmann's mount, and the horse exploded into action. Rearing sharply and flailing wildly with iron-shod forefeet, the horse tore itself loose from Pinov's grasp and rose into the air. Taken completely by surprise, the oberstleutnant tumbled backward from the saddle, landing in the sandy soil so common to all Russian roadsides. A landser dashed forward and seized the panic-stricken animal by the reins; others moved to assist the officer to his feet. Brushing aside their offers of assistance, Katzmann struggled to his feet and recovered his frightened horse. Glaring at me for several seconds, he turned and regained his mount before abruptly turning and riding past our now-silent, horrified ranks, followed by his escort.

The remaining portions of schnapps were collected by the gefreiters to be traded for candy and cigarettes. A sizable amount of forbidden firewater made its way to Favoli, Aigner, Binow, and the various company commanders, where it was consumed in quantity. So generous were some of our company members in distributing the surplus that eventually the source of this breach of regulations was traced, and I received a verbal reprimand from the regimental commander. I did not hear another word concerning the roadside incident, although I waited with dreadful expectation to be summoned for disciplinary action. It is likely that Oberstleutnant Katzmann, though short-tempered and often tactless in his resolution of certain situations, was fully aware that to make an issue of the incident would have served no positive purpose under the given circumstances.

The company commanders were called to battalion headquarters to be briefed on our current situation by Hauptmann Schmalfeld, the battalion commander. He solemnly advised us that farther to the south the enemy had broken through our front, and we were assigned to protect the open flank of Army Group North from the massive Russian forces pouring past us toward the west.

The battalion was hurriedly loaded into transports, and we were driven south over roads choking with dust. By late afternoon we had already relocated south of Duna. Following a short pause to organize the battalion, we advanced toward the south before dismounting from the vehicles. The landsers prepared for action, securing chin straps to their steel helmets, checking canteens of water, ensuring that magazines were fully loaded and that weapons were once again functioning faultlessly. Canvas sacks of hand grenades were distributed, and the infantrymen shared the burden of reserve machine-gun ammunition. Suddenly a kuebelwagon sped by our position, and from the front passenger seat of the vehicle Oberstleutnant Katzmann called above the clatter of the Volkswagon's air-cooled engine, "Leutnant Bidermann! Now show us what you can do!" I brought my hand to the rim of my helmet in acknowledgment as he disappeared in a cloud of dust.

We struck south without artillery support, penetrated the blocking fire of a Soviet howitzer battery, and shortly thereafter came under a concentrated mortar barrage, but miraculously we suffered no casualties. I led the company forward at a run, and as we cleared a small rise we suddenly found ourselves on a road occupied by Russian engineers busily engaged in laying box-mines in the evening twilight. The Russians scrambled for cover while opening fire with submachine guns in an attempt to protect themselves, but the detachment was raked by a machine-gun burst Aigner fired from the hip.

The enemy attempted to scatter, and we took two pony carts and a truck under fire with our small arms and hand grenades. Within seconds the incident was over and the guns had fallen silent. We immediately began searching the corpses strewn in the road, and in the passenger seat of the bullet-riddled truck I found a dying Russian colonel. I searched for and quickly located his blood-spattered map case in the last light of the sunset, and along with bars of sweet-smelling soap and Papyrossi cigarette packages, I uncovered the documents and maps. Stuffing the contents back into the leather case, I slung it over my shoulder and rallied the landsers, who were engaged in searching the pony carts for additional material. Of more importance to the hungry grenadiers for the moment, they had discovered several pasteboard boxes marked in English in black-stenciled letters, and they enthusiastically stuffed their pockets and bread bags with the tinned meat found in the containers.

The intelligence officer of the division later confirmed that the documents found on the fatally wounded colonel had revealed the detailed battle plans for the Third White-Russian Front, and from the maps the main points of penetration against our defenses could be determined. The documents also outlined a new system of attack to be implemented against us: the attacks would be opened by a heavy artillery barrage, followed closely by a low-angle blocking fire on the flanks of a corridor. Following closely within the two walls of bursting shells, in an area often no greater than one hundred meters wide, tanks and infantry would advance. The enemy was again adopting our tactics.

We deprived the enemy the use of the road for the remainder of the night, and the next morning we again moved toward the south and arrived at the location of an abandoned Soviet howitzer battery position. Dozens of spent shells lay scattered among piles of empty and discarded tins marked "Oscar Mayer—Chicago."

Our sister battalion was simultaneously fighting toward the south. Through the barrages from this Russian battery they had sustained heavy losses; and the battalion commander, Major Schnepf, his adjutant, Leutnant von der Stein, and many others had fallen.

With this attacking movement we had thrust ourselves thirty kilometers within the open flank of the Russian army, whose units in this area were targeted directly toward part of our homeland, the Baltic Sea, and East Prussia.

"Onward to Berlin!" was the watchword of the Soviets. "Father Stalin has commanded, and the Patriotic Front storms westward to destroy the hated German invaders. To the west must you attack, to avenge your fatherland, the land of the workers and farmers. The women of the enemy will be yours; there flows water from the walls; and you can wash yourselves and drink from porcelain containers." Instinctively we sensed the disaster that lay ahead, but even the most skeptical among us could never imagine the fury that our opponents from the east would deliver upon our homeland.

The regiment holding positions to the south had been bypassed and was threatened with encirclement. During the night of 30 June–1 July we received orders to march in a southerly direction toward Mioriya. The battalion was divided into two groups. With two rifle companies, an alarm company, two self-propelled Flak guns, and a heavy antitank gun, I was assigned as a group leader under the command of Battle Group Ambrosius. Oberst Ambrosius had recently been the commander of the NCO school in Riga, and one recent afternoon he had simply been pulled from there with his staff and students and thrown into battle.

This front, like so many others we had experienced, could be only thinly defended, and even then defense was limited to specific strategically important sectors. Our battle group was assigned to defend a sector approximately two kilometers in length. I positioned the antitank gun and the 20mm Flak guns on our left flank to cover the road that led through our positions to the southeast. The remaining area had to be defended by the rifle companies. Four heavy machine guns and two 80mm mortars reinforced the right wing.

With the rising sun the Russians probed our positions in company strength. In the early afternoon heavy-artillery rounds began to fall in our sector, and we soon found ourselves under a torrent of shells that abated only when the enemy attempted to penetrate our positions again. We clung to our line through 4 July, when the Russians plunged through the positions south of our right flank. The First Company, holding our southern sector, was compelled to counterattack in an attempt to close the penetration, and the company commander was among those killed in this action.

At 1400 our radio fell silent. We were no longer able to establish contact with Oberst Ambrosius and his staff of academy instructors in Mioriya. A reconnaissance platoon from my old company was dispatched in the direction of our right flank in an attempt to contact them, and they returned only to report that they had observed the town to be occupied by Russians.

Our battle group continued to hold its positions, despite the repeated Russian attempts to break through the left sector with infantry reinforced with armor. In the evening twilight, as the landsers lay behind their weapons, I crouched together with the radio operator who, bent over his communications equipment, vainly attempted to establish contact on the old frequency: "Mina, Mina, please come in. . . . Mina please report."

As darkness settled over us I received instructions, relayed through the forward observers of a 150mm artillery unit, to pull back five kilometers north-northwest. We feverishly organized for the withdrawal, and under cover of night we abandoned our positions. Leading the way was one of our self-propelled Flaks, the chassis piled high with members of the rifle company. The remainder of the rifle company followed with the antitank gun, the additional Flak, and, bringing up the rear, the other two companies. I joined the rear guard with two groups from the Second Company. The concise orders had demanded that we withdraw at exactly 2000, without leaving a rear guard in the positions. Prior to our movement more fire was exchanged, with infantry weapons and the two heavy machine guns firing tracers into the darkness. As we departed, the Russian mortar platoons fired sporadic salvos that impacted behind us. They received no reply.

We followed a trail through a thickly wooded area that eventually turned north. Just prior to 2200 we arrived at the eastern outskirts of a burning village. The forward element came to a halt and I hurried forward. After assessing the situation, we realized that we were now encircled and that we had no time to lose if we were to survive. From our location we could observe the village swarming with Russians, silhouetted against the fires that illuminated the area in a ghastly light. Near the edge of the forest, about one hundred meters from the first burning house, I stood next to the gunner of the 20mm. Aigner had rested his machine gun across the fender of the vehicle and was prepared to fire. The remainder of our group remained behind us, hidden in the shadows of the forest. After a moment's hesitation we moved forward and passed the village to the east, the flames from burning huts sending ghostly shadows among the trees. Despite the grinding of the engine that powered the self-propelled Flak, we remained unnoticed as we left the Russians behind us and eventually arrived at a forest-covered swamp.

In the dim glow of a field lamp I could see that my map outlined the northern edge of the swamp, beyond which was only a blank quadrant, void of the information we now required. Nevertheless, I realized that even this poorly executed map exhibited more information than many of our units would have had of the area. We proceeded through the forest until we entered a small clearing in the canopy of thick trees. From a small rise I looked toward the north and northwest, and at approximately ten kilometers' distance it was possible to observe a number of flares hanging silently in the sky. Russian aircraft had released them in preparation for a bombing run. There were the front lines; that must be our target as well. I advised the men of our objective, and we moved on through the darkness.

A summer-fresh sunrise brought a new day, 5 July 1944. The first morning rays danced on the meadows and wheat fields of a softly undulating landscape as we departed the perimeter of the forest. Barely one hundred meters distant a hill came into view on which was perched a primitive wooden shed. I cautiously approached the structure with the point element, intending to brief my second-in-command of our next movement. Barely thirty meters from us, a tall Russian major suddenly sprang from the waist-high wheat with drawn pistol and shouted in broken German, "Surrender, Fritz! You're surrounded!" For only a heartbeat the air remained still, and without warning a burst from Feldwebel Uschakow's submachine gun sawed across the major's breast.

The air instantly filled with the roar of gunfire. Russian submachine guns fired on us from almost point-blank range, hand grenades from both sides detonated around us, and we attempted to return fire while lying on the open ground. Still concealed in the forest barely one hundred meters behind us and yet unseen by the Russians, the first 20mm Flak opened fire, the rounds snapping viciously through the air above our heads. We could clearly see the tiny clouds of gray smoke as they exploded in the field before us. The second 20mm was soon brought into action, and, taken by surprise by this overwhelming firepower that had suddenly surfaced in their midst, approximately one hundred Russians fled before us to take cover in a protecting depression.

The rifle companies swarmed to the right and left of the road, plunging forward through the green stalks of wheat. With the Flak guns and the antitank gun in tow rumbling along the road, we pushed frantically toward the north. The seriousness of our situation, made desperate by our short-lived firefight, was apparent to every member of our group. I shouted over my shoulder to the men hurrying behind me, "Whoever wants to surrender can stay here. The rest of us will break through." There was no need to glance back toward our rear to know that no one remained behind as we urgently hurried on.

In the early afternoon we arrived near a settlement situated on a small rise that commanded the area. Dismissing the possibility that the village was occupied by the enemy, I prayed that from this location it was only a few kilometers to the Duna, where our lines would be.

The settlement was defended with two aging but still formidable T-26 tanks, which, belching clouds of black smoke, maneuvered to meet us with swinging turrets as we neared. Exhibiting great skill and bravery, Feldwebel Binow managed to get close enough to destroy one of them with a shaped charge. One of our Flak guns received a direct hit in the engine, and I crouched alongside the smoking chassis while the gunner continued hammering with uninterrupted fire at the enemy, a crimson stream of blood running from the sleeve of his tunic. The second Russian tank ground to a halt, and as the crew attempted to abandon the vehicle they tumbled to the ground under a hail of our small-arms fire. We rose from our positions and stormed into the village, screams erupting from our throats as we opened fire and threw hand grenades into the cottages.

A machine gunner barely twenty years old received a shoulder wound. Pausing long enough to grab the MG-42, I yelled for him to make his way toward the antitank gun so that they could take him aboard the self-propelled vehicle. Firing from the hip, I sprinted ahead with the others, and we broke through to the opposite side of the village.

We plunged ahead, leaving the burning dwellings behind us, and we soon arrived at the next settlement. There were no Soviet soldiers to be seen, but the inhabitants had everything prepared to welcome their liberation by the Red Army. We were suddenly among them before they were able to recognize our ragged uniforms and camouflage-bedecked helmets, and they were leaning from the doorways and windows of the huts, cheering and waving bits of white and red cloth. The women had prepared to greet their liberators with bowls of sweet cream, and the excited children stood nearby with wooden spoons. Horrified, they suddenly realized that the heavily armed arrivals were not members of the Red Army but were the enemy. Exhausted, hungry, and in torn uniforms caked with mud and sweat, we quickly downed the food and drink intended for our antagonists, otherwise ignoring the terrified inhabitants.

As the sun descended on the horizon we made our way closer toward our objective. Suddenly from our right flank we received a burst of machine-gun fire that snapped harmlessly overhead, and in the distance along the edge of the road we could make out the distinctive helmets of a heavy machine-gun crew crouching low behind their weapon. Our hearts pounding with elation, we drew cautiously nearer, calling to them in German. As we neared they gazed at us with wide-eyed astonishment.

While attempting the breakthrough back to our lines, the men of the rifle companies had requisitioned or captured pony carts into which the machine guns and wounded were now loaded. Some of the men were marching barefooted, their worn-out boots hanging across the backs of the horses. The uniforms were in tatters, white bandages stained with red-brown standing out starkly as a testament to the battles we had fought.

The exhausted group entered the positions of the oberst who had been assigned to defend Mioriya. Surrounded by officers of his staff, he stood in an immaculate uniform next to a table at a small crossroads. A tent had been erected in the background. On legs trembling with weariness, I reported the return of my unit. A large map was spread on the table, and I attempted to show him our route of retreat. For three days and nights we had been constantly on the move, without a moment's rest, and my eyelids grew heavy as I directed him across the map. Suddenly and without warning the colonel began roaring at me in a manner such that I had not heard since the war school.

I became instantly wide-awake. As he berated me for my appearance and bearing, I found myself resisting the urge to toss the table and the map at him and the surrounding officers, some of whom were glaring at me grimly; others appeared to suffer embarrassment at the outburst. He ended the tirade by requesting that I remove my dirty finger from his map and to use a twig of grass if needed for briefing him on our route. I ended the briefing abruptly, and wordlessly departed their gracious company as quickly as possible. I returned to the ragged column of landsers standing in the dusty roadway, and we moved on. Despite our immense relief at having returned to our lines, we were overcome with an intense longing to be back with our old regiment, to be again in the company of our family. We were attempting to find the route to our unit when we spotted an artillery carriage with the circular tactical insignia of our division, and we knew in which direction we must march.

The following morning, 6 July, we occupied a security line in the area of Druya, and in the course of the next several days we shifted our positions to cover a line ten kilometers south of Druya-Antonovka-Sossnovka-Malinovka. On 12 July we lay near Krasnogorka on Snudy Lake before again launching an attack toward the south into the open Russian flank. This attack from 13 to 19 July carried us to Strussto Lake and Dundele near Plusy.

On 12 July the regiment was situated fifty kilometers southeast of Dunaburg, before a terrain feature that offered an excellent field of fire for our antagonists. I was with the Second Company in a depression that could be taken under fire from the nearby Soviet positions. During daylight hours we could barely show our heads from the muddy holes we had dug without drawing enemy mortar and small-arms fire. We repeatedly requested artillery and assault-gun support, as without this reinforcement it would be next to impossible to ever silence the guns that terrorized us. We were acutely aware that even to attempt to do so would result in disaster.

Oberst Sepp Drexel came to our rescue with Regiment 436. He had been given the assignment to close the gap between our division and our southern neighbor southwest of Plusy. To my immense relief, Uncle Sepp assumed leadership of both regiments, and with two assault guns at his disposal the experienced commander pushed deep into the enemy flank. Following this action we were able to storm the heights from our low-lying positions, overrun the Soviet positions, and push far to the south in the direction of Strussto Lake.

This action afforded the army command a temporary and short-lived respite, as a major part of the right wing of Army Group North, which a few days previously had been fighting on the western heights before Polozk, could be withdrawn to a less threatened area. For his initiative and action taken in stabilizing the situation on the southern wing, Oberst Drexel was awarded the Knight's Cross, which he most highly deserved.

On 29 July we moved to Aknista. We maintained our positions for a week, during which time Hauptmann Schmalfeld was killed, and I assumed command of the battalion. We were then ordered south, and the long columns of ragged landsers wound their way to Stockmannshof in the Duna bridgehead. Here we remained, holding a thin line for almost two weeks before moving again, back toward the north and crossing the Duna over a wooden pontoon bridge. Following our crossing of the river we attacked toward the north near Ergli.

Twenty July 1944. Count Claus von Stauffenberg placed his bomb in the headquarters of the Fuhrer to destroy the brown dictator. Repercussions of this assassination attempt, the attentat, on the Supreme Commander of the German Wehrmacht and the Greatest War Lord of All Time were felt even on our foremost lines of the Eastern Front.

Our decimated companies had been engaged in constant battle since 30 June 1944. The opportunity to sleep, to close our eyes and momentarily escape the horror, came by the hour, by the minute, by the second. We remained drained and exhausted. The environment had ravaged the landsers physically and psychologically; the front demanded that each individual fight to survive from minute to hour. Then, in addition to the adversity and losses we were experiencing, came the news of the assassination attempt.

Simple words cannot express the thoughts we held at the news of the attempt on the life of Hitler. For years we had continued to fight bitterly for the survival of our homes and our families, but as the rumors of the actual situation in our homeland increased, combined with the exhortations of the political leaders far from the guns, we began to further question the integrity of our leadership in Berlin. We had become painfully aware that our sacrifices, the years of constant exposure to suffering, deprivation, and death had left these leaders indifferent and emotionless to everything except whatever would benefit and enrich them as individuals. We began seeking and praying for an end to the conflagration into which so many millions had been thrust.

A week later I learned from the forward observers of an artillery regiment that the son of General Lindemann had been arrested by a field-police unit. He had been assigned to an artillery regiment of the 132d Infantry Division, and when the news of the failed attempt on Hitler was announced, he was supposedly overheard saying, "Too bad that he isn't dead." He had then been denounced by one of his own men.

It was confirmed that General Lindemann, our former commander, was a member of the resistance group, and it is highly likely that the arrest of his son was the result of the so-called Sippenverhaftung that was carried out zealously and without mercy by the men of the party.

General Lindemann was an officer of the old school, an excellent leader of troops who had the refined mannerisms of an aristocrat. While serving as division commander he had gone to great lengths to ensure that his troops received the best available care, and he had exhibited the most meticulous professionalism throughout the offenses at Feodosia, Kertsch, and Sevastopol. He had always ensured that artillery, Luftwaffe, and all additional means of support were arranged and carried out to the utmost degree possible in order to reduce casualties.

Several times during the fighting at Gaitolovo he had risked his reputation and career by insisting that a delay or a rescheduling of an attack be implemented, in the face of much opposition from the higher command, after a careful study of the situation. This may have cost General Lindemann some prestige in Berlin; however, it certainly reduced the number of casualties that might have been incurred while ensuring the same successful results. It was also while under his command that the great Soviet offensives at Smerdynia and Lake Ladoga were broken.

And now it was revealed to us that General Lindemann was a member of a resistance group. From that moment, all reason for self-sacrifice, for loyalty to the country and to the National Socialist Government, all the reasons with which we were constantly imbued for making the sacrifices on the front would be forever in question. This one act, more than any other factor, revealed to us that the war was lost. The knowledge that a number of our most talented and trusted military leaders would attempt to kill our head of state, albeit a ruthless dictator, proved to us that militarily we could not win against the massed, combined might of the Allies.

The one remaining factor that steeled us to fight ever harder was the knowledge that our Soviet enemy would show no commitment to civility or to the common laws of humanity should they invade our homeland. The other outcome of the attempt on the Fuhrer's life was that it could not be denied, regardless of the lengths taken in justification, that Hitler, the one-time idol of millions, became in the eyes of many nothing more than a dictator in brown who would take any sadistic and brutal measures against his political opponents. Our own commanders in the field, to whom we entrusted our lives and who controlled our destiny, fell among the ranks of his victims as well. In the eyes of the soldiers, the aura of the Fuhrer was destroyed. The explosives placed by Oberst Count von Stauffenberg did not kill the dictator, but the act undermined, if it did not destroy, the idolatry that had been so carefully instilled and nurtured by the government throughout our youth.

For some time there had been National Socialist political officers assigned to military units. In the previous months and years, hardly anyone within the ranks on the front had taken them seriously. In the beginning they were usually experienced, trusted veterans of the frontline units who, because of serious wounds, were no longer able physically to serve in the lines. Nevertheless, as the fortunes of the war began to turn, it became apparent to us that they increasingly came to resemble their counterparts in the Red Army, and they came to be known among the landsers as "politruks."

Following the 20 July assassination attempt, the military salute was changed. The traditional salute, universally recognized as bringing the hand to the cap visor or rim of the steel helmet, was now forbidden. Reichsmarschall Hermann Goring, the highest ranking military officer of our nation, deemed the Nazi Party salute as more appropriate for demonstrating the loyalty of the Wehrmacht to the ruling system. This party salute, the thrusting of an outstretched right arm forward, was observed with contempt and resentment by soldiers who honored military tradition, and the order was taken as an insult by those who valued high standards and character. Indeed, in the eyes of the soldiers, the mandated use of this salute served to implicate them, to identify the soldiers with those enthusiastic members of the party who had developed a talent for sitting out the war at home, and it represented those who were now to be held in such contempt. Even prior to this order, within the military environment this salute had been regarded as ridiculous and impractical. Following the order it was not uncommon to observe entire companies carrying their mess tins in their right hands to avoid being compelled to demonstrate their "loyalty to the party."

In view of the circumstances we were facing on the front, our concern for the politics of the attentat was short-lived. The average soldier on the front was so immersed in the difficulties of survival that little time was spent on brooding over its consequences. In later years, among circles of friends, we revealed to one another that the entire affair caused not a tear to be shed among us. Any sympathy for politicians, regardless of the situation, had been eliminated through years of deprivation and suffering on the front and during the endless months and years of captivity that followed. Above all, however, we were bound to our duty by the oath we had sworn as soldiers of Germany; to swear, with weapons in hand, to defend our country even to the sacrifice of our lives. Not even a change in command or policy could free us from this oath. The attentat was not necessarily considered by the soldier to be a betrayal, as through the natural course of events on the front we had come to place our loyalty with our own and thus differentiated between the armed forces and the brown-clad leaders in Berlin.

It was fifteen years later that I learned the story behind the death of our general, who, in my mind, had served as an extremely brave and talented division commander, a fine officer, and an unforgettable leader in the memories of those who knew and served under him. The report of what had occurred was generously provided to me by the general's son and his widow, who had received the information in a letter from Frau Dr. Charlotte Pommer of the Staatskrankenhaus in Berlin.

The general had taken refuge in the home of an architect in Berlin, a deed for which both the man and his wife paid with their lives. The government of the Reich had placed a bounty of 500,000 Reichsmarks for information leading to his capture, and the Gestapo was set in pursuit.

According to the former German Red Cross nurse Gertrud Lux, General Lindemann had been shot by one of the Gestapo officials who brought him to the State Police Hospital, Berlin NW 40, Scharnhorststrasse 13, on 3 September 1944. This particular official wore a ring bearing the initials AT or TA. She was informed that these security service officials, while serving under the direction of Kriminalrat Sarde, had entered the residence on Reichskanzlerplatz in which General Lindemann was hiding. After their arrival, the general managed to lock himself in a room on the uppermost floor and then attempted to climb out the window onto the roof. The Gestapo official managed to kick in part of the door and quickly fired two shots toward the figure as he was attempting to climb through the window. At this point the general obviously collapsed, and the official then asked if he had been hit, to which Lindemann replied, "Yes . . . I think twice."

At 1430 the general was brought to the hospital with a gunshot wound in his abdomen and a flesh wound in his upper thigh. The hospital staff was instructed to care for the wounds he had received during his arrest, and the handling of the patient was classified as top secret and was to be dealt with accordingly. While preparations were being made to care for his wounds, he took a seat on a stool and was then placed on an operating table where his right wrist was secured. He expressed concern about the binding of his hand, and it was explained to him that the precaution was normal procedure prior to surgery. An anesthesia was then intravenously administered, and as he slipped into unconsciousness the general spoke in a loud voice, "I am General Lindemann . . . I am innocent . . . I am dying for Germany!!! Please greet my wife."

The operation, which lasted one hundred minutes, revealed that the colon had been penetrated twice, causing poisonous leakage that later infected his internal organs. The flesh wound in his upper thigh was tended as well. Following the operation he was taken to room 116 of the surgical unit, where two Gestapo officials remained constantly on watch. While he was still under narcosis, both his hands were bound to either side of the bed. It was then arranged that an interrogation would take place when his condition would permit and he was strong enough to withstand questioning.

On the following day the condition of the patient was much improved. The night nurse Gertrud Lux explained to the SD officials that the patient could not receive proper care as long as his hands remained bound and managed to convince them to free the bonds during the morning and evening washing, which lasted for approximately an hour and a half.

On 4 September it was attempted through Frau Alexandra Roloff and Dr. Maria Daalen to notify the relatives of the patient's status. On 5 September the bonds were removed from his wrists, and a postoperative examination revealed that peritonitis had set in, which made any immediate interrogation inadvisable. Despite the seriousness of his wound, his circulation and blood pressure remained relatively acceptable.

During the numerous air-raid warnings with which Berlin was plagued at this time, he was removed from his room and taken to the operations bunker, and he noticed that the SD official went to lengths to ensure that he was always taken to a very safe area, probably as much for the security of the SD personnel as for the security of the general. One time when the SD guard momentarily left his charge alone with the nurse to relieve himself, General Lindemann asked her, "Nurse Gertrud, how is the situation at the front?" In view of the recent events, the nurse was unsure of how to respond to this curious question and hesitantly asked, "Aren't you aware of what is happening to you?"

"Of course, but it is not of importance, while so many are dying," he responded. On another occasion he thanked her for caring for him and mentioned that he had two sons at the front.

The isolated peritonitis developed into a general abdominal infection, and the general's condition began to worsen. On 11 September a blood transfusion was ordered. At noon of the same day the Gestapo personnel received a phone call to warn them that a plan to free the general could be in progress. For several days afterward the SD officials kept a loaded pistol within quick reach on their night table.

On 13 September Professor Hoche, chief surgeon of state hospitals, examined the patient in the surgical ward. When he introduced himself, General Lindemann simply closed his eyes and did not reply. The professor opened the wound and drained an abscess without administering anesthesia. The general did not speak or utter a sound during or after the examination.

Following the examination, Professor Hoche contacted Kriminalrat Sarde by telephone and explained to him that the condition of the patient was serious and that an interrogation must be conducted as soon as possible if they wished to gain any information at all from him. Following this conversation, Dr. Charlotte Pommer contacted Dr. Tietze, the director of the internal section of the hospital. It was decided that the patient would be given a large dose of Pantopon rather than the regular hourly application of circulatory medicine during the night. This decision was never put into effect as approximately one-half hour later more Gestapo officials appeared and interrogated the general for a period of approximately two hours.

On the evening of 13 September news of his arrest was broadcast over the radio networks, and the next morning the incident first appeared in the newspapers. On the afternoon of 21 September he was interrogated once again for a short period of time, and on that evening his condition worsened considerably. At approximately 0300, 22 September his blood pressure dropped, and about two hours and fifteen minutes later he lost consciousness, never to awaken.

Throughout his interrogation and during his internment at the hospital he never expressed any outward sign of physical pain. After his death his body was confiscated by the Gestapo, and his last resting place remains unknown.

THE FINAL RETREAT

During the days of July and August we became specialists in withdrawal and retreat, despite our lack of formal training in the practice of this art. The old gefreiters thoroughly fulfilled their roles as the backbone of the battalions. Split up into small combat units, we were no longer routinely assigned to our own division but were constantly shifted from unit to unit with seemingly little planning or organization. We became in large part reliant on our own ingenuity for supply and support, and we learned that any given situation was likely to change without warning. Earlier it had been standard procedure to establish a proper supply and support organization whenever new positions were occupied, which would involve the prepositioning of ordnance and rations for all personnel, including a systematic plan for caring for the wounded. With the breakdown of the standard order of battle, such systematic planning was no longer possible, and we found it increasingly necessary to provide for ourselves without expecting or relying on support from the higher command.

We had developed a sensitive, self-reliant intelligence network that could inform us of the general conditions of our front. On a large scale, the lack of mail deliveries for an extended period of time became a sure sign that another major catastrophe had occurred. From our frontline positions it was not always possible to discern what might have been occurring several kilometers distant from our location; but as battle-hardened veterans, the landsers could quickly assess the situation around them and instinctively become aware of impending disaster. From a distance we could hear the heavy-artillery barrages as the enemy prepared to strike a sector of the front; and from the far-off gunfire and the customary sound of throbbing engines and grinding of tracks associated with heavy armor we could determine a breakthrough on our right or left flank, thus giving us only a few precious minutes hastily to prepare a withdrawal, the order for which would inevitably arrive at the last possible moment.

In the early morning hours I arrived at our new defense sector in the area of Dunaburg and set about establishing our defensive line and briefing the remains of the battle group and the First Battalion, Regiment 437. I was assisted by several NCOs and obergefreiters. Several hundred meters behind our position we located a storage depot where a supply feldwebel was guarding a large cache of provisions that had not yet been transferred farther to the rear.

We asked him if we could be permitted to draw some of the supplies for the use of the landsers and carefully advised him that within a few hours this very location would become the front lines, adding that from our experience the first mortar rounds would begin falling around midday. He replied that he would be more than willing to open his depot to us, as we still had sufficient time to distribute the goods to the combat troops, but added that he had been instructed to wait for a relief column to evacuate what he admitted were immense stores of flour, liquor, and cigarettes.

I immediately reported the situation to the battle-group headquarters and requested instructions regarding the supply depot, but I received no decision or orders concerning the supplies. Meanwhile our Second Company had begun arriving to occupy their positions before the depot, and word of the riches waiting to be taken spread like wildfire among the troops.

The commander of the Second Company neared with his entourage of landsers. As the supply feldwebel hedged and hesitated, platoons of infantrymen began approaching in bleached, ragged uniforms and battered, camouflaged helmets shielding their unshaven, sunburned faces. The dirty, gray-green columns came onward, battle weary, with grenades in their belts, submachine guns swinging at their hips. The machine gunners appeared with long belts of linked 7.92 ammunition gleaming in the sun and antitank rockets slung over their shoulders. The feldwebel suddenly seemed to realize the full seriousness of the situation. The front was coming to him. He immediately leaped into his vehicle and disappeared toward the rear in a cloud of dust, abandoning the depot and its entire contents to us.

The pony carts were quickly organized, and under the command of the machine-gun company the soldiers entered the depot to evacuate the stores. Huge quantities of cigarettes, food, and liquor were removed and placed by the roadside to enable the troops of other units to help themselves as they marched by. A large percentage of the supplies was distributed before late afternoon, when the depot came under the inevitable fire from the Russian artillery batteries and was destroyed.

During the next several days, Obergefreiter Hohenadel, my former recruit commander, destroyed his ninth Soviet tank in close combat while serving as platoon leader with the Fourteenth Infanterie-Panzerjaeger Company. In the late afternoon he had received the assignment to take three antitank "stovepipe" personnel up the road in a vehicle. This road marked the perimeter between them and the neighboring division, and we were assigned to block the route to any enemy tanks that might attempt to use this road. Approximately halfway to the assigned point they were met by a large number of infantrymen from the neighboring division who were withdrawing toward the rear, and they warned the four landsers not to proceed farther up the road, as a column of Russian tanks was approaching.

Heeding the warning, they were in the process of seeking a good defensive position when the transmission on the truck failed. With two of the men accompanying him, Hohenadel proceeded forward on foot. Rounding a curve in the road, they suddenly found themselves facing a number of Russian tanks a few hundred yards distant. In the evening dusk the obergefreiter could see that the tanks were piled high with heavily armed infantrymen, and the landsers immediately dove into a hedge near the roadside, praying that they had not been seen. As the column neared, the gefreiter with one of the stovepipes shouldered his weapon, took careful aim at the first tank, and scored a direct hit.

The entire column instantly pulled to a halt, and infantrymen leaped from the tanks and poured into the thick undergrowth approximately twenty paces from Hohenadel's hidden location. Hohenadel opened fire on the group of Russians with his submachine gun. The almost point-blank range from which they were suddenly being fired on, combined with the growing darkness, resulted in momentary chaos within the enemy ranks. They returned the fire, but in the darkness the antitank crew had already sprinted to the other side of the road where the other men were waiting, and the hand grenades thrown by the Russians exploded harmlessly on the position abandoned seconds earlier.

The landsers quickly shifted positions again and dove for cover in a roadside ditch. After several seconds the column began moving again, and the landsers were instructed to allow the first two tanks to pass before opening fire on the third. After several minutes the column could be heard clattering toward them; and as the enemy ranks neared, one of the men fired his stovepipe and scored a direct hit on the lead tank, which immediately burst into flames.

The remaining tanks held back and remained farther toward the rear, still accompanied by a large number of troops. Although greatly outnumbered, Hohenadel's group opened fire with machine pistols and assault rifles and charged onto the road. Despite the overwhelming odds against the landsers, the Russians fled in panic.

Meanwhile, the landsers could hear more tanks approaching to within one hundred meters of their location, and the next vehicle that they were able to observe in the flickering light of the already blazing tank was a type Stalin, a sixty-four-ton colossus that plunged into view from the protection of the darkness.

Another stovepipe was fired, and to the landsers' horror the projectile struck the target but failed to penetrate the armor. Luckily the tank halted, shifted into reverse, and retreated into the darkness. Hohenadel followed close behind with a panzerfaust after observing that the infantry had abandoned the vehicle when it had received the first hit. Making his way to within a few meters of the enemy vehicle, he fired the panzerfaust at point-blank range. The head of the projectile penetrated the thick steel wall and detonated within the tank. It quickly began to burn, and explosions from the fuel and ammunition soon followed.

A number of our own infantrymen arrived to reinforce the group, and they held the road until the following morning. This allowed enough time for the engineers to destroy an important bridge behind the tiny force, and with that move the enemy's attempt to drive a wedge between our two divisions along this road failed.

Midsummer 1944. During the fighting south of Drissa-Druya we attempted to link up with Army Group Center's Third Panzer Army with a drive that took us thirty kilometers over the Duna. Despite all efforts, this attempt was in vain. On 10 July, a gap twenty-five-kilometers wide was torn between our Army Group North and the devastated Army Group Center. In the Bobruisk pocket the Red Army destroyed twenty German divisions. This catastrophe could only be compared to the destruction of the Sixth Army at Stalingrad; but the German propaganda machinery made little mention of the disaster other than to attempt to convince the population that this ignominious defeat was in reality a victory of sorts, even though with this enemy offensive thousands of Germany's soldiers on the Eastern Front had fallen.

Following this great victory against Army Group Center, the Soviet army held a triumphal march in Moscow. Later, while incarcerated as a prisoner of war, I met a number of the soldiers of this debacle who had survived and had experienced the subsequent march into captivity. The German survivors—those who had managed to remain alive following the surrender—were transported to Moscow. Many had died from thirst and exhaustion on the long journey or, unable to continue due to wounds or sickness, had been summarily shot where they collapsed during the endless march. Eventually the prisoners were collected in massive camps near Moscow in preparation for the victory procession. In order to strengthen the starving prisoners for the ordeal, they were fed a ration of grease-laden soup, which they devoured ravenously.

In rows of twenty-four abreast they were then compelled to file through Moscow. They marched past the Soviet generals on reviewing stands, the city population lined the streets by the thousands, the Allied embassy personnel and dignitaries were present as honorary guests, and the victory march was captured on film by journalists from all corners of the globe. After weeks of deprivation, the digestive systems of the prisoners were no longer tolerant of the fare rationed to them, and during the march through the city the ragged columns became stricken with acute diarrhea, which served to weaken them to an even greater extent. Thousands of the "Voyna-Plennys" were unable to control their tortured bowels throughout the victory parade, and later in the United States a film was released showing the filth of the "Fascist invaders" being cleaned from the streets of Moscow—as an example of "the agony of defeat."

During ancient times it was common for the victorious forces to parade their prisoners through Rome or Carthage. The prisoners would become slaves of the victors, but there was nevertheless often a semblance of protection through laws and basic rights. In the twentieth century prisoners were often afforded little or no protection in any form and remained free game for the victors. One could beat them, work them to death, shoot them, or simply let them starve.

It was widely accepted within the ranks of those fighting in the east that death on the battlefield was preferable to an unknown destiny in a Soviet prisoner of war camp. This mentality often played a role in the many acts of bravery demonstrated by individuals or entire units. During the closing days of the war it was not at all uncommon for entire companies, battalions, and battle groups to fight to the last man, the survivors going into captivity only when ammunition was exhausted and wounds were too grave to allow further resistance.

In July, a massive force of twenty-nine Russian infantry divisions and an armored corps of the First Baltic and Third White-Russian Front pushed through the gap in the defenses of Army Group Central and streamed westward toward the Baltic Sea. With this thrust, the fate of Army Group North, composed of twenty-three German divisions, was sealed. These doomed divisions, isolated and totally cut off from Germany, were later to be designated Army Group Courland and would hold out against overwhelming odds until the bitter end.

ERGLI

In July 1944 the front of the Army Group in the south ran west of Schaulen to Mitau. The Soviets succeeded in pushing twenty divisions through this line, and on 29 July they arrived at Tukkum and were then standing on the Baltic Sea. Although the German divisions fought bitterly at Aknista, on the Duna bridgehead at Stockmannshof, and in the area of Ergli, they were nevertheless severed from the only possible land route to Germany.

In August General Graf Strachwitz attempted to recapture Tukkum behind us with his panzer group. On 20 August he succeeded in taking this strategically important sector, and for the moment we breathed more easily. This victory was recognized as an overwhelming accomplishment not only for Graf Strachwitz and his panzer crews but also for the sailors of the cruiser *Prinz Eugen* and escorting destroyers and torpedo boats, who had bombarded the Russian positions at Tukkum from the sea.

On 21 and 22 August we attacked the town of Ergli with the weakened First Battalion of Regiment 437. Near the banks of the Ogre we captured the forward positions and assaulted the Russians through the cemetery of Ergli. We sought shelter between the gravestones as we came under mortar and artillery fire, with shrapnel hissing and smashing against the stone memorials where we lay. Knowing that to remain at this location was to invite imminent death or wounding, Volle and I fired our submachine guns on the run as we advanced with the battalion staff through the barrage. A short distance ahead a row of underbrush offered cover, and I dodged through the grave markers toward the concealment, when suddenly from no more than two paces I was surprised by a set of wide eyes staring from under a round olive-colored Russian helmet.

Our eyes seemed to lock on one another's for an eternity. Instinctively I managed to shout a quick "Stoi!" and the Russian sergeant's submachine gun clattered at my feet. Volle, only a few meters distant, rapidly kicked a grenade that landed near him into the underbrush and captured a Russian private who stumbled forward, hands above his head.

A cursory search of the area revealed that the sergeant had a field telephone hidden in the row of bushes, and Gefreiter Treiber from the battalion staff took it for our own use, but not before dialing the Soviet unit at the other end of the communications cable and shouting, "Fritzen here, yes!" into the telephone as they came on the line.

The communications wire disappeared into the undergrowth, revealing to us the direction in which we needed to advance. The Russian sergeant had been directing the mortar and artillery fire that had threatened to cut off our attack, and with his capture his unit could no longer receive information regarding our movement or position.

We called in 80mm mortar fire as well as 150mm artillery support from the Thirteenth Artillery Battery on the commanding height south-east of Ergli, and behind this curtain of fire we assaulted the hill with fifty men. Volle, a former artillerist who had served with the 132d Artillery Regiment in the Crimea, established liaison between our location and two of our division's batteries that had taken up positions behind Ergli during the night.

As a means of holding the heights against overpowering opposition, we developed a new but dangerous tactic. With only a weakened means of defense, it was obvious that we would not be able to hold our positions without the unfailing support of the artillerists.

During the night we would establish two machine-gun posts forward of the crest. As dawn began to break, we would evacuate these positions, withdrawing the landsers to the lee side of the height, approximately two hundred meters from the crest. Predictably, the Soviets would advance in the wake of our withdrawing units, and as soon as we observed the first Russian helmets appearing on the crest of the heights, I would order 105mm barrages directly on our previous positions. This was unfailingly successful in driving the enemy back to their line, and in the evening light we would again occupy the positions.

In this manner we were able to hold our positions on "Egg Hill" before Ergli for nearly two weeks. In the last days of August Leutnant Steinhardt reported to us with eighty men from the Luftwaffe as reinforcements for the battalion. They were assigned to Grenadier Regiment 438 and adjusted quickly to their new role as infantrymen, proving themselves reliable and brave fighters. Throughout this period we maintained an excellent relationship with the regimental commander Oberst Sierts and his adjutant, Hauptmann von Daimling.

In the closing days of August we were pulled back to serve as the regimental reserve to the old Ergli estate. After a long period of fighting rearguard actions we had finally been placed under the command of our old regiment again. It was now commanded by one of the old "hatchets" from Regiment 436, Major Ochsner. He had heard of our defense of Egg Hill, and he approached us as I and 120 men from the battalion lay resting in the churchyard of Ergli. He greeted me warmly and, with his arm about my shoulders, we spoke briefly of old times that we had both enjoyed with the regiment. It remained unsaid, but we remained fully aware that in all likelihood we were approaching our last and final battlefield. As we spoke of so many of our comrades that now lay buried in

Russian soil, he paused long enough to gaze on the tattered, filthy survivors lying on the earth exhausted, and with moist eyes he suddenly turned and departed.

The days of the heldenklau descended on us. The rear support personnel were being rounded up in ever greater numbers and pressed into service as infantry. Luftwaffe personnel still wearing their blue-gray uniforms and without a single day's training in infantry tactics and only cursory instruction in the use of automatic weapons found themselves reporting to us, fully unprepared yet willing to face an ever-stronger enemy. For those in the rear, far from the Russian guns, the term "transferred to the infantry" had taken on a new, ominous meaning. The threat of serving in the front lines, where the mortar and artillery rounds burst, where snipers considered killing the unwary as a rewarding but deadly sport, and where men slaughtered one another routinely from almost within arm's reach was enough to make the blood run cold in the veins of many a rear-echelon warrior. The phrase "punitive transfer" was heard among the troops more often. This term was regarded with disgust and contempt by the older infantry veterans and survivors of many battles, and the practice as a penalty for a perceived or real infraction served to promote ill feelings between the battalion veterans and those troops who had been transferred to us for disciplinary reasons. As that became more commonplace, the professional infantrymen were obliged to ask themselves if the years spent in the foremost lines, the deprivations suffered, and the horrors experienced had been regarded as nothing more than a disciplinary action.

There was one generaloberst in particular whose highly esteemed rank insignia could, in the minds of those who had personally experienced his peculiar style of leadership, only be credited to the golden party badge he wore and to his philosophy of placing his loyalty to the National Socialist Party above his loyalty to the troops whose lives were entrusted to him. Generaloberst Schoerner made a practice of punishing landsers, noncommissioned officers, and officers with immediate transfer to the infantry for any insignificant infraction. It was generally agreed that this high-ranking gentleman obviously understood nothing of the code of honor held by the German infantry. By sending offenders to the infantry as a form of punishment, he contributed to the degradation of the soldiers' willingness to sacrifice themselves for what they had been taught was right and just.

One evening a noncommissioned officer, trained as a weapons specialist, reported to me for duty from battalion headquarters. He informed me that he was reporting as ordered by the generaloberst and was to be demoted in rank and placed in the foremost lines. The following day we received the punitive report carefully printed as an official document bearing the letterhead of Army Group North, signed by the generaloberst with an oversized S as the initial for Schoerner.

This highly trained feldwebel had been a precision toolmaker by profession, had attended the Army Weapons School, and as such could be considered an irreplaceable asset to his battalion. The generaloberst, so he explained, was not concerned with how the battalion would keep its machine guns and assault rifles in repair but with the idea that discipline must be maintained and that infractions would be severely punished.

The perceived infraction had occurred when this feldwebel was en route to a rearward weapons depot to obtain urgently needed parts for his unit's weapons. He had been riding on the running board of a regimental vehicle when he observed a high-ranking general at a crossroads, and he had dutifully leaped from the vehicle to report. He removed his pipe with his left hand and held it at his side as he rendered the customary salute. He was unable to put the pipe in his uniform pocket, as it was lit and would thus burn his tunic. As he saluted, the general demanded to be shown the item he was holding in his hand. He showed the officer with crimson and gold collar insignia his pipe and was immediately told to toss it away.

The feldwebel then dutifully tapped the pipe against the sole of his boot and quickly stuck it into his tunic pocket, an action that would have been considered perfectly acceptable by any reasonable officer. For this grave offense he was to be punished. He remained with us for several days at battalion headquarters, where he found employment repairing and refurbishing our battle-worn weapons.

Almost one week later I was approached by a one-armed staff officer who appeared unexpectedly at our headquarters. This leutnant had been assigned the unenviable task of confirming that the sentence of the soldier involved in this incident was indeed being carried through. It was at this time that I made my first and only false report during my entire military experience: "The man was killed in action . . . two days ago."

The officer then disappeared and I never regretted the false report. It was the duty of every officer to ensure the welfare of his men, and I considered the feldwebel's skill and his ability to keep our weapons in the best working order to be far more valuable to the war effort than simply to obey this preposterous order.

During the last weeks the division had been pulled back over the Russian-Baltic border, and once again we had European soil under our feet. The area had served as a geographic buffer for centuries between central and northern Europe as well as between east and west. To the casual observer, the softly undulating terrain renders a peaceful atmosphere. The hilltops are loosely crowned with pines, maple, and oak. The shallow valleys are carpeted with grass, damp moor, and small lakes surrounded with birch trees. The landscape is interspersed with small, fast-moving streams that flow into the Duna River, which meets the Baltic Sea at Riga.

The inhabitants were primarily engaged in farming or forestry. The earth is fruitful, and for eastern Europe the climate is comparatively mild. Cattle, pigs, and sheep are raised in abundance, and the people live in wooden houses with a large living quarters, a bathing room, and solidly built barns for the animals. Large, well-constructed cellars are usually built in close proximity to the houses. During the fighting in the areas of Stockmannshof, Aknista, and Ergli and from Riga to Courland we used the cellars for battalion and company headquarters when possible. The local estates, somewhat smaller than those of their Prussian cousins to the west, are scattered throughout the land, with villages alongside primitive roadways that are constructed more for use by horse-drawn carts than for motorized vehicles. Although the farm and village dwellings display a distinctive eastern architecture, the larger structures in the cities and towns are of definite German design. The cities contain churches and public buildings of lower German baroque style from the Middle Ages.

The peaceful landscape with clean homes, villages, and towns reminded us of our own homeland, to the extent that it made our current situation, being severed and isolated from our familiar surroundings and families, somewhat easier to bear. The field kitchens welcomed supplies of fresh vegetables, new potatoes, and pork, and the supply officers and each company spiess strove to enhance their reputations as they competed with one another to provide the best possible provisions to the soldiers at the front.

The last days of August found the battalions and regiments of the

132d Infantry Division engaged in battle west of Modohn and near Ergli against an enemy immensely superior in material and manpower. Following this heavy fighting, it was necessary to disband the 437th Grenadier Regiment due to the heavy losses suffered without hope of replacements. On 14 September, the last commander of Regiment 437, Major Ochsner, holder of the Knight's Cross, was killed in action at Ergli. During the war in Russia he had been wounded no less than eight times and had hardly recovered from his most recent wounds when he met his fate on the battlefield.

At the beginning of September, Hauptmann Dedel assumed command of the battalion. He was a genuine Bavarian, with a sense of humor and a strong, athletic build. He was known for his short-stemmed pipe, which he referred to as his "nose-warmer." I remained on the staff serving as battalion adjutant, and Volle was assigned duties as the ordnance officer. Gerd Pirner was our medical officer, and the machine-gun company was commanded by the blond Hauptmann Fred Fuchsius, whom we had nicknamed Peer Gynt.

The few survivors within our old circle of friends had become inseparable, and only wounds or death could break the bonds of comradeship among us. It must be said that this remained the only positive aspect that we experienced during our "total war." Following the dispersal of Regiment 437, the units were reassigned to the staff, to the Thirteenth Infantry Company, to the Fourteenth Panzerjaeger Company of Grenadier Regiment 436, and to Infantry Regiment 438. Only one grenadier battalion remained intact, and it was permitted to continue carrying the designation II Grenadier Battalion, Infantry Regiment 437, although it was now assigned to Infantry Regiment 436. Those of us from the 437th took pride in continuing to wear our old numerical designation.

The regimental commander of 436, Knight's Cross winner Oberst Sepp Drexel, was one of the few commanders to have fought through both World Wars and survived. He had a sterling reputation for the absolute fairness and loyalty he consistently exhibited to his troops. He was a commander with a rare talent for knowing when the situation required a stern disciplinarian or when permissiveness could be accepted. The troops referred to him unofficially as Papa Drexel, and those with a close relationship to him often took the liberty of calling him Uncle Sepp. The new officers and men immediately developed an excellent relationship with him.

Once again we narrowly escaped disaster. On 14 September enemy forces heavily supported by armor broke through our right flank. They pushed onward, and on 16 September they bypassed Ergli, thus severing us from the main body of forces in the west. With this serious development it was no longer possible to hold our positions, so once again we broke through the encirclement and occupied the heights to the west of Ergli. We held these positions for a number of days.

The leaves in the trees began to take on the hue of autumn. In long columns we marched westward along the cobblestone roads, "capturing ground further to the west," as our withdrawal was jokingly referred to with a soldier's gallows humor. Despite the losses we had suffered in breaking the Soviet ring that had recently closed around us, we continued to conduct an orderly retreat as we drew ever closer to the sea, from where we could·withdraw no farther.

Far to the north the Russians had launched their offensive at the end of September between Narva and Pleskau. This offensive forced the withdrawal of all German forces north of the Duna, and the plans for the evacuation of Riga were set into motion. The long march marking our final retreat to Courland had begun.

Riga is the ancient seat of the Order of Hanseatic Knights. We were provided the dubious distinction of observing the once-beautiful city at our backs experiencing its death throes. The primitive roads were choked with the dusty columns of trucks and tanks. Lines of refugees with wagons and handcarts piled high with belongings filed through the Latvian capital day and night. The bellowing of confused and weary herds of cattle filled the air as they were driven westward over the brick-paved streets. The foreboding sight of Russian fighter-bombers became a constant reminder of our dire situation as they screamed over the tiled rooftops, the five-pointed red star clearly visible on the shining silver fuselages.

Autumn 1944 brought wind, rain, and cold nights. As we had so often experienced wherever the war had taken us, many of the roads had again become bottomless mires. Exhausted, incessantly hungry, and always cold, the men mechanically withdrew from one position to the next line of defense. The only relief from the hounding enemy would arrive with the setting sun, when the encroaching darkness would shield us from the relentless eyes of death. The enemy forces who quickly followed any withdrawal would fill the void after our departure, swarming in endless numbers through the towns and villages. The clusters of infantry piled high on the giant T-34 tanks, the raging artillery, and the low-flying aircraft would seek out our next line of defense, and again we would halt and turn to face our relentless pursuers.

October 1944. Operation Thunder—the final withdrawal of the German forces to Courland and the evacuation of Riga—was carefully planned by the staff of Army Group North. At the beginning of October 1944 Generalmajor von Natzmer signed the order that would concentrate the German forces remaining in the Baltic region into our final battlefield.

On 5 October Operation Thunder was put into motion. As the operation was executed, the 132d Infantry Division held its positions southeast of Riga. Beginning on 6 October, an entire army filed westward behind us and marched through the city and over the Duna bridges. The Army Group was able to hold only a narrow corridor forty-five kilometers long and six kilometers wide between Riga and Schlock, which offered the only passage to Courland. All refugees and military units withdrawing before the Red horde were compelled to cross the Duna and Aa within this stretch of territory. It was necessary for two divisions, plus a mixture of various splintered units, to pass daily through this gauntlet, which had been within range of indirect Soviet artillery fire since the first days of October. The operation was a masterpiece in terms of planning and organization, and this planning was composed by the able Generalmajor Frankiwitz of the 215th Infantry Division. His forces provided one thousand officers and men for organization and control of the columns, which slowly but methodically wound their way toward Courland.

Some officers from the reserve were assigned to maintain control during the evacuation, and Gustl Hickl informed me later that stringent measures were taken in an effort to maintain a flow of traffic and to save as many lives as possible. Any vehicle, regardless of whether the occupants were high-level staff officers or ragged landsers, that became disabled due to aircraft strafing or artillery barrages or that simply had run out of fuel was unceremoniously pushed off the road to sink into the marshes lining the roadsides. Any abandoned equipment was destroyed to deny its use to the enemy, and pony carts piled high with wounded, intermingled with civilian refugees—the flotsam of war—creaked slowly toward the sea in a vain effort to escape the Red Army.

Cool and somber, the night of 12–13 October settled on the men occupying the machine-gun and infantry positions in the suburbs of Riga.
As a drizzling rain began to fall, the last infantrymen with our battalions,
which had received the dubious distinction of serving as a rearguard, finally wound their way through the burning city.

At the approach to the large Duna Bridge, General Wagner, commander of the 132d Infantry Division, stood silently together with Papa
Drexel. They wordlessly observed the field-gray forms filing past, the
steady rhythm of worn boots on the cobblestones broken only by the
occasional clank of a rifle barrel or submachine gun against a mess tin or
helmet hanging from the heavy leather field belts. The flames rising in the
heart of the city from the opera house danced against a black sky, casting
ghostly shadows on the gray columns treading over the ancient bridge as
a once-conquering army withdrew in tatters.

At exactly 0030 my column approached the Duna Bridge spanning
the river, which appeared black and forbidding in the night. At the head
of those troops entrusted to me to guard the battalion withdrawal, I
knew we represented the last forces of the German Wehrmacht to cross
from east to west over the Duna in Riga. Nearing the two solitary figures
whose dim silhouettes were visible on the bridge against the flickering
light of a dying city, I drew to a halt and saluted. After a brief pause, during which we watched the ragged column pass in silence, the last general,
major, and leutnant passed to the other side. It suddenly occurred to me
that at this very spot twenty-five years earlier, Schlageter had stood with
his cannon in a valiant struggle to prevent the Red Revolution from
sweeping through the old Ordensland.

At 0500 the dawn brought a wet and cold day. As the sun attempted
to penetrate the thick gray horizon, an officer from a pionier unit pushed
the charging handle of an electric blast machine wired to the demolitions
placed within the Duna Bridge. A gigantic ball of flame shot into the air
over the river, and the atmosphere was rent by an enormous explosion as
the bridge finally collapsed into the Duna, severing us once again from
the Soviet army.

Some one hundred meters distant a ferry carrying the last remnants of
the rear guard was completing its crossing of the river. As the bridge sank
into the swiftly moving current with a roar, large pieces of stone rained
on the vessel, striking and severely injuring some of the withdrawing soldiers. Thus Operation Thunder had reached its ominous end.

CHAPTER TEN

Courland: The Last Front

Bravery and fear are

emotions of the sane and have no place in the suicidal

quagmire into which we had been thrust. . . .

We had arrived at our new and final battlefield—Courland. For three-and-one-half years, almost without relief, the 132d Infantry Division had faced the enemy on the Eastern Front. This last front not only provided our final resistance against an overpowering enemy a geographical location but also served as the final culmination of our operations. As our homeland far away collapsed in fire and death during these last months of war, the divisions constituting Army Group Courland continued to hold ground, albeit growing ever weaker from many wounds.

Ammunition was scarce. Our artillery batteries were allotted only two limited rations of shells daily for expenditure. Machine guns were permitted to fire only in the semi-automatic mode. The firing of entire belts was allowed only when the situation required the repelling of attacks. Our latest assault rifles, newly developed and distributed in the final months of the war, were sometimes rendered useless when the initial allocation of intermediate-sized ammunition was expended. The troops often resorted to relying upon carefully concealed caches of supplies hidden for such contingencies. This system pertained not only to munitions but also to gasoline and food. The resourceful drivers had always held a few carefully hidden canisters of fuel in reserve. An extra sack of barley or dried rhubarb was always put aside for the horses. As our supply lines were disrupted more often, the movements of entire companies would sometimes depend upon the resourcefulness of the individual soldiers.

Within the horse-drawn units, the condition of the animals was taken very seriously. All reports required statements regarding the status and condition of horses as well as of troops. As with the soldiers, the ranks of the horses, on which every troop movement now depended, grew ever smaller. It was not unusual for the horse-drawn supply carts to cover a distance of twenty kilometers or more to the front per day, during which they were compelled to dodge artillery barrages and run gauntlets between squadrons of strafing fighter planes.

In the closing months the troops in the Courland pocket received little meat for their diet, and many of the horses suffering from debilitating shrapnel wounds were turned over to the cooks to be slaughtered for food. With these desperate measures our dire situation became quite clear to us.

The cooks learned to prepare baked horse liver with onions. Horse-meat goulash was added as a welcome respite to our otherwise meager and bland diet. In the first days of January 1945, I was granted a rare furlough for valor, and I received from my company a large quarter-section of smoked horsemeat to carry as rations while en route to the homeland. It was dark red in color, hard and sweet-tasting, but was nevertheless eaten with great relish.

Following the evacuation of Riga we had the opportunity once again to savor fresh sausages, which had been salvaged from a warehouse in the Latvian capital. While packed into Wehrmacht trucks and wagons en route to our new destination, we feasted upon the hard sausages and filled our bread bags with the delicacy. To deprive the advancing Russians of all foodstuffs, even the entire contents of a schnapps distillery was taken with us.

We had been on the move for several days; our withdrawal consisted of movement by night, digging in prior to the onset of daylight to hinder any sudden Soviet assault upon our open rear should the enemy attempt a massive push toward the Baltic. Ahead of our withdrawing forces, the roads remained packed with refugees fleeing from the Red menace that followed at our heels, the ox carts and farm wagons, the women, children, and elderly marching through the sodden roads in files of misery and sorrow.

The regiment took up positions in the new line of defense on Lithuanian soil far to the southwest of Frauenburg. The Second Company of Regiment 437 occupied the town of Pikeliai. The commanding presence of an ancient wooden church dominated the center of the town, and approximately one hundred meters distant was a smaller wooden sanctuary, also at least two hundred years old.

I inspected the buildings in the tiny settlement as we prepared to establish our positions and chose a small log structure behind the sanctuary in which to locate our communications center. The building was not imposing but was sturdily built of thick timbers with several small rooms that could serve as administrative office areas. Adjoining our communications office I found a small room approximately three-by-four meters in size. One small window provided light, and on the rough-hewn wall directly opposite the window hung a seventeenth-century oil painting of the Madonna in a worm-eaten wooden frame. A large, ancient wooden bed occupied the end of the room next to the painting, complete with a threadbare but inviting mattress. Other than the Madonna and the bed, the room had been completely stripped of all furnishings by its previous inhabitants. A soft breeze floated through the open window; the shattered remnants of the glass panes that had once sealed it lay scattered on the floor beneath the gaping windowpane.

Unslinging my submachine gun, I hung the weapon on a hook that protruded from the wall beneath the painting, and in full uniform stretched out for a moment's respite on the bed to momentarily savor the unaccustomed luxury. In the distance I could faintly hear the movement of the landsers as they worked to prepare and reinforce their positions. I attempted to concentrate on our withdrawal and the rearguard actions conducted throughout previous days, and as I gazed at the ceiling in the dim light of the room I soon fell asleep.

I awakened as evening descended on the settlement near Pikeliai, and the setting sun cast a dim, golden glow through the solitary window of the room. Raising myself slightly from the comfort of the mattress, I vaguely discerned the soft sound of footsteps running rapidly but quietly among the buildings. I was abruptly jolted upright by the explosions of several hand grenades against the side of the log structure, and in the dim light I struggled to gain my feet and locate my weapon. I lunged forward and frantically sought my MP-40. From the corner of my eye I caught the motion of a helmeted figure in khaki-brown appear at the window. The unmistakable, ventilated barrel of a Soviet submachine gun was instantly thrust through the window, and a blinding muzzle blast filled the confined area with a deafening roar.

Throwing myself on the floor, I desperately scrambled and clawed at my weapon hanging above me as bullets slammed into the wall. With my eyes fixed on the window, I could observe the rounded helmet of the Soviet infantryman behind the intense flash of the barrel, below which was the clear silhouette of a circular drum magazine. As I frantically attempted to gain my own weapon, the burst from the enemy submachine gun continued to impact against the wall immediately above me, filling the confined space with smoke, cordite fumes, brass cartridge cases, and wooden splinters.

I found myself grasping my MP-40 and instinctively rolled onto my back and fired into the muzzle flash of the enemy gun. Praying that no Russian grenade would follow, I held the trigger and emptied a full magazine directly into the window. Within seconds my ammunition was expended, and as I pulled another magazine from my belt I became aware of the silence that had descended on the room. The smoke and dust slowly settled in the dim light, and in the distance I could hear the rapid firing of automatic weapons and isolated explosions of hand grenades, accompanied by the shouting of the landsers as they defended their positions against the Soviet incursion. Releasing the spent magazine and inserting a fully loaded one into the magazine well of the submachine gun, I crawled to the window and chanced to gaze through the shattered panes into the village.

Within seconds it was over. The enemy soldier who had fired into my room had disappeared; the only trace of his presence were the dozens of 7.62mm cartridge casings that littered the ground near the window and the floor of the room. Badly shaken, I inspected our positions and was relieved to learn that we had suffered no casualties. The Soviets had left behind two dead and several wounded. I returned to the log building, intent on abandoning the deceptively inviting shelter that had so nearly become a death trap. On inspecting my quarters, I discovered that the oil painting had received the full burst from the enemy weapon; the frame was shattered and destroyed. It was obvious that the enemy soldier, when hurrying past my window, had discerned movement at the very moment I sat upright on the bed. In his haste he had instinctively thrust the barrel of his weapon through the window and had opened fire on the silhouette of the first human figure observed in the dim light. In the heat of the decisive moment the silhouette of the painting had drawn his full attention, and he had concentrated his fire on it at a close, deadly range within the confined space. Only this had allowed me vital seconds to re-cover my weapon and defend myself.

Several days later the village came under intensive artillery fire that set the building ablaze, and I pulled the bullet-riddled painting from the wall and removed it from the shattered frame, resolved to prevent further de-struction of the Madonna whose painted countenance had saved my life. Later I unrolled the painting to further inspect the damage inflicted on the centuries-old canvas. It was then that I discovered that, despite the extended burst fired point-blank into the painting, not a single bullet had struck the face or body of the Holy Virgin. Numerous bullets had perfo-rated the background area in a deadly halo of fire, but the countenance had remained untouched. This painting remained constantly with me until my last furlough to Germany, where I chose to leave it in safekeep-ing with my family as a reminder that, whatever outcome the war was to bring us, I had perhaps been protected on this day.

The clergy in Pikeliai had served as a conduit of German culture to Lithuania two centuries ago, and in the rough-hewn building I discov-ered spiritual books from the seventeenth and eighteenth centuries as well as a lengthy manuscript describing the art of chemistry as being "the source of all knowledge" by Dr. Johann Caspar Ellenrieder, printed in Hamburg in 1723. I took advantage of our momentarily quiet sector and spent nights reading by candlelight. The candles were manufactured lo-cally of pure beeswax and emitted a pleasant aroma. We later removed the candles, together with the beautifully worked candelabra, to the cel-lar in hopes that at least these works of art might survive the conflagra-tion of Russian artillery shells, which we had learned was inevitable.

One evening one of the landsers sat at the ancient organ—it required two men to pump the massive leather bellows—and played a chorus and the Song of Mary, which was audible even to the men in the foremost po-sitions. Throughout the concert not a shot was fired from either side. For some days the tiny chapel remained untouched by the shells, as if the Russian gunners had made a conscious decision to respect a religious ob-ject of beauty. Eventually it, too, fell prey to the vicious bombardment from unseen guns and was soon completely devoured by flames.

On this same day a civilian appeared at our position, and in great dis-tress he introduced himself as the priest of the chapel. When we turned over to him the sacral cups, the candelabra, bedding, and other items of economic and spiritual value that we had previously removed to a secure place within the cellar, he expressed joy and relief at having recovered the things so dear to him and his congregation. He later made many trips through the falling artillery shells to take with him what he could carry away to safety.

The inhabitants of the town sought refuge in the surrounding forests in anticipation of the Soviet offensive and the inevitable capture of the town by the Russians. The priest left us to accompany them to their haven of relative safety, but not before giving us his blessing. In view of our very uncertain and ominous situation, we were grateful for his words of comfort.

Apart from enemy attacks in company strength during the first battle for Courland and the intermittent artillery barrages, our sector remained ominously quiet. It was not until mid-October that Russian tanks appeared near Polangen, to the north of Memel on the Baltic, which lay to our west, and we were brutally reminded once again that our lifeline to our homeland had been severed. The ranks abounded with rumors and news from mostly dubious and unconfirmed sources: "We will break out toward the south and make our way to our lines as a moving pocket . . . ; strike the Russian flank as a levering force to push them out of East Prussia . . . ; we will shove the Red Army back over the borders of the Reich to keep central Europe free from domination and slavery under the Red Soviet star."

Indeed, toward the end of October a desperate plan for breaking out of the pocket was actually conceived by some of the units located to the south of Libau, but before it could be put into effect the Soviets struck with an offensive of such ferocity that the surviving units had to consider themselves fortunate to have endured the attacks thus far and continued occupying their defensive positions.

Through an order from the commander of Army Group North it was forbidden to use the phrase "Courland pocket." It was even rumored, although to my knowledge never carried through, that a death sentence could be conferred on any of the landsers that were heard to speak of our hopeless situation in a "pocket." Since the destruction of the Sixth Army at Stalingrad, the word had carried ominous connotations of impending, inescapable disaster. With the issuance of this regulation, however, even the most optimistic among us, those of us who continued to cling to the belief in a "final victory," now realized the hopelessness of our situation. That said, however, the will to resist the Soviets, the fighting spirit within the ranks of the Courland fighters, remained unbroken.

The term "Courland bridgehead" became the official name for the trapped army. From the strategic viewpoint a bridgehead is regarded as a jumping-off point for the launching of offensives. The use of this term served as a dubious attempt to provide the impression that our positions would later be used as a bridgehead for an offensive to free East Prussia, thus the requirement that we continue to cling tenaciously to our shrinking positions.

In October some units were prepared to depart Courland on board ships for transport to the East Prussian front; however, such plans were canceled when it was realized that the heavily battered divisions, with few tanks remaining, lacked the strength to launch an attack of any measure. Thus the Courland troops were destined to remain in their positions and to conduct themselves on the principle of "fighting to the last round."

The strength and resolve of the men in the trenches could by no means be credited to the generaloberst with the golden party badge. The attributes, the will to resist, and the sacrifices made had been instilled in the individual soldiers in the three and one half years of war the division had faced on the battlefields of southern and northern Russia. For these qualities we had no need of the guidance from a political officer.

We saw the true sense of our operation in Courland as having one clearly defined objective: the defense of European culture. We believed that our presence on the northern flank of the Soviet army could prevent the Red tanks from thrusting deep into the heart of Europe. Perhaps the hour of birth for a new Europe was at hand and remained solely dependent on our will to resist the Soviet army to the last hour. Little did we realize that the western politicians had shut their eyes to the tragedy unfolding in eastern and central Europe. Communism descended on an entire culture as the western armies demobilized and effectively ceased operations. The guns had long fallen silent, and the survivors of Courland were decaying in the Russian prison camps, surrounded by the four towers perched on tall posts and the high barbed-wire enclosures of the death zone.

The OKH chief of staff in the Fuhrer Headquarters, Generaloberst Guderian, attempted desperately to persuade Hitler to evacuate the troops from Courland and employ them in the defense of Berlin. The Soviet propaganda had made it clear for years through the tons of leaflets dropped into our lines that the final goal of the Red Army was the capture of Berlin, made even more obvious by the printed scene of attacking Soviet soldiers storming the Brandenburg Gate, complete with tanks and waving banners.

Rather than choosing to follow strategic reason and face reality, Hitler insisted on sticking to his order to hold all ground in Courland. Generaloberst Schoerner vowed the impossible—to hold the front along the lines of October 1944. Although the navy prepared detailed plans that would have made the evacuation possible, Hitler stuck firmly to his belief that the Courland positions would be needed for a future offensive. He had found in Schoerner a general who would bow to his every demand, who would promise miracles. The professional opinions of Guderian and other senior officers were dismissed, often accompanied by hysterical outbreaks of rage, and Hitler would again launch into quixotic plans for new offensives using divisions and men long since decimated in the expanses of Russia. Promises of new and revolutionary weapons would steer the course of plans and strategic decisions, even as the German industry was crashing in ruins under the weight of overwhelming fleets of bombers. In December 1944, the Ardennes offensive ground to a halt, and the impending disaster became obvious to all realists.

Thus the 132d Infantry Division in Army Group North, now referred to as Army Group Courland, stood to the bitter end on the "last front." For nearly seven months the regiments on the Baltic prevailed against enormous odds in terms of men and material. We were resolved never to surrender, and the troops in Courland were to bear the ominous distinction of being the only combat units in the German army that were never defeated in open battle.

In November 1944, the last front in Courland extended from the banks of the Baltic thirty kilometers south of Libau in a general direction toward the east, turned past Moscheiken and swung again toward the north of Tukkum to the Baltic area of Riga Bay. The position of the division was very similar to the situation faced by the units of the Eighteenth Army during the battle for Leningrad, in the sense that the Red Army was attempting to reach the supply channel in Libau and thus cut the pocket in half. The entire front extended a length of approximately two hundred kilometers, in which our division, from the end of 1944, was centrally situated to the southeast of Frauenburg. The Venta, or "Windau" as it was named in German, roughly followed the defense lines of the division. On 1 November 1944, the division occupied the positions on the Windau, and within a few days the sector was reinforced by a number of companies. Despite the newly arrived supporting units, the situation on 19 November had become so critical that we were required to defend a sector of the line eleven kilometers in length. This roughly averaged a total of two beleaguered landsers for every one hundred meters of line that had to be defended in our sector.

One afternoon in early November I received a message from the Second Battalion of the 437th Regiment to expect the arrival of Generaloberst Schoerner. This dreaded and feared officer would be touring our positions and would expect a briefing of our situation on his arrival. Schoerner was notorious for his obsession concerning communications details. It was also widespread knowledge that when he found something to his dislike, a hail of reprimands, demotions, and like punishments were immediately to follow. He would sometimes demote or promote on impulse, as the situation suited him. It was rumored that his driver kept three uniform tunics in the staff kuebelwagon and that on several occasions the driver had started the day as a feldwebel, then for a minor infraction or perceived mistake was degraded to schutze, only later to be promoted to feldwebel again later that afternoon. Every visit to the front would be accompanied by threats, and those who served in the rear areas could expect to be punished by immediate transfer to the foremost lines.

General of Mountain Troops Dietl, a professional officer in every sense, had once said of Schoerner that he was better suited to serve as a field-police feldwebel, known to the landsers as chained dogs, than as a general. This opinion was widely shared by the troops, who remained ever perceptive of their leaders. Ironically, this very same general, who had exhibited no understanding of the troops at the front and who had callously condemned thousands of men to their deaths with his orders to hold untenable positions at all costs, was captured by American troops at the end of the war in an alpine hut where he had fled in an attempt to avoid facing his responsibilities when Germany surrendered. When captured, he was wearing a traditional Bavarian alpine costume, for which he had exchanged his uniform and golden party badge. Only weeks earlier he had subjected untold numbers of soldiers to summary execution for similar displays of cowardice.

The generaloberst did indeed make an appearance to inspect our position. His kuebelwagon arrived in the late afternoon, bearing the impressive checkerboard pennant of a field commander, and I correctly greeted him in the prescribed manner, saluting him sharply as he approached. He responded with a surly, impersonal salute, after which he did not offer a handshake. I was immediately struck with the impression that he had arrived specifically to create problems for us.

I had prepared the unit carefully for his inspection. At the dug-out entrance were two sentries, meticulously outfitted in complete field uniform with helmets and rifles as required. The communications NCO, Feldwebel Stenitzer, was personally occupying the field desk to ensure that everything went as planned. The radiomen had repeatedly inspected and tested their equipment beforehand. All contacts with the artillery liaison command and the forward observers were flawless.

The general requested a status briefing on our sector, which I had prepared for presentation in advance. I had committed myself to portraying our situation exactly as I judged it, and I presented this picture to him frankly and honestly. Daily a Russian observation balloon would appear on the horizon. Despite our repeated requests, no German aircraft appeared to disrupt the activities of the enemy observers; thus, the Soviet artillery fired uninterruptedly on chosen targets as they desired. Moreover, we were of the belief that a number of positions along the Windau in our sector were being taken under fire in preparation for a tank assault, which we expected to occur within the next several days. The number of troops were too few to hold the assigned sector; our defenses were too thinly spread along the line. The lack of heavy weapons, above all antitank weapons, was critical. Our supply of Model 42 teller mines could not be used, as they lacked the necessary detonators.

The esteemed generaloberst was obviously not pleased to receive such a negative report from a junior officer. He abruptly departed, leaving us with the distinct impression that he was less than satisfied. It was later rumored that while visiting the positions in the rear he had shared bottles of wine with Artillery Battalion Schonzki and had openly complained about the attitudes of the infantry units on the line. He certainly had not aroused my trust or faith in his leadership but had only confirmed the reports we had previously heard of his peculiar style of command. Not one single encouraging word had been spoken, either to me personally or even to those men shouldering weapons for him in the defense positions.

I was accustomed to a different type of German general. Furthermore, he had ridiculed my assessment of the situation, rebuking my prediction of an oncoming tank assault with the remark that if and when such an attack did take place it would be far to the west, toward Libau.

The great strategist was mistaken. On 20 November a Russian artillery barrage pounded our positions and those of the regiment to our left, and large concentrations of Soviet tanks pushed over the Windau. In what was to be the second battle for Courland, the Russians tore through the front in several locations, including the sector held by our division. Only with reinforcements from various units was the offensive halted near Frauenburg several days later.

Similar to our great panzer offensives early in the war, the standard tactic for the Russians was to attack the line at various locations along a front, and wherever the front was penetrated all additional resources would be concentrated to gain a bridgehead from where all available forces would be thrust through the gap. On occasion a false attack would be launched, and in another sector a massive push would attempt to penetrate defenses after the defender's reserves had been committed to the feint. In order to gain control of the situation it was often necessary to move entire divisions within hours to weak points where a breakthrough had occurred or was considered imminent. This was made even more difficult because of poor road conditions during the fall rainy season, when roads and positions were churned to a morass beneath convoys of heavy vehicles and columns of countless men and horses.

During the second battle for Courland our units were successful in containing the Russian onslaught; but immediately thereafter the rains began, and all movement, regardless of how insignificant, was conducted only with great effort. Along the line the terrain became a vast, swampy morass, to which even the Russians, with their overwhelming motorized units, had to yield.

The German reconnaissance units reported that Soviet tank units had retreated to the south and were concentrating in the vicinity of Vainode-Pikeliai. This marked the end of the second battle for Courland. The troops were exhausted and worn. The line consisted mostly of shallow muddy holes half-filled with water from melting snow and ice, in which the landsers alternated sentry duty while attempting to remain physically able to further resist the enemy. Resupply, when at all possible, became sporadic due to the impassable roads and constant disruption from the artillery barrages and the relentless, strafing aircraft that appeared suddenly and without warning from the gray sky. The horses were now often collapsing from lack of nourishment; and for the landsers in the earthworks, warm food had become a rare luxury.

STEDINI AND PAMPALI

In early December I was shocked to learn that I was to be placed under two weeks' quarters arrest. Generaloberst Schoerner had obviously been displeased with my negative, albeit honest and accurate appraisal of our situation and had demanded this punishment following his inspection of the positions. It is also possible that he was displeased with my Swabian dialect, revealing to him that I was from Württemberg, which served to remind him of our famous Desert Fox—Generalfeldmarschall Rommel, whose fame and reputation he probably envied and resented. Our division commander, General Wagner, arrived at our battalion headquarters to inform me personally of my impending punishment. This thoroughly professional and responsible officer advised me that under no circumstances would this report negatively reflect my service to the army and that only with great reluctance was he carrying out these orders as directed. Furthermore, he stated that my service, backed by years of combat experience, was badly needed elsewhere behind the front.

I then reported to the operations officer of the regiment, Major Dechamp, who advised me that construction battalions and various parts of other units had been collected deep within the center of our pocket. It was necessary to initiate construction of defensive positions in the rearward areas during lulls in the fighting. Past experience had proven that in the event of a breakthrough, rear-based units such as artillery troops had become a critical asset in halting the enemy penetration. Thus, I was assigned to plan and construct a second and third line of defense. It was to contain deep interconnecting tank traps, area defense trenches, gun positions, and an interlocking earthwork system that extended one thousand meters between positions.

Far to our rear was a network of rearguard positions to be prepared for an eventual evacuation by sea of the Courland divisions should the order from the highest command ever be received. The solution was relatively simple in the minds of the landsers: "Better to dig trenches than graves." My work was enhanced by the acquisition of a tractor-powered machine that was capable of digging trenches up to 80 centimeters deep, and 500 meters long in one night.

Throughout the hours of daylight we remained engaged in poring over and developing plans for additional defenses; and during the hours of darkness, when we could work without the danger of the ever-present fighter-bombers, we constructed miles of bunkers and earthworks in anticipation of a final, massive Soviet push through our lines to the Baltic.

Our work was interrupted abruptly in mid-December by a deep, sudden frost. The earth froze to the consistency of stone. The muddy roads were once again passable, and a forbidding atmosphere of expectation swept over the ragged army. The companies far in the front and the artillery observers reported the sound of heavy movements of vehicles coming from within the enemy lines. Throughout the nights the grinding of tank tracks was clearly audible. Our artillery remained powerless to fire on targets of opportunity, as munitions had become scarce and were carefully rationed.

Bands of fighter planes and squadrons of bombers displaying the red five-pointed star on their fuselages and wings flew over us at random. With impunity they made daily excursions during these clear, frost-laden December days on their way to bomb the supply harbors of Libau and Windau in attempts to disrupt our tenuous lifelines. The Flak units and the few fighters remaining with the Army Group battled valiantly against the endless numbers of enemy aircraft. Our fighter squadrons were commanded by Luftwaffe General Pflugbeil, and during 15 and 16 December alone they shot down twenty-five Soviet planes over Courland.

To better enable me to fulfil my assignment for constructing and planning the defenses, I was invited by the regimental medical officer of the 438th Regiment, Dr. Schlipp, to share the Latvian farmhouse he occupied. Two women and an elderly man continued to inhabit part of the dwelling, and the younger of the women, the daughter, spoke fairly good German. When asked why they did not take refuge farther toward the rear to seek safety from the daily artillery barrages, they replied, "To where? There no home more, only the sea."

They heated the washroom for us and fried potatoes while the old man chopped wood in a nearby shed, and he was once observed tacking the skin of a martin to a board. He had thus spent his entire lifetime here on this land. He once remarked, "We Latvians now have the dogs in our land . . . but soon we will have to have the wolves as friends." The meaning of his words required no explanation.

We had nicknamed the doctor Poldi, and his work was never-ending. Legions of wounded were brought to him in pony carts lying on scattered straw, often under the protection of darkness. They were wrapped in dirty, blood-encrusted bandages, weak, unshaven, and filthy, without hope or barely retaining a glowing ember of optimism. Poldi would take them under his care, and beneath the uncertain protection of the Red Cross flag he cared for the wounds, replacing bandages, administering pain-relieving injections, stitching torn flesh, and splinting broken bones. The serious cases would be loaded into the sankas to be driven to the division collection point a few kilometers behind the front for surgery. These assistants to the beaten and weary—the doctors and medical corpsmen who wore the staff of Caduceus on their shoulders and carried the scalpel in their tunic pocket—were to prove themselves indispensable many times in the future during the period of imprisonment in Russia.

Poldi and I shared many thoughtful conversations in his hut. I would appear in the dead of night from my work constructing the defenses and would sit next to the hearth near the warmth of the fire. In the flickering light he and his medical assistant would join me and drink a toast to my safe return. Here existed warmth and comfort, a part of home that exuded not only from the hearth but also from the heart. Poldi was a dark-haired, very serious doctor with deep brown eyes. I often imagined him a descendant of the Roman or Gallic legionnaires who occupied the area of Kastell-Mainz, which he called home. We would speak of our homes often and would ask ourselves if we would ever again stand before the ancient monuments of our homeland, if we would ever again step into the half-darkness of the Mainz Cathedral to pray.

Always again the specter of our fate would rise to loom over us and would surface during each conversation—how would it all end? Would the army in Courland be sacrificed to the overwhelming onslaught of Communism, bolstered by the immense industrial might of the combined Allied powers? Would it be later said over our graves, as was said following the Stalingrad debacle, that the Courland army had "fulfilled its true duty to its country and people to the last round, fighting against overwhelming odds to allow new defenses to be established, making it possible to protect the homeland?" The fate of the troops who were eventually isolated and abandoned far to the south on the Crimean

Peninsula, our former battleground, came to mind. It was said that as boats and ferries plunged toward the open sea on a course toward Odessa, the remaining defenders who were left behind had called to the departing vessels, "We are the honorary citizens of the nation!" They then marched the long bitter way into captivity.

A few days before the expected offensive, a new medical bunker was prepared near the regimental headquarters, enabling the wounded to be brought to a safe area for care. The Latvian farmhouse at Stedini, where Poldi and I had enjoyed temporary comfort, was later riddled by tank fire. We saw no more of its inhabitants and never learned of their fate.

A solid, passable road led through a sector of the division from the direction of Pampali toward Stedini, then split into a fork. One branch led northeast toward Frauenburg, the other toward Libau. It was at this junction that the Russians attempted to break through in order to split the Courland army and to capture Libau.

THE THIRD BATTLE OF COURLAND

At exactly 0600 on 21 December 1944, our sector of the division was enveloped in a firestorm. The horizon came alive, glowing with the muzzle flashes from countless heavy guns. It was confirmed that within the sector of Grenadier Regiment 438 alone, more than eight hundred barrels—consisting of a deadly combination of heavy artillery, rockets, and mortars—fired multiple salvos on our positions.

An incredible raging firestorm rained on the trenches. Machine-gun nests, earthworks, bunkers, and reinforced fire positions along our front collapsed in clouds of dust and smoke. The earth trembled, roared, heaved, and tossed. The bunkers collapsed; the trenches were leveled. For three long hours an unseen, unreachable force assaulted the earth with fury, seeking out our last refuge in the shadow of battle. First the heavy fire was directed on the foremost positions; it then careened over the Stedini heights, after which it advanced into the wooded area to our rear to descend upon the regimental headquarters. The treetops were splintered, entire trees sailed into the sky, shells struck the reinforced bunkers and completely enveloped our surroundings. Minutes became an eternity.

The first wounded appeared, stumbling and staggering aimlessly, often without helmets, uniforms covered with blood. Those unable to walk arrived wrapped in shelter-quarters, carried by landsers straining against the load. The wounded screamed in agony and thrashed wildly on the ground as they awaited the care of the medical officer. Poldi and his assistants worked feverishly. I attempted to assist them by plastering an air-tight bandage to a sucking chest wound. Some of the wounded who remained coherent reported that Ivan had broken through the nearby left sector, and concentrations of tanks piled high with infantry had been sighted.

Suddenly the barrage on our position lifted. In the distance, to our right and left flanks, the shells and rockets continued to fall with indescribable fury. I looked across the makeshift operating table at Poldi and felt the nerves at my neck tingle with anticipation. He glanced up at me from his work, nodded knowingly, then wordlessly resumed repairing the wounds of his patient. The silence in our sector was an ominous sign, which I had experienced in battles past. The Soviet artillery had lifted in our area and was now concentrating on our flanks. We were occupying the corridor through which the enemy armor would attempt to thrust toward our open rear sectors.

I dropped the roll of bandages and dashed toward the door of the medical bunker, seizing a carbine along the way. At the entrance I detected the sound of roaring engines and the screeching of tracked vehicles, accompanied by ear-splitting explosions. Red fighter-bombers were overflying the woods, releasing bombs and firing with wing cannons and machine guns. The sound of engines grew louder, and through the rolling thunder of explosions I recognized the unmistakable grinding of Soviet T-34s. From the ruins of the headquarters I caught sight of several landsers running in panic past our location with carbines at their sides. Racing headlong toward the bunker, they collapsed upon the ground with burning lungs, rasping "Panzer! Panzer!"

I dashed outside and immediately stumbled over the splintered branches of large trees that had been torn from the now-naked stumps rising vertically in the air. On all sides shells were bursting, and close to the communications bunker I came upon my longtime friend Leutnant Rech, the son of a rector from Saarbrucken. An exploding tank projectile had torn open his abdomen, and as he sank to his knees I caught him and lowered him slowly to earth. As I looked into his dying eyes, an intense feeling of rage overcame me, a rage I had known only rarely from previous battles and other deaths—a consuming rage without reason, that only barely recognizes a distinction between enemy and friend, an overwhelming sense of anger that knows no limits, a feeling that reaches far beyond the simple emotions of bravery or fear. Bravery and fear are emotions of the sane and have no place in the suicidal quagmire into which we had been thrust. One felt overcome with the simple, primitive obsession for revenge.

"Revenge . . . revenge," hammered through my brain. "Destroy the attackers, kill them, those who have destroyed those close to you. When so many have perished, why should I survive? Better to die now, killing the enemy, than to await the inevitable."

I leaped to my feet and charged blindly forward. I became vaguely aware of two of Rech's men running alongside me. As we approached the Fourteenth Company headquarters, I observed several members of an antitank unit frantically preparing their panzerfaust stovepipes for close combat. Several of the antitank weapons were primed and leaning against the wall, next to the door of the bunker.

"Come on!" I shouted desperately. "Let's go! Let's go! They're coming!" I seized one of the long, gray-green tubes loaded with the blunt, bulbous projectile and lunged through the trees for a distance of approximately fifty paces to the edge of the wood line, toward the sound of the heavily armored vehicles. The shrill whine of bullets filled the air around me, and exploding shells continued to burst in the treetops, sending white-hot fragments whistling and thudding dully into the earth.

Suddenly, at approximately twenty meters' distance, I observed through the undergrowth the long barrel of a T-34 moving slowly but steadily forward. Acutely aware that the tank was normally accompanied and supported by at least a platoon of infantry, I backtracked in a long arc through the woods and turned to approach the massive silhouette from concealment. Jumping into an opening in the trees near the huge tank, I knelt with burning lungs between piles of splintered branches from where, at about thirty paces, I could now clearly see the steel colossus that displayed several large numbers painted next to a red star on the turret.

I quickly pulled the safety pin from the panzerfaust and flipped up the perforated sights. I held my breath in a vain attempt to calm my fluttering pulse. I was aware of my pounding heart throbbing with tension in my throat, and I concentrated on aiming correctly.

I centered the quadrant of the sight directly in the middle of the giant red star bordered with white on the turret. With my last strength of will I forced myself to remain calm and to hold the sight picture steady against the target, and I slowly but firmly squeezed the trigger. With a loud explosion a ball of flame erupted behind me from the open breech of the weapon into the woods. The projectile flew forward with a roar, clearly visible to the naked eye, and struck squarely on the turret. The warhead detonated flawlessly, spraying the interior of the heavily armored vehicle with fire and white-hot shrapnel.

Immediately a large, round hatch flew open and a fine wisp of smoke rose from within the tank, followed only by an overwhelming silence. Pressed tightly against the earth, I observed a second tank, previously unseen, some fifty paces away, crashing through the trees in reverse gear as it backed away from its destroyed attendant. It broke through the tree line into an open field where a company of Russian infantrymen were now lying in view, prone upon the ground. The two men who had accompanied me from the panzerjaeger company destroyed this tank with their weapons just as I had dispatched the lead vehicle.

From the concealment of the tree line, the two men and I opened fire with carbines upon the Russian company lying on the frozen ground some two hundred meters distant. We exchanged a short burst of fire, and the Russians began to withdraw, pulling their wounded with them. We sank to the ground, physically and psychologically benumbed by the experience. We had successfully repelled a reinforced enemy company . . . and we were alive.

The self-propelled guns of Hauptmann Brandtner arrived. One of them received a direct hit while on the road; the other was able to position itself and open fire on the column of oncoming Russian tanks on the heights of Stedini. On the first day of the Battle of Courland at Stedini, the Russians lost more than twenty tanks to Regiment 438 during the fighting at the tiny crossroads that led to Frauenburg and Libau.

My panzerfaust had destroyed the lead tank at the head of the assault group, and the second had been knocked out by the two men of the Fourteenth Panzerjaeger Company. Three additional tanks were destroyed by other grenadiers in close combat, and the self-propelled gun had accounted for the remainder of those that were left burning and exploding on the battlefield. Thus on the first day, the spearhead of the attacking force had been broken and a major catastrophe was thwarted. On 10 December Knight's Cross holder Hauptmann Zoll, commander of the

Fourteenth Company, Regiment 436, received the assignment to march toward Pampali as Battle Group Commander with a strength of approximately one hundred men. It consisted of two infantry platoons, one heavy machine-gun platoon, one five-man Pak crew, a small number of pioniers, and one or two forward artillery observers.

On 12 December the day remained quiet; the sky remained dark with low-lying clouds as Zoll's Battle Group began constructing defense positions. They waited expectantly for the Russian attack; days came and went as they feverishly reinforced their positions. On 16 December heavy-artillery fire burst on the earthworks, forcing the landsers to seek shelter in the narrow trenches and makeshift bunkers. The artillery fire continued sporadically for several days, with barrages impacting without warning, only to lift for several hours before resuming. On 21 December the Russian attack was launched, proceeded by heavy-artillery fire that rendered all movement impossible. The positions near Pampali were penetrated by the infantry and tank units by midday, and that afternoon the beleaguered landsers were isolated and surrounded. The numbers of dead and wounded continued to rise, the dead lying in the trenches where they fell, the wounded receiving only cursory care under relentless fire from an overwhelming enemy. Ammunition, medical supplies, and food supplies were quickly exhausted. Radio contact with the regiment or division was no longer possible; the last orders received repeatedly stressed to hold the positions at any cost.

The pocket continued to shrink. Facing total annihilation within hours, a breakout and withdrawal to the division was planned. Ammunition for the heavy weapons was expended, and lacking prime-mover resources, the guns were to be destroyed and abandoned. Transport for the wounded was quickly organized. Despite all efforts, repeated attempts to contact the division met in failure; thus, official approval for the withdrawal was lacking. The decision to break out before dawn was made without command from higher authority. Columns formed for the transport of the wounded on sleds or in shelter-quarters as makeshift stretchers. The exhausted survivors prepared to break through to our lines.

At 0330, 22 December, the order was given for the evacuation. The columns launched out toward the German lines an hour later to the west of Pampali through an unoccupied depression and headed in a northerly direction. The ragged column was sparsely scattered, a point element forward, the wounded in the middle, and a rear guard following. Progress was slow but successful, and with no movement noted from the enemy they gained the German lines. On initial contact with the Army Courland positions, the point element was taken under fire, having been unable to give the password; but they were quickly recognized as German troops, and at 0700 the main column crossed into friendly lines. The survivors of the battle group had entered a sector occupied by the Second Battalion, Infantry Regiment 436, and were quickly taken to the regimental headquarters to be greeted. There they celebrated a successful escape and were offered the opportunity to receive food and a short rest before being sent into the line.

The fighting raged through the end of December. This sixth and last Christmas of the war remained muted and depressing for the troops. Our thoughts were constantly occupied by the tenuous if not hopeless situation in which we found ourselves. We received solace only in our numbers and in being with comrades with whom we had shared so many experiences over the weeks, months, and years. On 24 December, Christmas Eve, a fusilier battalion from another division marched toward the line to reinforce the sector, and only the steady rhythm of worn, muddy boots upon the frozen ground could be heard. As the column slowly passed the trenches, above the marching ranks of ragged landsers the faint sound of "Silent Night, Holy Night" could be detected. There remained no peace on earth.

The division had suffered heavy losses in the recent fighting, many soldiers having fallen victim to the Russian artillery batteries and machine guns, and we had been forced to surrender some territory to the Soviets to avoid annihilation. At the end of December the division was relieved and transferred to a quieter sector south of Libau. The third battle for Courland had become another test of the troops' ability to withstand overwhelming odds, and again we had passed the test, albeit with pyrrhic success.

The official reports of OKW thus cited our last battle of 1944: "Army Group Courland has destroyed 513 tanks, 79 field guns, and 145 aircraft." In the center of the heaviest fighting had been not only our division but also the 225th North German Infantry Division, which held the area to our left.

A total of twenty reinforced enemy divisions was thrown against the thinly held positions of the Twenty-fourth, 205th, 215th, 290th, 329th Infantry Divisions and the Thirty-first Volks Grenadier Division. The

912th Army Assault Gun Brigade, a unit of the Twelfth Panzer Division, and the Schutzen-Panzerwagen Battalion of the Fifth Regiment, led by Hauptmann Gauss, who on many sectors of the front was known simply as "the man with the visored cap," were constantly thrown into the counterattack. Without the reliable reinforcement of the self-propelled guns and the few remaining tanks in the Courland army, the great defensive battles could never have succeeded in holding the enemy at bay. During the second and third battles for Courland, our already weakened division had lost in excess of one thousand irreplaceable men killed, wounded, and missing.

CHAPTER ELEVEN

The Bitter End

At exactly 1200 we received a

radio report from the regiment that struck like lightning from

the heavens . . .

January 1945. Our homeland was collapsing in fire and smoke. Waves of Allied bombers covered the skies over the cities and industrial centers. Homes and streets burned nightly with flowing streams of glowing asphalt. The innocent, the women and children, were dying by the thousands, their bodies reduced to glowing embers in the phosphorescent maelstrom. The borders of the homeland we had known were shrinking before a relentless combination of powerful enemies; the destruction and defeat that we had for so long refused to acknowledge was becoming reality.

On 2 January of the new year I stood with the four other members of the division who had also been credited with the destruction of enemy tanks in close combat. At the Eighteenth Army Headquarters, the commanding officer, General der Infanterie Ehrenfried Boege, had summoned us to his headquarters to recognize our actions.

The general's staff was situated in an old, picturesque estate, with an ancient manor built in the style of an eighteenth-century fortress surrounded by a beautiful park. The branches of the massive trees that bracketed the imposing structure lay heavy with snow. In a small, neighboring dwelling we received haircuts and were shaved by the staff barber in preparation for our meeting with the general. An aide waited patiently for the barber to complete his task, and we were then briskly led into the hall of the castle.

A heavy, paneled door opened, and we sprang to attention as the arrival of our commander was announced. We were presented to a gray-haired gentleman in whose eyes one could clearly recognize the heavy burden of responsibility, especially in these waning days, that he was carrying for so many in our beleaguered Courland army. He warmly shook hands with each of us, pausing momentarily to ask obligatory questions as he awarded each member of our party with the silver and black tank-destruction badge. He then presented us with a small quantity of cognac and tobacco, thanking us again for our valuable service to the fatherland before advising us of our additional reward of furlough, and we were then dismissed to return to our units.

A widespread prohibition on furloughs had been in effect since the summer months. Travel to Germany was no longer permitted, possibly due in part to the massive destruction of our cities and industrial centers by Allied bombers, which was evident in all densely populated areas. This ban had been in effect for the Courland army, with an exception for those who had earned special merit, which included the destruction of an enemy tank with small arms or explosives. This was by definition limited to special antitank shaped charges, mines, or panzerfausts. In these special cases home leave would be permitted.

The following day, 3 January, accompanied by the four men—a feldwebel, two obergefreiters, and a gefreiter—I boarded a fishing vessel at midday that had been pressed into the service of the Kriegsmarine in the harbor of Libau, and we were soon steaming west over the Baltic toward the homeland. Packed into an Alpine Corps rucksack were my few belongings and a portion of smoked horsemeat to serve as "march rations" on my journey. I had also carefully packed the oil painting of my protecting Madonna, which had remained by my side since our withdrawal from Pikeliai.

We steamed to the ancient port city of Danzig, where we arrived following an uneventful eight-hour transit through the Baltic. There we departed the ship during the night, and after taking quarters in the hotel Stettiner Hof, the following morning we began the journey home toward south Germany and the Rhine. While en route we observed firsthand the destroyed cities and factories; we experienced the hopelessness of the people, the innocents who suffered for the folly of others, the pain of the women and children whom we were supposed to be protecting in the trenches of Courland. Knowing that our relatives and others lived in daily terror of the bombs left us with no joy at being home again. We had escaped one inferno to be thrust into another, different form of purgatory, where our personal risk facing the enemy was slight; however, we remained powerless to stop the waves of bombers that flew over us with impunity. Here there was no taking up a panzerfaust or an assault rifle to repel the enemy. One could only helplessly wait.

There was little pleasure in being away from our accustomed environment. While visiting my father I received an indication of the extent of the evil practices that our leaders had brought upon the world. My father, who served as a police official, confided in me his questions and assumptions regarding the fate of our citizens considered as "undesirable" by our brown-clad leaders. He spoke of numerous death certificates for people held in custody by the government, received in the past months from various government agencies, sometimes accompanied by the sparse belongings of the deceased. "It cannot be possible," he stated to me in confidence, "that so many people could die of heart failure. Something is terribly wrong." This observation, accompanied by more subtle evidence occasionally detected in our daily lives, served to reveal crimes committed by the government that could not be denied.

I was shocked to see the destruction that had befallen the city of Stuttgart. Accustomed to the sight of burned villages and destroyed facilities on the Eastern Front, I was nevertheless distressed to observe that entire population centers had been reduced to blackened piles of rubble. Hit especially hard during the bombing campaign of September 1944, much of Stuttgart lay in ruins. The residence of the former Württemberg royal family, the New Palace, was totally destroyed, and from gaping, shattered windows the once-elegant draperies could be observed waving softly in the wind that whistled through the blackened ruins. Throughout the city, labor units consisting of prisoners of war, Hitler Youth groups, and conscripted foreign workers toiled to clear streets and facilities of rubble. Signs were posted on buildings and street corners advising that looters would be shot. Photography of any damage was strictly forbidden and punishable by severe penalty. The city I had known in my youth had disappeared in a hideous pile of ash and rubble.

I journeyed to the Black Forest town of Dornstettin to visit my grandparents, and I was relieved to find the outlying towns and villages still intact, relatively untouched by the catastrophe that had befallen the larger cities. Encouraged to visit relatives, I took a commuter train to

Mullacker. En route we came under attack by a single American fighter-bomber, which strafed the length of the slow-moving, defenseless train. The aircraft's board weapons disabled the locomotive, which slowly screeched to a stop, steam and smoke pouring in great clouds toward the crystal-clear winter sky. Panic-stricken, the passengers fled from the carriages to seek shelter in the surrounding terrain as the plane banked and, with motor howling, began a second strafing run. I attempted to assist several passengers in their efforts to disembark before throwing myself onto the ground as the plane passed overhead, machine-guns rattling as the low-flying aircraft struck the locomotive again with impunity.

Within seconds the attack was over. I had experienced my first and only direct contact with the American enemy, and that on my home soil. Miraculously, only a small number of passengers suffered slight injuries, and after some hours we were able to continue our journey.

In the first days of February I reported to the Generalkommando, which had been transferred to Ludwigsburg following the destruction of the headquarters in Stuttgart. It was necessary to report back from leave to the military officials and thus initiate my return to my unit in Courland. At the front desk in the duty office I was met by a stabsfeldwebel who commented on my decorations. Learning that I was returning from leave and would be reporting back to my division in Courland, he remarked that my experience at the front, particularly in close combat against enemy armor, would be put to better use here. He added that personnel with such experience were being sought to train Hitler Youth members in the use and tactics of panzerfaust weapons, in preparation for the impending invasion of Germany by the western Allies.

The proposal that I was to train fifteen- and sixteen-year-old boys to engage enemy armor made my blood run cold. I was of the steadfast conviction that, regardless of our military situation, to send children to meet a certain death in close combat with shoulder-fired weapons would serve no purpose and could be considered as murder at best. Furthermore, this practice would have little or no effect in stemming an armored advance by a determined, seasoned enemy.

The stabsfeldwebel must have sensed my outrage at this suggestion, and he added that I could also be needed on the Western Front where the Anglo-American forces were penetrating the Reich's defenses. I inquired as to the situation in the east, and he advised me that the Soviets had now breached the defenses at Oderbruch. I then replied that I was needed with my division in Courland and that I must return to my unit.

On 8 February I was accompanied by my father to the Stuttgart train station, where I was presented with a container of coffee by a young Red Cross worker before boarding the train to Berlin. The train took me through a thoroughly destroyed country, with intermittent stops that extended the journey to approximately twenty hours. While in Berlin I came dangerously close to being held by officials from Wehrkreiskommando V and sent to the Upper Rhine front, where replacements were badly needed to stem the American advance. I was also directed to report to the Oder front by other authorities. Determined to return to my division, I refused to obey. My desire was to end this war alongside those with whom I had experienced so much, with my old friends and comrades.

At the Anhalter train station I observed officers and field police stopping all personnel in uniform and carefully inspecting identification papers and documents. Numbers of soldiers were being sorted into various groups, where they stood under guard while they waited expectantly in ranks for further instructions. Due to my decorations I was bypassed by the military police patrols; however, I was soon approached by a senior SS officer who was accompanied by several kettenhunde, and he politely but firmly instructed me to report to the city commander's office near Potsdamerplatz. I located the commander's office amid the ruins of central Berlin, the blackened, crumbling walls fading ominously into the night sky. Crowds of soldiers stood in ranks at various locations near the headquarters; officers were observed reporting and departing in confusion as the air was rent by the wailing of air raid sirens. Through the turmoil an officer informed me that the Russians were only seventy kilometers from Berlin and had already reached Frankfurt am Oder and that I was to be placed in charge of an alarm unit to be dispatched to this front. My papers were returned to me, and I was further instructed to report to a Flak center near the Berlin radio tower and to board the bus outside for transport to that location.

As I exited the makeshift headquarters, I noted the presence of a large military bus that I had been ordered to take to the Flak center. Approximately fifty meters beyond the waiting vehicle I observed a dim blue light, and I could barely discern the word "S-bahn." Striding past the bus without turning my head, I proceeded to the streetcar stop and disappeared into the stairwell leading underground. With a pounding heart I soon boarded the car to the Berlin suburb of Zehlendorf-West, where I located the residence of my cousin, Dr. Gertrud Broesamle. Zehlendorf had suffered very little damage in the course of the countless bombing raids, and in the neighborhood of imposing villas I spent the night discussing events with my cousin. In the neighboring house lived Theo Lingen, the actor.

The following afternoon Gertrud accompanied me as I proceeded to the Stettiner train station to continue my journey back to Courland. In this station, as I had experienced at the Anhalter station, patrols were methodically inspecting documents of military personnel. In an attempt to avoid contact with the kettenhunde and SS patrols, Gertrud and I walked arm in arm, appearing to be a romantic couple deeply engaged in an emotional, departing conversation, both of us avoiding eye contact with those around us. Mysteriously, the ruse was effective, for we were not confronted by the authorities.

After several minutes we observed the arrival of a general who was accompanied by a feldwebel, and I instinctively remained by his side, hoping that his presence could protect me from the squads of military police who appeared to be intent on investigating solitary individuals in uniform. At length I approached him, saluted, and introduced myself. I then explained that I was attempting to return to my unit in Courland, and I asked if I might be permitted to remain with him for a short period of time.

"Of course, my son!" he exclaimed. "I understand how important it must be for you to return to your comrades." With this I bid Gertrud farewell, and she quickly departed from the oppressive surroundings. With my irreproachable position next to the general I was no longer delayed by the police patrols, and as the train began to move I was invited to remain with him in his coach. He was very friendly, and he informed me that his name was Mueller and that he was en route to Danzig to serve as the city commander. His aide, the feldwebel who had arrived with him, accompanied us. The following morning I arrived at Stettin without further delay. Years later I was informed that following the capture of Danzig by the Soviets, General Mueller had been hanged in that city.

Following our arrival in Stettin, I took quarters in the hotel Danziger Hof, which was under administrative control of the German navy. For several days I enjoyed life such as I had seldom experienced in the military, confirming to me the widespread belief that our navy made every effort to care for military personnel. The food was plentiful and delicious, and in the evenings we were entertained by a theater group, consisting primarily of attractive young women from Vienna. Despite the superficial luxury enjoyed in these surroundings, we were ominously aware of the oncoming Russians, who now stood only a short distance from the harbor. The city was packed with refugees who had fled from the onslaught of the Red Army. Numerous makeshift military units consisting of a mixture of individuals drafted from antiaircraft crews and work brigades or released from military hospitals were to be seen everywhere.

Every morning I reported to the Stettin harbor control, and after four days a convoy was organized to steam to Courland by way of Danzig. During my final morning en route to the harbor I observed an elderly man clothed in a no longer fashionable SA uniform who had obviously been drafted into the Volkssturm. Bent beneath the weight of a World War I vintage rifle that was slung across his back, he carried a single panzerfaust over his shoulder with which he expected to engage the Soviet army. We had reached the end of our strength.

Various fishing boats, a destroyer, torpedo boats, minesweepers, and two U-boats constituted the escort that was still at anchor in Danzig. While there we observed warships openly engaged in gunfire support for the units locked in battle beyond the sight of the ships. As we proceeded outbound it became necessary for the minesweepers to clear the area, as it was reported that the British had sown the waters during the night with mines; at midday we broke out onto the open sea near the heights of Memel.

The convoy received numerous air attacks from Soviet fighter-bomber squadrons. A bomb damaged the rudder of our ship, which had been a former freighter and was the slowest ship of the convoy. One of the other transports received a vital hit on the starboard side aft, and within fifteen minutes the ship had disappeared beneath the dark waves. Only half the soldiers who had embarked on this vessel were pulled from the water and rescued.

During my absence, the fourth Battle of Courland had taken place between 24 January and 3 February. My division had not been heavily committed to this battle, as the Soviet drive had occurred in the areas of Preekuln and Schrunden. The men of the 132d Infantry Division continued to languish in the positions south of Libau. Except for the enemy's minor probes into our lines and some isolated incidents, our sector had remained relatively quiet during my final trip home of the war.

With the onset of February the weather turned mild and springlike, with blue skies and sunshine accompanied only by a light frost in the morning hours. The soggy earth within the positions and the streets began to dry, and the roads were soon passable once again for a short period. The idyllic weather soon ended with a warm wind out of the south and west, which brought darkly clouded skies and unending thunderstorms. The soldiers from farming families had predicted a "stable frost" as stated in the "Hundred-Year Calendar" for the months of February and March 1945, but even specialists err, and this year nature showed little inclination to follow the calendar.

The battle-hardened Courland soldiers, especially those survivors from previous winters farther to the east where weather is much more severe than near the Baltic, remained in good health. Few illnesses were reported, and those who received light wounds would return as soon as possible to the old caves with their units. The few "old men" remaining at the front wore silver or gold wound badges pinned to their tunics below their close-combat insignia to indicate five or more wounds received during the course of our odyssey.

The positions south of Libau, in which I located my old unit with the 438th Grenadier Regiment, were well constructed. The remainder of the First Battalion of Regiment 438—now reduced to little more than a combat group—was situated almost against the Baltic. Positioned in a marshy, low-lying area, the soldiers had constructed a log palisade with a floor of sand that was somewhat higher than the surrounding terrain. Warm bunkers had been constructed up to the very front line, and those who had no iron stove had fabricated chimneys and fireplaces of stone and clay. There remained an abundance of firewood, and the troops preferred to burn split birch, as it created little smoke to betray their location. The men remained cautious about creating any smoke that would disclose their positions to the enemy, but we could observe many columns of smoke daily that revealed the enemy's warm fires in the trenches and forests opposite us.

With my first inspection of our positions I noticed that the quarters were more than just comfortably warm. When one entered the bunkers from the cold and damp air outside it was as though one had stepped into an oven. The troops nevertheless found these hot-houses suitable and protested loudly when the bunker door or shelter-quarter hanging over the entrance was left open to the cold air outside. The loud, vociferous protests usually implied that the soldiers would "rather stink than freeze," and I respected their wishes.

Our experience in constructing defenses on the northern front was put to good use in this sector. It was always interesting to observe how throughout this war, in which the most modern weapons and equipment were employed by all combatants, the use of primitive systems that harkened back to hundreds or even thousands of years were used in the bunkers and positions that wound through the swamps and woods. The blockhouses and palisades constructed by the troops were similar in appearance to those used on the frontier during the American Indian wars. Bombs, mortar rounds, and medium-caliber artillery shells that impacted on the flanks or corners of the positions were capable of inflicting some damage, but the core of the fortresses remained intact. Shell splinters and small-arms fire usually could not penetrate the thick logs. As a replacement for the now-scarce barbed wire, the troops had used pointed stakes and logs in the marshy woods before us as a means of hindering the enemy assault forces.

On 20 February the Russians again attacked our positions with reinforced companies. We came under a medium-strength barrage from artillery batteries, katyusha rockets, and mortars that impacted within our positions and in the open fields behind us. The barrages increased through the morning until the explosions reached a steady crescendo.

Believing that the deluge of firepower brought upon us would suffice in putting the foremost lines out of action, the riflemen of a Soviet division assaulted our positions, coming forward in masses as the barrage swept over us. In the wooded sector they advanced to within twenty meters of our positions before drawing our defensive fire. The attackers were met with a deadly crossfire from machine guns and assault rifles, hand grenades, and panzerfausts. Our own artillery opened fire on the Russian positions to the rear of the attackers, and while under fire I directed the fire from our mortar platoon into the heaviest concentration of fighting. The few men holding the foremost line stood and knelt behind the splintered barricades, shooting into the fleeing brown-clad figures who were now retreating into the swamps and woods.

The mortar rounds followed the path of their retreat, and as silence descended on the line I secured the positions to assess our situation. With a handful of infantrymen I moved forward between the lines to search the dead scattered before us. As twilight descended we returned to the safety of our positions, bringing documents and numerous weapons back into our lines.

A number of officers were found among the enemy dead wearing new leather belts and holsters. We retrieved documents from new map cases similar to our own. The uniforms consisted of quilted jackets and pants of excellent quality, and the steel helmets were freshly painted with a new, matt surface. We collected a large quantity of pistols and automatic weapons, which revealed 1944 as the year of manufacture. Upon the bodies of the enemy soldiers were found bundles of grenades and molotov cocktails, with which they had hoped to destroy our defenses once the perimeter had been penetrated.

Some of the Russian wounded left lying before our positions who had feigned death or had lingered while unconscious now attempted to make their way back to their lines in the growing darkness. Our posts and reconnaissance patrols brought them back into our lines, and they appeared strong, healthy, and well-fed. Our landsers appeared to be ragged scarecrows in comparison, worn and thin from harsh living conditions, but the morale of the Courland troops remained unshaken. Nevertheless, not a day passed in which skirmishes did not take place, and the enemy forces opposite us continued to grow stronger.

Just as our own army had done, the Red Army had previously transferred many units to the East Prussian front, considered an area of higher priority. Now new units appeared to face us on the Baltic. After suffering such a defeat before our positions in this sector, they did not attempt further penetration through our battalion but continued to probe and test our defenses with reconnaissance patrols and isolated artillery fire. Construction continued in the positions; new ones were being built and old ones were reinforced. Little enemy activity was observed, but occasionally a more daring or foolhardy Russian would be shot by our ever-watchful snipers.

New and more spectacular "latrine rumors" continued to surface. Many had heard that Army Group Courland was to be ordered to break out to the south toward East Prussia. Others had learned that we were going to be sent to Libau and Windau, the two supply harbors for Courland, to pull back from prepared withdrawal positions and be taken by ship to Germany.

The inevitable questions became more dominant in every conversation. What will become of this? How will it end? Is it to be an endless horror, from which there will be no escape? Propaganda Minister Goebbels had effectively ensured that we were all aware of the Americans' proposed Morganthau Plan. Germany would be splintered, divided into many feudal-like territories, and would become a purely agrarian pastureland—a "goat field." The intelligentsia and officers were to be liquidated, it was said. The living standards of the people would become lower than even that of the Russian peasants under the Bolsheviks. Faced with these macabre predictions of what the future held for Germany, the landsers in the trenches remained resolute in their determination to fight to the very end. Later, on the day of the capitulation, some soldiers and officers chose to take their own lives rather than face this bleak future without hope.

The cities and villages of the homeland sank under a hail of bombs into soot and ashes. Tens of thousands of refugees from eastern Germany and East Prussia poured into the endless, tearful columns of masses fleeing toward the west before the onslaught of the Soviet army pushing relentlessly toward Berlin.

With the beginning of 1945 the situation continued to deteriorate from week to week. The army in Courland remained fast in the grip of an enemy whose resources in men and material were overwhelmingly superior and were growing constantly stronger. The troops in the forward positions, as well as those in the rear echelons, were fully aware of the now-hopeless situation. They had come to know well this enemy that was threatening to overwhelm them, and everyone remained conscious of the fact that behind our backs and at our flanks the Baltic offered the only escape to Germany.

The sparse news from Germany became even more erratic. We no longer received deliveries of mail after the first days of March. It was necessary to rely on the Wehrmacht reports as a source of information, and occasionally one would hear news of the situation in Germany, carefully couched in optimistic overtones, from the "Soldiers' Program" in Libau. Sometimes news briefs published on the front were shared. Finally, as we no longer fully trusted our own sources of information, small circles of friends would share what had been surreptitiously heard over the Swedish radio broadcasts. It was through these bits and pieces of news that we remained informed of the continued massive air attacks of the Anglo-American air corps as well as of the new Soviet offensive between the Oder and the Weichsel.

Trapped in Courland with weapons in hand, we could do nothing further to prevent the cataclysmic fate befalling our country. Despite the bitter news, which grew ever worse from day to day, the Courland army continued to hold their positions as ordered: "Tie down enemy forces in the Baltic, to lighten the task of defending the borders of the Reich."

For those troops holding out in Courland a special award was authorized in the form of a "Courland" cuff band. This band was manufactured in a small mill in Goldingen, and Latvian women were contracted to complete this last German war decoration by hand in small groups in their homes. The band was thirty-eight millimeters in width and bore upon it an embroidered crest—the Teutonic Knight's Order with the Balkan Cross against a silver-gray background—and the elk head, borrowed from the city seal of Mitau. Between the two crests were the stark, black letters spelling KURLAND.

March and April passed with little activity. It was not until the fifth Battle of Courland that we again saw heavy action. We relieved the greatly weakened 126th Infantry Division in the area west and northwest of Preekuln, and this area on the Vartaya was to be our last stand until the day of capitulation.

In the left sector before Bunka, the Red Army once again massed a large force to attack the German front and to push through toward Libau. The assault suffered a severe defeat, and the Soviets withdrew under heavy fire from Nebelwerfer Regiment Seventy and the Army Flak Battalion 276. The Fourteenth Panzer Division, together with the Twenty-first Luftwaffe Field Division, secured the sector, and the Soviets withdrew only after suffering heavy casualties, leaving large numbers of dead and wounded on the battlefield in front of the German positions. The Red Army did not appear to recover fully from the defeat in this sector, and after 28 February the enemy no longer attempted to penetrate this limited area with a large-scale attack.

Mid-March brought a thaw, reducing the streets and roads to little more than bottomless quagmires over which nothing could travel without great exertion. The earthworks and machine-gun positions seemed to be devoured by the gray-black mud, and even the activity on the Soviet side came almost to a halt, the impassible roads spoiling any immediate plans for a further attack.

On 18 March a short but heavy artillery barrage fell on our positions, as if to announce the opening of the last great Battle of Courland. Units from the division were sent into action near Frauenburg and Schrunden, where they battled the Soviet attack until the offensive ground to a halt, the enemy tanks and support vehicles sinking in the swampy morass. The adverse conditions for the landsers holding the line had become indescribable, and words cannot express the sacrifices and suffering of the troops during these final days. Following another breakthrough by the Soviet Eighth Guards Division, the Russians were beaten back by the division on our left flank, situated to the south of Schrunden, the enemy suffering great losses. More than 500 prisoners, 263 tanks, 249 machine guns, 185 field guns, 29 mortars, and 27 aircraft were taken, exemplifying the determination of the landsers to hold to the last.

In mid-April the Eighteenth Army awaited another large-scale attack. The First Battalion of Regiment 438 was relieved at the front and assigned as reserve in preparation for the battle. The battle did not come. The enemy had begun placing all efforts and resources in the battle for central Europe and was no longer willing to continue sacrificing large numbers of troops against the stubborn German defenses between Riga and Libau.

Thus we also were compelled to wait. The front remained relatively quiet but did not sleep. Our lines were penetrated constantly by Russian reconnaissance units who exhibited great skill in their ability to slip past the thinly held positions, which still averaged two men per one hundred meters of line to defend. These reconnaissance squads were invariably infiltrating and joining numerous secret partisan units in the rear areas, which displayed more activity as the weeks passed. On the Courland front there was no rest, and simply to lie and sleep had become a foreign, unknown luxury as we struggled to survive. The grenadiers in the foremost positions hardly took notice that spring had arrived.

On the evening of 1 May 1945, we learned that Grofaz, the Greatest War Lord of All Time, was dead. In general, news of the death of Hitler was received by the troops with indifference; however, it must also be said that some breathed a sigh of relief. During one of the nights shortly thereafter, a barrage broke forth from the enemy lines, and after a short pause we heard the raucous voice of a Russian propagandist blaring from a loudspeaker, "Berlin is ours!" Early the following morning I observed in the dim light of the sunrise large letters of wood or cardboard impaled on posts spelling out "Russians in Berlin!" at the edge of the woods four hundred meters opposite us. Before dusk a heavy machine-gun crew opened fire on the offending message and hacked the sign to pieces.

On 5 May the battalion received instructions to send out a reconnaissance team to bring in prisoners in order to learn which unit lay opposite our positions. I selected several trusted landsers, and after nightfall we departed our lines. Before dawn we returned with two terrified Russians who were turned over to the division for interrogation.

In carrying out this assignment, Kurt, my communicator, received the dubious distinction of having been the last member of the company to be wounded during the war. He was grazed across his shoulder by a bullet fired from a Soviet submachine gun, and the superficial wound required only a tetanus shot and bandage. He insisted on remaining with us in our forward positions, despite my efforts to send him to the rear.

Eight May 1945 opened with brilliant sunshine. Throughout the previous days and weeks remarkable rumors had consistently surfaced in the desperate hope that we would be spared. It was said that the Courland army was finally to be evacuated. Supposedly the western Allies were standing at rest on the Elbe River and the remnants of the German Wehrmacht were reorganizing and massing to throw the Russians back over the old borders of the Reich and out of the heart of Europe. The Americans, the English, and the French had at last recognized that the Bolsheviks surging toward the west posed a threat to all of Europe. We were not to be betrayed and sold out to the Red Army after all. Other reports stated that the English and American fleets had been dispatched to evacuate the troops in Courland and even that we were to join with the Americans, who were now engaged in open battle against the Russians on the Elbe.

We were soon advised of another decision via reliable channels, and this devastating news served to extinguish any optimistic hopes of evacuation within the near future. British Field Marshal Montgomery had accepted the terms of surrender of Admiral von Friedberg in the North German Zone, but these terms were to be valid only for the Western Front. The only hope remaining was that the Supreme Allied Commander, General Eisenhower, would also agree to such terms and that it would also be considered as valid for the army in the eastern sectors. To do so would have served to extricate the long columns of refugees from the horror descending on them in the form of the Soviet army as well as saving the troops still opposing the Soviets from the insufferable fate of languishing for years in gulags and prison camps.

We belatedly received word that on 1 May the commander of Army Group Courland, Generaloberst Hilpert, had released a status communiqué, which passed verbally through the positions to the foremost lines:

TO CONTINUE PURSUING THE WAR IN THE WEST HAS LOST ALL REASON AND HAS THUS COME TO AN END. THE BATTLE IN THE EAST IS TO CONTINUE WITH THE SAME TENACITY WE HAVE CONSISTENTLY DISPLAYED. THE ARMY COMMANDERS AND THE FATHERLAND, THOUGH BLEEDING FROM MANY WOUNDS, FULLY EXPECT THE COURLAND SOLDIERS TO FULFIL THEIR DUTY TO THE LAST. OFFICERS AND MEN MUST CONTINUE TO HAVE FAITH! THE ARMY GROUP IS LATER TO BE SENT INTO ACTION ON THE ELBE AND THE EVACUATION PLAN FOR THE COURLAND ARMY CONTINUES TO REMAIN IN EFFECT.

Our 132d Infantry Division held the battle sector to the west of Preekuln in the southern part of the Courland front, approximately thirty kilometers from Libau. While we continued to repulse Russian troops probing the front lines, behind us marched units of the Eleventh and Twenty-fourth Infantry Divisions toward the harbor at Libau. Throughout the last three days Kriegsmarine vessels of all types in Libau and Windau took on board as many personnel as possible. The naval commanders received by radio this message from the Oberkommando der Wehrmacht:

TO HELA, LIBAU, WINDAU AND BORNHOLM: FROM 5 MAY 08:00 GERMAN SUMMER TIME, A CEASE-FIRE WITH THE OPPOSING UNITS OF FIELD MARSHAL MONTGOMERY WILL BE IN EFFECT. ALL AVAILABLE TRANSPORT AT SEA SHALL CONTINUE AS ORDERED BY THE KRIEGSMARINE TO SAVE GERMAN PERSONNEL FROM THE EAST. DO NOT ENGAGE, DESTROY, OR SINK ANY VESSELS. SAFETY IS PARAMOUNT.

The naval communicators on board ships and vessels received this message on 6 May from the German Sea Command:

TO ALL SHIPS IN THE BALTIC: DUE TO IMPENDING SURRENDER ALL SEA AND SECURITY FORCES AS WELL AS FREIGHTERS MUST HAVE LEFT THE HARBORS OF KURLAND AND HELA NO LATER THAN 0:00, 9 MAY 1945. THE TRANSPORT FROM THE EAST OF GERMAN CITIZENS SHALL BE CARRIED OUT WITH THE HIGHEST PRIORITY.

The German sailors of the Kriegsmarine attempted to save what little remained. The Fifth Patrol Boat Flotilla fought a final sea battle against Russian motor torpedo boats and was successful in sinking one of them in combat.

But the dice had been cast to decide our destiny. General Eisenhower would recognize the cease-fire on the Western Front only if the remaining German forces still opposing the Soviets in the east were to lay down their arms as well. The Allies possessed an immeasurable superiority in aircraft, armor, and artillery with which they were fully capable of totally destroying the remnants of the German forces. It was reported that in order to end the resistance of the German units stubbornly holding out in Courland, the Russians had already transferred armored regiments from Berlin to set in motion against us.

On 7 May the commander of Army Group Courland sent an offer to surrender by telegraph to the Russian command. The Soviets agreed only under the conditions that the surrender be conducted by Hilpert in person. They wanted their victory in the last hour to be as politically valuable as possible. In this manner the favored general of the Courland fighters followed the most difficult path of his life, that of obeying his last orders to surrender his soldiers to an unspeakable fate. He was never again to see Germany, perishing in 1946 behind the barbed wire of a Soviet prison camp.

During the night of 7–8 May our division received the order,

TO ALL FORCES: MARSHAL GOVOROV HAS AGREED TO A CEASE OF HOSTILITIES TO BEGIN 14:00, 8 MAY, 1945. ALL UNITS ARE TO IMMEDIATELY HEED THIS COMMAND. WHITE FLAGS ARE TO BE DISPLAYED FROM ALL POSITIONS. LOYAL OBEDIENCE IN THE EXECUTION OF THIS ORDER IS EXPECTED BY THE SUPREME COMMANDER OF ALL TROOPS. THE DESTINY OF ALL PERSONNEL IN COURLAND IS DEPENDENT UPON CLOSE ADHERENCE TO THIS ORDER.

Two days prior to the capitulation each battalion was permitted to select twelve soldiers—fathers with many children—to be sent to the rear to await transport to Germany. The chosen individuals reported in full marching equipment to the battalion headquarters to await their final assignment.

Not a murmur was heard from those whose fate it was to remain behind. Throughout the ranks the discipline and strong sense of comradeship prevailed to the last minute. Thirty-five aging Tante JU-52 aircraft arrived in direct flight from Norway to Courland to take these men on board. The men filed onto the planes. As the glittering fuselages with thundering motors lifted from the Grobin airfield, the soldiers who were left behind followed the departure with moist eyes. No one could have imagined the fate that would befall this last airlift from Courland. Shortly following the departure, the planes were attacked by a band of Russian fighters who shot down thirty-two of the slow-moving, defenseless aircraft. They were the last planes of the German Luftwaffe, which, with all evacuees on board, went down in flames to find their graves on foreign soil and in the cold waters of the Baltic Sea.

Other unnerving scenes took place on 8 May at the loading docks in the harbors of Libau and Windau. Members of the Eleventh Infantry and the Fourteenth Panzer Divisions, the two "fire brigades" of the Courland army, filed aboard the hastily assembled vessels of the Ninth Kriegsmarine Security Flotilla. The sailors manning the minesweepers, fishing boats, ferries, and harbor cutters jettisoned all excess equipment and freight in order to make room for as many men as possible.

The soldiers patiently waiting to depart exhibited another enduring display of iron discipline. Under the murderous strafing fire of Russian fighters and through the explosions of bombs there were no complaints, no panic, no turbulent scenes. As the load of human cargo on board the ships reached dangerous levels, the naval officers halted the columns of troops filing onto the low-lying vessels. A number of the younger men, seeing that there was no more space available, voluntarily surrendered their places on board and departed the ships to enable older soldiers with families to be rescued. As the lines were cast off, the vessels slowly steamed toward the open Baltic. The commander of the Eighteenth Army, General der Infanterie Boege, called to those departing Libau: "Greet the homeland for all the Courland fighters."

With foaming bows the ships plowed against the high waves of the Baltic en route to the western ports. Suddenly Russian fighter-bombers appeared in the sky and descended like birds of prey on the slow-moving vessels. During the initial attacks, some evacuees lost their lives to the machine guns and cannons of the aircraft, and in strict obedience to orders not a shot was fired in defense. As the planes banked and approached for a second attack, however, they were met with a murderous barrage of defensive fire, and they turned and disappeared over the horizon.

Three of the vessels transporting the Forty-fourth East Prussian Grenadier Regiment were unable to keep pace with the convoy and made port in Traelleborg. Despite the ostensible neutrality practiced by Sweden throughout the war, these soldiers were later delivered to the Soviet Union.

Some of the ships that departed the Windau harbor were intercepted by Russian torpedo boats on the high sea. The leading ship *Rugard* turned and faced the oncoming vessels to allow the two accompanying minesweepers to break away and attempt escape. The thirteen hundred men on board waited with baited breath as they anticipated the worst. The sailors of the *Rugard* reassembled the dismounted breech block of the 88mm deck gun. As the enemy craft continued closing, their intentions to halt the vessel became obvious. The first shot left the barrel, and simultaneously they received the order over the radio-telephone from the fleet admiral to continue steaming forward. With this shot the leading Soviet boat received a direct hit, and accompanied by the others turned and retreated, leaving the *Rugard* to continue its journey. Thus ended the last sea battle in Europe, and more than twenty-five thousand men of the Courland army made their way over the Baltic to German harbors in Holstein.

In early May the men in the foremost positions were not fully aware of the events taking place far to the rear of the 132d Infantry Division. They did not hear the words of the last Wehrmacht report sent on 9 May 1945, which was to be the last official command from Germany:

OUR ARMY GROUP IN COURLAND, WHICH HAS SUCCESSFULLY RESISTED OVER-WHELMING ARMOR AND INFANTRY OPPOSITION FOR MONTHS, HAS DEMON-STRATED COURAGE AND ENDURANCE WITHOUT EQUAL IN SIX MAJOR BATTLES.

In the early morning hours I stepped from the bunker of the Fourth Heavy Machine-Gun Company at the Vartaya streambed and blinked in the sweet, cool air of a new spring day. In sparse patches where the earth was not torn by the battle that had raged for months around us, nature began to show new growth, bright green sprouts shooting from the dark soil. Even the saplings and bushes, torn by shrapnel and shell splinters, revealed tiny buds breaking forth as if to display that despite the insanity mankind had wrought upon itself, life would continue. I was startled from these foreign thoughts by several mortar rounds that impacted in quick succession nearby.

The company still possessed six heavy machine guns, four 80mm mortars, and two heavy 120mm mortars on the battlefront. And the men had received no wounds since Kurt had received the shoulder wound during action two days previously.

At the mortar position, which I had situated in a depression two hundred meters behind the headquarters, we received isolated rifle fire from the enemy positions. Using two heavy machine guns situated deep within the battle line, I opened fire on the opposing tree line from where most enemy activity was observed. The Russians replied with artillery; our own gunners returned fire. At approximately 0900 a band of fighters overflew the battalion positions and released bombs from the shining, silver fuselages. Several of the fragmentation bombs exploded behind the mortar position without causing any damage. The forward observers reported strong enemy movement in the hinterland of the opposite enemy rifle brigade. The communicators reported to me that our land lines with the battalion were temporarily cut by the shelling, and we prepared our weapons and waited for an attack. At exactly 1200 we received a radio report from the regiment that struck like lightning from the heavens:

AT 14:00 THE COURLAND ARMY WILL CAPITULATE. WHITE FLAGS ARE TO BE DISPLAYED ALONG THE FRONT LINES. ALL PERSONNEL WILL REMAIN IN POSITION UNDER ARMS; WEAPONS ARE TO BE UNLOADED, MAGAZINES REMOVED AND BARRELS CLEARED. OFFICERS ARE TO CONTINUE TO COMMAND THEIR UNITS.

At 1300 I heard for the last time over the field telephone the voice of Hauptmann von Daimling, the regimental adjutant. He sharply instructed me not to do anything irrational, to stop the shooting immediately, and to exhibit responsibility in ensuring that the capitulation order, which he repeated verbally, was carried out. He emphasized that strict compliance would determine "the fate of the entire front sector."

The news of the order for unconditional surrender raced throughout the ranks. For years we had been fighting desperately, burying our dead and refusing to capitulate to a vicious enemy whom we still wholeheartedly opposed.

I made the rounds of our position, speaking to the men of the unknown fate that lay before us and attempting to calm their nerves. We no longer feared the prospect of death, for we had lived and dealt intimately with it for years, to the extent that death on a battlefield in the east was an eventuality that was to be expected, that our inevitable fate was to find a final resting place in an unmarked grave in Russia. The fear that possessed us was the fear of the unknown, of not knowing what was to become of us and, more important, of our families in Germany. We had long been aware of what had happened at Katyn in Poland, where the Russians had liquidated thousands of Polish officers, and we had no reason not to expect a similar fate should we fall into the hands of the enemy. The philosophy of fighting to the death had become so ingrained within us during the past years that to surrender, as we were now being ordered to do, was inconceivable.

The silence that had fallen on the front was broken by the report of a pistol shot a short distance away. On investigating, I discovered that one of our officers, receiving word of the capitulation order, had pulled his Luger pistol from the holster, laid it on his map case, and on his note pad had written, "Without an army there is no honor." He had then calmly pressed the muzzle of his pistol against his temple and squeezed the trigger.

A company commander ran toward me wildly waving his pistol and screaming, "I won't surrender!" I ordered him to holster his weapon and to return to his company, to which he responded with threats. I then pulled my own pistol, and he disappeared into the undergrowth of the Vartaya streambed, still screaming, "No surrender! I refuse to surrender!" I was later to learn that he had raced toward the rear, where he had confronted the commander of a self-propelled gun, and with still-drawn pistol attempted to force the officer to advance toward the line with the heavy weapons, all the while screaming, "They are surrendering up on the line!" One of the landsers eventually clubbed him with a rifle butt, and he fell unconscious to the ground. He did in fact go into captivity; however, while in the prison camp he was also to remain something of a psychiatric case for the Russians.

The enemy had launched a final assault on our sister regiment, Infantry Regiment 436, on the last morning of the war in Europe. The order for capitulation was received by Uncle Sepp Drexel during the course of the attack, and it was necessary for him to use every art of persuasion upon the battalion commander to obtain a cease-fire.

That afternoon Oberst Drexel received General Radyonov, the commander of the Soviet division opposite Drexel's own sector. The Russians were standing with massed artillery and an entire division of infantry opposite Drexel's positions and made this pointedly clear to the German oberst. The Soviet general was accompanied by his intelligence officer, who compared maps with the German staff officers. The extent to which they were informed of our positions was remarkable. Several weeks before the surrender, the intelligence officer had penetrated our thinly held lines and, disguised as a civilian, had surveyed the entire hinterland of the front. Oberst Drexel could only chuckle at the intruder's notes, in which he was often referred to as Uncle Sepp. The intelligence officer was also aware that blond Fred, the battalion commander of First Battalion, Infantry Regiment 436, enjoyed tipping a glass on occasion.

The Russians expressed surprise that our lines had been so thinly defended. One of the causes of their astonishment was the fact that in the Soviet army for every three men on the front line, one remained in the rear as support. In the German army the opposite was true.

The Russian officers were then taken to General Demme for the official surrendering of the division. The bulk of the division was assembled on the evening of 8 May at the division headquarters, from where the men then marched for many days en route to the prisoner assembly camp at Telshay.

At 1400 our position was marked with ragged shirts, socks, and bandages stuck on the ends of rifle barrels. With this sign of surrender, a khaki-brown wave surged forth from the forest's edge opposite us. The Russians swarmed into our positions, their new uniforms and well-fed bodies a striking contrast to our ragged appearance, our bodies thin from malnourishment and bleached pale from months of living beneath the earth in bunkers.

The Soviets ignored the weapons and equipment and ran among the soldiers still standing in their positions, ripping decorations and insignia from uniforms and tearing watches and rings from the upraised arms. I was still wearing my camouflage battle smock over my tunic and was thus spared this plundering.

I immediately ordered all personnel to assemble at the company command post and stationed a soldier approximately every ten meters along a perimeter with an assault rifle, the bolt open and without a magazine in the weapon. With this action the Russians ceased their plundering and wandered elsewhere in search of loot.

A young Russian artillery lieutenant appeared at my company headquarters. He was of impeccable appearance, wearing a clean, well-fitting uniform. He had a slender face from which two wide, blue eyes gazed steadily at me as I approached. From his appearance, he could have been one of many German students in Heidelberg or Tübingen. We greeted one another with a salute, and he drew a map from a thick leather case, stating that he needed to be advised of our artillery positions. I was able to provide him with only the approximate information, and he expressed amazement that our batteries were positioned so far to the rear.

He continued to ask, "Why? Why did you keep shooting? Hitler long kaput!" Roving bands of Russian soldiers had reappeared, and they danced about the unmoving ranks of the grenadiers, singing, "Gitler kaput! Voyna kaput!" A childish naivete beamed from their round faces as they danced and sang. The nightmare of war was now erased from their consciousness. The ranks of landsers could reply only with stony silence, their faces reflecting the bitterness and frustration of the moment.

Eventually the victors departed, and we received no further reports from the regiment, the last order having been to remain in our positions. At approximately 1500 a pony cart appeared before our bunkers and drew to a halt at our command post. Alone on the cart was a squat Soviet major with oriental features and a pockmarked complexion. He sprang to the ground and approached my position on bowed legs, a row of medals hanging from ribbons on his tunic. We greeted one another with a traditional military salute, his coal-black eyes darting furtively over our surroundings.

From a former container for mortar fuses he pulled a strip of paper from a section of *Pravda* and a pinch of Machorka tobacco, and offered me a cigarette. I politely refused and extended to him a German Eckstein, which he accepted with a nod. I then called for Lehmann, one of our soldiers who spoke fluent Russian, to serve as a translator. As he translated the words of the major it was made clear that we were to march across the lines to the Soviet positions. He added that officers would retain their sidearms for maintaining discipline. I explained that I could not comply, as my last orders were to remain in position, and no other orders had been received. He nodded thoughtfully, climbed back on the pony cart, and returned to his lines.

About thirty minutes later he reappeared and again through the translator ordered me to march the men across the lines. I repeated that no orders from our regiment had been received, and with this he pulled his pistol from the holster at his side and responded, saying that if I refused, then he would shoot me and the men would follow him. To this I could only reply, "Da, da," in acknowledgment; I then gave the order for the men to form a column and marched the battalion forward.

We marched several kilometers along the road through the forest in the direction of Preekuln, and we were amazed at the overwhelming numbers of Russians who had opposed us. The forest was filled with T-34 tanks, the supply units were crowded with Studebaker trucks parked bumper to bumper. As we proceeded along the road we encountered an oncoming column of T-34 tanks, heavily camouflaged with tree branches and protected from our antitank weapons by thick logs lashed to the chassis. The lead driver swerved sharply toward the column of prisoners, and we stepped aside and marched past the Soviet tank crews, who glared down at us from the dark turrets.

We soon came to a small clearing in the forest where a Russian colonel had assembled his staff. In a half circle stood the staff officers; among them were a number of women wearing immaculate, tight-fitting uniforms, their eyes wide in amazement as they viewed us from under wide fur caps. The unfamiliar and long-forgotten smell of perfume wafted toward us. The column was brought to a halt, and I strode forward to formally surrender the First Battalion, 438th Regiment, to the enemy. After several long seconds of silence I heard a low voice from the ranks of Soviet officers remark, "Karoschi discipline! Nonoga discipline!" (good discipline! much discipline!).

The colonel greeted me with a salute followed by a handshake, something that I had not expected. He asked repeatedly, "Patschevu? Why did you continue to fight? Hitler is long dead." I replied simply, "Because we are soldiers."

I was then approached by a staff officer wearing the blue-piped cap of the NKVD, who inquired as to the fate of the two Russians we had captured several days previously. I explained that they had been turned over to the regiment in good health, and he replied in broken German, "If not true, then . . ." and he slapped his holster threateningly.

I was then asked if all weapons had been surrendered. I unbuckled my pistol belt and handed it to one of the officers, then turned and asked the men standing motionless in ranks if any arms were still carried. An NCO stepped forward and attempted to give a Russian officer a P-38 pistol, to which the officer responded, "Nyet, Nyet!" shaking his head vigorously. I then took the proffered weapon, removed the magazine, cleared the chamber, and tossed it onto the roadside.

It was explained to me that we would be treated correctly and that we would soon be released and returned to our homes again. I clung desperately to these words with a glimmer of hope that perhaps the long nightmare was indeed coming to an end.

I was then escorted a short distance from the column and invited to eat at a table piled high with food. I was amazed to see condiments of every description, including the cases of canned goods bearing the familiar label, "Oscar Mayer—Chicago." I politely refused the invitation, explaining that a German officer cannot eat unless the men are fed as well. The colonel appeared surprised at this response, and I was unceremoniously escorted back to the waiting column of prisoners.

We were then assigned a mounted Cossack as an escort, and he repeatedly raced along the length of the column without a saddle at breakneck speed. Shortly after leaving the clearing we were again descended upon by swarms of Russians who poured from the forest, falling on the column to tear wedding rings, watches, and military decorations from the prisoners.

I motioned for the Cossack, who galloped up to me and brought his mount to a sharp halt. I then removed my watch and offered it to him, explaining that he had been given responsibility to maintain order and that in violation of this order the men were being plundered of personal belongings. He nodded grimly, and springing to the ground, he selected a stout stick from the forest's edge and leaped back on the horse. He then galloped headlong into the ranks of plundering Russians. Wielding the stick like a saber, he swung wildly at the mob, viciously striking them on their hands, arms, and backs until they retreated to the protection of the forest.

As the sun was setting behind us, we were marched to a prisoner collection point in an old cemetery, and as darkness descended the Russians began to celebrate their final victory. Wildly firing over our heads with submachine guns, rifles, and pistols, they danced in the light of flares fired into the sky while we were forced to lie flat on the ground to avoid being struck as tracer bullets bounced and ricocheted among the tombstones. The Soviets gathered around us, rejoicing in their victory with a macabre dance, chanting, "Gitler kaput! Voyna kaput!" in an unending chorus, leaping and springing in ecstasy while firing into the air.

At dawn the officers were separated from the enlisted men. The pain of defeat had begun. The heads of the soldiers were shorn, and the ranks formed into massive columns to be herded like cattle toward the east. Small groups of German soldiers captured earlier in the war appeared before us, representing the "Antifa Organization" (the National Committee for Free Germany), and spoke of the benefits of Communism. The presence and words of the collaborators were met with cold silence from the Courland veterans.

After several hours we were again on the march. After three days of steady marching we received our first rations: a thin broth in which floated bits of cabbage leaves. This was only an indication of what our future would bring. The illusion of good treatment first assured us soon came to an end as the rear-echelon units did not recognize the fairness observed by soldiers at the front. The endless march along the primitive roads through swamps and forests had begun. The column moved painfully between heavily armed guards lining the roadsides, through the shroud of total defeat toward the east, to a final end of the war and to an unknown destiny.

EPILOGUE

On 8 May 1945, the surviving soldiers of the Courland army marched into captivity. Thus began the final phase of the war, a struggle that proved to be vastly different from the battles we had previously experienced. A bitter fight for survival began, a battle for which there exists little defense.

Herded together like cattle, we were first confined in open fields and forests clearings. As our hunger increased we desperately attempted to draw nourishment from grass in the fields, and we chewed bark from trees in attempts to stave off the gnawing pains of starvation that overwhelmed and weakened us.

We were eventually marched to a large camp situated in a former paper factory near the town of Sloka, on the Bay of Riga. Here we received our first sparse rations, which were accompanied by an issue of a dozen Papyrossi cigarettes and ten grams of sugar. It was explained to us that the cigarette and sugar rations were the same afforded the junior officers in the Soviet army, and we were surprised that this distinction existed within the "worker's and farmer's army." In the German Wehrmacht all ranks had always received identical rations.

At length we were addressed by a Flak officer who had been taken prisoner at Stalingrad in January 1943. A member of the "National Committee of German Officers," which was led by another, better-known Stalingrad survivor, General von Sedylitz, the leutnant had received training as a "politruk" in a Moscow prison camp. He implored us to embrace the Communist-Leninist ideology, speaking tirelessly of the new world in which we must live, a world that could be made better only through the Communist system. His remarks were met mostly by indifference from the Courland soldiers; however, the political rhetoric was greeted with enthusiasm by a few individuals, some of whom perhaps perceived a better chance of surviving the ordeal by cooperating fully with the authorities in whose hands our destiny lay.

Over the next several days propaganda documents were distributed. To relieve boredom some soldiers began to study Russian. Others attempted to mend threadbare clothing while some fashioned crude "Kurland" arm bands from bits of uniform material.

At last we were permitted to write letters. Due to a lack of writing material and envelopes, we wrote on whatever scraps and bits of paper we could find within our sparse belongings. Written with stubs of previously concealed pencils, the letters were folded into compact triangles and carefully addressed to family members. More than one thousand letters were painstakingly written to inform family members that the writers had survived the last months of the war; however, none reached the homeland. The letters did provide information to the NKVD officers who, unbeknownst to the prisoners, confiscated them and combed through the contents, gleaning information for the exhaustive files that would remain to haunt us throughout our captivity.

On one occasion we stood shirtless in ranks with an uplifted left arm as Soviet intelligence officers searched for the blood group tattoos that were characteristic only of members of the Waffen SS. Those prisoners found to have the identifying mark below their left armpit were quickly separated from the ranks, and they simply disappeared into the void of the Soviet Union.

One morning in mid-July we were ordered to prepare to march. Formed into long gray ranks, six abreast, we were flanked by Soviet soldiers wearing sweeping overcoats, despite the heat of summer. Across the breasts of many guards were slung submachine guns with the round, drum-shaped magazines that had become so familiar to us during the war. Other guards carried infantry rifles at the ready, with mounted bayonets gleaming menacingly in the sunlight.

We marched in a long column toward the Sloka railway station. A rumor circulated through the ranks that a large number of enlisted prisoners from a nearby camp had been engaged in preparing cattle cars to transport us toward the east. On our arrival at the marshaling yard, roll call was taken again, and we were assigned into groups to board the train. Uneasiness swept though the ranks as we realized that a new, more ominous phase was beginning.

Glancing desperately about, I realized that it was impossible to avoid climbing into the dark opening in the side of the car, and I reluctantly boarded the cattle car as a pair of armed guards, accompanied by an officer, methodically checked each name against a roster. After the car filled with an allotted number of prisoners, the large door was slid shut, leaving us in semidarkness. A dim light was provided by a narrow opening in the wall of the car near the door, where a provisional toilet, made of two rough-cut boards hammered together at a right angle, emptied alongside the rails.

We stood packed within the railcars until after nightfall. Slowly the cars began to move, the inhabitants swaying silently with the movement of the train, packed closely together, each member of the group lost again in private thoughts of home and survival. We traveled throughout the night, and as the train slowed to a crawl I was able to discern the horizon growing light with dawn through the crack near the door. In the early morning hours I could vaguely identify the city of Riga silhouetted against the sky. We passed slowly over the Duna, creaking over the hastily repaired railway bridge where, during the night of 13–14 October 1944, I had briefly stood with my commander before the bridge was demolished behind us during our retreat to Courland.

We continued toward the east. The train rolled toward the area east of Vitebsk, and our sojourn was interrupted by numerous, inexplicable stops of varied duration. During the journey we were provided with a ration of one salt herring and one slice of bread per man. A small container of water was occasionally passed through the door of the car at some stops. As the suffering from thirst grew in intensity, attempts to bribe guards during the stops became commonplace. Gold wedding rings, carefully hidden from the enemy soldiers during the initial phases of surrender, were offered in exchange for a small canteen cup of water. This misery became especially acute in the rear sections of the train, where the sparse rations of water often failed to reach the inmates before the container was emptied. During this phase of the journey my "soldier's luck" remained with me, as I was situated only a short distance from the car reserved for the guards. Thus I was able to trade some carefully hoarded Papyrossi cigarettes for cups of water during the occasions when we were commanded to "na borni!" (get out).

We eventually reached a bivouac area far to the east of the Volchov, where we had fought the vicious winter battles in the previous years south of Lake Ladoga. Here we were provided large, American-made tents for quarters. Rations were delivered—large wooden casks of salted fish and crates of cabbage. I was assigned by the senior German officer to establish a field kitchen for rationing and preparing the fish and cabbage. A number of enlisted prisoners from a nearby camp were detailed to us as cooks and kitchen workers.

The distinctive Nazi emblem of the German Wehrmacht—an eagle clutching a wreathed swastika—was soon ordered removed from the breast of our tunics and from our caps. The routine plundering by the guards and Soviet intelligence personnel continued. Anything of monetary value or any object that could be regarded as a souvenir was taken. I had hidden a small wristwatch behind the cockade insignia on my officer's visored cap, which escaped seizure. Our paper money was confiscated whenever found by the authorities. Due to lack of toilet paper, a number of prisoners had resorted to using our now-worthless military pay script at the latrines, and this currency was plentiful among the prisoners as there had been nothing available for purchase on the battlefront. One morning several of us were astonished to observe a Soviet lieutenant and sergeant slink into the slit trench that served as a latrine and fish out a number of these bills, which they washed clean in a nearby stream. We later heard that there existed a lucrative trade in exchanging this German currency for rubles, which accounted for their enthusiasm in collecting the bills.

I quickly became obsessed with the idea of escape. Despite the sparse rations of fish soup and bits of bread, I managed to hoard enough dried crumbs to collect a small emergency ration, which remained concealed at the bottom of my Wehrmacht-issue bread bag. I was certain that the Bay of Finland lay between one hundred and two hundred kilometers' distance, and I began to formulate an escape plan to the north. These hopes were soon dashed after consulting with my friend Vollrath, who had served as a geologist with the Courland army staff. He advised me that our location lay at least eight hundred kilometers from the sea and reminded me that winter would soon be upon us. Despite my enthusiasm to escape I was soberly aware that an attempt to traverse that distance in winter, without proper food or clothing, would ultimately end only in death through recapture or starvation.

The camp of tents was broken in late summer, and the imprisoned officers were separated into groups for the transfer to various penal camps. The majority were sent to Borovitschi, including my longtime friend and prison companion Dr. Leopold Schilpp, the cheerful staff doctor from Mainz who would later, while serving as camp physician, keep me alive during periods of grave illness due to malnourishment. The method of determining how the prisoners were segregated into groups remained a mystery to us, and I was assigned to a small body of forty officers ranging in rank from leutnant to hauptmann, including a Luftwaffe medical doctor.

Many prisoners were already compelled to wear crude wooden clogs as replacements for their officer's boots, which were eagerly sought by the Russian "soldateska" and were often surrendered to the guards at gunpoint or traded for food. The loose clogs were worn on the long march through swampy terrain to the railhead for the transport to new camps. I had already been compelled to cut off the upper parts of my knee-length boots in order to use the fine leather to reinforce my now threadbare breeches at the knees and thus had managed to retain the lower part of the footwear for the march. After several hours of labored marching we arrived at a single-track rail junction, where we were loaded onto a train consisting of a primitive steam engine to which was attached several railcars. Our journey further to the east began.

The train was also occupied by a number of poorly dressed civilians, men and women of various ages. As the train began to move toward the east, an approximately forty-year-old man with a mouth full of silver teeth began to berate us strenuously. The curses directed at the silent ranks of prisoners soon turned to gestures and threats that increased in intensity until a sergeant of the guard interrupted and silenced him.

GULAG "HOZZI"

At the end of this journey we were brought to a forest clearing, in which stood a number of wooden barracks constructed from rough-hewn logs. As we stood in ranks, we were addressed by a young, blond lieutenant and a political officer accompanied by a group of soldiers. The political officer, who was recognizable by his green peaked cap, was always accompanied by a young woman. We were instructed that it would be our duty to construct the prison camp, the most important aspects being the construction of four watchtowers. The towers were supported by four log pillars and were approximately eight meters in height. At the top of each tower was a small platform, roofed with rough board shingles. We then moved barbed-wire fencing into place to complete the crude enclosure.

Several days following our arrival at this camp we observed a long train pull to a stop, and approximately two hundred German prisoners dismounted. They shuffled mournfully through the gates of the enclosure, in ragged ranks, apathy etched clearly upon their faces. They were older prisoners, soldiers who had gone into captivity in 1944 when the

Soviets had captured the island of Oesel near the Bay of Finland in the Baltic Sea. A few of them had surrendered near the border of East Prussia.

As the columns of prisoners approached, I was shocked by the condition of the men, their close-cropped skulls and hollow cheeks. Their lifeless, glassy eyes stared straight ahead from shallow, gray faces. The ranks shuffled toward us, most men wearing the familiar, rough-hewn wooden clogs, their malnourished bodies appearing lost in the remnants of uniforms that were little more than rags.

A sauna was soon constructed, considered a necessity for protecting the prisoners from typhus. We remained in constant danger from this disease, carried by lice and spreading through the camp populace. The lice tormented us incessantly, laying clusters of tiny gray eggs in our head and body hair. The forty officers assigned to a separate barracks were compelled to remove all hair from their heads and bodies in an effort to thwart the lice infestation. The sauna was used both as a delousing station and bathing facility, and we were permitted access in shifts, approximately every fourteen days.

Labor parties were organized, and it was planned that the work details for woodcutting in the forest would be led by men from the officers' barracks under the watch of the armed guards. This plan was soon changed when a labor union functionary from Vienna, who wore a red-and-white-striped band on his cap, assembled the enlisted men and gave an inflammatory speech. Together with a self-proclaimed Communist from Hamburg, they were tireless in their efforts to unite the enlisted prisoners against the officers.

On the anniversary of the Red October Revolution—7 November 1945—the Soviet NKVD officer explained to us through his translator that the German Wehrmacht had ceased to exist. He further explained that hereafter there would be no officers among us and that in the future we were to repay through our labor the war damage inflicted upon Russia by the Fascists. In coordination with this declaration, we were required to remove all officer's insignia from our uniforms, including shoulder boards and collar tabs. Any medals and badges were to be confiscated, an order having been given to collect and turn in to the authorities any devices that were intended to "glorify Fascism." This order was hardly necessary, as all medals and badges had long since been stripped from the prisoners by the Soviet soldiers in their endless pursuit of souvenirs or items of trade. With this final order to remove insignia of rank, it was clear to us that we had been stripped of any rights and were at the total mercy of our captors. Any reference to rights of prisoners through the Hague Convention was useless.

Along with the old prisoners were Christian Burkhard from Wornersberg, Emil Glatz from Ebhausen, and others from the area of my hometown. One Sunday morning I attempted to organize a small choral group with these men. This displeased the Antifa group in the camp, who considered this effort a threat to their authority, and I was thus denounced as an escape risk. During the subsequent search of my belongings, the Russians found a tiny compass needle buried deep within a roll of socks.

Theoretically, this needle could have been mounted on a small splinter of wood to indicate magnetic north for an escape attempt through the swamps, and as punishment for this infraction I was to be placed in solitary confinement for an indefinite period of time. A passageway through the officers' barracks was divided by walls to form a space approximately two meters by two meters in size. The entrance to this cell was secured by a wide door nailed together from heavy planks, which could be barred from the outside by an iron rod. When the rod was slid into the secure position, the door could not be opened from the interior of the cell.

Once a day I was led from the cell to be given a slice of damp bread and a cup of thin cabbage soup. The temperature was dropping rapidly with the coming of winter, and the cell remained cold throughout the days and nights, despite the presence of a large iron stove that was missing a door. This oven had probably been used to heat the barracks before the construction of the isolation cell; however, we were not permitted to use it for warmth.

During one of my short respites from the cell, Christian Burkhard met me near the latrine and slipped me several splinters of firewood, along with a tiny amount of tinder material, a flint, and a rough piece of steel, with which I could light a small fire. I stuck the material into an inner pocket of my breeches unnoticed by the escorting guard, who did not discern anything out of the ordinary, as I had already been deprived of my belt and was required to hold up my pants by the waist. Thus I was provided the opportunity to light a small fire in the doorless oven. After several minutes of rest in luxurious warmth, I fell asleep on the floor next to the stove. A short time later I awakened, choking on smoke that filled the cell and gasping for oxygen. A small piece of burning wood had fallen from the stove and ignited the floor of the cell, and I was now in danger of asphyxiation. Luckily, a large number of prisoners who had been stricken with diarrhea were forming a steady stream of traffic to and from the latrines. I rolled over to the door of the cell, and through the crack between the door and the floor I deeply inhaled fresh air; then I began to yell "fire!" I was soon pulled unconscious from the smoke-filled cell with singed clothes and minor burns, and the fire was extinguished with snow-water.

When I awoke at midday I was surprised to find myself on my old bunk in the barracks, the building empty, as the occupants had been mustered out on a labor party. One of the guards, whom we called "One-eye" due to his cross-eyed appearance, soon led me at bayonet-point from the camp to the commandant's office. In the dim room I was greeted ominously by two men of the Antifa group, a German-Polish prisoner who served as translator, and the German and Russian camp medical officers. The latter was a Jewish doctor from Leningrad. Also present was the political officer and his ever-present female attendant.

The hearing was presided over by the commandant, and it was explained to me that I faced the serious charges of arson, sabotage, and attempted destruction of Soviet property and that I could expect severe punishment for these grave offenses.

My referral to the Hague Convention and the relevant conditions for the handling of prisoners of war with international rights gave me the opportunity to explain further to the commander what had occurred. I told him that sleep deprivation, combined with solitary confinement in freezing weather, without heat or warm clothing, could only be considered inhumane treatment; therefore I had taken the liberty of lighting a fire to prevent freezing to death. I spoke of the lack of nourishment that had been experienced by the prisoners, and in closing I remarked that if my death had already been determined, then as a military officer I should be afforded a bullet.

With this remark a great uproar ensued among those present. At length the translator relayed to me that the commandant had proclaimed that "no more German officers will die in Russian camps!" I was immediately escorted under guard to the camp kitchen, where I was provided a double ration of soup and bread.

The work details were dispatched into the snow-covered forests, where trees were felled by hand. All the labor in the forests was conducted without the benefit of machinery: the trees were cut with axes and cross-cut saws; the trunks were then split with mauls and wedges. The sparse rations could not provide enough nourishment for our bodies to enable us to conduct such strenuous labor, and we soon experienced the first deaths.

The ground at the perimeter of the camp was frozen to the consistency of concrete, and it was necessary to drag the corpses to the softer soil of the swamps for burial. Here we would scrape away the covering of snow and lay the dead to rest; during these burial details I sought out patches of wild cranberries under the ice, which provided a needed, albeit sparse, source of vitamins.

Among the dead was Sarotti. This was not his family name; however, he was from a well-known Hanseatic business family and had managed the Sarotti chocolate factory in north Germany. His bunk was located directly beneath me in the barracks, and one morning I awoke to find him lying with his head cocked to one side, a small rivulet of dried blood on his chin. We dragged him to the swamp for burial along with several others who had died during the night.

The ranks of the dead continued to climb, among them the teacher Hermann from Onstmettingen, the young Drescher from Endringen, and others. During the winter of 1945–1946 one of every three prisoners from our camp made the final journey to the makeshift cemetery.

On one warm spring day, Hauptmann Hermstruewer, Oberleutnant Heck, and Oberleutnant Schreiber, along with two others, attempted to escape, despite their weakened condition. We had previously discussed the possibility of slipping through the deep ruts created by the supply truck, which led under the gate, directly before the eyes of the guards. This small group had slipped under the gate and broken into a supply hut to obtain additional rations for the escape before stealing soundlessly into the forest. The ground was still covered with snow, and their attempt was clearly an act born of desperation. All of us were fully aware that under the current conditions we would soon die of exhaustion, disease, or malnutrition in the desolate camp.

Three days later Heck and Schreiber returned. They were paraded before the mustered ranks of prisoners, badly beaten and covered with blood. Their threadbare uniforms hung from their emaciated bodies in tatters. "This is what happens to those who attempt an escape!" we were told. Hauptmann Hermstruewer had suffered a severe skull fracture from the beating and died a few days later. Oberleutnant Heck was eventually released from the gulags many years later, and I met him during the 1960s after he had become Dr. Walter Heck, harbor commander in Kehl on the Rhine.

One of the reasons for the high rate of death in our camp was the total lack of bread for a period of approximately six weeks. This occurred during the middle of the bitter winter, when the need for nourishment was most critical to our bodies in the freezing temperatures. It was rumored that the baking facility, located several kilometers' distance, was not functioning. As a result, we were provided a small amount of bread meal mixed in warm water, which created a thin, milky soup almost devoid of nourishment. It was also said that we were made to suffer as punishment for the deprivations experienced by the population of Leningrad, where thousands of civilians had starved during the siege.

During one of the last days of March 1946, a gray, weary column made its way painfully to a railhead, as we used the last vestiges of strength in our bodies, our skeletal figures shivering as we weakly stood in ranks awaiting the transport. Fully aware that our only hope of escaping death lay with the transfer to a new camp, we prayed that this change would bring us better conditions.

At length we climbed into the railcars for a one-day journey to our new destination.

BOROVITSCHI

The large main camp, with approximately two thousand prisoners, was situated on a hill. It consisted of twenty barracks, which were sunken into the ground. These bunkers were previously used as a work camp and for the storage of potatoes.

There were numerous enlisted bunkers as well as the "Spanish barracks," which housed Spanish officers from Spain's volunteer legion. After spending a period of time in the medical facility I was assigned to Officers' Barracks II. A commission to determine the health and work capability of the prisoners was established. The prisoners quickly named these inspections "meat exhibits." We were required to stand naked before the Russian commission, and during the examination the medical officers would pinch the flesh on our buttocks between their thumb and forefinger to determine weight loss, which would indicate to them our ability to withstand heavy or light labor. Among the categories were "Rabotschi-Group III" (Work Group III), designated only for light labor, and "Rabotschi-Group IV o.K.," which was designated for those who could perform only the most menial and light tasks. The last group, "Distroph," was used to designate prisoners who were completely disabled from dystrophy and were often inflicted with dropsy.

When brought before the commission, it was diagnosed that I was suffering from a particular type of dropsy called edema. My luck remained with me at this examination, as our former staff medical officer, Dr. Schilpp, was assigned to assist the female Soviet medical doctor. This extraordinary woman did everything possible to improve the lives of the German prisoners, and we nicknamed her "Puppchen" (little doll). Following World War I she had worked as a pediatrician in Frankfurt, and she spoke fluent German. Through the recommendations of these two physicians I was assigned to the camp medical clinic, where I was provided a small piece of white bread, the first I had seen subsequent to our surrender.

Through the weakening of the digestive system and the months of starvation in the former Hozzi camp, I was suffering from constant diarrhea. Dr. Schilpp provided a treatment in the form of a tea consisting of charcoal mixed with caraway and yarrow or other herbs that were available. After several weeks of this treatment I had recovered sufficiently to be classified for Rabotschi-Group III and was released from the clinic.

I shared my bunk in the officers' barracks with my longtime friend Dr. Gustel Hickl. We slept on two tiers of wooden planks, upon which we would spread our threadbare winter clothing, which now consisted mostly of quilted Russian field jackets. The quilted clothing served as protection from the cold and was also used as mattresses; and, when necessary, we pulled small bits of cotton quilting from the material for tinder to ignite small, surreptitious fires. The keeping of fires for heating in the barracks was strictly forbidden, so we slept closely together during the bitter, freezing nights in attempts to keep warm.

Also with us was a young leutnant named Graf von der Schulenburg. This ancient title of Prussian aristocracy was well known to the Soviets, and until the outbreak of the war his uncle had served as the German ambassador in Moscow. One day Leutnant Graf von der Schulenburg was taken under guard from the barracks and led away, never to reappear among us. It was said that he had been taken to Moscow for "special treatment."

The camp authorities organized labor parties that were parceled out to various assignments. Prisoners were provided for labor to a factory that produced tiles and concrete piping. Another workplace was a nearby paper mill. During the summer months many prisoners labored to cut peat from the nearby marshes. I was assigned to cut peat, and we dug into the marsh with square shovels and stacked the peat into piles for drying. In the peat kolkhoz there were potatoes and turnips from which a thick soup was made. Despite the backbreaking labor we savored the rare opportunity to enjoy a healthy portion of soup.

Eventually a large steam-powered peat-cutter was engaged to cut furrows in the swampy ground, and the prisoners would then cut and stack layers of brown-black peat for drying and collection. A very unproductive machine dating from Czarist Russia was also put into use. This machine was powered by steam, the fuel for which was the peat previously won through hours of strenuous labor by the prisoners. In order to gain a pause in the heavy labor, we could occasionally find intact tree branches and stumps buried beneath the peat, pieces of which would be quickly thrown into the works of the machine to jam the mechanism. An hour or so of valuable rest could sometimes be won in this manner while the tightly wedged obstruction was being cleared.

We began to receive an officer's ration of ten to fifteen Papyrossi cigarettes and five grams of sugar per day. The enlisted prisoners received Machorka tobacco. The internal authorities of the camp now consisted of German Communists, and the prisoners remained under the watch of these groups of collaborators both inside and outside the camp. During excursions for work details we were escorted by these privileged individuals, who wore a special insignia on their sleeve. We referred to these escorts as "convoys." They were immediately identifiable by their better clothing and their healthy, robust appearance, and among other privileges they were always afforded generous portions of the rations. Unbeknownst to them at the time, their cooperation with the Soviets, in hopes of early release, was to have the opposite effect, as their collaboration was essential to the Soviet authorities for propaganda purposes and for administering the large numbers of prisoners. In some instances, much to their surprise and dismay, they were to be among the last prisoners to be released.

The prisoners received their soup in wooden bowls, and the issue of food was strictly administered to ensure that each prisoner received the same portions from the ten-liter buckets. One bucket of soup was made available to each organized group of ten prisoners. A small scale was used for weighing each slice of dark bread, and the receipt of the end crust was organized into shifts, each man taking his turn to receive the crust. We were aware that the crust contained more calories; thus this portion of bread was highly valued. Within the officers' barracks discipline, administered among ourselves, remained very strict, as we were aware that our self-discipline and cooperation with one another would contribute to our chances of survival.

POMASCHKI FABRIKYE — THE PAPER MILL

With the onset of winter our work detail was transferred to a paper mill. The strenuous, daily march by foot for several miles to the peat farm was discontinued. We were now afforded transportation to and from the paper mill, and every morning we would climb aboard the battered Ford truck to begin our ten-hour workday. We were now permitted to rest on Sundays, although this pause in our labor at the mill was interrupted by the requirement for a labor party to retrieve logs from the nearby river.

I was inevitably assigned to the logging detail. A thin sheet of ice covered the river, broken only in the areas where the heavy timbers, felled far to the north and borne to our location by the current, were lifted from the water for further transportation over land. For this labor we were issued hip-length linen stockings that were not waterproof, and I soon developed a disabling kidney infection from the hours spent in icy water. I was permitted to spend a number of days lying feverishly on my bunk, as the camp medical clinic was filled to overflowing with ill patients.

We continued to suffer losses in the camp; however, the death rate did not reach the levels of the previous year. One of the prisoners routinely assigned as a gravedigger was always recognizable by his large, imposing moustache and his completely bald head. One day he fell ill and died from intestinal blockage, caused by overeating. Upon investigation, it was discovered that he had broken gold teeth from one of the corpses prior to burial and had traded the gold to the guards or civilians in the area for food. He had proceeded to consume the full amount received for the gold and had quickly developed the fatal, agonizing complications.

While on the work detail in the paper mill I developed a close friendship with Hans Holzknecht, a mineworker from Tirol. Also present was Gustel Hickl. We were assigned to carry "klino"—piles of gray clay—on a wooden, two-man litter to an elevator. One day I discovered a data plate on the elevator, "Voith-Heidenheim 1898." After my eventual return to Germany I relayed this news to my Uncle Breuninger from Heidenheim who had worked many years for the Voith company. He had served as a chief engineer for this internationally known turbine and propeller manufacturer. During his apprenticeship in Esslingen he had received the assignment as a young, unpaid volunteer to dismantle the machinery at the paper mill in Kirchheim-Teck, which was to be replaced with more modern, efficient equipment. He was then dispatched to Czarist Russia to install the machinery at the paper mill near Borovitschi. My uncle had spent several months as a volunteer constructing the very same paper mill where I, many years later, was compelled to work as a prisoner of war.

Weeks and months passed. We received the first mail from our homeland after almost two years of captivity. Our replies to these desperately written letters were the first indication to our families that we had survived the war and were still alive in captivity. Eventually, our comrades from Austria and the prisoners from Alsace were taken from the camp and returned to their homes. International politics adroitly steered from Vienna was having an effect on our captors. It was rumored that prisoners from Germany were also being released. The rations improved as well but remained far below the minimum health requirements.

In this camp I also met the last general staff officer from our division, Major Dechamps. From him I learned of the fate of other members of my unit. At the time of our surrender, during the night of 8–9 May 1945, Hauptmann von Waechter from our division artillery had succeeded in climbing aboard a Kriegsmarine ferry, which took the passengers to the Swedish coast near Malmo. In June 1945 an agreement was reached between the Swedish government and the Soviet Union that these soldiers would be turned over to the Soviet authorities. The Swedish military strongly protested this decision but remained helpless to prevent the delivery of the interned soldiers. Upon learning that he was to be delivered to the Soviets, von Waechter slit his wrists and was unconscious when discovered. He was taken to a hospital in Malmo where he recovered, and he was eventually turned over to the Soviet Union.

On an early Sunday morning work detail I came upon a windfall when unloading a lumber cart that had previously been used to deliver poppy plants to a mill to be processed for hog feed. In the corners and in the cracks of the wooden floor I was able to recover whole, hard seeds, which, when chewed to separate the kernel from the chaff, provided badly needed nourishment. We were also able to retrieve small amounts of corn pulp from the paper mill, which was used for the processing of rough paper.

Hauptmann Walter Schaechterle had served as the communications officer with the Courland army. One morning Schaechterle, together with the Spanish officers, refused to muster for work in protest over the poor rations. It had also been planned that the enlisted men would participate in this protest; however, they came under immense pressure from the Antifa group and did not do so.

An enraged soldateska stormed into the barracks and with leveled submachine gun forced us to muster in ranks outside. Walter Schaechterle and two Spanish officers were then removed and taken to solitary confinement. They were sentenced to life imprisonment—usually a term of twenty-five years—for sabotage and were soon transferred to another camp far to the east in the Kirgesian steppe. I managed to speak with him one last moment before his transfer, and he requested that I advise his parents of what had occurred. I later was able to fulfill this promise. Walter's father was general director of the German linoleum factory in Bietigheim and spent more than two years attempting to learn the whereabouts of his son through a Swedish intermediary. He was eventually able to gain his release by surreptitiously paying large sums of U.S. dollars in bribes to Soviet authorities. Walter and I met once again in the 1950s and celebrated our reunion in the wine country near Fellbach.

We learned to expect sudden interrogations that would take place randomly and without warning. The former police officers, members of the Police Regiment Riga, and the few remaining soldiers from the Waffen SS were particular targets of the Soviet intelligence system. As a result of the interrogations, many prisoners would disappear from our ranks, transferred to other camps where they would undergo additional penalties. Included in the prisoners singled out were the commanders of regiments, staff officers, and generals. These targeted personnel who survived the ordeal in Russia were finally released in 1955 through the untiring efforts of the German chancellor, Konrad Adenauer.

My interrogations usually took place in the presence of two Soviet army officers, a woman in uniform of indeterminable rank, and two Antifa members as well as the ever-present interpreter. I was always asked to affirm my Fascist-officer's rank and where I had served throughout the war. The operational history of the 132d Infantry Division was known to the interrogators. One of the main questions seemed to concentrate on personal behavior: "What did you eat?"

"Konserv!" was always my reply.

"Konserv, da, Berlin?" the commission would ask.

"Da, da, Berlin! From the Heereszeugamt!" I would respond. The Heereszeugamt was the bureau responsible for providing uniforms for the army; however, this response seemed always to give them a sense of satisfaction, perhaps because they assumed they had received information from me about an official organization. Despite numerous threats, coercive behavior, and repeated interrogations, I never wavered from this response. The commission would attempt to draw me into confessing that I had on occasion requisitioned pork, beef, or poultry for my use. I steadfastly replied "Konserv."

Following one of my interrogation sessions the commission called for Oberleutnant von Postel, a former tank commander. Under duress he finally admitted that he had once slaughtered a hog, for which he was immediately pronounced guilty of "theft of Soviet property" and was sentenced to twenty-five years' hard labor. He was eventually released in 1955 through Adenauer's efforts.

THE TRANSPORT

In April 1947, cattle cars at the Borovitschi railhead were prepared by a work detail with bunks and makeshift latrines. A number of prisoners classified as "Rabotschi-Group III" were mustered together on a warm afternoon and taken to this location for transport. I was among them, and our hearts pounded with hope that we were, at long last, about to begin the journey to freedom. As the train began to move, I could discern from the position of the sun that we were traveling south toward Moscow.

On 1 May the train screeched to a halt at a switching station near Moscow, and we found ourselves positioned on a multilevel track on the west bank of the Moskva. Peering through the slits in the walls of the cattle cars we watched with amazement as unfamiliar aircraft crossed the clear blue sky from various directions, leaving vapor trails in the form of Soviet stars behind them. Approximately two kilometers' distance we could discern red flags flying above the walls of the Kremlin as the citizens celebrated May Day.

At length we were permitted to dismount between the tracks. No one thought of escape, and we remained full of hope that our journey would continue toward the west. After we spent a restless night, the train began to move, but to our disappointment we turned south, eventually crossed over the Don bridges, and proceeded into the heart of the Caucasus. It was now rumored that our destination was a recuperation camp, after which we could expect to be released.

CAMP "GAGRI"

We were greeted by a flat, endless landscape on a warm summer day as we continued rolling south. The string of cattle cars was now towed by a massive, red-painted diesel locomotive of American manufacture. On arriving at the Sotschi station we were ordered to detrain, and before us was an expanse of white buildings nestled among cypress trees stretching to the gray-green Black Sea on the horizon.

After several hours of marching on foot we arrived at a camp with large, clay-walled barracks. Our new quarters were immediately recognizable, surrounded by a perimeter of barbed wire and the familiar, tall watchtowers rising at each corner. There were already a number of prisoners in the camp. These unfortunates had recently been transported from prisoner of war camps in the United States to their hometowns in the Russian-occupied zone of Germany where, upon release, they were immediately taken into custody by the Soviets. In the United States these prisoners had experienced a confinement vastly different from our ordeal in the gulags. They were well-fed and in the best of health, and the former members of tank crews were still recognizable by their distinctive black panzer uniforms, albeit without insignia.

I rested against the wall of the barracks and gazed toward the west, where the fiery ball of the sunset sank on the horizon. The camp had remained vacant for an extended period of time prior to our arrival, and soon we began to feel the stinging of numerous bites from fleas as the vermin sought newly arrived victims. We discovered that our new dwelling was thoroughly infested with fleas, and as I attempted to sleep I was soon attacked by swarms of the parasites. The first night I slept outside under the open sky instead of lying on the rough planks that formed the wooden bunk. The following morning Rolf Kainz, a fireman from Esslingen, and I managed to obtain a small amount of kerosene from the Russians, which we poured into the cracks of the clay walls and ignited. The bodies of the fleas, swollen with the blood of the prisoners, popped audibly in the flames as we exterminated them.

It was at this camp that I experienced the most bearable period as a prisoner. The climate was mild, and the guards did not choose to exhibit the brutality that we had previously experienced. We were permitted more liberty in our movements than before, and the civilian populace in the area seldom exhibited animosity toward the prisoners. Large vegetable farms nestled below the cliffs were lined with green fig trees and citrus groves. Tobacco farms and cornfields beckoned to us, and we were able to slip from the confines of the camp secretly to gather small amounts of the crops to augment our diet. Although necessary to stave off the onset of starvation, these activities were undertaken at great risk, as theft of Soviet property held serious consequences.

The "death zone" between the double row of barbed wire marking the perimeter of our camp was approximately five meters wide. The prisoners designated for light labor worked in shifts to keep the sand in this zone raked smooth, for the purpose of revealing any footprints that would indicate whether prisoners had attempted to slip through the area during the night. We found such action to be hardly necessary, as it was not difficult to be assigned to an external labor party that was given work outside the confines of the camp. Additionally, a two-meter deep drainage ditch, which remained dry in the heat of the southern sun, led under the barbed wire and was blocked only by a crude barrier of tangled wire. This barrier was easily pushed aside to enable one to slip along the edge of the trench, allowing prisoners to make temporary excursions into the countryside. By this means we were able to obtain small amounts of fruit and green corn, which we then cooked into a soup in the barracks.

A labor crew was assigned to construct a road along the crest of the nearby mountains, and high supporting walls were required to retain the banks of earth as the road was cut through the terrain features. I had reported to the Russians that I was experienced in concrete finishing work, and under the command of a Hungarian cavalry captain I was assigned to this work brigade.

One day a Russian guard suddenly decided to prohibit any of the prisoners from leaving the immediate area of the work detail. He strictly demanded that we remain within his sight at all times, thus eliminating any hopes of wandering to a nearby vegetable kolkhoz. One late afternoon a ground viper appeared from the construction site and slithered rapidly toward the guard post. When the guard saw the snake it was already between him and his rifle, which he had leaned against the roots of a massive mulberry tree a short distance from his location. Hearing the cries of "Snake! Snake!" he sprang to his feet and fled in panic.

The prisoners quickly killed the poisonous viper with stones, and during the melee Rolf snatched the rifle and hid it in thick undergrowth some one hundred meters distant. Returning from his place of retreat, the guard discovered his rifle was nowhere to be found, and he angrily demanded the return of the weapon. The demands, which were met with indifference from us, quickly softened, and he was soon pleading with tears in his eyes for the return of his weapon. It was apparent that he could expect a severe punishment and would probably be subjected to confinement if the incident were to be discovered by the authorities. Despite his pleas we continued working without acknowledging his predicament, until at length Rolf retrieved the rifle and returned it to him. Thereafter he became very permissive in his treatment, and we were able to slip away from the labor party for short periods of time.

Using a broken piece of a hacksaw I carved tiny chess figures from small pieces of cedar. In manufacturing the crude tool, it was necessary to spend countless hours grinding the blade against stones to sharpen a point and a cutting edge from the thin piece of steel. The possession of knives was strictly forbidden, and the tool remained hidden within a hand-sewn inner pocket of my left trouser leg for many months.

I was again stricken with acute diarrhea and was ordered to report to the clay-walled barracks that served as the camp clinic. Dr. Kohler, from Heidelberg, who was later portrayed in the film *The Doctor of Stalingrad,* prescribed charcoal. Here I also saw for the first time large candy containers that had been provided by the international Carita charity organization. These containers held vitamin B tablets marked with English writing. I was also surprised to experience daily inspections in the clinic by a Russian major who was the camp physician. I referred to him as "Gospodin Major" instead of using the usual term "tovaritsch" (comrade). The title "gospodin" was a term taken from old Russian for "lord" or "master," and the use of this term, together with a small gift of carved figures, pleased him immensely. I also presented him with a charcoal landscape sketch that delighted him.

While being treated for the diarrhea that seemed to plague me continually, I was again placed into Work Group III. In the predawn hours, the labor parties would depart on the assignments, and I was permitted to leave the camp unescorted to walk the short distance to the Russian barracks where the major's room was located. In his simple room I was allowed to copy illustrated instructions from a medical book that had been printed in Vienna in 1900. I made brushes and pens from cattle hair obtained from nearby farms. The major provided india ink in tiny, dried cubes that had to be mixed prior to use; and small pieces of condensed colors were obtained from the paper mill, which enabled me to color the drawings. The Gospodin Major then distributed these drawings to medical doctors located in the neighboring political clinics, which had been established as rest and recreation areas for the Soviet working classes.

On New Year's Day 1948, a currency reform was set into motion by the Soviet government. The mineworkers from the Caucasus regions flocked to the exchange markets on small horses and donkeys to exchange large wads of paper currency where they had previously traded tobacco leaves and merchandise. Many of them found themselves arrested and taken into custody for illegal trading in currency, despite their ignorance of having committed any crime. The workers, having unknowingly committed a serious offense, were often sentenced to hard labor and dispatched to Siberian camps. These measures, undertaken by a government far away in Moscow, served to further alienate the population, who valued their independence from central authority.

Among the patients in the camp clinic was Sepp Kartzer, a former paymaster from Augsburg. He eventually died from malnutrition; however, before he died an order had been received from Moscow requiring that all future deaths of prisoners of war be thoroughly investigated for cause. This measure was most certainly taken because of pressure from the International Red Cross.

On the morning of Kartzer's death, I and several other prisoners were ordered to place his body in the back of a Studebaker truck. The German camp physician and Gospodin Major took their places in the cab of the vehicle, and we were ordered to ride in the back with the corpse. The driver then sped over rough-paved roads in the direction of Sotschi, and it was necessary to hold tight to Kartzer to keep his body from sliding from the open bed of the truck.

Our destination was a horseshoe shaped clinic situated in a grassy area. The building had three levels of large, wooden verandas, and white-clothed medical personnel were seen gathering to peer from the upper floors as we unloaded Kartzer's body from the truck. We carried his body into the building and laid him on a table, where we were immediately surrounded by doctors and nurses who gathered to witness the event as Dr. Kohler began to open the body for autopsy. During the process the doctor made statements about the findings, which were noted by one of the attendants.

During this examination I slipped out the door and explored the clinic grounds, where I soon discovered the kitchen. I was able to obtain a ration of Kascha, which I ladled into my ever-present mess tin. A large well was located near the door of the kitchen, and in the nearby garden I found garlic and red peppers. I was stuffing handfuls of these delicacies into my bread bag next to my mess tin when I heard the call "Vidermann, suda! Voda nada!" In response to their request I grabbed a pail of water that was located just inside the kitchen door. Gospodin Major and Dr. Kohler proceeded to wash their hands in the pail following the "operation," and Dr. Kohler then handed the pail to a medical assistant who was waiting nearby. The assistant walked to the kitchen door, tossed the water into the garden, refilled the pail from the well without rinsing it, and returned it, filled with water, to the kitchen without further cleansing.

We soon departed with Kartzer in our custody. A large pink stain appeared on the middle of the white sheet that covered his body during our journey back to the camp. After we arrived, he was carried to a small hill where the camp cemetery was located and laid to rest among our other comrades who had perished as prisoners. Local inhabitants had told us that in 1917 prisoners of war had been incarcerated in the camp while building roads through the mountains and that their graves were also located in this cemetery.

With the changes in politics it was ordered from Moscow that the graves of prisoners would be identified with their names. From Gospodin Major I received a list of names of prisoners who had recently died; and we nailed together rough crosses, upon which I painted the names from the list, using paint mixed from chalk and kerosene. I was later able to smuggle the list of approximately fifteen names, hidden in the sole of my wooden shoe, back to Germany, and the names were given to the Red Cross. Thus a final explanation was provided for the fate of a tiny number of those listed as missing in the east.

GAGRILOVO

At length Gospodin Major ensured that I was assigned to a small special camp near Gagrilovo. This camp, also under his responsibility, contained about fifty sick prisoners. An enormous work camp had been located in the shadows of the Caucasus nearby, and it had only recently been disestablished. It had been planned that prisoners would be concentrated at this location as labor for the construction of a massive hydroelectric dam. These plans had only recently been abandoned after consulting a team of German prisoners consisting of engineers and related technicians, including the geologist Vollrath from my hometown. After inspecting the site they advised the Russians that the flow of water available, combined with the rate of evaporation in the warm climate, would never produce enough energy to power the turbines. A high commission from Moscow was dispatched to the scene, and the Russians then determined that an error in plans had been made; thus the power plant was to be constructed at another location. In the nearby mountains were large stores of equipment that were to have been used in the construction of the dam.

One afternoon I was sitting in front of the barracks filing a piece of aluminum into a comb, as I had begun to regrow my hair, which the Soviets had once required to be close-shaven. Gospodin Major passed by and as usual asked me how I was doing. "Nitschevo, plocho," I responded.

"Why you doing bad?" he retorted. "You very sick. You go home soon!"

And so it happened. In summer 1948 I was permitted to board a boxcar that was filled with approximately forty prisoners for what was rumored to be our final trip to freedom. The journey was said to have taken about one week; however, I was again stricken with severe diarrhea and raging fever. Lying weakly within the dark car, my condition seemed to worsen with each passing hour, and I was soon too weak to stand for more than a few minutes' duration. Through a feverish veil I remained barely able to discern between daylight and dark and was hardly able to comprehend the events taking place around me. At long last we reached the border.

We were herded from the railcar onto the parade ground of a military base on the banks of the Oder near Frankfurt, where we stood in ranks, the chill of an early morning penetrating the ragged bits of various, now-obsolete uniforms that hung from our emaciated bodies. Silence hung heavy in the air as we stood motionless, painfully aware that freedom lay only hours, perhaps minutes, away. Through burning eyes I watched a Soviet officer, flanked by a guard with an ever-present submachine gun, pace slowly along the ranks of prisoners. We had been ordered to lay all possessions at our feet. The officer carefully examined each prisoner, then shifted his gaze to the meager belongings piled onto threadbare Wehrmacht rucksacks and bread bags as he moved down the line. I shivered uncontrollably from the fever; however, my weakness was momentarily forgotten as his expressionless gaze shifted from my face to my clothing, then concentrated on my sparse belongings piled at his feet. A sense of relief swept over me and I attempted to still my pounding heart as he then turned and stepped to the next prisoner.

Next to me stood Oberleutnant Hans Hirth from Reichenbach, a small town near my home in Stuttgart. The Soviet officer inspected Hans carefully, then looked at the belongings piled before him. He turned on his heel as if to move on but hesitated and then stopped. Bending down, he picked up a small, crudely carved wooden box that Hans had fashioned from pieces of cedar in the camp. Examining the box curiously, he suddenly tossed it to the ground and brought his booted heel upon it, splintering the box and spilling the contents. Hidden within a false bottom was an Iron Cross that Hans had managed to conceal during more than three years of searches and inspections in captivity. The officer picked up the decoration, raised it slowly, and examined the object before looking at Hans.

"Fascist!" he exclaimed loudly. Two guards with rifles suddenly appeared from the perimeter; the officer snapped commands as he glared at Hans. They took positions on either side and pushed Hans forward, leading him away with shoves and unintelligible shouts. Hans glanced over his shoulder at me, his haggard face white with terror. "Tell my parents what happened!" he shouted desperately. Oberleutnant Hans Hirth did survive and was eventually released from captivity many years later.

The journey continued. With a high fever I was transported through Saxony, and near Hof an der Saale we departed the Russian Zone and crossed into Bavaria, bringing my 1,080 days of Soviet captivity to an end. In an ever-weakening condition and stricken with edema, I remained barely conscious as I lay for several weeks in a former military clinic in Ulm. The central area of this ancient city had been reduced to rubble by the heavy bombing raids, and the crests of ragged walls remained marked with wooden crosses to indicate where civilians lay dead beneath the ruins.

Under the care of Red Cross nurses I slowly regained my health, lying for many hours in the shadows of the clinic. I had returned to a world yet torn asunder, and I was determined to leave my past, with its many horrors, behind me. Despite my efforts, I remained lost in the weeks, months, and years of a past that I was resolved to forget. My thoughts wandered to comrades lying in unmarked graves, the enemy dead, and the overwhelming challenge of facing a changed world. It remained impossible to comprehend that the long ordeal was over and that with so much death and destruction our world had witnessed, I had somehow survived. Contrary to my long-held expectations, there was no outpouring of emotion. I felt no elation with the slow realization of survival, only overwhelming emptiness when reflecting on the victims lost to the apocalypse.

Of the twelve members of Gottlob Bidermann's antitank crew who marched into Russia in June 1941, three survived to return to their homeland.

Gun Captain – Gefreiter Bidermann, twenty-two years old.
    Multiple wounds (7). Surrendered 8 May 1945.

Gun Layer – Gefreiter Ohler, twenty-one years old.
    Lost eye near Gaitolovo, September 1942. Discharged with severe wounds.

Gun Loader – Gefreiter Albert, twenty-one years old.
Multiple wounds, killed in action near Dunaburg, 1944.

Munition Handler 1 – Gefreiter Spinnler, twenty-one years old.
Multiple wounds, killed in action south of Lake Ladoga, 1943.

Munition Handler 2 – Gefreiter Eichler, twenty-one years old.
Twice wounded, killed in action on the north front, 1943.

Munition Handler 3 – Obergefreiter Krenz, twenty-nine years old.
Severely wounded, battle of Smerdynia, arm and leg amputated, 1943.
Discharged with severe wounds.

Munition Handler 4 – Oberschutze Wacker, twenty-two years old.
Killed in action near Gaitolovo, 1942.

Machine Gun Crew Leader – Gefreiter Hafner, twenty-one years old.
Previously wounded, killed in action at the Parpatsch position,
February 1942.

Gunner 1 – Obergefreiter Brendel, thirty-two years old.
Killed in action south of Lake Ladoga, 1943.

Gunner 2 – Oberschutze Eigner, nineteen years old.
Killed in action on the north front, 1944.

Gun Mover – Obergefreiter Fehr, thirty-five years old.
Killed in action near Dunaburg, 1944.

Munition Handler – Gefreiter Fahlteich, thirty-five years old.
Killed in action on the north front, 1943.

We learned to scorn death,
but to love life with fervor.

APPENDIXES

Chronology of Engagements, 132d Infantry Division, 1940–1945

October 1940–March 1941: Assembly, organizing, and training of the division; headquarters located in Landshut

28 March–9 April 1941: Security duties on the Germany-Yugoslav border

6–9 April 1941: Penetration of the Yugoslav border fortifications

10–12 April 1941: Engagements associated with the capture of Agram and Belgrade

13–18 April 1941: Capture of Belgrade; follow-on engagements at Sarajevo

18 April–9 June 1941: Security duties in the former Yugoslav territory

10–27 June 1941: Training in Karnten in the areas of Villach-Klagenfurt

28 June–31 July 1941: Transport and initial engagements in the Russian campaign

1–5 August 1941: Follow-on engagements to the Dnieper

6–20 August 1941: Engagements for capturing the west bank of the Dnieper in the area of Kanev-Tripolye

6–16 August 1941: Battle near Kiev and Boguslav

21 August–27 September 1941: Battle near Kiev

21 August–15 September 1941: Security of the west bank of the Dnieper in the area of Tripolye-Reschischtschev

18–27 September 1941: Engagements in the area east of Kiev

28 September–28 October 1941: March into the Crimea

29 October–4 November 1941: Follow-on engagements in the Crimea

5–6 November 1941: Engagements for the outer fortress positions of Sevastopol

17 November–16 December 1941: Engagements for the encirclement of Sevastopol

17–31 December 1941: Assault on Sevastopol

1–2 January 1942: Engagements associated with the siege of Sevastopol

5–7 January 1942: Repelling of Soviet landing attempt near Yevpatoria

3–18 January 1942: Engagements at Feodosia

3–15 January 1942: Defensive action west of Feodosia

15–18 January 1942: Battle of Feodosia and capture of the city

16–28 January 1942: Repelling of Soviet landing at Ssudak

19 January–7 May 1942: Defensive battles in the Parpatsch positions and coastal security

8–20 May 1942: Recapture of the Kertsch Peninsula

8 May 1942: Breakthrough of the Parpatsch positions

9–20 May 1942: Follow-on engagements on the Kertsch Peninsula

15 May 1942: Capture of Kertsch

19 May 1942: Assault on Burnu

25 May–1 June 1942: Coastal security at Ssaki-Mamaschay

2 June–1 July 1942: Assault and capture of the Sevastopol fortress

2–6 June 1942: Preassault artillery preparations

7–30 June 1942: Assault on the fortress

7 June 1942: Breakthrough of the first line of defenses; storming of Olberg

9 June 1942: Storming of Neuhaus heights

17 June 1942: Capture of Bastion I and Maxim Gorki

18 June 1942: Destruction of the Russian bridgehead at Lyubimovka

19 June 1942: Capture of Fort Schischkova

20 June 1942: Capture of Fort Lenin

21 June 1942: Capture of Fort Nordfront

27 June 1942: Capture of Langer Berg

28 June 1942: Establishment of Inkerman bridgehead

29 June 1942: Capture of heights south of Inkerman

30 June 1942: Encirclement of southern perimeter of city of Sevastopol

1 July 1942: Capture of Sevastopol city and harbor

2 July–28 August 1942: Coastal security along the Straits of Kertsch

28 August–10 September 1942: Rail transport of the division to the Leningrad front; route taken over Cherson, Nikolayev, Berditschev, Rovno, Kovel, Brest, Byalistock, Lyck, Insterburg, Tilsit, Schaulen, Mitau, Riga, Walk, Pleskau, Luga, Lissina

11–21 September 1942: Reassembly of the division in the areas of Mga, Sogolubovka, and Schapki

The following entries were taken from the notebook of Stabsfeldwebel Stenitzer and from the diary kept by the author while he was serving with Infantry Regiments 436 and 437. Due to the incompleteness of available records, the engagements conducted by the entire division during those periods listed cannot be given in full, especially those conducted during the last half of 1944.

22–30 September 1942: First battle south of Lake Ladoga; assault on and capture of Gaitolovo; closing of the pocket conducted by Third Company, Infantry Regiment 437

1–13 October 1942: Assault on Tschernaya and near Gaitolovo to the west of Mga; mopping-up actions of rear areas to clear isolated pockets of resistance

October 1942–January 1943: Engagements in the eastern area of Pogostya pocket

January 1943: Partial engagement of Infantry Regiment 437 on Volchov front

11–28 February 1943: Onset of the second battle south of Lake Ladoga; defensive operations and counterattacks near Smerdynia

March–June 1943: Defensive operations in areas of Pogostya pocket, Klosterdorf, and the Tigoda positions

June 1943: Rest and training period in the areas of Lyuban, Schapki, Uschaky

July–August 1943: Defensive engagements in the Maluksa positions near Pogostya

10–17 August 1943: Third battle south of Lake Ladoga; defensive engagements at Stichdamm and Vornovo; counterattacks for reestablishing the main battle line

End August–September 1943: Engagements on the Volchov front and Kirischi bridgehead

1–4 October 1943: Evacuation of the Kirischi bridgehead

5 October–November 1943: Transfer by means of vehicles and rail assets to battle area of Pustoschka west of Nevel; engagements also conducted in support of the Thirty-second, Eighty-first, Eighty-third, and 290th Infantry Divisions

November/December 1943–mid-January 1944: Defensive engagements and counterattacks in the areas of Pustoschka, Idritsa, Drissa, and Yasno Lake; security of the right wing of Army Group North

12–18 January, February 1944: Defensive engagements in the areas of Sagatya, Schulyatino, and Dyatly

11–13 March 1944: Assault operations and defensive engagements near Schwary

13–19 March 1944: Assault operations and defensive engagements near Rog

19–21 March 1944: Assigned as reserve near Mutovosovo

End March 1944: Holding positions near Baravucha

29 March–14 April 1944: Defensive engagements near Neschtscherdo Lake

14–19 April 1944: Defensive engagements in area of Puschkinskiye-Gory in support of Thirteenth Luftwaffe Field Division

19 April–24 June 1944: Engagements in the Ssorot positions, Yuchnovo positions, the Kussel heights, and Point 96.0

24 June–1 July 1944: (Grenadier Regiment 436 in support of Eighty-third Infantry Division); Velikaya bridgehead, assaults, and defensive engagements in areas of Novy-Put, Katzenbuckel, Stubben heights

June 1944: (Grenadier Regiment 437 with 132d Infantry Division); engagements near Koskatschevo

29–30 June 1944: Relieved in positions and transported to Dissna and Mioriya

1–3 July 1944: Counterattacks and defensive engagements near Mioriya

4 July 1944: I Battalion, Regiment 437, and combat group isolated and
  encircled southeast of Mioriya

5 July 1944: Breakout toward Druya; independent movement and actions
  in conduct of breakout operations

6 July 1944: Defensive engagements near Antonovka, Sossnovka,
  Malinovka

12–19 July 1944: Engagements at Krasnogorka, Snudy Lake, Plusy; attack
  toward south to Strussto Lake

20 July 1944: Transfer to Dunaburg, Sarasei

End July 1944: Assaults and defensive engagements in area of Dunaburg,
  Sarasei

End July–mid-August 1944: Transfer movements toward north; movement
  up to Duna bridgehead south of Stockmannshof

20 August 1944: Movement toward north

21 August 1944: Assaults and defensive engagements near Ergli; defensive
  engagements in Duna positions

22 August–14 September 1944: Defense of Ergli and of Egg heights

15–16 September 1944: Counterattack with Fourteenth Panzer Division

17–25 September 1944: Rearguard actions and engagements toward the
  west along main route to Riga; transfer to the Sega Forest position

5 October 1944: Transfer to the Suntazi positions

6 October 1944: Transfer to the B line

11 October 1944: Transfer to the F line before Riga

12–13 October 1944: From 2100, transfer movement
  through Riga, crossing of the Duna Bridge

14 October 1944: Transfer movement over the Courland River Aa

15 October 1944: First Battle of Courland; defensive engagements
  southwest of Frauenburg

17–30 October 1944: Regiment 437 in defensive engagements in area of
  Pikeliai, Lithuania; Regiment 436 in defensive engagements in areas of
  Losi, Bataiciai, Point 89.3

1–19 November 1944: Adjustment of main battle line to the Windau

19–27 November 1944: Second Battle of Courland south and southwest of
  Frauenburg

28 November–20 December 1944: Defensive engagements in Courland
  positions

21–31 December 1944: Third Battle of Courland at Pampali, Stedini, near
  Frauenburg

January–February 1945: Fourth and fifth Battles of Courland south of
  Libau near Preekuln

March 1945: Sixth Battle of Courland

April–7 May 1945: Defensive engagements southeast of Libau, west of
  Preekuln

8 May 1945: 1400, surrender to Soviet army; surviving members of the division taken into captivity. Prisoner of war camps: Preekuln, Sloka, Telshay, Riga, Novgorod, Memel, Dunaburg, Narva, Pleskau, Polozk, Borovitschi, Waldaihohen, Moscow, Minsk, Leningrad, in the Urals, in the Kirgisen steppe, on the Volga, Siberia, in the Caucasus near Suchumi and Tiflis. Complete information for additional camps and locations is unknown or unavailable

Military Cemeteries, 132d Infantry Division, 1941–1943

The following locations of the military cemeteries established by the 132d Infantry Division were recorded for burial records by the division's protestant chaplain, E. Wunderer. The cemeteries were established from the campaign in Yugoslavia through engagements south of Lake Ladoga. The last entry was recorded by the chaplain on 16 August 1943.

Engagement	Notes/description
Yugoslavia	Yayce
Yampol-Rossalyeff	Near the Russian garrison, encirclement at Kiev
Yusefovka	Along the road to Gorokovatko
Kusyeminzy	Along the road on the heights above Kusyeminzy
Reschischtschev	Along the main road
East bank of the Dnieper	Across from Balyka
Kargarlyk	At the northern perimeter of the palace park
Grigorovka	On the west bank of the Dnieper, town center
Kozani	Southern edge
Chanischkoy	West entrance, Crimean operations
Chanischkoy	Large military cemetery
Savk-Tabek	Single grave, roadside
Chaminsky-Bachtschisseray	Tartar palace park
Salanskoya	Hill and northwest entrance, along Height 278, four kilometers from Salanskoya
Kolkhoz Tolle	Seven kilometers southwest of Bachtschisseray
Beyuk-Syuren	Roadside
Otarkoy-Kesek	Near the town and ravine
Kamyschi	Eastern edge of the ravine
Karagoss	Near Feodosia, large cemetery
Kischlav	Military cemetery

Feodosia	Below the Tartar villa, very large cemetery
Vassilyeva	Near Kertsch; Gadschikoy, near Duvankoy
Sheglovo	Large cemetery from operations south of Lake Ladoga
Michailovski	Military cemetery
Mga	Military cemetery
Sogolubovka	Cemetery established by Infantry Regiment 437
Vyritza-Novinka	Rail crossing
Lipki	Southern edge; large cemetery, north
Ramzy	Large cemetery
Pomeranya	Near the Russian church

Table of Military Ranks

Germany	United States*	Great Britain*
Grenadier/Schuze	Private	Private
Obergrenadier/Oberschutze	Private	No equivalent
Gefreiter	Private First Class	Lance-Corporal
Obergefreiter	Corporal	Corporal
Unteroffizier	Sergeant	Corporal
Unterfeldwebel	No equivalent	No equivalent
Feldwebel	Staff Sergeant	Sergeant
Oberfeldwebel	Technical Sergeant	Sergeant
Stabsfeldwebel	Master Sergeant	Staff Sergeant
Hauptfeldwebel	Sergeant-Major	Company/Regimental Sergeant-Major
Leutnant	Second Lieutenant	Second Lieutenant
Oberleutnant	First Lieutenant	Lieutenant
Hauptmann	Captain	Captain
Major	Major	Major
Oberstleutnant	Lieutenant Colonel	Lieutenant Colonel
Oberst	Colonel	Colonel
Generalmajor	Brigadier-General	Brigadier
Generalleutnant	Major-General	Major-General
General der Infanterie, Kavalerie, etc.	Lieutenant-General	Lieutenant-General
Generaloberst	General	General
Generalfeldmarschall	General of the Army	Field Marshal

*Approximate equivalent

GLOSSARY

Attentat–Assassination attempt. Used in the text to describe the 20 July 1944 attempt on Hitler's life.

Aufklaerungsabteilung–Reconnaissance Battalion. The literal meaning of abteilung is "section" or "detachment." The German army also used this term to designate certain battalion-sized units.

Bolshevik or Bolsheviki–Bolshevist. Often used as a generic term for Russian soldiers; equivalent to "Kraut" in G.I. slang.

Drahtverhaue–Barbed-wire entanglement. Slang term used by German soldiers during World Wars I and II for a military-issue mixture of dried vegetables.

Esbit stove–A small, pocket-sized collapsible stove on which tins of food could be heated using a short candle or military-issue fuel tablet.

Fieseler Storch–A small, slow-flying observation and reconnaissance aircraft.

Flak–Acronym for "Flugzeugabwehrkanone." German term for antiaircraft gun. In the German army, Flak weapons were often used in a ground-defense role, including the famous Flak 88, a high-velocity 88mm weapon originally designed for air defense. The Flak 88 became a highly respected antitank weapon.

Golden pheasants–Derogatory term for high-ranking Nazi Party members. The term derived from the brown and red uniforms worn at official functions and rallies by party members that resembled the brilliant colors of the male pheasant.

Grofaz–German soldier's derogatory acronym for "Grossten Feldherr Aller Zeiten," a title publicized by Nazi propaganda to refer to Adolf Hitler during the early war years. Literal translation: "Greatest War Lord of all Time."

Gymnasiorka–A light-weight, loose-fitting shirt worn as a Russian uniform item.

Heimatschuss–Literal translation: "homeland shot." A wound not severe enough to be permanently disabling but of enough severity to require evacuation from the battlefront. The German soldier's equivalent to the American G.I.'s "million-dollar wound."

Heldenklau–Literal translation: "stealing of heroes," or "snatching of heroes." Slang term used to denote the practice of commandeering rear-echelon personnel for front-line service.

Hindenburg candle–A small stove or lamp created from a small ration tin or similar container, partly filled with sand, into which kerosene or diesel oil would be poured and ignited.

Hiwis–Abbreviation for German term "Hilfswilliger." Literal translation: "volunteer helper." This term was widely applied to foreign nationals in eastern Europe who served with the German armed forces.

Ivan–German slang for Soviet soldier.

Kettenhund–Literal translation: "chained dog," or "watchdog." German slang for a military policeman. The term derived from a metal gorget that was worn suspended around the neck from an aluminum chain. This field badge was the equivalent of the "MP" armbands of their U.S. counterparts.

Kindersaerge–Literal translation: "children's coffins." The term applied to small, wooden, antipersonnel box-mines.

Knobelbecher–Slang commonly used by German soldiers for the military-issue jackboots. The term is taken from the leather or pasteboard cylinder used to hold a pair of dice for the playing of games of chance.

Kolbenring–The insignia of rank worn by the senior noncommissioned officer assigned as "spiess" in a unit. The insignia consisted of two nine-millimeter strips of silver or gray braid worn on both sleeve cuffs of the uniform tunic. The two strips of braid encircled the sleeve and were positioned approximately five millimeters apart.

Kolkhoz–Collective farm as organized and established within the Soviet communal farming system.

Komiss bread–A military ration of dark, or "black," bread, usually in the form of a loaf.

Lafette–An adjustable field mount for a heavy machine gun. The lafette could be preadjusted to establish set fire zones to include right and left flanks as well as elevation; thus, fields of fire could be accurately determined during hours of darkness.

Landser(s)–Common slang used by German soldiers to denote infantrymen.

Landsknechte–Term used in reference to mercenary soldiers in central Europe during the Thirty-Years War. Used during World War II on the Russian front to describe men or units unkempt from hard service.

Luftwaffe–German air force.

MG-34–Official designation for German machine-gun model "Machinen-gewehr 1934." This weapon was produced in several variants and could be modified for use as a heavy or light machine gun. Often referred to as the "Spandau" machine gun.

MG-42–Official designation for German machine-gun model "Machinen-gewehr 1942." A complex machine gun of multiple uses, the weapon had an extremely high rate of fire. Like the MG-34, this weapon was often mounted on vehicles and could be used in a light or heavy machine-gun role. Often referred to by both Axis and Allied soldiers as the "Hitlersaege," or "Hitler-saw."

MP-40–Official designation for German submachine-gun model

"Machinenpistole 1940." This was a fully automatic, 9mm machine pistol that remained in use throughout the war. Often erroneously referred to by the western Allies as the "Schmeisser" submachine gun.

National Socialist–Political party from which the acronym "Nazi" derives.

NCO–Noncommissioned officer. The term applied to senior enlisted ranks below the rank of commissioned and warrant officers.

Nebelwerfer–Official designation for German rocket launchers and units employing those weapons.

OKH–Acronym for German term "Oberkommando des Heeres." Literal translation: "Supreme Command of the Army."

Old hares–Veterans on the front who had exhibited an ability to survive the hardships and deprivations forced upon them by both the enemy and their own army.

Pak–Acronym for "Panzerabwehrkanone," or antitank gun. Literal translation: "panzer defense gun." This term was applied to antitank guns designed for that purpose or to units employing those weapons.

Panzer–Literal translation: "armor." Used to denote tank or armored vehicles and those units equipped with armor.

Panzerfaust–A simple but highly reliable shoulder-fired antitank rocket manufactured in several variations. The panzerfaust weapons were the rough equivalent of the U.S. bazooka.

Panye–A small pony or horse used in eastern Europe.

Pionier–German military term for combat engineers.

PPSH-41–A submachine gun of very simple but efficient design produced in great quantities by the Soviet Union. This submachine gun used a 72-round drum magazine and fired a 7.62mm cartridge.

Rata–Official designation for the Soviet I-16 fighter, which was an obsolescent aircraft used early in the war. The term was widely used by German soldiers to denote any of the several types of primitive aircraft placed into service by the Russians, and the type described in the text was probably the PO-2, also referred to as the "sewing machine."

Reichsbahn–The railway system under the control and administration of Nazi Germany.

Sanka–Acronym for "Sanitaetskraftfahrtzeug," commonly used to designate German field ambulances.

Schmaltzbrot–Slices of bread on which a high-protein mixture of pork meat and fat is spread.

SD–Acronym to designate the "Sicherheitsdienst," the Nazi Party's internal secret police. Literal translation: "security service."

Shelter-quarter–A triangular, waterproof sheet of light canvas, usually printed with a light-green and tan camouflage pattern. A standard-issue item, officially referred to as a "Zeltbahn," these versatile sheets could be used singly as a rain poncho or, as a set of four, could be combined in the field to fashion a tent for four soldiers.

Sippenverhaftung–The practice in Nazi Germany of arresting members of a person's family for political crimes or treason committed by that person.

Sonderkommando–Literal translation: "Special unit." Official term that applied to certain German and foreign SS units that operated behind the front in the German-occupied areas, particularly on the Eastern Front. The Sonderkommandos were responsible for the rounding up and liquidation of inhabitants considered undesirable by the Nazi government.

Spandau–Term often applied to the German machine-gun model MG-34. The term derives from the Spandau arsenal near Berlin, which manufactured large numbers of German small arms.

Spiess–Colloquial name for the highest-ranking noncommissioned officer in a company. Usually a hauptfeldwebel, he was responsible for the company's administration, discipline, and morale of the troops. The spiess exercised more official authority than his American counterpart.

Stovepipe–Slang term used by front-line troops to denote the panzerfaust antitank weapon.

Stuka–Military acronym for the German term "Sturzkampfflugzeug." Literal translation: "dive-bombing aircraft." The term was used to designate the German JU-87 dive-bombers that were prevalent during the early war years. Stuka aircraft were outfitted with sirens that were activated at the beginning of the dive-bombing attack for the purpose of instilling fear and panic among enemy personnel.

Volksturm–The loosely organized military units that were poorly trained and rapidly placed into service in Germany during the closing months of the war. The Volksturm consisted primarily of teenaged boys from the Hitler Youth, elderly men too old for active military service, convalescents, and others not normally considered fit or qualified for duty.

Wehrmacht–Literal translation: "defense force." The term was used to denote the German Armed Forces during the Nazi period of government. The Wehrmacht consisted of the "Heer" (army), "Luftwaffe" (air force), and "Kriegsmarine" (navy).